Praise for *1 and 2 Timothy, Titus*

"Brilliant as usual, Kuruvilla puts his pericopal approach to work in this theological commentary for preachers. Conversant with scholarship, grounded in the original text, and acutely relevant—I love this commentary and will turn to it often. Highly recommended!"

—ANDREAS J. KÖSTENBERGER, Research Professor of New Testament, Director of the Center for Biblical Studies, Midwestern Baptist Theological Seminary

"Few commentaries on these Pauline letters rival this one for excellence in clarity, brevity, exegetical accuracy, theological acumen, and pastoral application. This is not to mention the author's remarkable homiletical vision—if you preach or teach the Bible, this book will fuel rather than frustrate as you prepare to present. Kuruvilla draws on thorough knowledge of the historical background (both Greco-Roman and Jewish), the history of interpretation, and the contemporary literature to arrive at a compelling account of these epistles. Serious readers at all levels will find canonical understanding, encouragement in personal growth, and fresh treasure for public proclamation."

—ROBERT W. YARBROUGH, Professor of New Testament, Covenant Theological Seminary

"In a rapidly changing and increasingly complex world, Professor Kuruvilla is to be commended for designing a commentary format that helps preachers and teachers prepare a faithful message as it is historically informed, rhetorically conscious, linguistically astute, theologically reflexive, hermeneutically sensitive, and practically oriented. Amidst the many commentaries available on the letters to Timothy and Titus, this one stands out as a reliable guide in bringing their theological message to the fore. As such, it deserves a wide audience."

—JERMO VAN NES, Senior Researcher in New Testament, Evangelical Theological Faculty, Belgium

"Dr. Kuruvilla has achieved in this commentary what most commentaries do not even attempt. He provides deep exegetical work while also delivering solid exposition and homiletic insights that aid teachers and preachers. If you are looking for a commentary that combines academic credibility with pastoral sensibilities, this is the commentary for you."

—BENJAMIN L. MERKLE, Professor of New Testament and Greek, Southeastern Baptist Theological Seminary

1 AND 2 TIMOTHY, TITUS

1 AND 2 TIMOTHY, TITUS

A Theological Commentary for Preachers

Abraham Kuruvilla

CASCADE Books • Eugene, Oregon

1 AND 2 TIMOTHY, TITUS
A Theological Commentary for Preachers

Copyright © 2021 Abraham Kuruvilla. All rights reserved. Except for brief quotations in critical publications or reviews, no part of this book may be reproduced in any manner without prior written permission from the publisher. Write: Permissions, Wipf and Stock Publishers, 199 W. 8th Ave., Suite 3, Eugene, OR 97401.

Cascade Books
An Imprint of Wipf and Stock Publishers
199 W. 8th Ave., Suite 3
Eugene, OR 97401

www.wipfandstock.com

PAPERBACK ISBN: 978-1-7252-7517-1
HARDCOVER ISBN: 978-1-7252-7518-8
EBOOK ISBN: 978-1-7252-7519-5

Cataloguing-in-Publication data:

Names: Kuruvilla, Abraham, author.

Title: 1 and 2 Timothy, Titus : a theological commentary for preachers /by Abraham Kuruvilla.

Description: Eugene, OR: Cascade Books, 2021 | Includes bibliographical references and index.

Identifiers: ISBN 978-1-7252-7517-1 (paperback) | ISBN 978-1-7252-7518-8 (hardcover) | ISBN 978-1-7252-7519-5 (ebook)

Subjects: LCSH: Bible. Timothy—Commentaries. | Bible. Titus—Commentaries.

Classification: BS2735.53 K87 2021 (paperback) | BS2735.53 (ebook)

04/02/21

To Susan
for her exemplary pastoral care
of our families

CONTENTS

Preface . ix

Introduction: Theology, Goals, Prolegomena . 1

1 TIMOTHY: SHEPHERDING THE SAINTS

Pericope 1 (1 Timothy 1:1–11): *Instruction for Godliness* . 17
Pericope 2 (1 Timothy 1:12–20): *Faithfulness in Ministry* . 29
Pericope 3 (1 Timothy 2:1–7): *Public Prayer for All* . 39
Pericope 4 (1 Timothy 2:8–15): *Corporate Roles* . 48
Pericope 5 (1 Timothy 3:1–16): *Leadership as Modeling* . 65
Pericope 6 (1 Timothy 4:1–16): *Devoted and Disciplined* . 83
Pericope 7 (1 Timothy 5:1–16): *Godly Care for the Needy* . 97
Pericope 8 (1 Timothy 5:17–25): *Maintenance of Godliness* . 108
Pericope 9 (1 Timothy 6:1–2): *Bestowal of Service* . 117
Pericope 10 (1 Timothy 6:3–21): *Giving to Get* . 127

2 TIMOTHY: COMPLETING THE COURSE

Pericope 11 (2 Timothy 1:1–18): *Suffering with Confidence* . 141
Pericope 12 (2 Timothy 2:1–13): *Working Hard, Pleasing God* . 154
Pericope 13 (2 Timothy 2:14–26): *Beneficial to God, Useful for Good Work* . 164
Pericope 14 (2 Timothy 3:1–17): *Continuing in Scripture* . 174
Pericope 15 (2 Timothy 4:1–22): *Preach the Word* . 185

TITUS: EXEMPLIFYING THE EXCELLENT

Pericope 16 (Titus 1:1–16): *Charitable Correction* . 199
Pericope 17 (Titus 2:1–15): *Being God's Own: Godliness in Community* . 211
Pericope 18 (Titus 3:1–15): *Showing God's Grace: Societal Godliness* . 222

Conclusion . 230

Bibliography . 233
Modern Authors Index . 239
Scripture Index . 241
Ancient Sources Index . 257

PREFACE

It has been a joy to explore the Pastoral Epistles, 1 and 2 Timothy, and Titus. Their relevance to current times is remarkable, their focus on godliness and good works energizing, their exhortations pertinent, and their anticipation and vision of a consummated divine household rousing! For one interested in all matters homiletical, I was also struck by the portrayal of the roles and responsibilities, joys and pains, and the undistractedness, uprightness, and untiring nature of the one called to bear the greatest burden for preaching in the local church. It does take a shepherd to preach!

And, as has been the case with all my writing endeavors in this series, digging through these three letters also was provocative and exhilarating, prompting me to align my own life to the character of the blameless shepherd of the people of God, the steward of the household of God, promoting the economy of God. May all who undertake leadership in the church at any level be marked by the godliness and devotion to the flock as called for in the Pastoral Epistles. And may the Holy Spirit, the source of God's inspired word in which preachers traffic, stimulate our minds, sensitize our hearts, and strengthen our wills for the edification of God's people for God's glory.

> And indeed it is my belief that the Spirit of God is certainly not only the best, but also the sole guide, since without him, there is not even a glimmer of light in our minds enabling us to appreciate heavenly wisdom; yet as soon as the Spirit has shed his light, our minds are more than adequately prepared and equipped to grasp this very wisdom.
> (John Calvin, "Preface to Chrysostom's Homilies," ca. 1540)

And may the Scriptures that the Spirit caused to be "God-breathed" be, in our lives and in the lives of those to whom we preach, "profitable for teaching, for reproof, for correction, for training in righteousness in order that the person of God may be capable, fully equipped for every good work."

Abraham Kuruvilla
Dallas, Texas
Pentecost 2020

INTRODUCTION

Theology, Goals, Prolegomena

> "*I solemnly charge [you] before God and Christ Jesus . . .:*
> *preach the word; be ready in favorable time, in unfavorable time;*
> *reprove, rebuke, exhort, with all patience and teaching."*
>
> 2 Timothy 4:1–2

The goal of preaching is to bring to bear divine guidelines for life from the biblical text upon the situations of the congregation, to align the community of God to the will of God for the glory of God. In other words, the ancient text is to be applied to the modern audience.[1] This is the preacher's burden—the translation from the *then* of the text to the *now* of listeners, with authority and relevance. This commentary is part of a larger endeavor to help the preacher make this move from text to praxis.[2]

Particularly pertinent is how this translation from text to praxis may be conducted with respect to the bite-sized portion of the scriptural text that is employed weekly in the corporate gathering for worship of the body of Christ—the pericope.[3] The pericope is the basic textual unit of Scripture handled in such assemblies, the foundational element of the weekly address from the word of God, and the primary way in which the people of God come into contact with their Scriptures. What exactly is the author of the text communicating in a given pericope that needs to be heeded by the listeners of the sermon?[4]

---

1. For more on this concept of preaching, see my *Privilege the Text!* and *Vision for Preaching*, as well as *Manual for Preaching*. The "Theology" and "Goals" sections of this introduction is modified from Kuruvilla, *Judges*, 1–7.

2. The other commentaries currently available in this series are those on Genesis, Judges, Mark, and Ephesians.

3. "Pericope" is employed here to demarcate a segment of Scripture, irrespective of genre or length, that forms the textual basis for an individual sermon and that has a discrete theological thrust, sermonically and applicationally distinguishable from the thrusts of pericopes preceding and following.

4. For the purposes of the commentaries in this series no particular distinction will be made between the divine and human authors of the biblical text.

INTRODUCTION

THEOLOGY

Elsewhere it was proposed that the critical component of the ancient text to be borne into the lives of the modern audience was the *theology of the pericope*, or what the author is *doing* with what he is saying in the text. This is what moves the people of God to valid application, for pericopal theology is the ideological vehicle through which divine precepts, priorities, and practices are propounded for appropriation by readers.[5] A biblical pericope is therefore a literary instrument inviting men and women to organize their lives in congruence with the theology revealed in that pericope. The goal of any homiletical transaction, thus, is the gradual alignment of the church, week by week, to the theology of the biblical pericopes preached. Pericope by pericope, the various aspects of Christian life, individual as well as corporate, are progressively brought into accord with God's design for his creation. This is the goal of preaching: faith nourished, hope animated, confidence made steadfast, good habits confirmed, dispositions created, character molded, Christlikeness established.[6]

All such discrete units of pericopal theology together compose a holistic understanding of God and his relationship to his people, and each individual quantum of pericopal theology forms the weekly ground of life transformation by calling for alignment to the demands of God, resulting in the assimilation of Christlikeness. I call this a *christiconic* hermeneutic.[7] In brief, if each pericope depicts a facet of God's ideal world, then each pericope projects an aspect of divine demand: the precepts, priorities, and practices of God's ideal world, or how that world is to run, as called for in that particular pericope. Since the only one to comprehensively and perfectly fulfill the requirement of every pericope in Scripture is Jesus Christ, the perfect Man, every pericope is, in essence, projecting what it means to be more like Christ, i.e., depicting a facet of Christlikeness, a pixel of the *Christicon*, with the whole canon portraying the plenary image of Christ. After all, it is God's ultimate design to conform his children into the "image" (εἰκών, *eikōn*) of his Son, Christ (Rom 8:29). In a sense, this week-by-week and sermon-by-sermon alignment to the divine demand in each pericope is an imitation of Christ, a movement by the children of God towards increasing Christlikeness. This is at the core of the theological interpretation followed in this commentary series: a hermeneutic specifically geared for preachers and their noble task—a *christiconic* hermeneutic. Because children of God are called to conform to the image of Christ, preachers everywhere are, in turn, to discern the theology of the pericope—i.e., the facet of Christlikeness depicted therein—and apply it to the widely diverse situations of believers across the globe, across millennia and across cultures, to enable them to emulate the perfect Man, their Lord Jesus Christ.[8] In other words, while pericopal theology tells us *what* Christ looks like, application in sermons directs us to *how* we can look more like him, in our own particular circumstances, thus becoming "capable, fully equipped for every good work" (2 Tim 3:16–17).[9]

---

5. See Kuruvilla, *Text to Praxis*, 142–90; *Vision for Preaching*, 91–109; and "Pericopal Theology," 3–17.

6. Modified from Tertullian, *Apology* 39.

7. See Kuruvilla, *Privilege the Text!*, 238–68; *Vision for Preaching*, 111–48; "Christiconic Interpretation," 131–46; and "Christiconic View," 43–70.

8. This, of course, is not to deny the fullness of the deity of Jesus Christ. But it must be remembered that it is into the likeness of his perfect humanity that God's people are being transformed.

9. All translations of Scripture in this work are my own. Please note that textual translations within the body of this work are intended to aid study; they are not necessarily smoothened out for devotional reading.

INTRODUCTION

Such a conception of preaching should not cause one to construe divine demand for holiness as merely a litany of dos and don'ts that a capricious God burdens his people with. Rather, God's call to be aligned with his requirements and standards is a gracious invitation to inhabit his ideal world by the power of the Spirit, to enjoy its fullness of blessing, in his presence. It is the biblical canon, preached by the leader of the people of God in the context of their worship of God, that portrays what this world of God (the kingdom of God) looks like, how it functions, and how the community is to inhabit it. Pericope by pericope, a theological picture of God's ideal world is unveiled. This is the world God would have; and that is the kind of people God would have us be.

GOALS

I come to the books of 1 and 2 Timothy and Titus, and indeed to all of Scripture, with a reading bias that is Protestant and evangelical. I take it that a biblical author writes purposefully, creating a text with intention, each part of it contributing to the overall theological agenda of the individual book. This commentary also assumes that every pericope in the canonical Scriptures may be employed gainfully for application by the church universal.[10] Thus, no pericope of the Pastoral Epistles (PE) may be disregarded for the purposes of sermons. And applicational response is, of course, the endpoint of the preacher's endeavors. The employment of the Bible as the foundation of the existence, beliefs, and activities of the church assumes that its interpretation *will* result in a response of application—life change for the glory of God.

Most Bible scholars and theologians have not been coming to the text of Scripture with the eyes and heart of preachers; therefore, the pericope has been disregarded as a textual unit of theological value, and the goal of life transformation—a pastoral concern—has tended to be subjugated to other academic interests. The aim of this commentary series, part of a long-term endeavor to rectify this misdirection, is to develop the theology of each pericope of the PE so that preachers may be able to proceed from this crucial intermediary to a sermon that provides valid application, both authoritative and relevant. There is, thus, a twofold aspect to the homiletical transaction: the discernment of the theology of the pericope, and the derivation of application, how the theology may be actualized in real life.

Text ▶ Theology ▶ Application

The first move, from text to (pericopal) theology, draws meaning *from* the biblical text with authority, and the second, from theology to application, directs meaning *to* the situations of listeners with relevance. The advantage of employing pericopal theology as the intermediary between text and praxis is that its specificity for the chosen text makes possible a weekly movement from pericope to pericope with a clear progression and development of distinct but connected theological thrusts as one preaches through a book. In sum, the theology of the pericope (a crystallization of which is labeled "Theological Focus" in this commentary) functions as the bridge between text and application, between the circumstances of the text

---

10. See Kuruvilla, *Privilege the Text!*, 65–86, for a set of "Rules for Reading" that respects the special nature and hermeneutics of the biblical text.

INTRODUCTION

and those of the reading community, enabling the move from the *then* to the *now*.[11] The resulting transformation of lives reflects a gradual and increasing alignment to the values of God's kingdom (or a gradual and increasing approximation of Christlikeness) as pericopes are sequentially preached. Thus, a pericope, as a quantum of the biblical text, is more than *informing*; it is *transforming*, for as the people of God adopt its theological values they are becoming rightly oriented to God's will, inhabiting God's ideal world as its citizens, and becoming more like Christ.

This series of commentaries does not intend to lead preachers all the way to a fully developed sermon on each pericope; rather, it seeks to take them through first move from text to (pericopal) theology: the *hermeneutical* aspect of sermon preparation. Though that is the primary focus, each commentary does provide two "Possible Preaching Maps" for every pericope, to advance preachers a few more steps closer to a sermon.[12] However, preachers are left to work out this second move from theology to sermon/application (the *rhetorical* aspect of sermon preparation) on their own, providing appropriate moves-to-relevance, specific application, illustrations, etc., all of which can be done only by the shepherd who knows the flock well.[13] Beyond a few general guidelines, it is impossible for a third party to determine what exactly specific application looks like for a particular audience. That task is between the preacher, the Holy Spirit, and the congregation. Therefore, this is not a "preaching" commentary, in the usual sense. Rather it is a "theology-for-preaching" commentary, a work that seeks to undertake an extremely focused interpretation of the text, one that moves the preacher from text to theology, en route to a sermon. In that sense, this is a "theological" commentary, with theology defined as pericopal theology.

The commentary on the PE is primarily geared for those interested in preaching through these three letters (in any context of the people of God) and seeks to help them proceed pericope by pericope, by isolating the theology of the pericope and discerning the trajectory of the whole. The three Epistles are broken down into eighteen pericopes—ten for 1 Timothy, five for 2 Timothy, and three for Titus: these pericopes may be preached in back-to-back sermons, or in two separate series—separating them by addressee. Nevertheless,

---

11. Permit me to add here that these theological foci are *not* the communicational goals of the sermon (à la the "Big Idea" modus operandi of traditional homiletics). These are merely tools to help the sermon preparer structure the sermon, stay focused while fleshing out the structure, and derive application. The goal of the preacher is not to create a masterpiece (that explains, validates, and applies the Big Idea/Theological Focus); rather the aim is to curate the Master's piece, the text in toto. For more on this see my *Manual for Preaching*, and "Time to Kill the Big Idea?" This latter essay, and a couple of rounds of responses (from others) and rejoinders (from me), are available on my website, at http://homiletix.com/kill-the-big-idea/.

12. I have chosen to call these "maps," rather than "outlines." An *outline* has some self-imposed constraints: its points are constructed as full sentences (usually propositions with subjects and complements), with main points subsuming subsidiary points, and so on, all of which pedantries are unnecessary for a *map* that aids the sermonic curation of "text+theology" (I see the pericope and its theology as a unified and inseparable entity). That does not deny that a sermonic undertaking deals with ideas, and even arguments, but simply points an accusatory finger at the dominant metaphor of the traditional approach and its complicit nomenclature that, in my opinion, have stultified the way we think about preaching, especially in light of our fast-advancing understanding of how language works and how the brain works to comprehend texts and speech. See Kuruvilla, "'What Is the Author *Doing* with What He Is *Saying*?'" 557–80 (available, with a colleague's response and my rejoinder, at https://homiletix.com/kuruvillajets2017/).

13. For more on these and other aspects of preaching, see my *Manual for Preaching*.

each of the three may be studied for its own depiction of facets (or pixels) of the *Christicon* which each child of God must adopt into his or her own life.

Commentaries were described by Ernest Best as "the backbone of all serious studies of scripture."[14] Therefore, it is hoped that not only preachers, but all interested laypersons, Sunday School teachers, and others who teach Scripture will find this commentary—a small vertebra in that spinal column—helpful. For that matter, if an applicational response is the goal of Bible study of any kind and at any level, a work such as this promises to be useful even for those working through the PE on their own.[15]

Needless to say, in all sermonic enterprises, quality and depth and intensity of preaching go only so far towards achieving the spiritual formation of listeners. Augustine (*On Christian Doctrine* 4.27.59) noted wisely: "But whatever may be the majesty of the style [of the preaching], the life of the speaker will count for more in securing the hearer's compliance," not to mention the divine work of the Spirit in the hearts of listeners.[16] Therefore, this commentary, along with the others in this series, is submitted with the prayer that preachers, the leaders of God's people, will pay attention to their own lives first and foremost, as they work through the PE, seeking to align themselves to God's demand in each pericope of these letters, thus becoming, in the power of the Spirit, more Christlike themselves.

PROLEGOMENA

The Cities

Ephesus, on the west coast of modern Turkey, was a provincial capital and commercial center in the ancient Near East, third in importance after Rome and Alexandria. With a population of about 150,000, it was Greek, though under Roman rule, and had a substantial Jewish population.[17] Ephesus boasted the Temple of Artemis that was severalfold larger than the Parthenon in Athens and one of the Seven Wonders of the Ancient World. No wonder the town clerk of the city claimed that Ephesus was the "keeper of the temple [νεωκόρος, *neōkoros*] of the great Artemis, of the image that fell from heaven" (Acts 19:35).

Crete, in the Bible, shows up in Acts 27, though Cretans were said to have been present in Jerusalem at Pentecost (2:11). It, too, was a Roman province, an island known for its seafaring merchants. Particularly distinguishing Crete was its retelling of the myth of Zeus who, Cretans alleged, was born and had died in Crete, giving a boost to the general sentiment that Cretans were liars. Debauchery was common and the island gave its name to such dissolute activities: to "cretanize" (κρητίζω, *krētizō*) signified living in this manner (see Pericope 16: Titus 1:1–16).

Endeavors to link references in the PE to historical events in the life, movements, and activities of Paul are many and varied, and none of them go much beyond speculation.[18]

---

14. Best, "Reading and Writing of Commentaries," 358.

15. Which brings me to another point: while a working knowledge of Greek will be very handy for the reader of this work, Greek terms and phrases (and the rare Hebrew ones), wherever referred to in the commentary, have been both transliterated and translated, in order to enable those not as facile with the original language to use this work efficiently.

16. *Nicene and Post-Nicene Fathers* 2:595.

17. Josephus, *Jewish Antiquities* 14.10.12–13; 16.6.1–7.

18. See Mounce, *Pastoral Epistles*, liv–lxiv.

INTRODUCTION

The fact that Acts never mentions Paul writing any letters makes attempts to correlate the histories recounted in the former with the provenance of the Pauline Epistles an exercise in futility.[19] In any case, such correspondences, if at all discoverable, do not, for the most part, make a difference to the thrust of the pericopes of the PE.

The Corpus

The PE, as we know them, were grouped together quite early in church history as the only Pauline Letters addressed to specific coworkers of the apostle (so Philemon is excluded from that category). Tertullian (*Against Marcion* 5.21) affirmed the existence of "two [letters] written to Timothy and one to Titus putting together the order/status of the church [*de ecclesiastico statu compositas*]."[20] However, the actual label "Pastoral Epistles" comes from the eighteenth century.[21] All the members of this trio have significant authorial autobiographical references, not to mention enough similarity at "linguistic and conceptual levels" to merit consideration as a group (see below).[22] As far back as the Middle Ages, Aquinas classed the letters to Timothy and Titus together, noting that "[Paul] instructs the prelates of the churches . . . on the foundation, construction, and government of ecclesial unity in 1 Timothy, on firmness against persecutors in 2 Timothy, and on defense against heretics in the letter to Titus."[23]

In keeping with this commentary series' acknowledgment of the canonicity of the books of Scripture, arguments for and against reception of the PE into the inspired corpus will not be rehearsed. Standard commentaries discuss these issues at length, should the preacher have the need to investigate such matters. In any case, once the books are recognized as authoritative, these issues do not affect the thrust of their pericopes. The question of authorship has also been adequately dealt with in other tomes. Because of the rarity of acceptable pseudepigraphy in those days and the historical particularities within the text of the PE, it is a fair assumption that traditional ascription of these letters to Paul's hand is accurate.[24]

Of the thirteen traditionally accepted Pauline Letters, the PE have the highest frequency of *hapax legomena* based on total number of words (in Greek): 8.2 percent in 1 Timothy; 8.2 percent in 2 Timothy; and 7.7 percent in Titus (the rest range from 4.6 percent

---

19. But see Porter, "Pauline Chronology," 65–88.

20. My translation from the Latin (http://www.tertullian.org/articles/evans_marc/evans_marc_11book5.htm). As well, see the strategic employment by Irenaeus of the PEs as a group, about which White noted: "The breadth of use to which Irenaeus put the Pastorals, as well as the ways in which the Pastorals were being used by other authors in the second century, suggests that they already fit comfortably within the proto-orthodox tradition by the time that Irenaeus writes" ("How to Read a Book," 148).

21. Guthrie, *Pastoral Epistles*, 17.

22. Towner, *Letters to Timothy and Titus*, 1.

23. Aquinas, *Super Epistolas S. Pauli*, prologue [11], 1:3 (translated in Sirilla, *Ideal Bishop*, 100, 100n105). The second-century Muratorian canon also brackets together the letters to Timothy and Titus, along with that to Philemon: "[Paul wrote] one [letter] to Philemon, one to Titus, and two to Timothy and these are held sacred in the esteem of the Church catholic for the regulation of ecclesiastical discipline" (translation in Metzger, *Canon of the New Testament*, 307).

24. See Schnabel, "Paul, Timothy, and Titus," 383–404; Wilder, "Does the Bible Contain Forgeries?," 165–82; and Lea, "Early Christian View," 65–75; as well as standard commentaries for more on this issue.

in Colossians to 2.5 percent in 2 Thessalonians).²⁵ As well, these three letters have a unique literary tempo:

> When their text is read aloud in Greek, the author's use of sound to accent his thought is often notable. The reader hears alliteration, assonance, rhyme, paronomasia, polysyndeton (for abundant expressiveness), asyndeton (for a vivid, impassioned effect, adding a certain brilliance to epistolary style . . .). Poetic citations ornament the composition [1 Tim 3:16; 2 Tim 2:11-13; Titus 1:12] . . . , and the prose has at times distinctly poetic rhythmic structure, particularly when prayers are alluded to or cited (thus 1 Tim 1:12-17).²⁶

Other similarities between 1 and 2 Timothy and Titus include: "this is a trustworthy statement" (1 Tim 1:15; 3:1; 4:9; 2 Tim 2:11; Titus 3:8); no mention of a scribe in any of the three (as in Rom 16:22; and assumed in 1 Cor 16:21; Gal 6:11; Eph 6:21; Col 4:7; 2 Thess 3:17); the presence of "virtue" and "vice" lists (1 Tim 1:9-10; 2 Tim 3:2-5; Titus 1:6-10; 2:2-10); considerable stress on teaching (see below) and on "soundness" of speech and faith²⁷; several prayers (1 Tim 1:12-17; 2 Tim 1:3-14, 16-18); and creedal/hymnic formulae (1 Tim 1:15; 2:13-15; 6:11-16; 2 Tim 2:8, 11-13; Titus 2:4-5, 11-14; 3:4-7). Besides, there is "almost a monopoly" in the PE on the use of εὐσέβεια (eusebeia) and its cognates; the theme of godliness is a major motif in these Epistles.²⁸ There is also a significant emphasis in the PE on "good works" which turns out be a critical aspect of the thrust of the corpus as a whole and of each letter individually. "Good works" are urged of believers in 1 Tim 2:10; 2 Tim 2:21; 3:17; Titus 1:16; 3:1 (with the adjective ἀγαθός, agathos; there is also οἰκουργοί ἀγαθαί, oikourgoi agathai, "good home-workers," in 2:5; and ἀγαθοεργέω, agathoergeō, "do good work," in 1 Tim 6:18); and in 1 Tim 3:1; 5:10, 25; 6:18; Titus 2:7, 14; 3:8, 14 (using καλός, kalos).²⁹

All that being said, the interpreter should not overrate these elements of style as evidence of authorship, whether of Paul or otherwise.

> In the Hellenistic world, the rhetorical ideal was expressed by prosōpopoiia, which means "writing in character," whether in speeches, drama, or narrative.

---

25. *Hapax legomena* counts are from van Nes, *Pauline Language*, 225–76 (percentage calculations are my own based on total word count in each Epistle in the *Novum Testamentum Graece*, Nestle-Aland, 28th edition). There are 284 New Testament (NT) *hapax legomena* in the three letters of the PE (80 of which show up in the LXX). Another 130 words appear elsewhere in the NT, but not in any of the other Pauline letters (Witherington, *Letters and Homilies*, 56).

26. Quinn, *Letter to Titus*, 6.

27. See 1 Tim 1:10; 6:3; 2 Tim 1:13; 4:3; Titus 1:9, 13; 2:1, 2, 8. The notion of "soundness" employing the verb ὑγιαίνω, *hygiainō*, for matters not health-related, is found in Paul only in the PE, and the adjective ὑγιής, *hygiēs*, only in Titus 2:8.

28. Witherington, *Letters and Homilies*, 58. These instances are: εὐσέβεια in 1 Tim 2:2; 3:16; 4:7, 8; 6:3, 5, 6, 11; 2 Tim 3:5; Titus 1:1 (and in the NT, only in four other instances in 2 Peter); εὐσεβέω, *eusebeō*, 1 Tim 5:4 (and elsewhere in the NT, only in Acts 17:23); and εὐσεβῶς (*eusebōs*) only in 2 Tim 3:12 and Titus 2:12 in the NT; as well as the synonym θεοσέβεια (*theosebeia*) in 1 Tim 2:10 (a *hapax* in the NT). The antonym ἀσέβεια (*asebeia*) is found in 2 Tim 2:16 and Titus 2:12.

29. Thus, "good works" is found in every chapter of Titus, and almost every chapter of both Epistles to Timothy. There is also εὐεργεσία (*euergesia*), "good work," in 1 Tim 6:2; as well as antonymous phrases ἔργον πονηρός (*ergon ponēros*), "evil work," 2 Tim 4:18; and κακοῦργος (*kakourgos*), "evil worker," 2 Tim 2:9. Other consistent themes in 2 Timothy: suffering (1:8, 12; 2:3, 9, 24; 3:11-12; 4:5, 14-15, 17-18); and future rewards (2 Tim 1:12, 18; 2:5, 6, 10, 12; 4:8, 18).

INTRODUCTION

> The same ideal applied to the writing of letters in antiquity. Style was a matter of being rhetorically appropriate to circumstances and followed definite conventions. . . . In Paul's time, style was less a matter of personal expressiveness and more a matter of social presence and rhetorical craft. Writers of such differing gifts and locations as Luke the Evangelist and Lucian the Satirist display a dazzling variety of "styles" that are controlled by a single writer in the service of "writing in character."[30]

In other words, the situation dictated the style; making too much of distinctions between Epistles written for different purposes is unwise. Besides, the size of the PE corpus is too small for the interpreter to make fine discriminations between these three and the rest of Paul's letters. So, while "the three letters share a common shape of vocabulary, style and method of argument which is somehow different from that of the other ten letters [of Paul in the NT]," I see no reason to reject the traditional acceptance of Pauline authorship of the PE.[31]

Church as a Divine Household

The PE have the author Paul—herald, apostle, and preacher (1 Tim 2:7; 2 Tim 1:11)—guiding his delegates, Timothy and Titus, in their roles as blameless leaders and stewards of the divine household. This concept of the church as a "household" (οἶκος, *oikos*) is congruent with what God is doing in the cosmos, "the economy of God" (οἰκονομία θεοῦ, *oikonomia theou*, 1 Tim 1:4).

> The term [οἰκονομία θεοῦ] envisions a divinely organized pattern of life—God's ordering of reality—and the opening instruction [in 1 Tim 1:4] suggests that it is apprehension of this pattern and the appropriate faith response to it that this letter will seek to explain. As Paul applies it to Christian existence, the term is expansive, encompassing the whole social, political, and religious world in much the same way that the emperor would take to himself the role of father or householder and regard the empire and its inhabitants as his household. Understood in this way, the whole of life is subject to the divine will (or is meant to be). The implications for a Christian understanding of the church in the world and mission are enormous.[32]

What God is doing in the cosmos on a grand scale is what "gospel" signifies in its broadest sense: "the administration [οἰκονομία] of the fullness of times, the consummation of all things in Christ—the things in the heavens and the things on the earth in Him" (Eph 1:10). And this glorious divine ordering is to be reflected in local bodies of Christ, as facilitated by "God's steward" (θεοῦ οἰκονόμος, *theou oikonomos*), the elder of the church (Titus 1:7) which is the "household of God" (οἶκος θεοῦ, *oikos theou*, 1 Tim 3:15).[33] In the LXX, οἶκος delineates God's abode: Deut 26:15; 1 Kgs 7:31, 37 (7:45, 51 English); 8:1; Ps 41:5 (42:4); Dan

---

30. Johnson, *First and Second Letters to Timothy*, 60.
31. Marshall, *Pastoral Epistles*, 63.
32. Towner, *Letters to Timothy and Titus*, 68–69.
33. For notions related to the church as God's household, see 1 Tim 3:4–5, 12, 15; 5:1–2; and 2 Tim 2:20 (and 1 Cor 3:9–10; 4:1; Gal 6:10; Eph 2:10, 19–22; 1 Pet 4:17; etc.). Interestingly enough, the "body" metaphor for the church is absent in the PE.

5:23; etc.[34] Thus we have the divine household that appears to be continuous with the domestic household, the latter a microcosm of the former. In keeping with that reality, there are instructions in the PE on how to treat older men (including elders of the church), older women (including widows), younger men, and younger women, besides slaves and the wealthy (1 Tim 5:1—6:2; 6:17–19; Titus 2:1–10). The mission of the domestic entity is "to extend this reality beyond its walls so that God's way of ordering life can be known and obeyed by more and more of the unbelieving world."[35] In this dispensation, as taught in the PE, the character of the private entity (οἶκος) is to be reflected in that of the public entity (ἐκκλησία, *ekklēsia*); one day, in the eschaton, that will be the state of the universal entity (κόσμος, *kosmos*)—God's kingdom come!

Teaching and the Pastoral Epistles

Overall, the PE seem to be characterized by Paul's response to false teachers and opponents, though not every aspect of each letter is directly related to them (or their activities). But Paul takes the opportunity to address ancillary matters as well, that are only tangentially, if at all, related to the provocations of those predators. After all, such missives were relatively rare in an age without phone calls, emails, or texts, not to mention the USPS (of the "neither snow nor rain nor heat nor gloom of night" fame).

The Jewish identity of these agitators is evident (1 Tim 1:4, 7; 4:7; 2 Tim 2:14, 23; 3:8, 13; 4:4; Titus 1:10, 14–16; 3:9); they are apparently Jewish-*Christians* (1 Tim 1:3, 6–7, 19; 4:1; 6:3; 2 Tim 2:14, 18, 20–21; 3:5) influencing fellow believers (1 Tim 5:13–15; 2 Tim 2:14, 17–18; 3:6–7; 4:3, 14; Titus 1:11), for Paul retains the hope of their restoration (1 Tim 1:20; 5:17–25; 2 Tim 2:25–26; Titus 1:13; 3:10–11).[36] In the PE there is a unifying thread of countering such heretical agitators firmly. Take for example, 1 Timothy, where, broadly, a pattern is followed with Timothy and his opponents alternating with specific church groups[37]:

---

34. In ancient Greek poetry, οἶκος also designated Zeus's abode on Mt. Olympus, as well as the household of gods over whom he ruled as father and king (Zamfir, "Is the *Ekklēsia* a *Household*?," 523).

35. Towner, *Letters to Timothy and Titus*, 69. Suetonius (*Lives of the Caesars 2: The Deified Augustus* 58) makes Augustus the *Pater Patriae* ("Father of the Country"); Dio Cassius (*Roman History* 56.9.3) calls him πατήρ (*patēr*); and Aelius Aristides (*Orations* 23.31) compares the Roman πόλις, *polis*, "city," to the οἶκος. Isocrates (*Nicocles* 41) observed that "if kings are to rule well, they must try to preserve harmony, not only in the states over which they hold dominion, but also in their own households and in their places of abode [τοὺς οἴκους τοὺς ἰδίους καὶ τοὺς τόπους ἐν οἷς ἂν κατοικῶσιν, *tous oikous tous idious kai tous topous en hois an katoikōsin*]." See Isocrates, *To Demonicus, To Nicocles*, 100–1.

36. Indeed, there are several Hebraistic hints in the PE, for instance: βασιλεὺς τῶν αἰώνων (*basileus tōn aiōnōn*; 1 Tim 1:17) suggests מֶלֶךְ עוֹלָם (*melek ʿolam*; Jer 10:10; Ps 10:16; 29:10); praying for kings and authorities (1 Tim 2:1–2) was an accepted practice among the Jews (Ezra 6:9–10; 7:23; Jer 29:7; 1 Macc 7:33; *Letter of Aristeas* 45; Josephus, *Jewish War* 2.10.4; 2.17.2; *Against Apion* 2.6.77; Philo, *Flaccus* 7.49); the credal statement εἷς γὰρ θεός (*heis gar theos*; 1 Tim 2:5) sounds like a declaration of the *Shema*, ὁ θεὸς ἡμῶν κύριος εἷς ἐστιν (*ho theos hēmōn kurios heis estin*; LXX Deut 6:4); and there is a strong allusion to the Decalogue in 1 Tim 1:9–10 (see Pericope 1: 1 Tim 1:1–11).

37. From Van Neste, *Cohesion and Structure*, 143.

INTRODUCTION

A	Timothy and Opponents (doxology, 1:12–17)		1:3–20
	B	Specific Church Groups	2:1—3:13
A'	Timothy and Opponents		3:14—4:16
	B'	Specific Church Groups	5:1–6:2
A"	Timothy and Opponents (doxology 1:12–17)		6:3–21

No wonder the διδασκ- (*didask-*) root shows up twenty-five times in the PE (elsewhere in Paul only twenty times in six other letters), indicating both the act of teaching and the content thereof, and those who engage in it: 1 Tim 1:3, 7, 10; 2:7, 12; 4:1, 6, 11, 13, 16; 5:17; 6:1, 2, 3; 2 Tim 1:11; 2:2; 3:10, 16; 4:2, 3; Titus 1:9 (×2), 11; 2:1, 7, 10.³⁸ Teaching is clearly central in the PE.

That Ephesus was a center for the magical arts in the ancient Near East also raises the possibility that the church in that city was infected with tendencies towards thaumaturgy. The Ἐφέσια γράμματα (*Ephesia grammata*) were well known inscriptions referencing magicians and curses. Magical amulets with Jewish elements have also been discovered in and around the ancient location of Ephesus. Indeed, magic and Ephesus were linked in Acts 19:11, 19; περίεργα (*perierga*, "magicians") occurs both in Acts 19:19 and in 1 Tim 5:13, the only two instances of the word in Scripture (the magicians Jannes and Jambres also feature in 2 Tim 3:8; and "sorcerers" in 3:13).³⁹ One also has to take into account the pervasive Artemis cult in Ephesus, one that was well known in Greco-Roman times.

> Artemis was considered to make the city safe and sound . . . and healthy [for ὑγιής and its cognates in the PE, see above] . . . . She is described as Lady [Κυρία, *Kyria*; and Κύριος, *Kyrios*, occurs 22× in the PE] . . ., Saviour [Σώτειρα, *Sōteira*; and Σωτήρ, *Sōtēr*, occurs 10× in the PE] . . ., a heavenly goddess and the Queen of the Cosmos. In contrast, 1 Timothy describes God as "the King of the ages, immortal, invisible, the only God" (1:17) and "the blessed and only Sovereign, the King of kings and Lord of lords (6:15). Finally, Artemis is described as "most manifest" [ἐπιφανεστάτη, *epiphanestatē*; and ἐπιφάνεια, *epiphaneia*, occurs 5× in the PE, and ἐπιφαίνω, *epiphainō*, 2×] . . . . It would appear that this language would have particular resonance for the original Ephesian audience of the letters to Timothy.⁴⁰

With all of these heresies prevalent in the environs of Ephesus, it appears these false teachers had infiltrated the church, bringing about the fulfillment of Paul's prophetic utterance in Acts 20:28–31 that "savage wolves will come in among you not sparing the flock."

---

38. Nouns with the διδασκ-root occur in the PE both as plural (1 Tim 1:7; 4:1) and as singular (1 Tim 1:10; 2:7; 4:6, 13, 16; 5:17; 6:1, 3; 2 Tim 1:11; 3:10, 16; 4:2, 3; Titus 1:9 [×2]; 2:1, 3, 7, 10). Strikingly, all of the former (with the exception of Titus 2:3 explicitly prefixed with "good": καλοδιδάσκαλοι, *kalodidaskaloi*) deal with false teaching, and all of the latter with sound doctrine. The use of "soundness" of speech and faith in the PE was noted above.

39. See Pietersen, "Women as Gossips?," 27.

40. Pietersen, "Women as Gossips?," 27–28.

INTRODUCTION

Mandata Prinicipis

Timothy and Titus are Paul's "children" (1 Tim 1:2, 18; 2 Tim 1:2; Titus 1:4) and overall, one might consider the PE as his final words to them, provoked, no doubt, by particular issues, but written with the consciousness of passing on the Pauline baton to delegates. Quinn notes that this model of the Pauline last will and testament in the PE was a sort of set piece in the OT, where we have those of Jacob (Genesis 49), Moses (Deuteronomy 33), Joshua (Joshua 23—24), and David (2 Sam 23:1–7), not forgetting that of Jesus himself in the NT (John 13—17).[41] Johnson's observation is apt:

> There is a body of letter writing that can be termed broadly "royal correspondence," and that is extant partially through inscriptions and partially through papyri fragments. The collections include a variety of communication between royal officials and cities, as well as between royal officials and their subordinates. The latter category is of special significance, for it provides an analogy to the social relationship in 1 Timothy: a superior writes to a representative or delegate with instructions concerning the delegate's mission.[42]

These are the *mandata principis*, "commandments of a ruler," correspondence that has a number of mandates and imperatives for the addressee, as do the PE. Though Johnson seems to restrict this label to 1 Timothy and Titus, there is no doubt that 2 Timothy could be included in the category, too: explicit commands to Timothy therein are found in 2 Tim 1:6, 8, 13–14; 2:1–9, 14–16, 22–24; 3:10–14; 4:1–5.[43] "Although addressed to an individual, the delegate in question, the letters had at least a quasi-public character, for the *entolai* ['commandments'] were to be heard by others as well as the delegate. In some instances, such mandates were accompanied by personal instructions and exhortations to the delegate having to do less with specific actions and more with general attitude and behavior."[44] This is evident in the PE, as will be seen in the body of this commentary. The final utterance of each of the PE, even the very personal one, 2 Timothy, has Paul invoking divine grace upon ὑμεῖς, *hymeis*, "you [all]" (2 Tim 4:22; also see 1 Tim 6:21; Titus 3:15 has πάντες ὑμεῖς, *pantes hymeis*, "you all"), clearly intending that these *mandata principis* be perused by the entire congregation, not just by its leaders.[45] Besides, these emissaries, Timothy and Titus, are to be models for the rest of the congregation to follow, just as they followed their mentor, Paul; and this schema of modeling is something Paul wanted the flock to be aware of.

> A delegate carrying such a letter from his superior and having it read aloud in the assembly of the city to which he was commissioned—even for such a short period as envisaged by 1 Timothy—would accomplish two things. First the

---

41. Quinn, *Letter to Titus*, 9.

42. Johnson, *First and Second Letters to Timothy*, 139.

43. But imperatives are not necessarily governed by grammatical structures; even narratives can have imperatival force. Indeed, the hermeneutic espoused in this commentary series recognizes that every pericope of every book of every Testament of Scripture has the imperatival force of divine demand, whether explicit or implicit: they all call upon God's people to respond and change their lives in order to be conformed to the εἰκών of Christ for the glory of God by the power of the Spirit.

44. Johnson, *First and Second Letters to Timothy*, 140.

45. Nonetheless, the personal nature of 2 Timothy cannot be denied. The frequency of first-person singular pronouns in the three PE is telling: 1 Timothy has six; Titus has four; but 2 Timothy has thirty-three! See Quinn and Wacker, *First and Second Letters to Timothy*, 784–85.

provisions for the community would be perceived as the will of the superior and not simply the whim of the delegate. As a result, the instructions would be legitimated. Second, those parts of the letter exhorting the delegate to good behavior provided the community with a norm by which to measure the delegate's behavior as the leader's representative. The populace would thereby have a basis for appeal to the leader if the delegate fell significantly below the standards established by the letter.[46]

Thus we have, in the PE, three *mandata principis* from one (Paul), to one and all (Ephesian and Cretan Christians, and via the canon to all God's people), through specific single individuals (Timothy and Titus), on how leaders at any level in the divine household are to promote God's economy, οἰκονομία θεοῦ (1 and 2 Timothy), and how such leaders are to be blameless stewards of the οἶκος θεοῦ (Titus). In other words, the PE are all about leading the household of God. Of course, all of God's people are to be leaders to some degree, in some fashion, to some extent, and in some arena. And, as leaders go, so do the people; therefore, what leaders are called to do (and model) is what God's people are called to do (and model, in turn). So while the primary addressees of the PE were the delegates, Timothy and Titus, the entire congregation had access to these missives: it was for them, too. All that to say, leading the household of God to further the economy of God is the task of all the people of God, blameless stewards empowered by the Spirit of God. Thus they become more like the Son of God, for the glory of God.

Theological Focus of the Pastoral Epistles

As expected from the conception of pragmatics as being specific for a particular text, the theological focus of each of the pericopes of the PE is unique, contributing a slice or a quantum of theology to the broad theological thrust of the book it is part of and the corpus it makes up. Together, the theological focus of the PE reflects how leaders of the divine household promote God's economy.

1 Timothy: Shepherding the Saints[47]

The pericopal segments for 1 Timothy deal with: promoting the economy of God by rightly handling Scripture, instructing for the goal of love, the manifestation of godliness (Pericope 1: 1 Tim 1:1–11); discharging one's ministry faithfully, while false teachers are disciplined for disastrous dereliction of duty (Pericope 2: 1 Tim 1:12–20); engaging in corporate prayer for all, that the people of God may live godly and that outsiders may be redeemed, thus furthering the divine economy (Pericope 3: 1 Tim 2:1–7); accepting the critical roles of men

---

46. Johnson, *First and Second Letters to Timothy*, 141.

47. "Shepherding the Saints" (1 Timothy: guidance for conduct in the divine household), "Completing the Course" (2 Timothy: guidance for passing the baton to the next generation, especially in the context of inevitable suffering), and "Exemplifying the Excellent" (Titus: modeling godliness and good works within and without the community), are attempts to provide an approximate heading that is specific for each of the PE. For both 1 and 2 Timothy, I have retained "promote of God's economy" as the opening clauses of the overall Theological Foci of each book (see below), in recognition of the focus on the gospel and all that God is doing ("gospel" is absent in Titus). Also, the unified Theological Focus of each of the three Epistles has "leaders" and "divine household" (the church).

and women in the corporate gathering—being godly: leading prayer (men), and learning with deference and embracing domestic responsibilities (women) (Pericope 4: 1 Tim 2:8–15); leading by modeling godliness (Pericope 5: 1 Tim 3:1–16); undertaking intense spiritual discipline and persevering in godliness for future reward (Pericope 6: 1 Tim 4:1–16); caring for the deserving needy in both domestic and divine households (Pericope 7: 1 Tim 5:1–16); celebrating godliness in others and thereby guarding the holiness of the church (Pericope 8: 1 Tim 5:17–25); serving one another selflessly with good works, thus enhancing God's reputation (Pericope 9: 1 Tim 6:1–2); and relentlessly pursuing godliness marked by humble contentment with basic needs and by a richness of generosity (Pericope 10: 1 Tim 6:3–21). Summing up the Theological Focus of the entire book of 1 Timothy we have:

> *The leaders of the divine household promote God's economy by rightly handling Scripture for the goal of love, the manifestation of godliness, discharging one's ministry faithfully, engaging in corporate prayer for all, accepting the respective critical roles of men and women in the corporate gathering, leading by modeling godliness, undertaking intense spiritual disciplining and persevering in godliness for future reward, caring for the deserving needy, celebrating godliness in others and thereby guarding the holiness of the church, serving one another selflessly with good works, thus enhancing God's reputation, and relentlessly pursuing godliness marked by humble contentment and rich generosity.*

2 Timothy: Completing the Course

The pericopal segments for 2 Timothy deal with: undertaking the divine commission, empowered by the Spirit and with confidence in God, thus faithfully and unashamedly enduring inevitable suffering (Pericope 11: 2 Tim 1:1–18); entrusting the work of God to other faithful ones and seeking to please God and further his economy, thus gaining eternal rewards (Pericope 12: 2 Tim 2:1–13); pursuing righteousness and being beneficial to God for good works, including right speech based on a clear expounding of Scripture (Pericope 13: 2 Tim 2:14–26); following godly models and trusting God for deliverance from persecution, while continuing in Scripture to make one fully equipped for good works (Pericope 14: 2 Tim 3:1–17); and preaching God's word at every opportunity, demonstrating lifelong faithfulness to God, confident of ultimate deliverance and eternal rewards (Pericope 15: 2 Tim 4:1–22). Summing up the Theological Focus of the entire Epistle of 2 Timothy, we see:

> *The leaders of the divine household promote God's economy by undertaking the divine commission faithfully and unashamedly, empowered by the Spirit, seeking single-mindedly to please God, pursuing righteousness and being beneficial to God for good works (especially right speech), continuing in Scripture that makes them fully equipped for good works, preaching God's word at every opportunity, and demonstrating lifelong faithfulness to God, thus being confident of ultimate deliverance and eternal reward.*

Titus: Exemplifying the Excellent

The pericopal segments for Titus deal with: holding firmly to the word of God as blameless leaders and correcting false teachers (Pericope 16: Titus 1:1–16); demonstrating exemplary

INTRODUCTION

godliness in community for the furtherance of God's economy, grounded in the work of God in Christ (Pericope 17: Titus 2:1–15); and likewise, in society, engaging in good works, exhibiting to others God's love for mankind that they had themselves experienced (Pericope 18: Titus 3:1–15). Summing up the Theological Focus of the entire letter to Titus we get:

> *The leaders of the divine household promote God's economy by correcting false teachers, manifesting exemplary godliness in community, and likewise in society, engaging in good works, expressing to others the love God had for them.*

Not surprisingly, there are areas of overlap between the three Epistles; however, they may be undertaken as an eighteen-part preaching series with profit, as the preacher discriminates between the pericopes and their thrusts as demonstrated in the commentary. I see the Letters to Timothy as an encouragement to leaders of the divine household to promote and further the economy of God. The Epistle to Titus is an exhortation to set things in order in the church, another task of a leader, a blameless steward of the divine household.

And thus we have these three unique letters, the PE, guiding leaders at any level in the body of Christ, the shepherds of God's people, in their undertaking of the most honorable task of stewarding the divine household to promote God's economy, for his glory!

1 TIMOTHY

Shepherding the Saints

PERICOPE 1

Instruction for Godliness

1 Timothy 1:1–11

[Right Handling of Scripture; Promotion of the Divine Economy]

SUMMARY, PREVIEW

Summary of Pericope 1: The first pericope of 1 Timothy (1:1–11) focuses on the august responsibility of the people of God and their leaders to handle Scripture rightly, in contrast to what false teachers do. Such a right handling of Scripture in accordance with the gospel (in its broad sense) seeks to apply the sacred writings for the development of godliness in listeners, thus promoting the economy of God and culminating in God's glory.

Preview of Pericope 2: The second pericope of 1 Timothy (1:12–20) has Paul putting himself into the category of those sinners mentioned in the previous pericope (1:1–11). He gratefully describes his wondrous salvation by grace wrought by a merciful God through Christ Jesus. Such a work of God for all believers is for the purpose of appointing them into his service, strengthened by him and persevering in ministry, unlike false teachers who face discipline.

1   *1 Timothy 1:1–11*

THEOLOGICAL FOCUS OF PERICOPE 1

1   The people of God, divinely and authoritatively commissioned, in their right handling of Scripture—congruent to sound teaching and in accordance with God's glorious gospel: his grand plan for his creation—promote the economy of God and his glory, for the goal of their instruction is love, the manifestation of godliness (1:1–11).

1 TIMOTHY

OVERVIEW

This pericope (1:1–11) and the next (Pericope 2: 1 Tim 1:12–18) are carefully centered around the law/Scripture, its misuse and its right use[1]:

Pericope 1 (1:1–11)
- **A** Heterodox teachers; Paul's opposition to them; ἵνα ... μὴ, *hina ... mē* **(1:3–4a)**
  - "instruction;" "good conscience"; "faith" **(1:4b–5)**
  - **B** "from which things [feminine plural] some, going astray" (relative pronoun + τινες, *tines* + aorist participle)
    - Condemnation of ignorant false teachers **(1:6–7)**
    - **C** μὴ νοοῦντες, *mē noountes* (present participle, 1:7) "not understanding"
      - **D** Right use of law; gospel **(1:8–11)**

Pericope 2 (1:12–20)
- Redemption of ignorant sinners **(1:12–17)**
  - **C'** ἀγνοῶν, *agnoōn* (present participle, 1:13) "unknowingly"
- "instruction;" "good conscience"; "faith" **(1:18–19)**
- **B'** "which [feminine singular] some, rejecting" (relative pronoun + τινες + aorist participle)
- **A'** Heterodox teachers; Paul's opposition to them; ἵνα ... μὴ **(1:20)**

1   1 Timothy 1:1–11

THEOLOGICAL FOCUS 1

1   The people of God, divinely and authoritatively commissioned, in their right handling of Scripture—congruent to sound teaching and in accordance with God's glorious gospel: his grand plan for his creation—promote the economy of God and his glory, for the goal of their instruction is love, the manifestation of godliness (1:1–11).

TRANSLATION 1

1:1   *Paul, an apostle of Christ Jesus according to the command of God our Savior, and of Christ Jesus, our hope,*

1:2   *to Timothy, genuine child in faith: Grace, mercy, peace from God the Father and Christ Jesus our Lord.*

1:3   *As I charged you to remain at Ephesus, when I left for Macedonia, so that you may instruct some not to teach falsely,*

1:4   *nor to attend to myths and endless genealogies, which promote useless speculation rather than the economy of God which is in faith.*

---

1. Structure modified from Johnson, *First and Second Letters to Timothy*, 173; and Van Neste, *Cohesion and Structure*, 124.

1:5 *But the goal of [our] instruction is love from a pure heart and a good conscience and an unhypocritical faith,*

1:6 *from which things some, going astray, have turned aside to fruitless discussion,*

1:7 *wanting to be law-teachers, not understanding either what they are saying or things about which they make confident assertions.*

1:8 *But we know that the law is good, if one employs it lawfully,*

1:9 *knowing this, that law is not appointed for a righteous person, but for the lawless and rebellious, for the ungodly and sinners, for the unholy and profane, for patricides and matricides, for murderers,*

1:10 *the immoral, homosexuals, kidnappers, liars, perjurers, and whatever else is contrary to sound teaching,*

1:11 *according to the gospel of the glory of the blessed God, with which I myself have been entrusted!*

NOTES 1

1   *The people of God, divinely and authoritatively commissioned, in their handling of Scripture—congruent to sound teaching and in accordance with God's glorious gospel: his grand plan for his creation—promote the economy of God and his glory, for the goal of their instruction is love, the manifestation of godliness (1:1–11).*

The sense of passing on a commission, characteristic of the *mandata principis*, is all the more emphasized as authoritative with Paul's self-identification as an apostle, himself commissioned by the "command" of God and of Jesus Christ (1:1), adding weight to the *mandata*—instructions to be conveyed, rebukes to be served, practices to be implemented, exhortations to be given, leadership qualities to be examined, and priorities to be promoted.[2] Paul's confident pulling of rank stands in contrast to the pseudo-legitimacy claimed by "some . . . wanting to be law-teachers" (1:6–7) without any warrant or support. The inclination to follow heretical leaders is likely to have generated Paul's claim to primacy right off the bat.[3]

Timothy is Paul's "genuine child" (1:1; as also is Titus, Titus 1:4).[4] It is a spiritual sonship, of course, not a biological one, a relationship born and bred "in faith," a kinship authentic and legitimate because he, Timothy, "followed my [Paul's] teaching, conduct, purpose, faith, patience, love, endurance, persecutions, sufferings" (2 Tim 3:10–11). He is the one being tasked with the *mandata* of the *princeps*, the charges of the leader. By extension,

---

2. "Command" (ἐπιταγή, *epitagē*, 1:1) is an assertive and compelling term, used elsewhere in the NT of divine commandment as here (also in Rom 16:26; 1 Cor 7:6, 25; 2 Cor 8:8).

3. This emphatic authority is also evident in Titus (1:3), another Epistle tackling false teachers; 2 Tim 1:1 has a less authoritative opening.

4. See also 1 Tim 1:18; 2 Tim 1:2; 2:1, as well as 1 Cor 4:17; Phil 2:20 for other affirmations of Timothy's filiation with Paul. Of all Paul's fellow workers, Timothy is the one mentioned the most: co-sender of letters (2 Cor 1:1; Col 1:1; Phil 1:1; 1 Thess 1:1; 2 Thess 1:1; Phlm 1), a "brother" (2 Cor 1:1; 1 Thess 3:2; Phlm 1), a "coworker" (Rom 16:21; 1 Thess 3:2), "kindred spirit" (Phil 2:19–22), a gospel proclaimer (2 Cor 1:19), and one "doing the work of the Lord even as I [Paul] am" (1 Cor 16:10).

all God's people, listening in on this correspondence, are enjoined to abide by the injunctions of God's authoritative apostle. After all, all of God's people are God's leaders, in some degree, to some fashion, in some arena—home, marketplace, office, playground, classroom, mission field. And so, what God through Paul intends Timothy to obey and live by, is what God intends all of his people to obey and live by.

Somewhat uncharacteristically for a NT Epistle, 1 Timothy and Titus (like Galatians) do not commence with a thanksgiving (see 2 Tim 1:3 for the exception in the PE), perhaps reflecting the seriousness of the issues in Ephesus and Crete, respectively.[5] Also indicating the urgency of the situation is the interrupted sentence in 1 Tim 1:3–4; it begins but does not formally complete its thought, though an imperative is implied: "As I urged you to remain in Ephesus, when I left for Macedonia, so that you may instruct . . ."[6]

The verb "to instruct" (παραγγέλλω, *parangellō*) in 1:3 is quite forceful, having the sense of "charge"/"prescribe" (also in 4:11; 5:7; 6:13, 17). This not only continues to underscore Paul's apostolic authority, but also implies that Timothy himself possesses Paul's authority as he undertakes to follow his mentor's "instruction" (παραγγελία, *parangelia*, 1:5; equally forceful: see Acts 5:28; 16:24; 1 Thess 4:2; 1 Tim 1:18). Timothy, by virtue of being Paul's proxy, is thus being instructed to instruct others, particularly the false teachers. On the other hand, "some" (1:3, 6, 19) have no such authority (and two of these characters are named in 1:20; for others, see 2 Tim 2:17; 4:14).[7] It appears that Paul had informed Timothy earlier ("as I charged you . . . ," 1 Tim 1:3) and that he is repeating himself here, likely for the benefit of the entire Ephesian church—another indication of this epistle being more public than one might suppose.[8]

The verb "to teach falsely" (ἑτεροδιδασκαλέω, *heterodidaskaleō*) shows up in the NT only here in 1:3 and in 6:3, in effect bracketing the entire letter. In several places in the rest of the Epistle, Paul will contrast falsehood and truth, as well as their respective proponents and the results of their particular propagations. Indeed, 1:3–7 is itself carefully structured, contrasting the false teachers with Paul and his cohorts[9]:

---

5. However, there is an extended and personal thanksgiving later in 1 Tim 1:12–17. Here, in the greeting, God is labeled "Savior" in 1:1, and also in 2:3 and 4:10, as well as in Titus 1:3; 2:10, 13; 3:4. Elsewhere in the NT, such a theme shows up only in Jude 25.

6. Such a discontinuity is called an anacoluthon, not entirely rare when Paul is the author (Rom 5:12–14; Gal 3:6; Phil 1:7).

7. "Some" (τινες, *tines*) is a fairly common quasi-pejorative designation by Paul for his opponents; also deployed in 1 Tim 1:19; 4:1; 5:15, 24; 6:10, 21; and in Rom 3:8; 1 Cor 4:18; 5:1; 15:12; 2 Cor 3:1; 10:2; Gal 1:7; 2:12; Phil 1:15.

8. The historical scenario behind 1:3, that mentions the situation of the writer and his recipient, is a bit obscure. It is sufficient to understand that Timothy had been separated from Paul and remained in Ephesus, as his mentor headed off to Macedonia.

9. Modified from Van Neste, *Cohesion and Structure,* 120. A table summarizing the contrasts between true and false teaching is provided below.

A	*False teaching*: ἑτεροδιδασκαλεῖν, *heterodidaskalein* **(1:3)** ("to teach falsely")
B	*Negative*: ἐκζητήσεις; προσέχω and παρέχω; γενεαλογία **(1:4a)** (*ekzētēseis; prosechō* and *parechō; genealogia*) ("speculation"; "attend" and "promote"; "genealogy")
C	*Right teaching; positive*: "the goal" **(1:4b–5)**
B'	*Negative*: ἐξετράπησαν; ἀστοχέω; ματαιολογία **(1:6)** (*exetrapēsan; astocheō; mataiologia*) ("turn aside"; "go astray"; "fruitless discussion")
A'	*False teaching*: νομοδιδάσκαλοι, *nomodidaskaloi* **(1:7)** ("law-teachers")

The ones propagating false doctrine, those who "teach falsely" (1:3), were the ones seeking to be "law-teachers" (1:7). They were plying "myths" (1:4, and also in 4:7; 2 Tim 4:4; Titus 1:14) and "genealogies" (1 Tim 1:4; also in Titus 3:9, the only two instances of the word in the NT). "Myths" likely dealt with deity-related fables; "genealogies"—that had no end and furthered no goal ("endless")—could have had something to do with fabricated accounts of characters in Genesis (as in Philo, *On the Life of Moses* 2.47).[10] The proximity of 1 Tim 4:1–3 with the reuse of "myths" in 4:7 may also suggest that the bogus content of those false teachers included these "teachings of demons" (διδασκαλίαις δαιμονίων, *didaskaliais daimoniōn*, 4:1); in contrast is Paul's "sound teaching" (ὑγιαίνουσα διδασκαλία, *hygiainousa didaskalia*, 1:10). While we may assume their Jewish connections, it seems that they were operating within the church: as we shall see in Pericope 2 (1 Tim 1:12–20), they undergo some form of excommunication; Paul even appears to have entertained hopes of remedying their disorientation to divine writing and their disregard of divine economy (1:20). In any case, though it is uncertain what Paul was referring to by those terms describing the heterodoxy in 1:4, he is clearly affirming its falsehood, deceptiveness, and utter inutility.[11]

These promoters of falsehoods were "attending to" (προσέχω) such perversions, thus "promoting" (παρέχω; note the paronomasia) "useless speculations" (1:4), the negative result of their errant pedagogy.[12] They ought, rather, to have been promoting "the economy of God"—his administration (οἰκονομία, *oikonomia*, 1:4b), i.e., his management and stewardship of his creation: "God's way of ordering things."[13] This administration and ordering, this

---

10. Perhaps all of this was linked to some form of Jewish allegory, since 1:7 shows these false teachers to be connected to the law ("law-teachers"). From Titus 1:10, 14–16; 3:9, we can gather that these were "of the circumcision" (1:10). Besides, Paul referenced the Jewish fable of Jannes and Jambres (2 Tim 3:8), using it as an example of the gaseous thinking of these promoters of heterodoxy. In any case, "genealogies" and "myths" were standard pairings in Greek literature: see Plato, *Timaeus* 22A–B; Strabo, *Geographica* 8.2; Sextus Empiricus, *Against the Professors* 253; Polybius, *Histories* 9.2.1; etc.

11. Why the false teachers were doing what they were doing is also uncertain. At any rate, I don't think their specific motives are particularly pertinent to the thrust of this pericope.

12. "Useless speculations," ἐκζήτησις, *ekzētēsis*, occurs only here in the NT; the related ζήτησις (*zētēsis*, "disputes") is found in 6:4 (linked with ἑτεροδιδασκαλέω, as was its cognate noun in this pericope in 1:3); 2 Tim 2:23 (1:17 has the verb, ζητέω, *zēteō*); and Titus 3:9 (where it is linked with γενεαλογία, as also here in 1 Tim 1:4), suggesting a uniformity of theme within the PE.

13. Johnson, *First and Second Letters to Timothy*, 157. Or "God's administration of an orderly universe which he arranged and continues to guide" (Reumann, "Use of *Oikonomia* and Related Terms," 391). Elsewhere, God's ruling over the universe is described with the verbs διοικέω, *dioikeō* (Wis 8:1, 14; 12:18;

governing of the divine economy, occurs in the realm/sphere of "faith" (1:4)—a faith-based, faith-promoting, faith-operated, and faith-controlled undertaking.[14] This is the "sound teaching" endorsed in this pericope—as opposed to the false teaching of some—congruent to the "gospel" (1:11). In other words, this "economy of God" is the gospel in its broadest sense of God's grand, eternal plan to consummate all things in Christ.[15] This is not merely a description of the atoning work of Christ; rather, it is the delineation of God's operation stretching from eternity to eternity. And this gospel, Paul avers in 1:11, is glorious, because it brings glory to God as the divine economy is transacted.[16]

Thus the rest of the "instruction" in 1 Timothy (and even in the rest of the PE) explains the economy of God, how things ought to be in church and in society and in life in general, in the *world in front of the text*—"God's plan for executing his purpose with respect to humankind and indeed all creation."[17] And this economy, administration, ordering of God—"the gospel of the glory of the blessed God" (1:11)—is facilitated by "God's steward" (θεοῦ οἰκονόμος, *theou oikonomos*), the elder of the church (Titus 1:7) which body is, itself, the "household of God" (οἶκος θεοῦ, *oikos theou*, 1 Tim 3:15).[18] So if those false teachers were themselves leaders of some sort in the οἶκος θεοῦ, we are being told that their heterodox activities exposed them as *not* being θεοῦ οἰκονόμοι (*theou oikonomoi*) and *not* furthering the οἰκονομίαν θεοῦ (*oikonomian theou*).

The contrast between false and true teaching continues with 1:5–7 (a single sentence), outlining the goal of Paul's instruction ("but the goal of [our] instruction," 1:5). That rightful "goal" or endpoint (τέλος, *telos*) was love sourced in "a pure heart and a good conscience and a sincere faith."[19] In other words, love manifest and expressed is achieved by a heart cleansed of sin, a conscience cleared of guilt, and a faith cultivated in truth (as opposed to one that is hypocritical and not genuine).[20] This love, directed both toward God and neighbor, the zenith of godliness and the greatest of the commandments (Matt 22:37–40; Mark 12:30–31; Luke 10:27), is the mark of a person of God, living life God's way, fully entrenched

---

1:5:1; *Letter of Aristeas* 234, 254) and οἰκονομέω, *oikonomeō* (Philo, *On the Creation* 2; *On the Confusion of Tongues* 21).

14. The anarthrous uses of πίστις, *pistis*, generally deal with the realm/sphere or domain of faith.

15. A plan for the entirety of the cosmos: see Eph 1:8–10 (see Kuruvilla, *Ephesians*, 20–35; also see introduction).

16. The chain of genitives in 1:11, τὸ εὐαγγέλιον τῆς δόξης τοῦ μακαρίου θεοῦ (*to euangelion tēs doxēs tou makariou theou*), is analogous to another genitive cascade in Titus 2:13: ἐπιφάνειαν τῆς δόξης τοῦ μεγάλου θεου (*epiphaneian tēs doxēs tou megalou theou*), "the appearance of the glory of the great God" (= "glorious appearance"). The two are best interpreted similarly, and thus 1 Tim 1:11 would then read: "the glorious gospel of the blessed God," the gospel that redounds to the glory of God.

17. Quinn and Wacker, *First and Second Letters to Timothy*, 76.

18. For notions related to the church as God's household in the PE, see 1 Tim 3:4–5, 12, 15; 5:1–2; 2 Tim 2:20; Titus 1:7; 2:2–6.

19. Quinn and Wacker, *First and Second Letters to Timothy*, 79, note that "the three phrases here in First Timothy . . . are substantially synonymous." So while there is no need to distinguish between them, it may be worth remembering that the heart is biblically the seat of godly intentionality (Gen 6:5; Exod 4:21; Deut 8:2; Rom 1:24; 6:17), the conscience the arbiter of godly behavior (that may be "good"/"pure," 1 Tim 1:5, 19; 3:9; 2 Tim 1:3; or "seared"/"defiled," 1 Tim 4:2; Titus 1:15), and faith the godly attitude with which the entirety of life is conducted. Hence, "love," sourced in these godly attributes, is the manifestation of godliness.

20. Modified from Mounce, *Pastoral Epistles*, 24. It is notable that in the PE, every occurrence of "love" is paired with "faith," except in 2 Tim 1:7 (see 1 Tim 1:14; 2:15; 4:12; 6:11; 2 Tim 1:13; 2:22; 3:10; Titus 2:2).

in, and promoting, the economy of God, becoming an inhabitant of God's *world in front of the text*.[21] But that, however, was not the goal of the false teachers, who only promoted "useless speculation" rather than furthering the economy of God. In other words, to further the divine economy, the people of God manifest love (the summative command of Scripture) in a life of godliness marked by "a pure heart and a good conscience and a sincere faith," i.e., the expression of a complete person of God. (This is going to be contrasted with a list of some insalubrious characters, entirely ungodly, in 1:9–10; see below.)

Notice the wordplay that brackets 1:3–10: ἑτεροδιδασκαλεῖν (1:3) and εἴ τι ἕτερον τῇ ὑγιαινούσῃ διδασκαλίᾳ ἀντίκειται (*ei ti heteron tē hygiainousē didaskalia antikeitai*, 1:10): those who "teach falsely" promote "whatever else is contrary to sound teaching." In 1:8–11, the contrast between Paul's ministry and that of the false teachers is detailed further: using "the law ... lawfully," recognizing that the law was for the lawless (1:8–9) vs. not using the law lawfully (implied of false teachers):

1:8	οἴδαμεν ... *oidamen* ... "we know	ὅτι ... *hoti* ... that	ὁ νόμος ... *ho nomos* ... the law ...	νομίμως *nomimōs* lawfully"
1:9	εἰδὼς ... *eidōs* ... "knowing ...	ὅτι ... *hoti* ... that	νόμος ... *nomos* ... law ...	ἀνόμοις *anomois* lawless"

The law here, though referring to the Mosaic Law, is best seen as a metonym for Scripture and all divine demand, no matter what the genre of the text.[22] The law is "good" when used "lawfully" (1:8), i.e., against the lawless (1:9) and against all manner of vices—all that is "contrary to sound teaching" (1:10). This "sound teaching," Paul declares, is the gospel (1:11), in its broadest sense equivalent to the grand scope of divine action in creation, i.e., the glory-bringing economy of God, which Paul's instruction was promoting (1:4–5).

"Lawfully" (in 1:8) "refers to application of the law that is in accordance with the purposes of the divine lawgiver."[23] No doubt there are multiple uses of the law, some of which, after the work of Christ, have been rendered anachronistic in the current dispensation. For instance, the law could point "prophetically" to the Savior, a function it does not necessarily have now (Gal 3:19—4:7). But other functions of the law still pertain to God's people, especially its ability to reveal sin (Rom 3:20; 5:13; 7:7–12; 1 Cor 15:56; Gal 3:19).[24] This is related

---

21. The only other collocation of "heart," "conscience," and "faith" in the NT occurs in Heb 10:22, where also the context deals with purity of life and engagement in holy living—the divine economy incarnated in community as godliness.

22. See Kuruvilla, *Privilege the Text!*, 151–209. In other words, divine demand encompasses *all* of God's law—pre-Mosaic commands, Mosaic Law, law of Christ, laws of his millennial reign, etc. And, by divine demand, I do not mean to exclude non-imperatives in Scripture; every pericope in every genre of every book in the Bible depicts God's ideal *world in front of the text*—its precepts, its priorities, and its practices: how the divine economy runs. In that sense, every biblical pericope makes a divine demand upon mankind and is imperatival. Divine demand is certainly a gracious invitation from God to his people to inhabit his ideal world; but let us not forget that the rejection of that call has consequences.

23. Thornton, "Sin Seizing an Opportunity," 147.

24. Another permanent property of the law is its inability to justify (Rom 3:20) or empower sanctification (Rom 8:3).

1 TIMOTHY

to Paul's intent in 1 Tim 1:9a: the lawful use of the law points out behavior that is divinely proscribed, thus condemning lawbreakers (the ones listed in 1:9b–10). Notice that it is not only doers of those extreme acts of sin who stand condemned, but also those who engage in doing "whatever else is contrary to sound teaching" (1:10), considerably broadening the scope of lawlessness (i.e., sin).

Standard commentaries are unanimous in reading 1:3–17 as decrying law and exalting faith and grace. Commentators expatiate on Paul's attitude to law vis-à-vis gospel; for e.g., "the law is not of use for the Christian but rather for the unbeliever."[25] But Paul has just affirmed that "the law is good" (1:8)! And elsewhere in Romans, he asserts that "the law is holy and the commandment is holy and righteous and good" (7:12), and "spiritual" (7:14). In fact, Paul "establishes" the law (3:31), and in it he "delights" (7:22; also see 7:16). Indeed, it is through obedience powered by the Holy Spirit that the "righteous requirement of the law is fulfilled" (8:4). Paul's attitude to the law cannot be pejorative when he refers to the Mosaic Law in this very epistle (1 Tim 2:13–15) and even cites it approvingly, drawing application from that older text (5:17). Indeed, "*every* [text of] Scripture is God-breathed and profitable" (2 Tim 3:16).[26]

Against this traditional understanding, I submit that when Paul is seemingly derogating the law, for instance in Eph 2:14–18, he is actually talking about the *condemnation* of the law—the sentence pronounced in/by divine law upon sin and sinners.[27] Historically, what God demanded of his people was enshrined in the Mosaic Law; later such divine demand included every one of the laws of Scripture, in both Testaments. It is the condemnation called upon sin by this generic law that has been removed by Christ's atoning work. It is not that God's demands/laws have been nullified, but only the condemnation of the law pronounced upon the sinner, for the price of sin has been paid. In Christ there is no longer any condemnation for sin that affects the standing of believers with God for everlasting life (Rom 8:1). Those who trust Jesus Christ as their only God and Savior from sin are finally and forever freed from condemnation for breakage of God's demand/law. All that to say, divine demand/law is not rendered inoperative for those in Christ—all of it is still valid; it is only *the condemnation for not abiding by the law* that has been removed by redemption in Jesus Christ.[28] Divine demand/law, in its theological sense, is always valid, for all humanity—it directs the behavior of those who (already) have become the people of God. This is the "lawful" use of the law that Paul is arguing for in our text.[29]

---

25. Towner, *Timothy and Titus*, 122.

26. Cranfield describes the common understanding of the law as being abrogated as a "modern version of Marcionism" that regards the biblical history as "an unsuccessful first attempt on God's part at dealing with man's unhappy state, which had to be followed later by a second (more successful) attempt (a view which is theologically grotesque, for the God of the unsuccessful first attempt is hardly a God to be taken seriously)" (*Romans*, 2:862).

27. See my *Ephesians*, 66–83, from which this discussion is abridged. On the other hand, the law has no condemnatory jurisdiction upon those who are believers (Rom 7:1–4; 8:1); release from the law (i.e., from its condemnation) is found in 7:6 (also see Gal 2:19).

28. Paul's declaration of believers as no longer under the condemnation of the law (Rom 6:14)—the law having come to bring about wrath, increase transgression, and arouse sinful passions (4:15; 5:20; 7:5)—is consistent with this view.

29. For an extensive discussion on the *theological* validity of all God's demands for all of God's people in all ages and all places, see Kuruvilla, *Privilege the Text!*, 151–209.

Such an understanding is in accordance with "the gospel of the glory of the blessed God" (1:11)—the divine economy. Of course, if one is not sinning and is a "righteous person," then one has no need of the law (1:9a). But the law cannot justify, and even more importantly, it cannot sanctify. Only the Holy Spirit can, and he *does* enable every child of God to that end (Rom 8:3–5). All that to say, obedience is all of grace, yet there is Christian responsibility.

> In sum, the child of God is never to attempt obedience with self-resources: that would be a self-glorifying, flesh-driven, merit-attempting, grace-rejecting, faith-negating obedience to divine law—the legalism Paul so often excoriated. Utterly futile. Instead, the "obedience of faith" (Rom. 1:5; 16:26) that God empowers is a God-glorifying, Spirit-driven, merit-rejecting, grace-accepting, faith-exercising endeavor. So, Christian life, in its entirety, is a function of divine grace, designed to bring glory to God: the Father's choice of men and women to become a holy people in Christ (justification), their empowerment by the Spirit to live lives that are Christlike (sanctification), and, one day, consummation of their transformation into the image of Jesus Christ (glorification).[30]

Thus, a "lawful" use of the law (1 Tim 1:8) directs it to appropriate malefactors and their activities (1:9–10)—no doubt also to believers who, unfortunately, also tend to sin, living by the flesh rather than by the Spirit—to facilitate cessation of the malfeasances deprecated in 1:9–10: all that is "contrary to sound teaching."[31] This is to direct God's people to align themselves to divine demand. The vice list of 1:9–10 names nefarious actors and their pernicious activities that are antithetical to God's requirements. It labels four pairs of sinners, then a series of six singly listed evildoers, and concludes not with a seventh villain, but with "whatever else is contrary to sound teaching" (1:10).[32] This list appears to reflect the Decalogue, offenses against deity (I–IV in the Decalogue) and offenses against humanity (V–IX)[33]:

---

30. Kuruvilla, "Christiconic View," 68. Also see Kuruvilla, *Privilege the Text!*, 195–204, for more on such an "obedience of faith."

31. Notice the opposing use of κεῖμαι (*keimai*, "is . . . appointed for"—relating to the right use of the law by truth teachers) in 1:9, and ἀντίκειμαι (*antikeimai*, "is contrary to"—relating to the wrong use of the law by false teachers) in 1:10.

32. So, 1:9–10 is not a list of *vices*, but mostly a list of the *vicious!* Paul begins 1:9 with δίκαιος, a masculine singular, follows it with a list of masculine plural substantives (the "vicious"), and ends in 1:10 with τι ἕτερον, *ti heteron*, a neuter singular (the "vice").

33. The tenth commandment, against coveting, is not represented here; the catch-all, "whatever else is contrary," would include it, of course. Other lists in the New Testament that parallel the Decalogue are also likewise incomplete: Matt 19:18; Mark 10:19; Luke 19:20; Rom 13:9; etc.

1 TIMOTHY

	1 Timothy 1:9–10	Correspondence with the Decalogue
I	ἀσεβής asebēs	ungodly = having other gods (Acts 13:43, 50; 16:14; 17:4, 17; 18:7)
II	ἁμαρτωλός hamartōlos	sinners = idolatry (Exod 20:4–6; Gal 2:15; Rom 2:22)
III	ἀνόσιος anosios	unholy = taking the name of God in vain (Exod 20:7; Matt 6:9; Luke 11:2)
IV	βέβηλος bebēlos	profane = anti-Sabbath (Exod 20:8; Lev 19:12)
V	πατρολῴας, μητρολῴας patrolōas, mētrolōas	patricide, matricide = dishonoring parents (Exod 20:12; Deut 5:16)
VI	ἀνδροφόνος androphonos	murderer (Exod 20:13; Deut 5:17)
VII	ἀνδραποδιστής andrapodistēs	kidnapper or slave dealer = stealing (Exod 20:15; Deut 5:19)
VIII	ψεύστης, ἐπίορκος pseustēs, epiorkos	liar, perjurer = false witness (Exod 20:16; Deut 5:20)
IX	πόρνος, ἀρσενοκοίτης pornos, arsenokoitēs	fornicator, homosexual = illicit sexuality (Exod 20:14; Deut 5:18)

"The list echoes the Decalogue in such a way that the relationship is close enough not to be missed and broad enough to appeal to the Hellenistic ear of the church that would have overhead this letter. Calling on the Decalogue at this point makes perfect sense since as the core of the Torah it establishes the essential criteria for making sin against God and people known . . .—the appropriate use of the law that Paul has in mind."[34] One might ask why Paul tweaked the Decalogue in this fashion without resorting to actual quotes from the Torah. "Two factors may account for this. The first is Paul's evident decision to express the commandments in single words, a phenomenon not present in the Hebrew OT and thus not in the LXX. The second may be his desire to express this list in the contemporary terms known to the hearers and false teachers."[35] There is also Paul's need to shock listeners: "Look at the effects of the unlawful use of the law!" Paul exclaims. While shocking the list might be, it is rhetorical in intent and, though hyperbolic, its thrust is evident. The list of 1:9–10 is polemical, to underscore the fact that the rightful use of the law is to aid right living; and, on the other hand, an unlawful use of the law, the way it was being used by the false teachers, was not at all conducive to keep evil/evildoing in check. So Paul's declamation "lays the blame for committing such crimes upon the false teachers" and their unsound teaching that, rather than further God's economy in accordance with the gospel and for the glory of God, move people away from such an ideal *world in front of the text*, inducing their engagement in debased behavior.[36]

So, to summarize, here are the contrasting terms related to "true" teaching and false teaching in this pericope:

---

34. Towner, *Timothy and Titus*, 125.
35. Knight, *Pastoral Epistles*, 87–88.
36. Marshall, *Pastoral Epistles*, 378.

True Teaching	False Teaching
Promotes the "economy of God" (1:4)	Furthers "useless speculations" (1:4)
Seeks love/godliness (1:5)	Strays from love/godliness (1:6)
Uses law lawfully (1:8)	Uses law unlawfully (implied)
Applies law to sin and sinners (1:9–10)	Attends to myths and genealogies (1:3–4)
Is "sound teaching" (implied)	Is "contrary to sound teaching" (1:10)
Is in accord with the "gospel" (1:11)	Is not in accord with the gospel (implied)
Brings glory to God (1:11)	Does not bring glory to God (implied)

Thus the law was given to combat sin and unlawfulness, so that God's people would live in accord with, or be measured by the standard of, "the gospel of the glory of the blessed God" (1:11). This "gospel" of divine glory—considered in its broadest sense as the "economy of God" (1:4), the entirety of his plans and purposes for his creation—is the benchmark of "sound teaching." And so it is such instruction, congruent to the gospel (i.e., the lawful use of the law: the right handling of Scripture), that brings glory to God—declaring and manifesting God's glory in the godly lives of his people, lives marked by love from a pure heart, a good conscience, and a sincere faith. Such a grave responsibility that was "entrusted" to Paul,[37] and which he was, in turn, entrusting to his "genuine child in the faith," Timothy, is by extension, being entrusted to all believers as well.

SERMON MAPS

THEOLOGICAL FOCUS OF PERICOPE 1 FOR PREACHING[38]

1 The people of God, in their handling of Scripture, promote the economy of God (in contrast to false teachers), for the goal of their instruction is love, the manifestation of godliness (1:1–11).

Putting like things in the text together in the sermon is a critical skill to master. Rather than being constrained to go verse-by-verse, be controlled by the homiletical map you choose: the ordering of your sermon is governed by that map, not by the text. The two communicational modalities, spoken sermon and scripted text, are vastly different and will not necessarily have an identical sequencing of content. This is particularly true for non-narrative biblical literature.

---

37. The phrase ὃ ἐπιστεύθην ἐγώ (*ho episteuthēn egō*, 1:11) is emphatic—"with which I *myself* have been entrusted."

38. This is a reduction of a reduction! Such reductions are *not* what must be conveyed to listeners or what is intended to be caught by them. Rather, the Theological Focus is an aid for the sermon preparer: it helps in the creation of a sermon map, as well as in the deriving of specific application. See Kuruvilla, *Manual for Preaching*, 57–112; and Kuruvilla, "Time to Kill the Big Idea?"

1 TIMOTHY

Possible Preaching Maps for Pericope 1[39]

I. Functioning of False Teachers
   The interests of false teachers (1:4)
   The failure of false teachers (1:6–7)
   Move-to-relevance: Mishandling of Scripture today[40]

II. Functioning of True Teachers
   Seriousness and urgency of the task (1:1–3)
   The goal of true teachers: love, manifestation of godliness (1:5)
   Scripture and the guidance of godliness (1:8–10)
   Move-to-relevance: Our failure to be goal-oriented in our instruction

III. Consequences
   The non-promotion of the divine economy by false teachers (1:4–5)
   The promotion of the divine economy by true teachers (1:5)
   Congruence with the gospel, leading to the glory of God (1:11)
   Move-to-relevance: Consequences for the church and the Christian

IV. *Teach truly!*[41]
   How we can handle Scripture rightly, for ourselves and our listeners

With some minor changes, one may create a Problem–Solution–Application map[42]:

I. PROBLEM: Mishandling of Scripture and its Consequences
   The interests of false teachers (1:4)
   The failure of false teachers (1:6–7)
   The non-promotion of the divine economy by false teachers (1:4–5)
   Move-to-relevance: Mishandling of Scripture today

II. SOLUTION: Right Handling of Scripture
   Seriousness and urgency of the task (1:1–3)
   The goal of true teachers: love, manifestation of godliness (1:5)
   Scripture and the guidance of godliness (1:8–10)
   The promotion of the divine economy by true teachers (1:5)
   Congruence with the gospel, leading to the glory of God (1:11)
   Move-to-relevance: Our failure to be goal-oriented in our instruction

III. APPLICATION: *Teach truly!*
   How we can handle Scripture rightly, for ourselves and our listeners

39. The maps provided are deliberately skimpy; they are intended merely to be suggestions for further thought—rough-hewn stones to be polished by the preacher. It is nigh impossible to prescribe a sermon map without knowing the particular audience it is to be used for, and therefore this commentary will refrain from micromanaging homiletics for the preacher. Needless to say, the preacher must also provide the congregation with specifics on how the theological thrust of each pericope may be put into practice so that lives are conformed to Christlikeness in the power of the Spirit, for the glory of God (application; see Kuruvilla, *Manual for Preaching,* 57–86).

40. Moves-to-relevance are critical in every major move of the sermon, relating the theological thrust (or portions thereof) to listeners and their particular circumstances.

41. Maps in this commentary will have an imperative as a major move—the application. The specificity and direction of that imperative is between the Holy Spirit, the preacher, and the audience.

42. This age-old rhetorical scheme is easy to organize and manipulate; perhaps the reason is because we tend to think that way. There might very well be a hardwiring in our brains for a Problem–Solution–Application sequence.

PERICOPE 2

Faithfulness in Ministry

1 Timothy 1:12–20

[Divine Appointment by Grace; Faithfulness in Ministry]

REVIEW, SUMMARY, PREVIEW

Review of Pericope 1: The previous pericope (1 Tim 1:1–11) focused on the august responsibility of the people of God and their leaders to handle Scripture rightly, in accordance with the gospel (in its broad sense), seeking to apply the sacred writings for the development of godliness in listeners, thus promoting the economy of God and culminating in God's glory.

Summary of Pericope 2: The second pericope of 1 Timothy (1:12–20) takes an autobiographical tone, as Paul, putting his past self into the category of those sinners mentioned in Pericope 1, gratefully describes the wondrous salvation by grace wrought on his behalf by a merciful God through Christ Jesus. Such a work of God for all believers is for the purpose of appointing them into his service, divinely strengthened, that they may persevere in ministry, unlike false teachers, who face discipline.

Preview of Pericope 3: The next pericope of 1 Timothy (2:1–7) begins a section on instructions for corporate conduct. Primary in importance is corporate prayer—all manner of prayer for all people, including all authorities, for the salvation of all people: the furtherance of divine economy. This is pleasing to God, who desires all to be saved through Christ, and who has appointed believers for the task of proclamation of the gospel, the grand plan of God.

2   1 Timothy 1:12–20

THEOLOGICAL FOCUS OF PERICOPE 2

2   God's superabounding, amazing, and awe-inspiring grace strengthens and appoints believers—once sinners, now mercifully saved—into service, to discharge their ministries faithfully (a divine charge and entrustment), while false teachers suffer remedial discipline for disastrous dereliction of duty (1:12–20).

  2.1   God's superabounding, amazing, and awe-inspiring grace appoints and strengthens believers—once sinners, now saved—into service, to discharge their ministries faithfully (1:12–17).

  2.2   God's people, divinely charged and entrusted, engage in ministry with perseverance and integrity, while false teachers suffer discipline for disastrous dereliction of duty, hopefully to be reinstated into service (1:18–20).

OVERVIEW

There are several links between 1:11, the last verse of Pericope 1: 1 Tim 1:1–11, and this pericope[1]:

1 Timothy 1:11	1 Timothy 1:12–20
Paul's entrustment: a special ministry ("gospel")	Paul's being "placed in ministry" (1:12)
"Entrusted" (from πιστεύω, *pisteuō*)	πιστ-root: 1:12, 13, 14, 15, 16, 19 (×2)
Only first person singular in 1:8–11 (after 1:3)	Ten first person singulars in 1:12–17
Only mention of "God" in 1:3–11	Only mention of "God" in 1:12–17 (1:17)
"glory"	"glory" (1:17)

As was noted in Pericope 1: 1 Tim 1:1–11, the first chapter of this Epistle is constructed chiastically[2]:

Pericope 1 (1:1–11)
- **A**   Heterodox teachers; Paul's opposition to them **(1:3–4a)**
-   **B**   "instruction"; "good conscience"; "faith" **(1:4b–5)**
-     **C**   Condemnation of ignorant false teachers **(1:6–7)**
-       **D**   Right use of law; gospel **(1:8–11)**

Pericope 2 (1:12–20)
-     **C′**   Redemption of ignorant sinners **(1:12–17)**
-   **B′**   "instruction"; "good conscience"; "faith" **(1:18–19)**
- **A′**   Heterodox teachers; Paul's opposition to them **(1:20)**

---

1. Modified from Van Neste, *Cohesion and Structure*, 80. After 1:11 ἐγώ (*egō*) occurs only four more times in 1 Timothy, three of which are in 1:12, 15, 16.

2. Modified from Johnson, *First and Second Letters to Timothy*, 173; and Van Neste, *Cohesion and Structure*, 124.

The clause ὃ ἐπιστεύθην ἐγώ (*ho episteuthēn egō* (1:11) is emphatic—"with which I *myself* have been entrusted." It primes the reader for Paul's amazement in 1:12–16 that such a person as he could be commissioned to proclaim the "gospel of the glory of the blessed God" (1:11) for the furtherance of the economy of God, as opposed to inutile activities of false teachers (1:4–5).

2.1   1 Timothy 1:12–17

THEOLOGICAL FOCUS 2.1

2.1   God's superabounding, amazing, and awe-inspiring grace appoints and strengthens believers—once sinners, now saved—into service, to discharge their ministries faithfully (1:12–17).

TRANSLATION 2.1

1:12   *I give thanks to the one who strengthened me, Christ Jesus our Lord, for He considered me faithful, appointing me into service,*

1:13   *though being formerly a blasphemer and a persecutor and an aggressor, I was shown mercy because I acted unknowingly in unbelief;*

1:14   *and the grace of our Lord was superabundant, with the faith and love which [are] in Christ Jesus.*

1:15   *The statement is trustworthy, worthy of all acceptance, that Christ Jesus came into the world to save sinners, of whom I myself am foremost.*

1:16   *But for this reason I found mercy, so that in me as the foremost, Christ Jesus may demonstrate His utmost patience as an example for those who were to believe in Him for eternal life.*

1:17   *Now to the King eternal, immortal, invisible, only God, honor and glory from eternity to eternity. Amen!*

NOTES 2.1

2.1   *God's superabounding, amazing, and awe-inspiring grace appoints and strengthens believers—once sinners, now saved—into service, to discharge their ministries faithfully (1:12–17)*

Paul's thanks in 1:12 is unusual —χάριν ἔχω (*charin echō*) literally "I have thanks," rather than his typical εὐχαριστέω (*eucharisteō*), "I thank" (Rom 1:8; 1 Cor 1:4; Eph 1:16; Phil 1:3; Col 1:3; 2 Thess 1:3; 2:13; Phlm 4). And besides, almost all of his standard thanksgivings are directed to God, but here it is to "Christ Jesus our Lord." He is exulting with gratitude! Notice that Paul gives thanks (χάρις, *charis*, 1:12) for Christ's grace (also χάρις, 1:14).

There is no reason to attempt an unraveling of the sequence of divine initiatives mentioned in 1:12–16: strengthening, consideration as faithful, appointment to service (1:12); showing of mercy (1:13, 16); superabounding of grace along with faith and love in Christ

(1:14); and the demonstration of divine patience in Paul (1:16). One will be hard-pressed to create an order of events out of these. It will be sufficient, in summary, to see Paul being saved (1:15) by the grace, mercy, faith, and love of Christ, and appointed to faithful service by divine strengthening (1:12). The entirety of Paul's ministry, then, was a demonstration of God's patience with sinners, a prototype and paradigm to those who would believe in Christ (1:16). And for this commissioning, Paul is thankful (1:12) and he celebrates with a joyful benediction (1:17).

Paul's recounting of his appointment into "service" (διακονία, diakonia, 1:12), is undoubtedly a reminder to Timothy of his own "service"—this protégé of Paul is himself called a διάκονος of Jesus Christ (diakonos, 4:6). By extension, all God's people have been so appointed as well, to discharge their ministries faithfully. This is also implied in the labeling of certain officers of the church as διάκονοι (3:8, 10, 12, 13).

Faithfulness is the mark of such servants. As was noted in the table above, there are several instances of the πιστ-root in 1:12–20: πιστός, pistos, "faithful" (1:12); ἀπιστία, apistia, "unbelief" (1:13); πίστις, pistis, "faith" (1:14, 19 [×2]); πιστός, "trustworthy" (1:15); πιστεύω, "believe" (1:16). All of this goes to show that Paul's life change, from "blasphemer," "persecutor," and "aggressor" (1:13)—the "foremost" of sinners (1:15, 16)—to one strengthened by Christ Jesus and appointed to his service (1:12), was furthering the economy of God ἐν πίστει (en pistei, 1:4). And likewise, the exhortations to Timothy to keep "faith" and the parallel condemnation of those who were shipwrecked in their "faith" (1:19) demonstrate the author's intent that a faithful discharge of duty by all of God's people who are in Christ's service furthers the economy of God "in faith."

Paul deliberately links his past self to the "sinners" in 1:9 (also here in 1:13), and to the false teachers in kind and species (as seen throughout 1 Timothy)[3]:

Paul	Opponents and Their Ilk
"blaspheme" (1:13)	"blaspheme (1:20; 6:1) "blasphemies" (6:4)
Unknowing (ἀγνοῶν, agnoōn, 1:13)	Without knowledge (μὴ νοοῦντες, mē noountes, 1:7)
Unbelief (1:13)	Rejected faith (1:6, 19; 4:1; 6:10, 21) Shipwrecked faith (1:19)
Foremost of "sinners" (1:13)	"Sinners" (1:9)

Just as the entrustment of the gospel to Paul was stated in emphatic terms in 1:11 (ὃ ἐπιστεύθην ἐγώ, "[with] which I *myself* have been entrusted"), so also is Paul's assertion of his past sinful status in 1:15: ὧν πρῶτός εἰμι ἐγώ, hōn prōtos eimi egō, "of whom I *myself* am the foremost." "Foremost" does not mean the worst, but the most prominent, in line with the reuse of the adjective in 1:16 to denote himself as the example and type of Christ's "utmost patience."

Interestingly enough, Paul confesses not that he *was* the foremost of sinners, but that he *is*, "as though still poised in that dazzling, overwhelming moment of his conversion-vocation, a moment which gave him an unforgettable and ever-present revelation of his own

---

3. Modified from Van Neste, *Cohesion and Structure*, 108.

sinfulness in the same instant that it revealed the even greater mercy of God."[4] He is truly awed! Perhaps it also emphasizes the universal and transtemporal truth of that trustworthy statement, deserving full acceptance, by everyone, everywhere: Christ came to save sinners (1:15)![5] In this extension of mercy to Paul, Christ also demonstrated his "perfect patience," making the apostle an example or a type for all who would trust in Jesus Christ for eternal life: this is how it would be for every believer. "Eternal life" in 1:16 is not just for the future but is the "abundant life" that begins in the present (John 10:10)—the life of the godly, now: "life indeed" (1 Tim 4:8; 6:19)—made possible by the work of God in Christ. "The concept of ζωή [zōē]. . . is a sharing of the eschatological age here and now in anticipation of life in the eschaton, a totally different kind of life."[6]

But most importantly, by calling himself the "foremost" of "sinners" (1:15, 16), he places himself in the forefront of those "sinners" in the "vicious" list of Pericope 1 (1:9). He was both like those in the list, and like those false teachers who perpetrated those sinful vices by their wrong use of the law (see Pericope 1: 1 Tim 1:1–11): Paul was the paramount sinner (see the table above)! But no matter the depth of Paul's vice (or the intensity of his viciousness), the grace of Jesus Christ superabounded (ὑπερπλεονάζω, hyperpleonazō, a neologism, 1:14). The verb is in an emphatic position, literally: "and it superabounded—the grace of our Lord." Not only was Paul proffered grace, but also faith and love (1:14)—a triad of gifts for the apostle's trifold viciousness as a blasphemer, persecutor, and aggressor (1:13). This was "grace abounding to the chief of sinners,"[7] faith instead of his "unfaith" ("unbelief," ἀπιστία, 1:13), and love instead of his hatred for Christians and their Christ. Knight notes that "in the πίστις καὶ ἀγάπη [pistis kai agapē] correlation elsewhere πίστις is directed to the Godhead and ἀγάπη to humans," a helpful reminder of what the grace of God can do to radically change a person, bringing that one into a right relationship with both deity and humanity.[8] All of this is the result of the mercy of God (1:13, 16)![9] Every child of God needs this merciful donation of grace, faith, and love to be saved, and strengthening to be put into divine service—all a remarkable demonstration of the patience of God (1:16).

It is notable that 1:12–17 breaks down into two sections, 1:12–14 and 1:15–17, each part rehearsing Paul's life-change as a result of divine "mercy" (1:13, 16). The first begins

---

4. Quinn and Wacker, *First and Second Letters to Timothy*, 135.

5. The πιστὸς ὁ λόγος (*pistos ho logos*)-formula ("the statement is trustworthy") is used in the PE in 1 Tim 1:15; 3:1; 4:9; 2 Tim 2:11; and Titus 3:8 to introduce key statements. The phrase was a commonly used trope in Greek literature; see Dio Chrysostom, *Discourses* 45 3; Josephus, *Jewish Antiquities* 19.16.132; Dionysius of Halicarnassus, *Antiquitates romanae* 3.23.17.

6. Mounce, *Pastoral Epistles*, 59. "This eternal life is envisioned as starting now, but being fully realized only in the future (1 Tim 6:12–15; 2 Tim 4:6–8; Titus 2:11–14)" (Witherington, *Letters and Homilies*, 208).

7. The title of a work by the Puritan John Bunyan (1666).

8. Knight, *Pastoral Epistles*, 98. See Eph 1:15; Col 1:4; 1 Thess 1:3; 2 Thess 1:3. The relative pronoun, τῆς (*tēs*, "which") in 1 Tim 1:14 is feminine singular; its nearest antecedent is "love," but it likely refers to both "faith" and "love": thus, "faith and love which *are* in Christ Jesus." The two nouns are tied by the conjunction καί, *kai*, "and," and introduced with the single preposition μετά, *meta*, "with." Thus, "in Jesus Christ" is the sphere in which Paul was gifted both faith and love. Grace and mercy are, of course, attributed directly to Christ in 1:13, 14a.

9. Paul's excuse of himself—not exculpation—is based on his ignorance in his days of "unbelief" (1:13; see Lev 4:1–35; 22:14; Num 15:22–31). Lack of knowledge does not remove guilt (Eph 4:18) but may mitigate it (Luke 23:34; Acts 3:17; etc.). One may assume, in light of Pericope 1: 1 Tim 1:1–11, that he was not taught the lawful use of the law (and probably was not using the law lawfully himself). So he was ignorant in his "unfaith."

with thanksgiving (1:12); the second ends with blessing (1:17). The movement is from the particular: Paul's personal case (1:12–14 has three first-person singular verbs, two first-person singular pronouns, two first-person plural pronouns, and a participle from εἰμί, *eimi*) to the general: true for all (1:15–17: note the plurals, ἁμαρτωλούς and τῶν μελλόντων πιστεύειν, *hamartōlous*, "sinners," and *tōn mellontōn pisteuein*, "those who were to believe"), though Paul does mention his own sinfulness again in these latter verses.[10]

	1:12–14	1:15–17
Work of "Christ Jesus"	1:12	1:15ab
Sin of Paul	1:13a	1:15c
"I was shown mercy"	1:13b	1:16a
Exaltation of "Christ Jesus"	1:14	1:16b
Particular vs. General	First-person singulars	Third-person
Begins/ends with:	Thanksgiving (1:12)	Blessing (1:17)

Christ's "superabundant" grace (1:14) was matched by his "utmost" patience (1:16) that was more than sufficient for the "foremost" of all sinners (1:15, 16).[11] This dual panel then asserts that what happened to Paul—the manifestation of superabounding, amazing, and awe-inspiring grace—is what happens to all who believe, and this is how they are appointed to divine service, as was Paul (1:12).

Paul is so moved by what he has written about that he breaks out into a blessing of his great God, the King eternal, in 1:17.[12] There is no verb in this doxology, and with three alliterated words, all alpha-privatives, αἰώνων, ἀφθάρτῳ, and ἀοράτῳ (*aiōnōn*, *aphthartō*, and *aoratō*; "eternal," "immortal," and "invisible"), the exclamation of 1:17 has a sense of poesy. The whole ecstatic utterance stresses the transcendence of God and thus the magnificence of divine mercy, superabundant grace, and utmost patience that could appoint even one like Paul into Christian service. And so the doxology ends with "glory" (1:17), as also did Pericope 1 ("glory" in 1:11).[13]

2.2   1 Timothy 1:18–20

THEOLOGICAL FOCUS 2.2

2.2   God's people, divinely charged and entrusted, engage in ministry with perseverance and integrity, while false teachers suffer discipline for disastrous dereliction of duty, hopefully to be reinstated into service (1:18–20).

---

10. Table modified from Knight, *Pastoral Epistles*, 92, Köstenberger, *1–2 Timothy and Titus*, 84.

11. With regard to divine mercy, 1:13b and 1:16a have the only uses of the verb ἐλεέω in 1 Timothy, and the only employment in the PE of ἀλλά without a preceding negation (as in "not . . . but . . .") (see Van Neste, *Cohesion and Structure*, 25).

12. "King" (βασιλεύς, *basileus*) is also found in 6:15; thus it shows up at the beginning and end of the Epistle, both times in a doxology.

13. 1 Tim 1:16 ends with "eternal life," and 1:17 begins with "King eternal"; also, 1:17 closes with "from eternity to eternity."

TRANSLATION 2.2

1:18   *This instruction I entrust to you, son, Timothy, in accordance with the previously made prophecies concerning you, so that by them you may fight the good fight,*

1:19   *keeping faith and good conscience, which some have rejected, and have been shipwrecked in faith,*

1:20   *among whom are Hymenaeus and Alexander, whom I have handed over to Satan, so that they may be taught not to blaspheme.*

NOTES 2.2

2.2   *God's people, divinely charged and entrusted, engage in ministry with perseverance and integrity, while false teachers suffer discipline for disastrous dereliction of duty, hopefully to be reinstated into service (1:18–20).*

The remaining verses of this chapter, 1:18–20, form a single sentence. The parallels between 1:3–6 (from Pericope 1: 1 Tim 1:1–11) and 1:18–20 in this pericope are depicted again the table below:

Pericope 1 (1:1–11)	**A**	Heterodox teachers; Paul's opposition to them; ἵνα ... μὴ (*hina ... mē*) **(1:3–4a)**
		"instruction"; "good conscience"; "faith" **(1:4b–6)**
	B	"which [feminine plural] some straying [from]" (relative pronoun + τινες (*tines*) + aorist participle)
Pericope 2 (1:12–20)		"instruction"; "good conscience"; "faith" **(1:18–19)**
	B'	"which [feminine singular] some rejecting" (relative pronoun + τινες + aorist participle)
	A'	Heterodox teachers; Paul's opposition to them; ἵνα ... μὴ **(1:20)**

The "previously made prophecies concerning you [Timothy]" (1:18; also in 4:14; and perhaps 2 Tim 1:6) are likely to be akin to those by which the Holy Spirit had set apart Barnabas and Saul for a divine work in Acts 13:2. This, then, was Timothy's commission from God by the mouth of leaders, a "divine decision communicated to him in the presence of others."[14] Such a reference also, no doubt, reassured Timothy of divine help for him to undertake that commission.

Just as God "appointed" (τίθημι, *tithēmi*) Paul into service with a responsibility in 1 Tim 1:12 (also in 2:7; 2 Tim 1:11), so in 1 Tim 1:18, Paul, in turn, "entrusts" (παρατίθημι, *paratithēmi*) instructions to his protégé Timothy. This verb "often has the double-sided nuance of both safekeeping and transmission to others [as in 2 Tim 2:2; Luke 12:48] . . . . One may possibly say, therefore, that Paul is not only entrusting a παραγγελία, *parangelia* ("instruction") to Timothy but also that he is entrusting to him the same παραγγελία that Paul himself has been entrusted with."[15] To add to the similarity between the entrustments

---

14. Towner, *1–2 Timothy and Titus*, 156.
15. Knight, *Pastoral Epistles*, 107–8.

of Paul and Timothy are the πιστ-root words: they occurred once in each of the verses of 1:12–16, dealing with Paul's autobiography (see above); they now show up in the section with regard to Timothy (twice in 1:19). The appellation "son," with the vocative "Timothy" (1:18), adds to the urgency and gravity of this passing of the baton, befitting a *mandata principis* letter.

The command to Timothy here is nothing new; it is a return to the charge in 1:3–5: παραγγελία in 1:5, and the verb παραγγέλλω, *parangellō*, in 1:3, are reflected in παραγγελία in 1:18. And "good conscience" and "faith" in 1:5 are also duplicated in 1:19, embedded in a similar syntactical structure (see table above). This command, essentially to proscribe false teachers and their heterodoxy, is nothing less than warfare, declares Paul as the stakes are raised: Timothy is to "fight the good fight" (1:18), conveying the sense of a military campaign.

The contrast between Timothy and the "some" (τινες, the false teachers, as also in 1:3, 6), is laid out clearly:

A	Paul entrusts (παρατίθημι, *paratithēmi*) Timothy with a command; "so that" (ἵνα-clause) **(1:18)**	
	B	Timothy—"keeps" (ἔχων, *echōn* [participle]) faith and a good conscience **(1:19a)**
	B'	False teachers—"reject" (ἀπωσάμενοι, *apōsamenoi* [participle]) conscience and shipwreck faith **(1:19b)**
A'	Paul hands over (παραδίδωμι, *paradidōmi*) false teachers to Satan; "so that" (ἵνα-clause) **(1:20)**	

The relative pronoun "which" in 1:19 is singular, likely referring to its nearest antecedent, "conscience" in light of the careful structuring of 1:19:

- **A** faith (Timothy's: "keep")
- **B** conscience (Timothy's: ["keep"])
- **B'** conscience (false teachers': "reject")
- **A'** faith (false teachers': "shipwreck")

Paul takes the actions (and attitudes) of the false teachers very seriously. Theirs was a straying from the goal of orthodox instruction ("love from a pure heart and a good conscience and a sincere faith," 1:6), a rejection of "good conscience" (1:19), and shipwrecking of "faith" (1:19). In turn, Timothy has just been urged to watch out for his own praxis in teaching and its goals, including the keeping of faith and of a good conscience (1:19). "A leader must possess the qualities he is trying to enforce in others."[16] This, then, is a warning to Timothy, even as correction is being issued to the false teachers (1:20).

While it was noted in Pericope 1: 1 Tim 1:1–11 that these false teachers were likely Jewish in orientation, we might go further here. It is likely they were believers, as well: Timothy is urged to instruct the false teachers not to teach heterodoxy (1:3), and these apparently were men who had "strayed from these things," i.e., from orthodoxy, and "turned aside" (1:5, 6; also see 5:15; 6:10). As well, these false teachers had rejected a good conscience, and

---

16. Mounce, *Pastoral Epistles*, 66.

had been shipwrecked in regard to their faith (1:19), again suggesting an apostasy from the faith they once embraced (also see 4:1; 6:21). Besides, Paul's response, the delivering over to Satan of at least two of their company (1:20), also implies that these were believers who were being disciplined (also see 2 Tim 2:17–18).[17]

In sum, this pericope deals with the magnificent grace of God that redeemed sinners and appointed them to his service, to discharge their ministries faithfully, thus promoting the economy of God.

SERMON MAPS

THEOLOGICAL FOCUS OF PERICOPE 2 FOR PREACHING

2   God's superabounding grace appoints believers—once sinners, now mercifully saved—into service, to discharge their ministries faithfully (1:12–20).

The two tasks of the preacher correspond to the two parts in the preaching paradigm that I espouse: text to theology and theology to application. Of the two, I believe the first part—text to theology—to be primary and "foremost." Therefore, most of the moves in the sermon maps (provided here and elsewhere) will facilitate listeners discerning the theology of the pericope from the text. A final move of the map discovers application for listeners.[18]

---

17. There is a sharp irony here: these would-be "law-teachers" (1:7) "teach falsely" (1:3) things contrary to sound "teaching" (1:10). But what these self-designated pedagogues needed was to be "taught" (παιδεύω, *paideuō*) not to blaspheme (1:20). And Paul hopes to do so by delivering them over to Satan. As in 1 Cor 5:5, he is exercising his apostolic authority in calling for what was likely a form of excommunication. It is obvious, however, that restoration is the goal of such discipline (here, as well as in 2 Tim 2:25–26; Titus 1:13; 3:10). Indeed, if Paul, a blasphemer himself (1 Tim 1:13), could be rehabilitated, surely there was hope for false teachers.

18. Does application need to be the last move of the sermon? Not necessarily, but it is the most natural place to put it—after listeners have gotten the thrust of the text, the pericopal theology, for only then will they know what they are going to respond to in application.

1 TIMOTHY

Possible Preaching Maps for Pericope 2

I. Reprobation (Past)
   Paul's former life (1:13, 15b)
   Move-to-relevance: Our former lives
II. Rehabilitation (Present)
   Mercy, grace, faith, love of God (1:13, 14, 16)
   Christ's salvific work (1:15a)
   Paul's appointment to service (1:12, 16); and his praise (1:17)
   Move-to-Relevance: What Christ has done for us
III. Responsibility (Future)
   Faithfulness and perseverance (1:18–19a)
   Failure of faithfulness (1:19b, 20)
   Move-to-Relevance: Our responsibility; our failure
IV. *Fight in the Future!*[19]
   How to be faithful and persevere in our divine appointments

Here's another option, creating moves based on the protagonists: Paul (his past, present, and "future") and all believers (and their past, present, and future).

I. Paul: Reprobate Rehabilitated for Responsibility
   Paul's former life (1:13, 15b)
   Mercy, grace, faith, love of God (1:13, 14, 16)
   Christ's salvific work (1:15a)
   Paul's appointment to service (1:12, 16); and his praise (1:17)
II. All Believers: Reprobates Rehabilitated for Responsibility[20]
   Move-to-Relevance: Our former lives
   Move-to-Relevance: Our salvation
   Move-to-Relevance: Our call to ministry
   Faithfulness and perseverance (1:18–19a)
   Failure of faithfulness (1:19b, 20)
IV. *Fight in the Future!*
   How to be faithful and persevere in our divine appointments

---

19. Application must be specific, spelling out exactly what the audience is expected to do. Specificity in application, as opposed to a nebulous abstraction, is essential. See Kuruvilla, *Manual for Preaching*, 57–86.

20. Note that this second move largely comprises moves-to-relevance. That is a break from the usual (and recommended) pattern, but who says we cannot break rules? By all means do so, but know what you are doing and why.

PERICOPE 3

Public Prayer for All

1 Timothy 2:1–7

[Corporate Prayer to Further Divine Economy; Pleasing God]

REVIEW, SUMMARY, PREVIEW

Review of Pericope 2: The previous pericope (1 Tim 1:12–20) saw Paul putting himself into the category of those sinners mentioned in 1:1–11. He gratefully described his wondrous salvation by grace wrought by a merciful God through Christ Jesus. Such a work of God for all believers was for the purpose of appointing them into the service of God, strengthened by him, that they may persevere in ministry, unlike false teachers, who face discipline.

Summary of Pericope 3: The third pericope of 1 Timothy (2:1–7) begins a section on instructions for corporate conduct. Primary in importance is corporate prayer—all manner of prayer, for the salvation of all people: furtherance of the divine economy. This is pleasing to God, who desires salvation for all through Christ, and who has appointed believers for the task of proclaiming the gospel, the grand plan of God.

Preview of Pericope 4: The next pericope (1 Tim 2:8–15) addresses the roles of men and women in the public gathering of the church: men are to be godly and to lead prayer; women, no less godly, learn with deference, and as part of their godliness, embrace their domestic roles and responsibilities.

1 TIMOTHY

3 1 Timothy 2:1–7

THEOLOGICAL FOCUS OF PERICOPE 3

3 Corporate prayer is critically important—for all authorities, so that peaceful, godly lives may be lived out; and for all people, so that the redeemability of all may come to fruition—and such prayers are to be extensive both in subject (all prayer), object (for all people), and content (the salvation of all), in order to please God by furthering the economy of God, by facilitating the proclamation and teaching of the gospel for which the apostolic mission was instituted and the people of God appointed (2:1–7).

OVERVIEW

This pericope (2:1–7) and the next two (Pericope 4: 1 Tim 2:8–15 and Pericope 5: 1 Tim 3:1–16) are marked by the absence of any specific and explicit instruction to Timothy; rather we see exhortations to the entire community regarding corporate demeanor and behavior, with a focus on its leaders who are to ensure the maintenance of such conduct.

First Timothy 2, in general, details how Timothy (and other readers) must execute the command Paul had entrusted to him in 1:18–19: "fight the good fight, keeping faith and good conscience." First in importance in this campaign ("first of all," 2:1) was to be prayer for all people: "the instruction in 2:1–7 is the single most significant change Timothy can effect."[1] After dealing with how the people of God are to handle Scripture for instruction (Pericope 1: 1 Tim 1:1–11), and how they, in contrast to false teachers, are to persevere in their divine entrustment of ministry (Pericope 2: 1 Tim 1:12–20), it is fitting that Paul moves to conduct in the larger community setting of believers, specifically with regard to worship. Indeed, coming after the redeemability of a Paul (1:12–14), of sinners in general (1:15–17), and perhaps even of false teachers (1:18–20), this call to pray for "all people" (2:1) that "all people" may be saved (2:4; notice the "therefore" in 2:1) makes sense as an integral part of the praxis of God's people for the furtherance of his economy.[2] Thus, corporate conduct in worship forms the unifying theme in the two pericopes of 1 Timothy 2: prayer in worship, its scope and its rationale (Pericope 3: 1 Tim 2:1–7), and prayer and other aspects of behavior in the congregational gathering as they relate to men and women (Pericope 4: 1 Tim 2:8–15). Both pericopes are, thus, related:

---

1. Mounce, *Pastoral Epistles*, 78.

2. Many commentaries assume, from the instructions given in this pericope, that the problems with the church at Ephesus related to prayerlessness, or exclusivity/elitism of salvation, or some such: apparently these issues were being created by the false teachers and their heterodox operations. For instance, Mounce, *Pastoral Epistles*, 93: "Paul goes to the root of the Ephesian problem: a deficient understanding of salvation." Or Marshall, *Pastoral Epistles*, 417, who thinks that "the opposition to the gospel of Paul in the church was threatening not only the teaching but also and (first in importance) the effectiveness of the church's prayers." While these attempts to include this pericope (and others) under the banner of a polemic against false teachers are admirable, they go too far. No doubt there were some heterodox activities in Ephesus that prompted this missive as a whole, but one can be sure that as the letter took shape, a singular focus on false teaching was untenable; other issues, related tangentially or indirectly, won their own space in the Epistle, too.

	1 Timothy 2:1–7	1 Timothy 2:8–15
"pray[er]"	"Therefore, I urge …" "prayers … be made" "all [πᾶς, *pas*] people" 2:1	"Therefore, I want …" "to pray" "in every [πᾶς] place" 2:8
"quiet[ude]"	2:2	2:11, 12
"teach[er]"	2:7	2:12
"save"	2:4	2:15
πᾶς	2:1a, 1b, 2a, 2b, 4, 6	2:8, 11

First Timothy 2 begins with references to "all people," especially rulers and civic authorities (2:1–2) and ends with a mention of children (2:15b). In between are men and women (2:8–15a). One wonders if this is a deliberate move from civic society to ecclesial community, or even a depiction of hierarchies of authority: highest authority (kings and rulers), to non-authority (children), with "normal" authority (men and women) in between.

3 1 Timothy 2:1–7

> **THEOLOGICAL FOCUS 3**
>
> 3 Corporate prayer is critically important—for all authorities, so that peaceful, godly lives may be lived out; and for all people, so that the redeemability of all may come to fruition—and such prayers are to be extensive both in subject (all prayer), object (for all people), and content (the salvation of all), in order to please God by furthering the economy of God, by the proclamation and teaching of the gospel for which the apostolic mission was instituted and the people of God appointed (2:1–7).

TRANSLATION 3

2:1 *First of all, therefore, I urge that requests, prayers, intercessions, thanksgivings be made on behalf of all people,*

2:2 *on behalf of kings and all those who are in authority, so that we may lead a peaceful and quiet life in all godliness and dignity.*

2:3 *This is good and pleasing before God our Savior,*

2:4 *who desires all people to be saved and to come to the knowledge of the truth.*

2:5 *For [there is] one God, also one mediator between God and humanity, the man Christ Jesus,*

2:6 *who gave Himself a ransom for all, a testimony at the proper time.*

2:7 *For this I myself was appointed proclaimer and apostle—I am telling the truth, I am not lying—teacher of the gentiles in faith and truth.*

1 TIMOTHY

NOTES 3

3   *Corporate prayer is critically important—for all authorities, so that peaceful, godly lives may be lived out; and for all people, so that the redeemability of all may come to fruition—and such prayers are to be extensive both in subject (all prayer), object (for all people), and content (the salvation of all), in order to please God by furthering the economy of God, by the proclamation and teaching of the gospel for which the apostolic mission was instituted and the people of God appointed (2:1–7).*

There is a return to exhortation in this pericope: παρακαλέω (*parakaleō*, "I urge," 2:1) also began the previous chapter, after the epistolary greeting (1:3). The earlier one was an aorist; here it moves to the present tense: "The shift in tense suggests that one is moving from *ad hoc* guidance to Timothy (and through him to the believers of Ephesus) to materials that are of permanent significance for all."[3]

"Foremost" (πρῶτος, *prōtos*) described Paul's station among sinners in 1:15, 16. Here, in 2:1, it underscores the importance—"first of all"—of prayer for "all people." The emphasis on prayer is further underscored by a cluster of words ending with -ν (nineteen of them!) resounding in 2:1–3:

2:1	οὖν πρῶτον πάντων ... πάντων ἀνθρώπων *oun prōton pantōn ... pantōn anthrōpōn* "first of all, therefore, ... all people"
2:2	βασιλέων ... πάντων τῶν ἐν ... ὄντων *basileōn ... pantōn tōn en ... ontōn* "kings and all those who are in ..." ἤρεμον ... ἡσύχιον βίον διάγωμεν *ēremon ... hēsychion bion diagōmen* "we may lead a peaceful ... quiet life"
2:3	καλὸν ... ἀπόδεκτον ἐνώπιον ... ἡμῶν *...kalon ... apodekton enōpion ... hēmōn* "good ... pleasing before ... our"

First-person singulars in 2:1 and 2:7 form bookends for this pericope. But unlike in 1:3–4 (and 1:18–20), there are no second-person pronouns or verbs; the addressees, therefore, go beyond the individual, Timothy, to include the whole local body of believers.

As was noted, the word πᾶς, *pas*, shows up a number of times in 2:1–7, pointing to the breadth of these exhortations: 2:1a, 1b, 2a, 2b, 4, 6 (and also in 2:8, 11). To this one could add *all* manner of prayer, implied by the four synonyms used for this activity in 2:1—"requests," "prayers," "intercessions," and "thanksgivings." "The thought is one of completeness—every dimension and action of prayer being focused on the need at hand."[4] So one might read this exhortation this way: "I urge that [*all* prayers] be made for *all* people." Almost all of the New Testament terms for prayer are found here, all in the plural, and as an asyndeton. "Their asyndetic construction here as well as their coincidences

---

3. Quinn and Wacker, *First and Second Letters to Timothy*, 171.
4. Towner, *Letters to Timothy and Titus*, 166.

in sense demand that all be taken closely together, almost as if hyphenated to one another," creating a single world of prayer.⁵

Yet another "all" may be implied in Paul's appointment to the gentiles in 2:7, a vast throng of peoples/nations—"all the world." Following 1:12–20, "all people" in 2:1b no doubt includes Paul, the foremost of sinners (1:15–16), and even Hymenaeus and Alexander, "handed over to Satan" (1:19–20), because (as Pericope 2 implied), even these are redeemable. So "requests, prayers, intercessions, thanksgivings"—all manner of prayers (2:1)—are to be made for "all" people, because salvation is available for "all": 2:4, 6 (also 4:10; 2 Tim 4:17; Titus 2:11). Indeed, such *all*-prayer is to be made for even "kings and *all* who are in authority" (1 Tim 2:2).⁶ Therefore, God's people are to pray for "all!"⁷

It is best to see 1 Tim 2:1b, the exhortation to pray for "all people," as the thrust of the section (and the pericope; A below), with 2:2a, the exhortation to pray for authorities being parenthetical (A' below): πάντων ἀνθρώπων, *pantōn anthrōpōn*, in 2:1 links to πάντας ἀνθρώπους, *pantas anthrōpous*, in the sentence of 2:3–4, connecting the implicit missiological thrust of 2:1 (in light of Pericope 1: 1 Tim 1:12–20, and the "therefore" in 2:1) to the explicit missiological thrust of 2:3–4. The reason for the exhortation in 2:1 is given in 2:3–7 (B below): the making of a kingdom people by their salvation and their knowledge of the truth. Notice also the play on the word ἄνθρωπος: prayers are to be made for all ἀνθρώπων (2:1); God wants all ἀνθρώπους to be saved (2:4), and so he sends the one mediator between God and ἀνθρώπων, the ἄνθρωπος, *anthrōpos*, Christ Jesus (2:5)—one human for all humans! Thus, 2:1 is strongly bound to 2:3–7. That makes 2:2 an aside: prayer for authorities in this verse (exhortation, 2:2a; A' below) is for the primary benefit of the community of God's people—"that we may lead . . ." (reason, 2:2b; B' below). On the other hand, prayer for "all people" (2:1) is for the primary benefit of those "all people" (2:4–7, that they may be saved, as God desires). Thus we have an exhortation-reason (A', B'; 2:2a, 2b) nested within another exhortation-reason (A, B; 2:1, 3–7)

A	*Exhortation*: Prayer for all (2:1) πάντων ἀνθρώπων
	A' *Exhortation*: Prayer for all authorities (2:2a)
	B' *Reason*: lives of peace, quiet; in godliness, dignity (2:2b)
B	*Reason*: Citizenship for all in the divine economy (2:3–7) πάντας ἀνθρώπους (2:4); ἄνθρωπος (2:5 [×2])

The quality of community Christian life sought is one that is "peaceful" and "quiet" (2:2). The employment of the same adjective ἡσύχιος, *hēsychios*, to describe the deportment of women later in 2:11–12, and its occurrence in conjunction with πραΰς (*praus*, "gentle") in

---

5. Quinn and Wacker, *First and Second Letters to Timothy*, 172.

6. "The whole spectrum of government officials, municipal, royal, imperial, can be included in the phrase ['kings and all who are in authority'], whose widest application is emphasized by *pantōn, all*" (Quinn and Wacker, *First and Second Letters to Timothy*, 177). "Christians are not party to an emperor cult in which they pray to the king; they pray for him" (Wall, "Empire, Church, and *Missio Dei*," 13). In any case, loyalty to state, manifested at least by prayer, is being called for here (also see Ezra 6:9–10; 7:23; Jer 29:7; 1 Macc 7:33; Titus 3:1–2; Rom 13:1–7; 1 Pet 2:13–17 for similar sentiments). Considering that the Roman emperor at the time of this writing was the notorious Nero (54–68 CE), this exhortation is all the more poignant!

7. "All people," of course, means "all *kinds of* people," and not every single individual in existence (see Rom 12:17, 18; 2 Cor 3:2; Phil 4:5; 1 Thess 2:15).

1 Pet 3:4, suggest that the use of the word here in 1 Tim 2:2 (with ἤρεμος, ēremos, "peaceful," a *hapax*) denotes "not silence of speech but quietness, calmness of demeanor, serenity"—peacefulness.[8] This life is also characterized by "all godliness and dignity" (2:2). "Godliness" is a matter of emphasis in this letter: over half of the occurrences of εὐσέβια, *eusebeia*, in the NT occur in 1 Timothy (eight of the fifteen instances).[9] Mounce notes that εὐσέβεια is the NT equivalent of the OT "fear of the Lord/God": in the LXX of Prov 1:7; Isa 11:2; 33:6, אֱלֹהִים/יִרְאַת יְהוָה (*yirʾat yhwh/ʾelohim*) is translated as εὐσέβεια (or as θεοσέβεια, *theosebeia*, a related word, in Gen 20:11; Job 28:28, also found in 1 Tim 2:10).[10] The paired noun, σεμνότης, *semnotēs*, "dignity," is found only in the PE: 1 Tim 2:2; 3:4; Titus 2:7; its cognate adjective, σεμνός, *semnos*, shows up in 1 Tim 3:8, 11; Titus 2:2; and Phil 4:8. Considering εὐσέβεια and σεμνότης as almost equivalent,[11] what is being intended in 1 Tim 2:2 is a life of godliness.

After the "aside" of 2:2, Paul returns to the matter begun in 2:1—all prayer for all people. It is an integral facet of the Christian hope that "all people" who are being prayed for (2:1), and "all people" whom God wants to be saved (2:4), may, in actuality, become "all people" who *are* saved.[12] Right now, they are not—notice that deity is "*our* God and Savior" (2:3), not everyone's. Perhaps the prayer for authorities would facilitate the salvation of "all people" by creating a salubrious society in which Christians thrive in godly living, influencing "all people . . . to come to the knowledge of the truth."[13] Certainly praying for rulers is not simply restricted to their making the environment wholesome for Christians; in all likelihood, the prayer is directed to their salvation, too; these rulers are certainly part of "all people" that God desires be saved. In any case, being "saved" is not to be equated with "coming to the knowledge of the truth" (2:4). The phrase ἐπίγνωσις ἀληθείας, *epignōsis alētheias*, is found in the PE in 1 Tim 2:4; 2 Tim 2:25; 3:7; Titus 1:1, where it is applied to believers, some of whom were going astray.[14] Together, being "saved" and "coming to the knowledge of the truth" encompass the work of God in Christ, making those who were once rebels into a

---

8. Mounce, *Pastoral Epistles*, 82. The use of the related verb, ἡσυχάζω, *hēsychazō*, "remain quiet," in Acts 11:18; 21:14 confirms this.

9. Adding the cognate, there are twelve instances of the root in the PE, nine of which are in 1 Timothy.

10. Mounce, *Pastoral Epistles*, 83. A related verb, εὐσεβέω, *eusebeō*, is used in Acts 17:23; 1 Tim 5:4, with the equivalent sense of "to worship" or "to be pious."

11. The latter carries that sense of holiness related to deity in 2 Macc 6:11, 28. In 2 Macc 8:15, we have the "venerable [σεμνός] and sublime name" of God himself.

12. Distinguishing between θέλω (*thelō*, used in 2:4) and βούλομαι, *boulomai*, as "to wish" vs. "to intend," in order to differentiate between God's moral will (that he desires to happen) and his sovereign will (that he decrees will happen), is not linguistically appropriate. "Although there are some examples where these original meanings are still present, and while there is much to be said for distinguishing between God's preference [moral will] and what he wills to accomplish [sovereign will], it is the context that determines meaning and not the choice of words" (Mounce, *Pastoral Epistles*, 86). For the stronger use of θέλω, see Rom 9:18; 1 Cor 4:19; 12:18 (compare with βούλομαι in 12:11); 15:38; Col 1:27; etc. For an excellent discussion of the moral and sovereign wills of God, see Friesen, *Decision Making*.

13. Such intercessions for all manner of societal authorities are certainly appropriate, though 2 Tim 3:12 suggests that overdependence on the state to make society amicable and conducive to the church's faith and praxis is ultimately futile. But it is, no doubt, the case that creators of "unpeace" and disquiet—no matter who they are, whether civic authorities or churchly dissenters—are capable of preventing the primary function of the church in society: the salvation of souls and the enlargement of the kingdom, i.e., the furtherance of God's economy (1:4).

14. These are also the only occurrences of ἐπίγνωσις, *epignōsis*, in the PE.

people for his own possession exhibiting godliness. Thus, this making of a people of God should not be restricted to atonement- and cross-related events. The scope of God's purpose began in eternity past and will continue until all things in the cosmos are consummated in Christ (Eph 1:9–10)—the broadest sense of "gospel," the economy of God. And this "one God" accomplishes his grand design for "*all* ἀνθρώπους" (1 Tim 2:4)—as his people pray for "*all* ἀνθρώπους" (2:1) through the "one mediator"—the "*one* ἄνθρωπος" who gave himself as a "ransom for *all*": the single sentence of 2:5–6 lacking a main verb is aptly an exclamation![15] It is through the person of the Lord Jesus Christ that this vast and glorious scheme of God has been set in place; and it is through him that it will one day be consummated.

The thrust of this section (and this pericope) makes prayer of this sort not an optional activity for the church, but one that is integral to the proper functioning of the "household of God" (3:15) and entirely "good and pleasing" in the eyes of "God our Savior."[16] The adjective ἀπόδεκτος, *apodektos,* is found in the NT only here in 2:3 and 5:4; the related word δεκτός, *dektos,* is commonly used in the LXX of sacrifices to God that are "pleasing" (Lev 1:3, 4; 17:4; 19:5; 22:19, 20, 21, 29; 23:11; etc.). "The effect of placing the activity of prayer [in 1 Tim 2:1–2] into this OT legal and cultic framework is to underline its intrinsic importance to God and to his people by comparing it with the role of sacrifices in the old system. Prayer has replaced sacrifice for the messianic people of God," for the promotion of the economy of God, the consummation of his glorious purpose in Christ.[17] This grand plan and its furtherance was the "testimony" (μαρτύριον, *martyrion*) of Jesus—in deed and in word—at the "proper time," for the proclamation of which Paul was "appointed" (τίθημι, *tithēmi*) as "herald, and apostle, . . . [and] teacher" to the gentiles (2:7).[18] And he holds these portfolios and propounds these truths to his audiences "in faith and truth," i.e., faithfully and in accordance with divine truth. Elsewhere in the PE, μαρτύριον is used only in 2 Tim 1:8, where it explicitly refers to Jesus's testimony, with a proximal mention of Paul's "appointment" (again, τίθημι in 2:11) and his portfolio as (again) "proclaimer, and apostle, and teacher." In both instances, then, it was Jesus's "testimony"—his witness, in action and speech, to the gospel in its widest scope—for which Paul was "appointed."[19] The apostle's confession of his appointment to proclaim Jesus's testimony underscores his wonder: εἰς ὃ ἐτέθην ἐγὼ literally reads "for this I myself was appointed!"[20] Imagine that, he exclaims! And it is this amazement at his own commissioning for the announcement of God's awesome plan and purpose (the testimony of Jesus, the gospel) that makes him aver that he is telling the truth and not lying (2:7). After the self-description of his miserable status before God in Pericope 2: 1 Tim 1:12–20, it is no

15. 1 Tim 2:6 has the only NT use of ἀντίλυτρον, *antilytron,* "ransom."

16. "God our Savior" is found in the PE in 1 Tim 1:1; 2:3; 4:10; Titus 1:3; 2:10; 3:4.

17. Towner, *Letters to Timothy and Titus,* 176.

18. There may likely be a polemical function in Paul's labeling himself a διδάσκαλος, after the excoriation of the νομοδιδάσκαλοι in 1:7, who seek ἑτεροδιδασκαλεῖν (1:3) in contrast to promulgating sound διδασκαλία (1:10).

19. Couser notes that in Isa 55:4 LXX, "David's historical accomplishments 'bear witness' [μαρτύριον] to theological realities"; the uses of the word (also in Mark 13:9 and Luke 9:5 in conjunction with actions) "allow for an understanding of the term that embraces both acts and words; the whole of a life or an event can stand as a testimony" ("'Testimony about the Lord,'" 303). The verb μαρτυρέω, *martyreō,* in 1 Tim 6:13 suggests the "testimony" is something that was borne by Jesus Christ, again likely to have been both in word and in deed. But Quinn and Wacker, *First and Second Letters to Timothy,* 187, are right: "The sentence [1 Tim 2:5–6] is densely elliptical and has eluded definitive explanation."

20. A similar reinforcement of his being put into divine service was seen in 1:11: ὃ ἐπιστεύθην ἐγώ—"with which I myself have been entrusted!"

surprise that Paul has to emphasize that he isn't kidding here about the magnitude of the responsibility with which he had been entrusted, as a witness to the incredible transactions of God! One who had been described by a diametrically opposed triad—blasphemer, persecutor, and violent aggressor (1:13)—is now labeled with another triad—proclaimer, apostle, and teacher. We see here an unaffected and guileless simplicity of character on display: Paul just cannot believe his assignment and he figures his audience will not either. So he avows his veracity!

These emphases on Paul's personal appointment and sending also indicates the importance of what God is doing, not just in an isolated corner in the Levant for some unique peoples, but for *gentiles,* i.e., all peoples, and all across the world—"all ἀνθρώπους" (2:1, 4). What a grand and glorious plan of God! And what a way for the people of God to partner with him in this global and cosmic program—by prayer and proclamation![21]

SERMON MAPS

THEOLOGICAL FOCUS OF PERICOPE 3 FOR PREACHING

3   Corporate prayer for all people is critically important so that all may be redeemed; such prayers please God by furthering his economy, facilitated by the proclamation and teaching for which his people have been appointed (2:1–7).

You have already noticed that in my maps I include "moves-to-relevance" (actually sub-moves within each move) at the end of every move preceding the application move, which is itself a direct aspect of relevance. Without those "moves-to-relevance," we will risk losing our hearers if we leave them out for the bulk of the body prior to the application. Therefore, in those "moves-to-relevance," the preacher must thoughtfully consider how the lives of listeners—their spiritual walk, their circumstances, their world and culture, cares and concerns, victories and failures—are impacted by the textual content curated in the move.[22]

Possible Preaching Maps for Pericope 3

I. God's Pleasure
   God's desire for all to be saved (2:3–4)
   God's execution of his plan (2:5–6)
   Move-to-relevance: Is God's pleasure our pleasure?
II. Our Purpose
   Paul's appointment: Furtherance of the divine economy (2:7)
   Move-to-Relevance: Our appointment
III. Church's Prayer
   All manner of prayer for all (2:1–2a)
   Consequence of prayer (2:2b)
   Move-to-Relevance: Our failure to pray
IV. *Pray and Please!*[23]

21. I am including all manner of communication of Scripture under the banner of proclamation here.
22. See Kuruvilla, *Manual for Preaching,* 87–109.
23. Since the context of this pericope is the corporate gathering of God's people, it is appropriate to derive application that relates to that activity.

How to engage corporately in all prayer for all

One could of course, turn this around, shifting the sequence of moves to correspond with that of the text, though the preacher should not be under any constraint to follow the textual order. Ultimately, sequencing is the preacher's call, based on what creates the best sermonic flow for a particular audience[24]:

I. Church's Prayer
   All manner of prayer for all (2:1–2a)
   Consequence of prayer (2:2b)
   Move-to-Relevance: Our failure to pray
II. God's Pleasure
   God's desire for all to be saved (2:3–4)
   God's execution of his plan (2:5–6)
   Move-to-relevance: Is God's pleasure our pleasure?
III. Our Purpose
   Paul's appointment: Furtherance of the divine economy (2:7)
   Move-to-Relevance: Our appointment
IV. *Pray and Please!*
   How to engage corporately in all prayer for all

---

24. Spoken sermons are a different form of media than scripted biblical texts. The former do not necessarily have to follow the sequence of argument or parallel the narration of the latter. But there is something to be said for ease of following along (from a congregant's point of view) with a sermon whose order of moves closely parallels the sequence of the biblical text, for this means fewer ungainly leaps around the text. And the fewer these leaps, the greater the clarity, and thus, hopefully, the firmer the assimilation of truth in the hearts, minds, and lives of listeners.

PERICOPE 4

Corporate Roles

1 Timothy 2:8–15

[Responsibilities of Men and Women: Prayer, Learning, Domestic Management]

REVIEW, SUMMARY, PREVIEW

Review of Pericope 3: The third pericope of 1 Timothy (2:1–7) began a section on instructions for corporate conduct. Primary in importance was corporate prayer—all manner of prayer for all people, for the salvation of all people: furtherance of the divine economy. This is pleasing to God, who desires salvation for all through Christ, and who has appointed believers for the task of proclaiming the gospel, the grand plan of God.

Summary of Pericope 4: This pericope (1 Tim 2:8–15) addresses the roles of men and women in the public gathering of the church: men are to be godly and to lead prayer; women, no less godly, are to learn with deference and, as part of being godly, embrace their domestic roles and responsibilities as well.

Preview of Pericope 5: The next pericope (1 Tim 3:1–16) deals with the offices of the church: eldership and diaconate, members of which bodies guide and model communal and individual conduct of the people of God. Such exemplary behavior, both by leaders and followers, is grounded in the work of Jesus Christ that initiates and sustains the godliness of God's people.

4   1 Timothy 2:8–15

> **THEOLOGICAL FOCUS OF PERICOPE 4**
>
> **4** The critical roles of men and women in the serious matter of worship in the corporate gathering involve: men, being godly, leading prayer in the corporate assembly, rather than generating angry dissension; women, being godly, learning with deference rather than taking on authoritative teaching, at the same time embracing domestic roles and responsibilities (2:8–15).
>
> 4.1 The critical role of men in the serious matter of worship in the corporate gathering involves being godly in attitude and action, and leading prayer in the corporate assembly, rather than generating angry dissension (2:8).
>
> 4.2 The critical role of women in the serious matter of worship in the corporate gathering involves being godly in attitude and action, and learning with deference rather than taking on authoritative teaching, at the same time embracing domestic roles and responsibilities (2:9–15).
>
> 4.2.1 *The critical role of women in the serious matter of worship in the corporate gathering involves being godly in attitude and action* (2:9–10).
>
> 4.2.2 *The critical role of women in the serious matter of worship in the corporate gathering involves learning with deference rather than taking on authoritative teaching, at the same time embracing domestic roles and responsibilities* (2:11–15).

OVERVIEW

This pericope continues what was begun in Pericope 3: 1 Tim 2:1–7.[1] Corporate conduct is the issue of both pericopes, but here in Pericope 4 there is a narrower focus on the behavior of men and women in the public gathering of the church.[2] After all, 3:15 considers this Epistle to be a set of instructions on behavior in the house of God. And here, men's prayer is public, and women's clothing and behavior is public—both appropriate topics of instruction.[3] It is, perhaps, the exhortation to public prayer in Pericope 3 that has raised in Paul's mind the issue of the behavior of men and women at such corporate gatherings.

There are several linguistic parallels between 2:11–12 and 1 Cor 14:31–35; the latter clearly deals with activities in the corporate gathering; the similarities again suggest that an identical locale is in consideration here in Pericope 4[4]:

---

1. See Pericope 3: 1 Tim 2:1–7 for how that one and this current pericope are linked by verbal parallels.

2. If the corporate gathering were not the context for Pericope 4, males praying "in *every* place" (2:8) would rule out females praying anywhere *tout court*!

3. "Prayers" in the plural, and the other species of such addresses to God noted in 2:1, indicate that the context is the larger assembly of believers (as also does the exhortation to women to learn in silence [2:11]). Both 2:9–10 and 2:11–12 pick up from 2:2: "godliness" and "quiet/quietude" are shared between the earlier and subsequent verses. This again substantiates the context as being that of a corporate assembly.

4. Modified from Mounce, *Pastoral Epistles*, 439; Witherington, *Letters and Homilies*, 222. There are also several links between 1 Tim 2 and 1 Cor 10—11, another section dealing with matters of order in public settings: apostolic authority (1 Tim 2:7; 1 Cor 11:1–3); context of public worship (1 Tim 2:8; 1 Cor 11:4); men at prayer and implication of women at prayer (1 Tim 2:8, 9; 1 Cor 11:4, 5); hairdo and ornaments, head and veil (1 Tim 2:9; 1 Cor 11:5–6, 13–16); "proper" (πρέπω, *prepō*; 1 Tim 2:10; 1 Cor 11:13); and recourse to Genesis (1 Tim 2:13–15; 1 Cor 11:3, 7–9, 12) (modified from Zamfir and Verheyden,

1 TIMOTHY

	1 Timothy 2:11–12	1 Corinthians 14:31–35
"All"	"in every [πᾶς, *pas*] place"	"in all [πᾶς] churches"
"Women"	γυνή (*gynē*, 2:9, 10, 11, 12, 14)	γυνή (14:34, 35)
"Men"	ἀνήρ (*anēr*, 2:8, 12)	ἀνήρ (14:35)
Silence	ἡσυχία (*hēsychia*, 2:11, 12)	σιγάτωσαν (*sigatōsan*, 14:34)
Prohibition	"I do not *allow* ... to teach" (ἐπιτρέπω, *epitrepō*, 2:12)	"they are not *allowed* to speak" (ἐπιτρέπω, 14:34, 35)
Learning	"learn" (2:11)	"learn" (14:31, 35)
Submissiveness	ὑποταγῇ (*hypotagē*, 2:11)	ὑποτάσσω (*hypotassō*, 14:34)

It is quite possible that τόπος, *topos*, in 1 Tim 2:8, designating the locus of prayer, refers to the place of the formal gathering of the church. In the LXX, τόπος translates בית, *byt*, when the latter refers to a place of worship: 1 Kgs 8:42; 2 Chr 6:32; Ps 119:54; also see Isa 66:1; Zeph 2:11. In Mal 1:11, ἐν παντὶ τόπῳ, *en panti topō*, "in every place," explicitly points to the Temple.[5]

First Timothy 2:8–9 is directed to men and women in general, not to husbands and wives: there does not seem to be any reason to restrict corporate prayer to husbands only and to prohibit single men from that activity (2:8). Likewise, the restriction of public adornment to wives only, and permitting single women not to be so governed, would be odd (2:9; this would also excuse widows). The context seems to be addressing the particular roles of worshipers of both genders, not just of men and women who are married.[6]

The tone of strong exhortation in prior pericopes continues here in Pericope 4: παρακαλῶ in 2:1 (taking up from 1:3); and βούλομαι in 2:8 (and implied in 2:9) and οὐκ ἐπιτρέπω in 2:12. Just as Pericope 3 began with παρακαλῶ οὖν (2:1), Pericope 4 begins with βούλομαι οὖν (*boulomai oun*, 2:8). Also, the topic of prayer from Pericope 3 is resumed in 2:8, but ἄνθρωπος in 2:1 has changed to ἀνήρ (2:8) and γυνή (2:9–10).

4.1   1 Timothy 2:8

THEOLOGICAL FOCUS 4.1

4.1   The critical role of men in the serious matter of worship in the corporate gathering involves being godly in attitude and action, and leading prayer in the corporate assembly, rather than generating angry dissension (2:8).

TRANSLATION 4.1

2:8   *Therefore I want the men in every place to pray, lifting up holy hands, without wrath and dispute.*

"Text-Critical and Intertextual Remarks," 390–403).

5. Also see LXX Exod 20:24; Deut 12:13; Ps 103:22. So also in the Didache: "'In every place [ἐν παντὶ τόπῳ] and time offer Me a pure sacrifice; for I am a great king,' says the Lord, 'and My name is wonderful among the nations'" (14.3–5; my translation).

6. Reading this pericope as addressing spouses also raises the question, later on, whether single women can teach, if only wives are prohibited from doing so. Nevertheless, it must be admitted that ἀνήρ and γυνή (*anēr* and *gynē*), when employed together, can indicate the husband-wife relationship (1 Tim 3:2, 11–12; 5:9; Titus 1:6; etc.).

NOTES 4.1

4.1 *The critical role of men in the serious matter of worship in the corporate gathering involves being godly in attitude and action, and leading prayer in the corporate assembly, rather than generating angry dissension (2:8).*

One of the first elements of church praxis to be lost in the presence of "wrath and dispute" in the community is corporate (and perhaps individual) prayer, already emphasized as being crucial and "good and pleasing" before God (2:1). Purity on the part of men praying is what is being called for in 2:8, with the symbolism of "holy hands" raised being an allusion to Aaron and his sons washing their hands when they entered the tent of meeting (Exod 30:19–21). The image of "holy hands" thus became a metaphor for moral purity: "And so we should approach him with devout souls, raising pure and undefiled hands to him" (*1 Clement* 29:1).[7] Guiltlessness and abstinence from evil deeds are the particular connotations of holy/clean hands in the presence of deity (see Pss 24:4; 26:6; 73:13; Isa 1:15; 59:3; Jas 4:8). No doubt, this "lifting up [of] holy hands" is "the very opposite of raising clenched fists in anger and disagreement."[8] All this means that "lifting up holy hands" is symbolic and not to be taken literally.

Does 1 Tim 2:8 beingn addressed specifically to men have an implicit restriction on public prayer by women in the assembly? "It is possible that, because of the church's roots in the synagogue, where only men could pray, most of the public prayer in the church was done by men."[9] At any rate, Paul does not appear to be giving any explicit instruction here on *who* should pray; he assumes it will be men. Rather, *how* those who pray should be engaging in that activity seems to be his focus. Indeed, 1 Cor 11:4-6 assumes that all will pray in public, irrespective of gender. That being said, in the context of corporate leadership (which is the subject of the next pericope), while laypeople may (and should) pray in public, I would hold that a "pastoral prayer" conducted on behalf of, and for, the whole body (as well for the global scope of "all men"—see Pericope 3: 1 Tim 2:1–7) should be led by one of its shepherds/elders; of necessity, then, that kind of a representative prayer will be offered by men (on elders being men, see Pericope 5: 1 Tim 3:1–16).

4.2   1 Timothy 2:9–15

THEOLOGICAL FOCUS 4.2

4.2 The critical role of women in the serious matter of worship in the corporate gathering involves being godly in attitude and action, and learning with deference rather than taking on authoritative teaching, at the same time embracing domestic roles and responsibilities (2:9–15).

   4.2.1 *The critical role of women in the serious matter of worship in the corporate gathering involves being godly in attitude and action (2:9–10).*

---

7. Clement, *Apostolic Fathers*, 1:87.
8. Quinn and Wacker, *First and Second Letters to Timothy*, 214.
9. Mounce, *Pastoral Epistles*, 106.

1 TIMOTHY

> 4.2.2 The critical role of women in the serious matter of worship in the corporate gathering involves learning with deference rather than taking on authoritative teaching, at the same time embracing domestic roles and responsibilities (2:11–15).

TRANSLATION 4.2

2:9   Likewise, [I want] women to adorn themselves in appropriate adornment, with modesty and self-control, not with braided hair and gold or pearls or expensive clothing,

2:10   but with good works, which is proper for women professing godliness.

2:11   A woman should learn in quietude and with all submissiveness.

2:12   But I do not allow a woman to teach or to exercise authority over a man, but to be in quietude.

2:13   For Adam was formed first, then Eve.

2:14   And Adam was not deceived, but the woman, being fully deceived, fell into transgression.

2:15   But she will be saved through the bearing of children if they continue in faith and love and holiness with self-control.

NOTES 4.2

4.2.1 The critical role of women in the serious matter of worship in the corporate gathering involves being godly in attitude and action (2:9–10).

The two parallel infinitives, "to pray" (2:8, directed to men) and "to adorn" (2:9, directed to women) are linked with the verb "I want" (2:8, and implied in 2:9). Contrasts between what to do and what not to do in the assembly are seen in 2:8 (to pray, but without . . .), 2:9–10 (to adorn, but without . . .), and 2:11–12 (to learn, but without . . .). The construction is even more precise between 2:9–10 and 2:11–12, with addressee ("women") + prepositional phrase ("in appropriate adornment"/"in quietude") + verb ("to adorn"/"should learn"), followed by a proscription ("not . . .") and a prescription ("but . . .").

That the items women are discouraged from wearing include gold and pearls and expensive clothing indicates that Paul's exhortation was probably directed to the wealthy. Elsewhere in the NT, the harlot of Rev 17:4 is adorned with "gold" and "pearls" and garbed in expensive clothing ("purple and scarlet"). "The reason for Paul's prohibition of elaborate hair styles, ornate jewelry, and extremely expensive clothing becomes clear when one reads in the contemporary literature of the inordinate time, expense, and effort that elaborately braided hair and jewels demanded, not just as ostentatious display, but also as the mode of dress of courtesans and harlots."[10] Philo (*Special Laws* 1.19.102; 3.9.51) describes such a disreputable person as having abandoned "decent and chaste demeanor [σχῆμα κόσμιον καὶ σῶφρον, *schema kosmion kai sōphron*]"; she is a "stranger to decency, modesty, and temperance [κοσμιότης, αἰδώς, σωφροσύν, *kosmiotēs, aidōs, sōphrosyn*]."[11] And what Paul

---

10. Knight, *Pastoral Epistles*, 135.

11. Philo, *On the Decalogue*, 158–59, 506–7. Notice the obvious parallels in wording: 1 Tim 2:9–10 has κόσμιος (*kosmios*, "appropriate"), αἰδώς (*aidōs*, "modesty"), σωφροσύνη (*sōphrosyne*, "self-control"), and κοσμέω (*kosmeō*, "adorn").

was exhorting women in 1 Tim 2:8–9 was close to the prevailing norm for the acceptable deportment of women. For example, here is Plutarch in the first century CE (*Advice to Bride and Groom* 26): "That adorns or decorates a woman which makes her more decorous [κοσμεῖ δὲ τὸ κοσμιωτέραν, *kosmei de to kosmiōteran*]. It is not gold or precious stones or scarlet that makes her such, but whatever invests her with that something which betokens dignity, good behaviour, and modesty [σεμνότητος εὐταξίας αἰδοῦς, *semnotētos eutaxias aidous*]."[12] The *Sentences of Sextus* 235 (ca. third or fourth century CE) recommends: "Let moderation [σωφροσύνη, *sōphrosynē*] be considered adornment [κόσμος, *kosmos*] for a faithful wife."[13]

It is worth observing that in 1 Tim 2:9, we are given a general directive regarding women's attire (marked by "modesty and self-control"), and a number of specifics (no braided hair, gold, pearls, or costly garments). The general exhortation is straightforward. But the specifics are not: What if one were to wear silver and emeralds instead of gold and pearls? Clearly if the latter were ostentatious—immodest and unrestrained—the former, too, would be equally so. In other words, it is the general exhortation that dictates the specifics. Anything, whether gold or silver, platinum or titanium, that falls into the category of immodesty, is to be avoided. Like the specific "holy hands" in 2:8 symbolizing the call to be holy, the specifics in 2:9 are also symbolic of the kind of clothing that must be avoided. Thus, the exhortation for women is to don vestments with "modesty and self-control," whatever the specific garments and ornamentations may be. Indeed, true adornment is "good works" that befit women professing "godliness" (θεοσέβεια, *theosebeia*, 2:10). This, of course, is not to say men can get away with immodesty, lack of self-control, and neglect of good works![14] By that same token, women are not exempt from having "holy hands," either.[15] Ideally, *all* members of God's household are to exhibit these "godly" lifestyles (εὐσέβεια, 2:2), marked by "good works" (2:10; they are to be evident in the lives of all people: 5:10, 24–25; 6:18; Titus 2:7, 14; 3:8, 14). So even though these particular exhortations to men and to women are made in the context of a worship gathering of the local body of Christ, they do not exclude the need for godliness in every facet of every Christian's life, regardless of gender. In sum, worship is to be taken seriously by all who participate in it: those involved are to be godly in attitude and action.

4.2.2 *The critical role of women in the serious matter of worship in the corporate gathering involves learning with deference rather than taking on authoritative teaching, at the same time embracing domestic roles and responsibilities (2:11–15).*

The complex of 2:9–10 has "self-control" (in 2:9), and so does 2:11–15 (in 2:15); thus, this noun forms a bracket for the entire section on women (2:9–15; and these are its only two occurrences in the PE). And in both sections, 2:9–10 and 2:11–15, there are outward

---

12. Plutarch, *Moralia*, 2:317, 319. In fact, Paul opens the doors for women further than Plutarch, who only recommended that "a virtuous woman ought to be most visible in her husband's company, and to stay in the house and hide herself when he is away" (*Advice to Bride and Groom* 9 in Plutarch, *Moralia*, 2:305). On the other hand, see 1 Tim 5:9–10; Titus 2:4–5; etc., for women performing "good works," obviously in public (1 Tim 2:10).

13. Wilson, *Sentences of Sextus*, 240.

14. Indeed, "self-control" is a requirement for every Christian leader: 3:2; Titus 1:8; 2:2, 5.

15. No doubt there is a link between the exhortation to women requiring "godliness" (2:10) and that to men calling for "holy hands" (2:8).

manifestations ("good works," 2:10; "childbearing," 2:15) and inward character traits ("godliness," 2:10; "faith and love and holiness," 2:15).

After addressing the disruption/dysfunction caused by men's unholy hands and their anger and the dissension they were engaged in (2:8), and that caused by women's immodest appearance and focus on externals (2:9–10), Paul switches to another matter of importance—women and instructional leadership roles in the corporate gathering of the church. (And the next pericope goes directly to the issue of who ought to be leaders in the community with the responsibility of teaching: Pericope 5: 1 Tim 3:1–16.) The two verses, 2:11–12, are constructed as an *inclusio*:

A   "in quietude" (2:11a)
    B   To learn "with all submissiveness" (2:11b)
    B'   Not "to teach or to exercise authority" (2:12a)
A'   "but to be in quietude" (2:12b)

Thus, to be in quietude (*A*) and learning with submissiveness (*B*) are in parallel with not teaching or exercising authority (*B'*) but rather remaining in quietude (*A'*). In other words, women do learn—in quietude and with all submissiveness (to teaching authority: *A*, *B*), but women do not teach—not exercising (teaching) authority, but being in quietude (*B'*, *A'*). Clearly, ἡσυχία, *hesychia*, in 2:11, 12 does not indicate absolute silence (for which σιγή, *sigē*, would have been a better choice, as in Rev 8:1; 1 Cor 14:28, 30, 34 also use the verb σιγάω, *sigaō*) or prohibit interlocution (see Acts 11:18; 21:14). Rather it is a sense of quietude that is to "characterise both the woman's learning and her forgoing of teaching."[16] As was noted, ἡσύχιος, *hesychios*, "quiet," also occurs in 1 Tim 2:2, describing the kind of life that God would have *all* his people lead: quietude of public life is the aspiration of every congregation and every member thereof.

We should not forget that Paul asserts that women *are* to learn (2:11). On the other hand, according to Rabbi Eliezer, "May the words of the Torah be burned and not be delivered to women" (*y. Sotah* 3.4).[17] Indeed, even the recitation of a blessing over a meal was restricted to men: "One does not invite women, slaves, or minors" (*y. Berakhot* 7.2).[18] Women generally did not have many doors open for their education in those days, perhaps partly due to the early age—mid-teens—of their marriages and the resulting disparity in ages between spouses. Besides, "writers questioned their aptitude to reason, to deliberate and to preserve their self-control. Prejudice made its way into Roman legislation that deprived women of various rights because of the *infirmitas, levitas* or *imbecillitas* ['infirmity, irrationality, or imbecility'] of the sex."[19] Plutarch (*Advice to Bride and Groom* 31, 32) would have the woman "keep silence [σιωπῆς, *siōpēs*]. For a woman ought to do her talking either to her

---

16. Marshall, *Pastoral Epistles*, 452. Also see Luke 14:4 (quietness in teaching); 23:56; 1 Thess 4:11; 2 Thess 3:12; 1 Tim 2:2 (quietness in life); 1 Pet 3:4 (quietness in feminine adornment).

17. Guggenheimer, *Jerusalem Talmud: Tractates Sotah and Nedarim*, 148.

18. Guggenheimer, *Jerusalem Talmud: Tractate Berakhot*, 521. While these sentiments in the Midrash cannot be dated precisely, and neither are they representative of all the Talmud (elsewhere it is assumed that girls and women will learn the Torah: *b. Sanhedrin* 94b; *b. Baba Batra* 119b), they are illustrative of at least a few notable strands of thought in Jewish history.

19. Zamfir, *Men and Women*, 220.

husband or through her husband."[20] So Paul is already countercultural; he does not focus on the issue of *whether* women should learn (they should), but only upon *how* they should learn (in quietude and with all submissiveness to the teaching authority; see below). He obviously does not think less of the ability of women: they are certainly capable of learning.

The manner in which women are to learn in a public setting is ἐν πάσῃ ὑποταγῇ, *en pasē hypotagē*. The adjective πᾶς intensifies the submissiveness and heightens the concern of the author for this character trait.[21] The related verb ὑποτάσσω, *hypotassō*, when used of interpersonal relationships is often in the middle voice, indicating a submission that is voluntary and not imposed (Rom 13:1, 5; 1 Cor 14:34; Eph 5:21, 22; Col 3:18; Titus 2:5, 9; 3:1; 1 Pet 2:1, 18; 3:1, 5). Since the corporate assembly seems to be the locus under discussion, this submission is likely to be to authorized teachers, elders who are "able to teach" (1 Tim 3:2).[22] Thus the submissiveness called for here is the attitude of deference and posture of acceptance appropriate to any learning situation: a first reflex of charity extended towards the teacher and to the authority of that person. No doubt, men in a learning environment would also be expected to demonstrate that characteristic (1 Cor 16:16; and see Gal 6:6). If household hierarchies operate in God's economy (Eph 5:22; Col 3:19; 1 Pet 3:1–6), and since the church is but the larger household of God (1 Tim 3:15; or a corporate extension of the domestic version: 3:4–5, 12; 5:10, 12–15; and see 1 Cor 3:16; 2 Cor 6:16; Eph 2:21–22; 1 Pet 2:5; 4:17), then a hierarchy might operate in the divine household as well. In that regard, there are a number of similarities between this pericope (1 Tim 2:8–15) and 1 Pet 3:1–16.[23] The latter is obviously concerned about domestic relationships, the former about corporate ones; the similarities suggest that somewhat identical hierarchies characterize both households.

And then we have 1 Tim 2:12, "the single most scrutinized verse of Scripture in recent scholarship."[24] From a broad study of the use of οὐδὲ, *oude*, "neither," in biblical and extrabiblical literature, Köstenberger confirms that the construction "negated finite verb + infinitive + οὐδὲ + infinitive," as in 1 Tim 2:12 ("I do not allow" + "to teach" + οὐδὲ + "to exercise authority"), links two infinitives that are related in quality—here, "to teach" and "to exercise authority."[25] Thus, the two terms linked by such a conjunction, though they may be related, are not modifying each other so as to sum up a negative sort of teaching, an exercising-authority kind (see the other two instances of οὐδὲ in the PE: 1 Tim 6:7, 16). Instead one could read οὐδὲ as "even": "to teach or *even* to exercise authority," since the latter is an activity broader in scope than is the former—teaching appears to be but a specific

---

20. Plutarch, *Moralia*, 2:323.

21. For similar uses of πᾶς, see 3:4; 4:9; 5:2; Titus 2:15; etc.

22. All believers are to be subject to their leaders: 1 Cor 16:16; 1 Thess 5:12; Heb 13:17; 1 Pet 5:5; to one another: Eph 5:21; to God: Jas 4:7; and to secular authorities: Rom 13:1; Titus 3:1; 1 Pet 2:13. There is also the submission of children to fathers (1 Tim 3:4), and slaves to masters (Titus 2:9).

23. "Wives" (γυνή, 1 Tim 2:9, 10, 11, 12, 14; and 1 Pet 3:1, 5) and "husbands" (ἀνήρ, 1 Tim 2:8, 12; and 1 Pet 3:1, 5, 7); "pray" (προσεύχομαι, *proseuchomai*, Tim 2:8) and "prayer" (προσευχή, *proseuchē*, 1 Pet 3:7); "adorn" and "proper" (κοσμέω and κόσμιος, *kosmios*, 1 Tim 2:9) and "adornment" (κόσμος, 1 Pet 3:3); "braided" (πλέγμα, *plegma*, 1 Tim 2:9) and "braiding" (ἐμπλοκή, *emplokē*, 1 Pet 3:3); "gold" and "garments" (1 Tim 2:9; and 1 Pet 3:3); "quiet[ude]" (1 Tim 2:11, 12; and 1 Pet 3:4); "submissive" (ὑποταγή / ὑποτάσσω, 1 Tim 2:11; 1 Pet 3:5); Adam and Eve/Abraham and Sarah (1 Tim 2:13, 14; and 1 Pet 3:6). See Christian, "Women, Teaching," 287–88, and Hugenberger, "Women in Church Office," 355–56.

24. Blomberg, "Women in Ministry," 168.

25. Köstenberger, "Complex Sentence," 122.

instance of the exercise of authority.[26] Mounce concludes that "Paul does not want women to be in positions of authority in the church; teaching is one way in which authority is exercised in the church."[27] The object of the two infinitives, διδάσκειν and αὐθεντεῖν (*didaskein* and *authentein*) is "man"—"to teach [a man] or to exercise authority over a man."[28] That Paul is likely to be prohibiting the broad idea of women taking authority over the elders is substantiated by 1 Cor 14:34.

It is evident that 1 Cor 11:1–16 assumes that women *will* pray and prophesy in the public gathering (also implied in Acts 1:17–18). One would wonder, then, why teaching is prohibited here in 1 Tim 2:12. Moo notes that the authority of the prophet, uttering divine revelation, is more a derived or deputized one, rather than a personal one, as is the case with a teacher. The latter engages in an activity that calls for preparation, study, and a greater individual and corporate consciousness, not to mention strong exhortations that delineate application for listeners:

> In short, his [the prophet's] activity is more distinctly "vertical" than that of the teacher whose activity is more directly related to the Scripture and tradition. In other words, prophesying, as more directly "pneumatic" than teaching, involves an authority relationship between the prophet and his hearers less personal than is the case with teachers. This greater personal authority of the teacher is the reason, I would contend, why Paul allows women to prophesy with men present, but not to teach them.[29]

Saucy notes that the "central concept in teaching, that of molding the will, suggests that there is considerable authority in this function." The association of "exhort," "refute," "reprove," and "rebuke" (1 Tim 5:20; 6:2; 2 Tim 4:2; Titus 1:9; 2:6, 15) "and the realization that it would be hard to exercise any of them without some teaching of truth suggests that the teaching ministry in the pastorals, being primarily associated with the community leaders, was one of authority."[30] The teaching authority of the individual performing that ministry seems obvious from the descriptions in the PE of those occupying offices where teaching is an important role: elders (3:2; 5:17; Titus 1:9), apostles (Paul: 1 Tim 2:7; 2 Tim 1:11), leaders (Timothy and Titus: 1 Tim 4:11, 13, 16; 6:2; 2 Tim 1:12, 14; 4:1–2; Titus 2:1). Obviously, *all* Christians are to be teachers (Matt 28:19–20; 1 Cor 14:26; Col 3:16; Heb 5:12), but the exercise of this activity in public office is restricted to certain individuals. As far as preaching is concerned, its primary locus is the worship gathering of the local body of believers and historically it

---

26. For parallels, see Rom 8:7, where it is said of the "mindset of the flesh" that it "does not subject itself to the law of God, neither [οὐδὲ] is it able [or 'it is not even able'] to do so"; and 1 Cor 3:2, where the Corinthians, "infants in Christ," were "not able [to receive milk], but neither [οὐδὲ] are yet able [or 'even now are not able']"; also 4:3; 5:1; 11:14; 14:21; 15:13, 16; Gal 2:3, 5; 6:13.

27. Mounce, *Pastoral Epistles*, 130.

28. Wolters, in his study of αὐθεντεῖν, a *hapax* in the NT, concludes that in period literature it bears "its ordinary meaning of 'authority'" and "is overwhelmingly used in a neutral or positive sense." Indeed, the cognate noun, αὐθέντης (*authentēs*, "master"), is never used pejoratively to indicate tyranny or despotism; in fact, it is even used of Jesus Christ: Αὐθέντης γεγένητο Λόγω Πατρί, *Authentēs gegenēto Logō Patri*, "Master, begotten Word of the Father" (*Sibylline Oracles* 7.69; also see 8.309) (Wolters, "ΑΥΞΕΝΤΗΣ," 724, 727; and "Semantic Study," 45).

29. Moo, "Interpretation of 1 Timothy 2:11–15," 207.

30. Saucy, "Women's Prohibition," 81–82, 90. Also see the formal (and likely public) refutation of false teaching in the PE, the responsibility of church leaders: 1 Tim 1:3, 10; 4:1, 6, 11; 5:20; 6:3–4; 2 Tim 2:16–18, 23; 4:2–5; Titus 1:9, 11, 13; 2:15; 3:9–11.

has always been the responsibility of one ordained for the office of elder, ostensibly one also gifted for the task (1 Cor 12:27–30; 1 Tim 3:2; 5:17; Titus 1:9). It is the public dimension of the service rendered to a congregation as a whole that calls for this restriction, and perhaps even ordination (1 Tim 4:11–16; 2 Tim 4:1–2).[31] Luther pungently noted:

> Every Christian has the same power that the pope, bishop, or priest has.... [But] if everyone wanted to preach, who would want to listen? If they preached at the same time, it would become like a racket made by frogs: "Croak, croak, croak!" Instead, it should happen in this way: the congregation should set in place someone who is competent for it to preach, distribute the sacrament, etc. We all have the power, but no one should presume to exercise it publicly except for him who is chosen by the congregation.[32]

Arguing that this prohibition extended only to women under the influence of the false teachers in Ephesus is quite tenuous. If learning is to be for women in general, not just women who have been duped by false teachers, then it stands to reason that the prohibition from teaching is also for women in general, not just for the women who may have themselves been influenced by false teachers or become false teachers themselves. Besides, the PE uses ἑτεροδιδασκαλέω to indicate false teaching (1:3; 6:3), νομοδιδάσκαλος for purveyors of heterodoxy (1:7), and διδασκαλίας δαιμονίων for the content of their pedagogy (4:1). Almost always, words with the διδασκ-root that are not otherwise qualified indicate correct doctrine (except perhaps for 2 Tim 4:3 and Titus 1:11): thus, the teaching here in 1 Tim 2:12 is not a pedagogy of error. Also, if the warning in 2:12 was against false teaching, one wonders why would Paul prohibit *women* from teaching error, while not in the same breath condemning *male* purveyors of falsehood? And if the prohibition were of women teaching error, there would have been no reason for Paul to qualify, explain, or rationalize it in 2:13–15 (with γάρ; see below): the proscription of false teaching needed no excuse.

Once again, it is important that "1 Tim 2:9–15 should be read with one eye on 3:1–7"; proscriptions directed to women in 1 Timothy 2 followed by prescriptions directed to elders in 1 Timothy 3 seem to be reasonable grounds for women not being considered for the office of elder that bears the responsibility of teaching in the corporate gathering of the body.[33] It appears then that it is the context of the teaching event that is the issue: the corporate

---

31. See Kuruvilla, *Vision for Preaching*, 31–49.
32. Luther, "Sermon for the First Sunday," 330–31.
33. Barnett, "Wives and Women's Ministry," 231. Paul goes from plural ("women") in 2:9 to singular ("a woman") in 2:11, 12. This also moves the scope of the exhortation from the time-bound circumstances of the women in Ephesus to a more general one, addressing all women, exemplified by the singular "woman." That leads the reader to see ἐπιτρέπω, *epitrepō*, a present tense verb (2:12), as gnomic, implying universality. Discussing 1 Tim 2:12, Wallace comments that "the normal use of the present tense in didactic literature, especially when introducing an exhortation, is not descriptive, but a general precept that has gnomic implications.... Grammatically, the present tense is used with a generic object (γυναικί [*gynaiki*]), suggesting that it should be taken as a gnomic present" (*Greek Grammar*, 525). In other words, the present tense, "I am not permitting" (2:12), does not restrict the prohibition to Paul's day; rather, it indicates Paul's personal practice in churches where he is himself ministering, and he desires that Timothy follow his, Paul's, practice in Ephesus (and, by implication, the rest of God's people are also to do so elsewhere). Indeed, the present tense is also used of his similar exhortations in 2:1 ("I am urging") and in 2:8 ("I want"). Permanence of strictures in our text are also evidenced by: reference to prototypical/primeval biblical events as the creation, fall, and salvation; the statement "if *anyone* desires ... it is necessary" (3:1–2); and the understanding of the PE as guidelines for "how one must conduct oneself in the household of God" (3:14–15).

nature of the responsibility is restricted to men who are elders (2:12; see Pericope 5: 1 Tim 3:1–16). This is not to say that women are never to teach *anywhere*; the context of the matter in our pericope is clearly the corporate gathering of the local body of Christ. In other situations, women can and do (and should) engage in activities synonymous with teaching: Acts 18:26 (women teaching individuals); 2 Tim 1:5 and 3:14–15 (women teaching family; also Eph 6:4); Titus 2:3–4 (women teaching women); and Col 3:16 and Heb 5:12 (though the context is not specified, it could be extrapolated to women teaching in a larger body). According to the NT, women have gifts of the Spirit (1 Cor 12:7–11) with which they can edify the body of Christ; their service and ministry are therefore indispensable to the church (1 Cor 12:12–26). And they certainly can prophesy: Acts 21:9; 1 Cor 11:5. Besides, there is no indication that the teaching gift is restricted to men (Eph 4:11); however, it appears that the office of elder is (1 Tim 3:1–2; 5:17; Titus 1:5–9).[34] (Incidentally, there is a similar prohibition of teaching in Titus 1:10–11, directed towards "rebellious men, empty talkers, and deceivers," who are to be "silenced" [ἐπιστομίζω, *epistomizō*]—a far stronger proscription than what is directed to women in 1 Tim 2:11–12.) Moo's comments are apropos:

> Some writers on this issue argue as if any restriction on the ministry of women somehow deprecates their position in the church. "Ministry" becomes subtly defined in terms of the more "public" activities such as preaching and teaching. While the term is sometimes employed in the contemporary church, it is imperative to recognize that this is a significant departure from NT usage. For Paul, *all* ministries were significant and not to be slighted . . . (1 Cor 12:21–33a). To argue, as I do, that women are barred from *some* ministries, is not to say that women cannot be "ministers" (in the NT sense) nor to suggest that their ministry is somehow less significant. The impression sometimes given that women do not "minister" or minister in less significant ways than men is an attitude against which women properly protest.[35]

Of course, how one puts the thrust of this text into practical church polity is a vexing question. I take a slightly different tack than the rest of the boats on the dangerous reefs of this text. I see preaching in the corporate context of the worship of the body of Christ as a different species of communication altogether, unlike most commentators and scholars who view preaching and teaching as equivalent activities.[36] In my conception, preaching in this corporate context is restricted to those office-bearers of the church who are authorized to teach—the elders (and perhaps those qualified to be elders). Therefore, outside of this corporate preaching engagement, I do not see any restriction of teaching activity in the community of God, whether in a Sunday School class, an Adult Bible Fellowship, a small group, or any other gathering, whatever the gender of the teachers, or the composition of the gathering.[37]

34. Can women teach *under* the authority of men/elders? The text does not address this explicitly, but I would gather that, since the proscription is of the exercise of *teaching* authority and since teaching carries inherent authority over the ones being taught (and that includes men in the corporate gathering), regardless of deputization or authorization by ecclesial office bearers, such a teaching ministry in the public setting of the church would be out of bounds for women (see Moo, "What Does It Mean?," 187).

35. Moo, "Interpretation of 1 Timothy 2:11–15," 214–15 (italics original).

36. See Kuruvilla, *Vision for Preaching*.

37. For this reason, the institution that I am part of, Dallas Theological Seminary, includes women students in its preaching classes.

After commenting on women *teaching*, the issue of women *learning* seems to be what Paul returns to in 2:14 (linking this to 2:11), since the emphasis here is on the woman being deceived—a faulty "learning" that led to transgression, exemplified in the fall in which Eve had a part. One might therefore conceive of a chiastic structure for 2:11–14, with 2:11 (A) and 2:14 (A′) dealing with women learning, and 2:12 (B) and 2:13 (B′) dealing with women teaching:

A	"A woman should learn in quietude, and with all submissiveness" (2:11)	Learning
B	"But I do not permit a woman to teach ..., but to be in quietude" (2:12)	Teaching
B′	"For Adam was formed first, then Eve" (2:13)	Teaching
A′	"And Adam was not deceived, but the woman, ... fully deceived, fell into transgression" (2:14)	Learning

The linkage of 2:13 to 2:12 makes sense since, in the PE, a γάρ-clause (as in 2:13: B′) following a command (as in 2:12: B) almost always provides a rationale for that command (see 4:7–8, 16; 5:4, 11, 17–18; 2 Tim 2:7, 16; 3:5–6; 4:2–3, 5–6, 9–10, 11, 15; Titus 3:9, 12[38]). Paul is concerned here solely with a sequence of deception leading to transgression that he does not want repeated in Ephesus.[39] "The shift from the simple to compound form [from ἀπατάω to ἐξαπατάω (*apataō* to *exapataō*) in 1 Tim 2:14] may be nothing more than a stylistic variation, and yet a slight emphasis does fit the context."[40] Hence my translation: "Adam was not deceived, but the woman, being *fully* deceived . . . ." This is not an argument against women per se; there is nothing in Scripture (or anywhere else) to suggest that women are particularly susceptible to deception.[41] Chrysostom puts it poignantly:

> In matters of the world, [men] do not yield at all to [women]—not in wars, not in sports. But in spiritual battles they [women] gain the advantage and are first to seize the prize and soar higher like some eagles, while we [men], like jackdaws, are ever wandering around in steam and smoke [of cooking food]. For it is the essence of jackdaws—and of greedy dogs—to focus on servers and cooks [i.e., on matters entirely earthly].[42]

In sum, with regard to the exhortation to women to learn with deference (2:11, A above), Paul simply cites the primordial example of sin (2:14, A′) as a dangerous potential: he does

---

38. The only exceptions might be 1 Tim 3:13 and 2 Tim 2:11. See Mounce, *Pastoral Epistles*, 132.

39. In 2 Cor 11:3–4, Paul makes a similar argument: deception leading to straying from Christ is linked to the serpent's ensnaring of Eve in the garden.

40. Mounce, *Pastoral Epistles*, 142.

41. Unlike what was expressed by Philo (*Questions on Genesis*, 1.33; LCL 380: 20): "Woman is more accustomed to be deceived than man. . . . and because of softness she easily gives way and is taken in by plausible falsehoods which resemble the truth." A similar sentiment is expressed in Sir 25:24: "From a woman was the beginning of sin, and because of her we all die" (my translation). But Paul blames *both* parties for the fall (Rom 5:12, 17).

42. Chrysostom, *Homilies on Ephesians* 13.11–17 (my translation from the Greek).

not consider any possibility of intrinsic deficiency on the part of women, with regard to learning or propensity to be deceived.[43]

As regards the prohibition of women from teaching, Paul grounds his mandate in 2:12 (*B* above) simply on primogeniture in 2:13 (*B'*): "Adam was formed first, then Eve" (2:13). The verb "formed" (πλάσσω, *plassō*, 2:13) shows its dependence on Gen 2:7, 8, 15, 19 LXX, likely a deliberate pointing to the Genesis text. In addition, the use of ἡ γυνή, *hē gynē*, in 1 Tim 2:14, instead of "Eve," is likewise deliberate; that was what was used in Gen 3:1, 2, 4, 6, 12, 13, 15, 16, 17 LXX ("Eve" shows up only in 3:20 after the fall). In referring to the Genesis accounts of creation and the fall,[44] Paul may have connected the present context of corporate worship with Adam's primary responsibility to "cultivate and keep" the garden of Eden, the sacred space of Yahweh, the Holy Place of the cosmic Temple (Gen 2:15). The verbs "cultivate" and "keep" are derived from עבד and שׁמר (*'bd* and *shmr*) respectively, that have corporate cultic and covenantal connotations (= "serve" and "worship"), especially when collocated, as in Num 3:7–8; 8:26; 18:7; Deut 11:16; 12:30; 13:4–5; Josh 22:5; 1 Kgs 9:6; Jer 16:11; Mal 3:14. So much so, "the Genesis garden is an archetypal sanctuary where God dwells and where man meets with God for worship."[45] That might also help explain the references to Genesis accounts here in 1 Timothy 2, where also the context appears to be the corporate gathering for worship.

> In light of the specific responsibilities assigned to the man in Genesis 2 that are exclusively associated with his creation in context, it seems more likely that Paul is directly referencing the man's service and guardianship in the worship of God. Accordingly, when Paul argues in 1 Timothy 2:13 on the basis of the fact that Adam was created first, he is using a summary citation of the creation mandate in the Genesis 2 pericope with respect to the service and guardianship responsibilities that God assigned to Adam.[46]

Thus, it was Adam's role as the primary caretaker of God's sacred space, with Eve a helper for Adam's assigned role. Paul draws from this historical stance to make his case for the corporate authority of man over woman as the primary teaching leader in the larger local body of believers.

Frequently, the argument has been made that since the Bible teaches equality among the genders, the notion of hierarchies should be abandoned by the church. But Blomberg is right: "There should be no doubt that Genesis 1—3 teaches a fundamental, ontological equality of male and female both before and after the Fall. Nevertheless, equality of being and personhood in God's eyes does not determine the question of whether or not any

---

43. Clearly, the male false teachers (aka the "serpents") were more culpable in this matter of deception leading to transgression. In Titus 1:10, the false teachers/"rebellious men" are labeled "deceitful" (φρεναπάτης, *phrenapatēs*), as was the serpent in the garden (Gen 3:13 uses the verb ἀπατάω of the snake; that word and the related ἐξαπατάω are employed in 1 Tim 2:14 and in 2 Cor 11:3, as well). Besides, Adam was certainly not devoid of blame for the fall (see Rom 5:12–20; 1 Cor 15:21–22). If anything, he—not being deceived—sinned willfully! And so, God questions Adam first after the fall (Gen 3:9–12), emphasizing his primary responsibility in the matter. Eve, on the other hand, confessed to having been deceived (3:13).

44. And, perhaps, the curse (1 Tim 2:15; Gen 3:16).

45. Cooper and Caballero, "Reasoning through Creation Order," 34. See Kuruvilla, *Genesis*, 29–51.

46. Cooper and Caballero, "Reasoning through Creation Order," 36.

functional differentiation (or even subordination) of roles or responsibilities remains."[47] There is no suggestion anywhere in Scripture of any *ontological* hierarchy, i.e., of essence: man and woman are equal, as Gal 3:28; 1 Cor 12:13; and Col 3:11 declare. Besides God himself is called a "helper" (Pss 10:14; 30:10; 54:4; 72:12), indicating that there is no existential subordination in that label from Gen 2:18. Therefore, Snodgrass observes "that equality and hierarchy are not necessarily antithetical ideas."[48] Schreiner notes that "it is a modern, democratic, Western notion that diverse functions suggest distinctions in worth between men and women. Paul believed that men and women were equal in personhood, dignity, and value but also taught that women had a distinct role from men."[49] In sum, for the prohibition of women from teaching in a public context (1 Tim 2:12, *B* above), no reason other than primogeniture is given (2:13, *B'* above): the author does not consider that there was, on the part of women, any heretical teaching, lack of education, or improper pedagogical style.[50]

On 2:15, Quinn and Wacker lament the "awkward, even bizarre Greek of this verse."[51] Paul begins: "but she will be saved/delivered [σωθήσεται, *sōthēsetai*, future singular[52]]"—the future tense from the perspective of Eve. But then he finishes: "if *they continue* [μείνωσιν, *meinōsin*, aorist plural] in faith and love and holiness with self-control." Who exactly the "they" are is unclear—children? wives and their husbands? women in general? Since Paul is on the topic of women, it would be best to remain on that track and assume Paul is going from Eve ("she") to all women ("they"), an extrapolation from one individual to a whole gender. Thus, for every person in this general group, the truth holds. In fact, the last plural noun before μείνωσιν is in 2:10: "women."

Of course, then there is the question of what kind of "salvation/deliverance" is on offer here—spiritual? physical?[53] In an extensive study, Köstenberger showed that "the passive of σῴζω plus διά was in literature surrounding the writing of the Pastorals regularly used in the context of a person's escape or preservation from danger by way of a given route."[54] For Köstenberger, this deliverance in 2:15 is from the clutches of Satan because: the fall is in view; Satan is mentioned in the parallel in 5:14–15; and concern for the believer's preservation from Satan is an ongoing one in the PE (1:20; 2:14–15; 3:6, 7; 4:1–5; 5:14–15; 6:9–10; 2 Tim 2:26).[55] In sum, it appears that σῴζω could well be spiritual deliverance here, but focusing

47. Blomberg, "Not Beyond What Is Written," 406.

48. Snodgrass, "Galatians 3:28," 175.

49. Schreiner, "Interpretation of 1 Timothy 2:9–15," 201–2.

50. Primogeniture is also adduced for women wearing a symbol of their being under authority (1 Cor 11:8–10).

51. Quinn and Wacker, *First and Second Letters to Timothy,* 231.

52. It could be read "*he* will be saved/delivered," but after the reference to Eve in 2:14 that forms the nearest antecedent, this is unlikely.

53. It has been argued that "*the* childbirth" (ἡ τεκνογονία, *hē teknogonia*) might refer to the birth of Jesus, as the early church fathers held (as also do a number of modern interpreters, for instance, Witherington, *Letters and Homilies,* 230). But there is no precedent for this use of τεκνογονία (a *hapax*).

54. Köstenberger, "Ascertaining Women's God-Ordained Roles," 129. See especially 1 Cor 3:15 (saved "through [διά] fire") and 1 Pet 3:20 (saved/brought in safety [διασῴζω, *diasōzō*] "through water [δι' ὕδατος, *di' hydatos*]").

55. Köstenberger, "Ascertaining Women's God-Ordained Roles," 130–32. And 1 Tim 2:15 may also indicate the use of the divine passive (σωθήσεται) to counter the "diabolical passive" (ἐξαπατηθεῖσα, *exapatētheisa*) in 2:14 (Köstenberger, "Ascertaining Women's God-Ordained Roles," 123).

on sanctification rather than justification: ongoing and increasing deliverance from the evil one's influence, and from the flesh and evil works, with increasing faithfulness to God, his Spirit, and good works—i.e., growth in godliness, a prominent theme in the PE.[56]

That leaves τεκνογονία to tell us the means of this spiritual deliverance (= sanctification). *Thesaurus Linguae Graecae* offers only two uses of τῆς τεκνογονίας before the first century—by Hippocrates (fifth century BCE) and by Chrysippus (third century BCE). The latter describes patriots as those "eager even to submit both to marriage and to childbirth [καὶ εἰς γάμον καὶ εἰς τεκνογονίαν, *kai eis gamon kai eis teknogonian*] for its sake and of the homeland, and to endure for it, if fitting, both anguish and death."[57] This use of τεκνογονία as a synecdoche—people patriotically embracing the duties of marriage and raising children—helps one understand the employment of the word in 1 Tim 2:15 as also potentially a metonym for the duties of a home. In 1 Tim 2:15, "the definite article joins with the author's choice of the noun [τῆς τεκνογονίας, *tēs teknogonias*] rather than the verb [τεκνογονέω, *teknogoneō*, as in 5:14] . . . suggesting that a general concept is in view, 'procreation,' i.e., the woman's participating in the multiplication of the human race." So Köstenberger renders 1 Tim 2:15 as "she (i.e., the woman) escapes (or is preserved; gnomic future) [from Satan] by way of procreation (i.e., having a family)," discharging her God-given domestic, biological, and societal responsibilities.[58] An almost similar argumentation is employed in 5:14–15: there, Paul would have younger widows avoid the wiles of Satan by getting married, bearing and rearing children, and keeping house. On the other hand, the abandonment of these domestic, biological, and societal engagements would counter the divine command to "be fruitful and multiply and fill the earth and rule over it" (Gen 1:28). Köstenberger concludes:

> It is inaccurate to view 1 Tim 2:15 merely from the perspective that it excludes the woman from all ruling functions in family, church, and society: the woman rather participates in this rule by adhering to her specific God-ordained role as indicated in the original creation account. . . . Rather than viewing this question primarily in terms of "confining" women to the home, it may be more productive to focus on the issue of determining the essence of a gender's calling from God, with women and men helping each other to live out their respective roles. The need of the hour is for an increasing number of individuals who model integrated relationships and ministry in the local church as well as in other Christian settings.[59]

Seeing σῴζω in 1 Tim 2:15 as primarily deliverance (= sanctification), it is not at all unusual to have it linked to a role (see also 1 Tim 4:11–16; also 1 Cor 15:2; etc.). Good

---

56. Of course, justification by works is rejected all along in the PE (1 Tim 1:15, 16; 2:3–6; 2 Tim 1:8–10; Titus 3:3–7).

57. Chrysippus, *Fragmenta Moralia*, 9.7.611 (158) (translation from Köstenberger, "Ascertaining Women's God-Ordained Roles," 140; see 140–42 for his excellent discussion on this issue from which I have borrowed liberally).

58. Köstenberger, "Ascertaining Women's God-Ordained Roles," 141–42. The Latin Vulgate translates τεκνογονία with *procreatio*.

59. Köstenberger, "Ascertaining Women's God-Ordained Roles," 139–40, 144. The choice of "childbearing" as the metonymous element of women engaging their divinely allotted roles in life is not surprising—after all it is the most distinguishable biological function of the female gender. "To select childbearing . . . indicates that the argument is transcultural, for childbearing is not limited to a particular culture but is a permanent and ongoing difference between men and women. The fact that God has ordained that women and only women bear children indicates that the differences in roles between men and women are rooted in the created order" (Schreiner, "Interpretation of 1 Timothy 2:9–15," 222).

works are essential for sanctification, as the PE amply testifies (also see Eph 2:10). Of course, 1 Tim 2:15 does not rule out such sanctification-deliverance for single women, who are not necessarily exercising themselves in family-related endeavors: Paul is simply emphasizing in general the supremacy of kingdom values and virtues (and their acceptance); for women as a gender category, he is stressing the importance (and acceptance) of domestic engagements. Needless to say, the other traits in the verse—"faith," love," "holiness," and "self-control"—are required of *all* believers: "faith" in 1 Tim 1:2, 4, 5, 14, 19; 2:15; 3:13; 4:1, 12; 6:10, 11, 12, 21; 2 Tim 1:5, 13; 2;18, 22; 3:8, 10, 15; 4:7; Titus 1:1, 4, 13; 2:2, 10; 3:15; "love" in 1 Tim 1:5, 14; 2:15; 4:12; 6:11; 2 Tim 1:7, 13; 2:22; 3:10; Titus 2:2; "holiness" in 1 Tim 2:15; and "self-control" in 1 Tim 2:9, 15.

In sum, I concur with Köstenberger: "While this is a difficult teaching in some respects, it appears to be what 1 Tim 2:15 is saying, and at least this writer does not feel at liberty to shrink from its apparent overt message merely because of the difficulties in implication and application of the passage in contemporary church and culture."[60] Thus, practically, for teaching in a public context we have certain restrictions being set with regard to gender, age, maturity of walk, quality of life, and content of pedagogy (1 Tim 2:12; 3:1–7; 4:11–12; Titus 1:6–9).

SERMON MAPS

THEOLOGICAL FOCUS OF PERICOPE 4 FOR PREACHING

4 The critical roles of men and women in the serious activity of corporate worship involve: men, being godly, leading prayer in the corporate assembly; women, being godly, learning with deference, at the same time embracing domestic roles and responsibilities (2:8–15).

This pericope deals with the role of women in the corporate gathering that has been a lightning rod in recent decades. No matter how this is preached, expect brickbats. In the pulpit, in the context of a worship service, it might be best to focus on the godliness/holiness aspect, touching only briefly upon the other issues. One could allot another venue and occasion for more of a "teaching" session on this, including a question-and-answer time. Other ideas include inviting experts to be part of a panel; making available books and articles for reading; detailing the church's stance on the issue and having elders address the reason for that position; etc.

Possible Preaching Maps for Pericope 4

I. Responsibility of Men
   Public Prayer (2:8a)
   Holiness (2:8b)
   Move-to-relevance: Men in society and in the church today
II. Responsibility of Women
   Public Learning (2:11–14)

60. Köstenberger, "Ascertaining Women's God-Ordained Roles," 138. At least in my reading of such scriptural texts, in my understanding of ecclesiology, and in my conception of homiletics, the practical aspects are fairly straightforward and were stated earlier: preaching is a different species of communication altogether, and the engagement of that activity in the corporate gathering of the whole church is reserved for the office of elder. Outside of this, I can see no restriction of preaching (or teaching) in other locations and to other audiences.

Holiness (2:9, 10, 15)
Move-to-Relevance: Women in society and in the church today
III. *Be Godly Publicly and Privately!*
Specifics on such godliness

A simple alternative:

I. Specific Public Responsibilities: Prayer and Learning
Men: Public Prayer (2:8a)
Women: Public Learning (2:11–14)
Move-to-Relevance: Taking our responsibilities seriously
II. General Public Responsibilities: Holiness
Men: Holiness (2:8b)
Women: Holiness (2:9, 10, 15)
Move-to-relevance: Taking holiness seriously
III. *Be Godly Publicly and Privately!*
Specifics on such godliness

PERICOPE 5

Leadership as Modeling

1 Timothy 3:1–16

[Elders, Deacons, Deaconesses; Leadership and Modeling of Christlikeness]

REVIEW, SUMMARY, PREVIEW

Review of Pericope 4: The fourth pericope of 1 Timothy (1 Tim 2:8–15) addressed the roles of men and women in the public gathering of the church: men are to be godly and to lead prayer; women, no less godly, learn with deference, and as part of their godliness, embrace their domestic roles and responsibilities as well.

Summary of Pericope 5: This pericope (1 Tim 3:1–16) deals with the offices of the church—eldership and diaconate—holders of which guide and model communal and individual conduct of the people of God. Such exemplary behavior, both by leaders and followers, is grounded in the work of Jesus Christ that initiates and sustains the godliness of God's people.

Preview of Pericope 6: The next pericope (1 Tim 4:1–16) warns of a time when false teachers, in their focus on, and devotion to, doctrines demonic, will deceive many. To counter these nefarious tendencies, the people of God remain focused on Scripture and discipline themselves for godliness, based on truth and by the Spirit, being examples to others.

1 TIMOTHY

5 1 Timothy 3:1–16

THEOLOGICAL FOCUS OF PERICOPE 5

5   Corporate conduct in the divine household is guided by elders (teachers and shepherds) and deacons and deaconesses (ministers and servers), who are characterized by virtue, including being irreproachable to outsiders and capable caretakers of the domestic household, as they model exemplary traits for the faith and praxis of members of the divine household, all based upon the work of Christ that initiates and sustains the godliness of believers (3:1–16).

  5.1   Corporate conduct in the divine household is guided by elders (teachers and shepherds) and deacons and deaconesses (ministers and servers), who are characterized by virtue, including being irreproachable to outsiders and capable caretakers of the domestic household, as they model exemplary traits for the faith and praxis of members of the divine household (3:1–13).

   5.1.1 Corporate conduct in the divine household is guided by elders (teachers and shepherds) who are characterized by virtue, including being irreproachable to outsiders and capable caretakers of the domestic household, as they model exemplary traits for the faith and praxis of members of the divine household (3:1–7).

   5.1.2 Corporate conduct in the divine household is guided by deacons and deaconesses (minsters and servers) who are characterized by virtue, including being irreproachable to outsiders and capable caretakers of the domestic household, as they model exemplary traits for the faith and praxis of members of the divine household (3:8–13).

  5.2   The core truth of the work of Christ with regard to his Person (incarnation, resurrection, and ascension) and with regard to his people (proclamation, reception, and exaltation) initiates and sustains the godliness of believers (3:14–16).

OVERVIEW

This pericope moves from the Epistle's most recent concern: who should *not* teach in the corporate context (2:12–15), to its current issue: who should (3:1–7). Both topics, of course, deal with conduct in the "household of God" (3:15). Connections with Pericope 4: 1 Tim 2:8–15 include: σωφροσύνη and σώφρων (*sōphrosynē* and *sōphrōn* 2:9, 15; and 3:2); κόσμιος and κοσμέω (*kosmios* and *kosmeō*, "honorable," 2:9 and 3:2); "likewise women" in 2:9 (ὡσαύτως γυναῖκας, *hōsautōs gynaikas*) and "women likewise" in 3:11 (γυναῖκας ὡσαύτως); and πάσῃ ὑποταγῇ and ἐν ὑποταγῇ (*pasē hypotagē* and *en hypotagē*, "in submission"; 2:11 and 3:4). The tenor and contours of 3:2–7 resemble those of Titus 1:6–9, so it is possible that traditional matter is being utilized in both these texts, though tweaked for the particular issues under consideration and for the specific audience being addressed in each letter.

Virtue Lists

Secular virtue lists of the day share several items with the lists in 1 Timothy 3 and Titus 1. For instance, the first-century-CE philosopher, Onasander, has in *The General* (1.1) eleven attributes for that eponymous official, several of which are either identical or notionally similar to the criteria for church elders in the PE: σώφρων ("self-control," 1 Tim 3:2; Titus 1:8); ἀφιλάργυρος (*aphilargyros*, "free from the love of money," 1 Tim 3:3); ἐγκρατής (*enkratēs*, "discipline," Titus 1:8); νήπτης, *nēptēs*, "alert" (νηφάλιος, *nēphalios*, "temperate," in Tim 3:2); πατέρα παίδων, *patera paidōn*, "father of children" (τέκνα ἔχοντα, *tekna echonta*, "keeping children" in 1 Tim 3:4; and a similar phrase in Titus 1:6); "a ready speaker" ("able to teach" in 1 Tim 3:2); and "a man with a good reputation" ("have a good testimony" in 1 Tim 3:7).[1] In the second century BCE, Polybius (*Histories* 10.22.5) averred that "it was impossible for a man who was careless about the conduct of his own life to administer [προστατέω, *prostateō*] public affairs well" (a related verb προΐστημι, *proistēmi*, is found in 1 Tim 3:4, 5, 12).[2] Paschke has also demonstrated how ancient texts listing qualifications of Roman magistrates (*cura morum*) touched on marriage, children's obedience, alcoholism, and religion, areas of identical interest in the qualifications for church elders, with verbal, semantic, and conceptual parallels.[3] Of course, there are considerable differences between the secular and sacred texts, for the latter are plainly Christian.

Interestingly enough, the *mebaqqer*, a leader in the Qumran community, was described as a father and shepherd, as well as the teacher of doctrine (Qumran *Rule of the Community* 6:10–20; 9:19–22; Cairo Genizah *Damascus Document* 13:8–10), as also was the elder (Acts 20:29–30; 1 Tim 3:2; Titus 1:9).[4] In the NT and in the church fathers, the elder was often considered a shepherd (1 Pet 5:1–5; Acts 20:28–29; 1 Clem. 44:4; Polycarp, *Philippians* 6:1), who cared for his own household as a father (1 Tim 3:4–5; Titus 1:6).

All that to say, even though Paul was unlikely to be borrowing from contemporary sources, similar ideas and concepts were certainly floating around the milieu of first-century thought, both Greco-Roman and Judaistic. Clearly, alignment of the character of church leaders with that of civic leaders would lend credibility to the former and prevent the church from being brought into disrepute. It is notable that the elder list commences and concludes with the demand that an elder be "irreproachable" (1 Tim 3:2; also in 5:7; 6:14) and one who, having a good testimony with outsiders, "will not fall into disgrace" in their eyes (3:7).[5] Thus the public image of the elder forms a bracket for all his qualifications. In essence, in the elder list, the many adjectival qualities in 3:2–3 "specify what is meant by the requirement that the overseer be above reproach."[6] One might therefore see the elder list as one with eleven items, with the first, "above reproach," being the heading. As Chrysostom noted, "every virtue is implied in this word" (*Homilies on First Timothy* 10).[7]

---

1. Onasander et al., *Aeneas Tacticus, Asclepiodotus, and Onasander*, 374–75.
2. Polybius, *Histories*, 4:175, 177.
3. Paschke, "Cura Morum," 105–19.
4. See Thiering, "*Mebaqqer* and *Episkopos*," 71.
5. "Dignified" commences the deacon list in 1 Tim 3:8, and the description of the deaconesses in 3:11 (also see 3:4). Besides, deacons also are required to be "blameless" (3:10; also in Titus 1:6, 7).
6. Malherbe, "Overseers as Household Managers," 563.
7. *Nicene and Post-Nicene Fathers* 13:438. As for the entire list comprising elder and deacon requirements, "good work" (3:1, of elders) and "good standing" (3:13, of deacons) form an *inclusio* for the whole section, 3:1–13.

1 TIMOTHY

Modeling for All Believers

No specific to-do items for elders or deacons are provided in these lists; rather than duties, we are given mostly character qualifications, behavioral traits, and dispositions that are not particularly Christian.[8] But what is striking in these lists is how the various items are to be demonstrated in the lives of *all* believers. Thus the role of leaders is to model godliness for the flock, as instructed in 1 Pet 5:3, and explicitly noted in the PE in 1 Tim 1:16; 4:12; and Titus 2:7. In the first century, the Roman stoic philosopher, Seneca the Younger (*Epistle* 94.40), opined: "For the frequent seeing, the frequent hearing of them [good men] little by little sinks into the heart and acquires the force of precepts."[9] So it is not surprising that the traits of church leaders are required to be demonstrated by all believers; for instance: νηφάλιος, "temperate," and σώφρων, "self-controlled" (1 Tim 3:2, 4, 11; Titus 1:8), also describe old men and young women and men (Titus 2:2, 5, 6; also see 1 Tim 2:2, 9, 15; 3:4; Titus 2:4); κόσμιος and σωφροσύνη (1 Tim 3:2) are also required of women (3:9); hospitality (3:2; Titus 1:8) is to characterize widows (1 Tim 5:10), as well as all Christians (Rom 12:13; Heb 13:2; 1 Pet 4:9); "honorable" is a trait of leaders (1 Tim 3:2), but all women are to manifest it (2:9); ability to teach (1 Tim 3:2; Titus 1:9) is to be visible in all, whether they occupy church offices or not (2 Tim 2:2, 24; Heb 5:12)—perhaps the only item in the elder list that details an ability.[10] Then there are the prohibitions of wine addiction (1 Tim 3:3, 8; Titus 1:7), and all believers are to eschew drunkenness (Eph 5:18; 1 Thess 5:7–8); leaders are not to be pugnacious or quarrelsome but gentle (1 Tim 3:3; Titus 1:7), and so, too, all the people of God (2 Tim 2:14, 24; Titus 3:2, 9); elders and deacons are not to love money (1 Tim 3:3, 8; Titus 1:7; and 1 Pet 5:2), and neither are believers (Heb 13:5; also see 1 Tim 6:6–10, 17–19). Malicious gossips are reprimanded in 3:11 (among deacons) and Titus 2:3 (among all believers). Of course, keeping the faith/being faithful (3:11) is to mark every child of God (1 Tim 1:12; 4:12; 2 Tim 2:2; Titus 1:6). And διάκονος, *diakonos,* "deacon/servant/minister" (1 Tim 3:8, 12) is applied to Jesus himself, usually accompanied by the call for all believers to serve likewise (Matt 20:28; 23:11; Mark 9:35; 10:43–45; Luke 22:26; Rom 15:8; etc.).

The Offices

The NT uses only two titles for offices—elders and deacons (but with a variety of labels; see below).[11] For elders, teaching appears to get prominence (1 Tim 3:2; 5:17–18; Titus 1:9, 11, 13; also seen in Eph 4:11; Acts 20:28), along with shepherding (see especially 1 Tim 3:5; 1 Pet 5:1–5).[12]

In their ecclesial capacity, elders (ἐπίσκοποι and πρεσβύτεροι, *episkopoi* and *presbyteroi*) are mentioned in the NT in Acts 11:30; 14:23; 15:2–6, 22–23; 16:4; 20:17, 28; 21:18; Phil 1:1; 1 Tim 3:1–7; 4:14; 5:17–25; Titus 1:5, 7, 9; Jas 5:14; 1 Pet 5:1–5; 2 John 1; and

---

8. Notwithstanding the oversight function connoted by ἐπίσκοπος, *episkopos*.
9. Seneca, *Epistles,* 3:37.
10. See Himes, "Rethinking the Translation," 191.
11. Apostleship is another office, obviously restricted in time and to a few individuals.
12. Whether the single office of elder constituted two orders, that of preaching-teaching elder and that of ruling elder, will be addressed in Pericope 8: 1 Tim 5:17–25. Spoiler: I don't think so!

3 John 1. The term ἐπισκόπος was also used of Greek civic officials.[13] On the other hand, πρεσβύτερος may have had its origin in Jewish communities.[14] The former was more a functional term, indicating oversight; the latter dealt more with standing and position. Acts 20:17 and 28, as well as Titus 1:5 and 7, suggest the terms are equivalent[15]; the verses in Acts 20 also seem to incorporate the responsibility of shepherding (ποιμαίνω) into the office of elder, as also does 1 Pet 5:1–5.[16] Of course, πρεσβύτερος can simply indicate one who is elderly, as in 1 Tim 5:1 and Titus 2:2. In fact, it is quite likely that church elders were older men. While ἐπισκόπος is always singular (1 Tim 3:2; Titus 1:7; in addition to a singular cognate indicating the office, ἐπισκοπή, *episkopē*, 1 Tim 3:1), the other term shows up both in the singular, πρεσβύτερος (1 Tim 5:1, 19), and the plural, πρεσβύτεροι (1 Tim 5:17; Titus 1:5). However, the singular in both cases is likely to be generic (as is obvious in 1 Tim 5:1), rather than indicating a "monarchical" episcopate, with a single elder/bishop in a city with other leaders beneath him. Plurality of leadership among God's people seems to be the norm in the New Testament (Acts 14:23; 1 Cor 12:28; Eph 4:11; Phil 1:1; 1 Thess 5:12–13; 1 Tim 5:17; Heb 13:7, 17, 24; etc.).[17]

Deacons in an official capacity are mentioned in the NT in Acts 6:1–6 (where διακονία, *diakonia*, is used); Phil 1:1; and 1 Tim 3:8–13.[18] In Greek literature, besides the sense of "servant" or "messenger," διάκονος was also used of an "*attendant* or *official* in a temple or religious guild."[19] Though at least two of the "deacons" of Acts 6 do not appear to have been only servers—Stephen, a miracle worker (Acts 6:8) and Philip, an evangelist (Acts 6:8–10)—it is fair to assume the diaconate in its early days underwent changes in its organization and portfolios. The use of the term, however, indicates its primary role of serving.

In sum, "the working hypothesis, provided primarily by the self-defining terms, is that the ἐπίσκοπος is an 'overseer,' one carrying out a ministry of oversight, while διάκονοι are 'servants,' those carrying out a ministry of service," dealing with the day-to-day exigencies of church life.[20] Mounce thinks that the relative sparseness of discussion on church leader-

---

13. Beyer, "ἐπισκέπτομαι, κτλ.," 611–14.

14. See, for instance, *Codex Theodosianus* 6.8.14, where presbyters are identified with archisynagogues.

15. Also see 1 Clem. 44:1–5 that uses both terms; as well, 42:4, 5; 47:6; and Irenaeus, *Against Heresies* 3.2.2; 3.3.1–3.

16. One could add Eph 4:11 to this list that mentions "pastors and teachers" (ποιμένες καὶ διδάσκαλοι).

17. Timothy himself is not explicitly labeled an elder, but 1 Tim 4:14 suggests an early form of ordination to that office; if Paul was involved in such a process (as 2 Tim 1:6 asserts), he, too, was likely an elder, certainly qualified to be one (Acts 13:1–3 calls Paul [Saul] a "teacher"). Other designations for elders include "leaders" (προϊστάμενοι, *proistamenoi*; 1 Thess 5:12–13; 1 Tim 3:4–5, 12; 5:17; and also see Rom 12:8; and ἡγουμένοι, *hēgoumenoi*; Heb 13:7, 17, 24); "shepherd" (Acts 20:28; Eph 4:11); as well, "teachers" and those with the gift of administration (1 Cor 12:28). It is best, however, to distinguish between spiritual gift and ecclesial office: the latter are fewer and limited to apostles, elders/overseers, and deacons/deaconesses, while the former are many and unrestricted (1 Pet 4:10); offices are by appointment or election, while gifts are entirely sovereign in bestowal (1 Cor 12:11, 18, 28); every believer has a gift, but not everyone holds an office; office-bearers are not to be recent converts and elders are to be men, while gifts are not so constrained (see Hoehner, "Can a Woman Be a Pastor-Teacher?," 761–71).

18. Titus has no mention of deacons, perhaps reflecting the relative newness (and size) of the church. The word διάκονος or its cognate shows up in Luke 22:26 (and parallels); John 12:26; Rom 13:4; 16:1–2; 1 Cor 3:5; 2 Cor 3:6; 6:4; 11:15, 23; Eph 3:7; 6:21; Col 1:7, 23, 25; 4:7, 17; 1 Thess 3:2; 1 Tim 4:6; etc.

19. "διάκονος," in Liddell and Scott, *Greek-English Lexicon*, 398 (emphases original).

20. Knight, *Pastoral Epistles*, 151.

1 TIMOTHY

ship structure "may simply be due to the ad hoc nature of the NT literature."[21] Besides, notions of leadership from extant Greek and Jewish societal and communal structures would have been familiar to Paul's readers without need for much explication.

5.1 1 Timothy 3:1–13

THEOLOGICAL FOCUS 5.1

5.1 Corporate conduct in the divine household is guided by elders (teachers and shepherds) and deacons and deaconesses (ministers and servers), who are characterized by virtue, including being irreproachable to outsiders and capable caretakers of the domestic household, as they model exemplary traits for the faith and praxis of members of the divine household (3:1–13).

  5.1.1 Corporate conduct in the divine household is guided by elders (teachers and shepherds) who are characterized by virtue, including being irreproachable to outsiders and capable caretakers of the domestic household, as they model exemplary traits for the faith and praxis of members of the divine household (3:1–7).

  5.1.2 Corporate conduct in the divine household is guided by deacons and deaconesses (ministers and servers) who are characterized by virtue, including being irreproachable to outsiders and capable caretakers of the domestic household, as they model exemplary traits for the faith and praxis of members of the divine household (3:8–13).

TRANSLATION 5.1

3:1 The statement is trustworthy: if one aspires to the office of overseer, it is a good work he desires.

3:2 The overseer, then, must be irreproachable, a one-woman man, temperate, self-controlled, honorable, hospitable, able to teach,

3:3 not addicted to wine, not pugnacious, but gentle, not quarrelsome, free from the love of money,

3:4 one managing his own household well, keeping children in submission with all dignity

3:5 (but if one does not know how to manage his own household, how will he take care of the church of God?),

3:6 not a new convert, so that he will not become conceited and fall into the condemnation of the devil.

3:7 And he must have a good testimony with those outside [the church], so that he will not fall into disgrace and the snare of the devil.

3:8 Deacons likewise [must be] dignified, not double-tongued, not given to much wine, not covetous of sordid gain,

3:9 keeping the mystery of the faith with a pure conscience.

3:10 And these must also first be tested; then let them serve as deacons if they are blameless.

3:11 Women likewise [must be] dignified, not slanderous, temperate, faithful in all things.

---

21. Mounce, *Pastoral Epistles*, 154.

3:12   *Deacons must be one-woman men, good managers of children and of their own households.*

3:13   *For those who have served well as deacons gain for themselves good standing and much confidence in the faith that is in Christ Jesus.*

NOTES 5.1

5.1.1 *Corporate conduct in the divine household is guided by elders (teachers and shepherds) who are characterized by virtue, including being irreproachable to outsiders and capable caretakers of the domestic household, as they model exemplary traits for the faith and praxis of members of the divine household (3:1–7).*

Structurally, 3:1, a single sentence, provides a sort of introduction to the section on elders; 3:2–6 is another single sentence (with a parenthetical query in 3:5); and 3:7, yet another sentence, gives a conclusion, with a warning to the elder-to-be to maintain a good reputation.

The list begins in 3:1 with "the statement is trustworthy" (one of five such assertions in the PE; the others are in 1 Tim 1:15; 4:9; 2 Tim 2:11; Titus 3:8). It is best to see the trustworthy statement as an underscoring of the value of *good* leadership in the divine household: "good" (καλός) occurs 3:1, 4, 7 in the elder list, as well as in 3:12, 13 in the deacon list. To function as an elder is a "good work" (καλός ἔργον, 3:1). Because it is a "good work"—"therefore" (οὖν, *oun*, 3:2)—the following traits "must" (δεῖ, *dei*, 3:2) characterize elder (3:2–7) and deacon candidates (3:8–13; the δεῖ is implied in 3:8 and 3:11 with "likewise").[22]

Below, I will deal briefly with some of the individual requirements, and then expound on two specific ones: the call for an elder to be a "one-woman man" (3:3; also for deacons, 3:12), and the indispensability of the candidate being a good household manager (3:4–5).

Perhaps there is a chiasm in 3:3, with negations using μὴ in A, B, and α-privatives in B', A'. Thus the central element, "gentleness" (C), might be the focus of the structure, with drunkenness, pugnacity, contentiousness, and money-love being marked by *ungentleness*.

---

22. While, no doubt, countering false teachers was a motivating factor for this letter and the elder list, one wonders about the requirement for managing one's household, being a "one-woman man," and not addicted to alcohol, etc. Were the false teachers poor fathers, promiscuous husbands, and inveterate imbibers? Nonetheless, there seem to be a number of contrasts being made between the elders of 1 Tim 3:1–7 and the opponents of 6:3–10: able to teach (3:2) and teaching heterodoxy (6:3); ἐπιθυμέω (*epithymeō*, "desire," 3:1) and ἐπιθυμία (*epithymia*, "lust," 6:9); ἀφιλάργυρος (*aphilargyros*, 3:6) and φιλαργυρία (*philargyria*, "love of money," 6:10); "conceited" (3:6 and 6:4); "snare" (3:7 and 6:9); "fall" (3:6 and 6:9); and ὀρέγω (*oregō*, "aspire/long for," 3:1 and 6:10). The last three pairs employ words found only in those instances in 1 Timothy. See Van Neste, *Cohesion and Structure*, 108.

> A   μὴ πάροινον, *mē paroinon*
>   "not addicted to wine"
> B   μὴ πλήκτην, *mē plēktēn*
>   "not pugnacious"
> C   ἀλλ' ἐπιεικῆ, *all' epieikē*
>   "but gentle"
> B'   ἄμαχον, *amachon*
>   "uncontentious"
> A' ἀφιλάργυρον, *aphilargyron*
>   "free from the love of money"

In 3:6, the elder candidate is required not to be a "new convert" (νεόφυτος, *neophytos*, only here in the NT), lest that one be consumed with "conceit"; perhaps it was the allure of the authority of office that oft lead bearers astray. The result of such conceit would be the "condemnation of the devil." This is likely to be in the subjective genitive, i.e., condemnation [of God] induced by the devil, as was warned in 1:20. Besides, Satan shows up again in the next verse, 3:7, actively causing mayhem: the "snare of the devil" is one that he sets for others, another subjective genitive (also in 2 Tim 2:26), thus making it likely that he was equally active in a maleficent way in 1 Tim 3:6.[23]

In 3:7, the elder candidate is called to (δεῖ) maintain a good testimony/reputation with those outside the church (see 1 Cor 10:32; Col 4:5; 1 Thess 4:12; 1 Pet 2:12, for similar sentiments with regard to the lives of all believers). Thus the elder list begins and ends with δεῖ (1 Tim 3:2, 7).[24] Since 3:2–6 is one sentence and 3:7 another, this last verse is likely a return to, and an emphasis upon, the opening theme of being "irreproachable" (3:2)—here in 3:7, avoiding "disgrace." Good work leads to good reputation!

"One-woman Man"

What does μιᾶς γυναικὸς ἀνήρ (*mias gynaikos anēr*, 3:2, 12; Titus 1:6) mean? If Paul were ruling out polygamy, then the related ἑνὸς ἀνδρὸς γυνή, *henos andros gynē*, in 5:9 would have to be ruling out polyandry—an extremely rare marital arrangement in those days (and in ours). If he were ruling out celibacy, it is surprising that he would endorse it in 1 Cor 7:32–40 (as also did Jesus in Matt 19:12). The additional problem with such a reading is that marriage alone would be insufficient to qualify an elder/deacon; the candidate would also have to have had at least two children—τέκνα is plural (3:4, 12). Besides, taking the phrase as prohibiting celibates from office would render 1 Tim 5:9 somewhat circular in argument when applied to widows, tautologically calling for them also not to be currently single, but (re)married, at which point they would no longer be widows! If marriage itself were a requirement for church officers, it would have been easier for Paul to have employed the verb γαμέω, *gameō*, than the convoluted "one-woman man." And such a mandate for candidates being married would likely eliminate Paul, too (and perhaps Timothy) from being a church

---

23. There is also the repeat of ἐμπίπτω, *empiptō*, in 3:6 and 3:7, warning of the shared satanic dangers these unqualified candidates might plunge into.

24. Note also the repetitions of καλός (*kalos*, 3:1, 7; also in 3:13) and the adverb καλῶς (*kalōs*, 3:4; also in 3:12, 13).

officer, not to mention Jesus, himself, the Chief Shepherd of all the elder-shepherds (Heb 13:20; 1 Pet 2:25; 5:4). And if μιᾶς γυναικὸς ἀνήρ meant that candidates for church office should have been married only once in the past, remarried aspirants for church office would thereby be barred from eldership and deaconship, though Paul had no problem with remarriage itself (Rom 7:1–3; 1 Cor 7:8–9, 39–40; 1 Tim 5:14).[25]

Clearly, sexual promiscuity (suggested, perhaps, by 2 Tim 3:6) would be a disqualifying factor for church leadership; that Paul did not expressly prohibit πορνεία (*porneia*, "immorality") in these lists leads one to conclude that a requirement for sexual purity is how μιᾶς γυναικὸς ἀνήρ is to be understood—morality and chastity, purity and propriety, all wrapped in the virtuous demeanor of men towards women. And thus, we have the adjective-like description: "one-woman man." In other words, even single people, equally prone to πορνεία as married ones, would be included in its fold. Demosthenes, the fourth-century Greek orator, declaimed: "Mistresses we keep for the sake of pleasure, concubines for the daily care of our persons, but wives to bear us legitimate children and to be faithful guardians of our households" (*In Neaeram* 59.122).[26] In all likelihood, it was this banality of marital infidelity in Greco-Roman culture that prompted the penning of this clause in the elder-deacon lists, to counter any hint of turpitude in those candidates for leadership. Topping the elder list and preceded as it is by a call to irreproachability, "the main point of the requirement would seem to be first the avoidance of any appearance of immorality."[27]

In light of the value being placed on visible virtues in these elder and deacon lists, one might ask if single people ever have the opportunity to display such spousal fidelity. They do. Note the emphases in the PE pro-purity and anti-immorality in all its forms—and this for *all* believers, married or otherwise: 1 Tim 1:10 (avoiding immorality); 2:8, 15 (living holy lives); 3:2, 11 (being temperate and self-controlled); 4:12 (exemplifying purity); 5:2 (treating younger women in purity); 5:22 (keeping free from sin); Titus 1:8 (being self-controlled); 2:2 (being temperate); 2:5 (demonstrating purity); 2:12 (denying worldly desires and living in godly fashion); 3:3 (not being enslaved to lusts and pleasures); and, of course, similar demands all throughout the NT. In other words, whether married or single, the candidate for church office should have demonstrated all these qualities, described by the catch-all, "one-woman man."[28] Note also that these visible aspects of faithfulness are what are being implicitly referred to when Paul tells the Corinthians that he "betrothed you to one husband [ἑνὶ ἀνδρί, *heni andri*], to present you a pure virgin to Christ" (2 Cor 11:2). Merkle concludes: "Consequently, Paul's intent in stating that a man must be the 'husband of one wife' is not that a man must be married, but that if he is married, he must be faithful to his wife."[29] And, I would add, if he is single, he must still demonstrate such values in his life. On the similar text in Titus 1, Quinn observes: "The emphatic position of 'one' here and

---

25. Likewise, if ἑνὸς ἀνδρὸς γυνή (5:9) meant that those currently widows were to have been married only once in the past, it would be quite strange for Paul to prescribe remarriage in 5:14 for younger widows, knowing that if they were widowed a second time, their second marriage (i.e., their remarriage after their first widowhood) would render them ineligible for subsequent ecclesial assistance.

26. Demosthenes, *Orations*, 6:45, 447.

27. Johnson, *First and Second Letters to Timothy*, 214.

28. Considering, as I do (see below), that 1 Tim 3:11 deals with female candidates for the diaconate, it is interesting that women are called to be "temperate, faithful in all things," but not to be ἑνὸς ἀνδρὸς γυνή (as widows were, in 5:9). The reason is obvious: these descriptions are synonymous.

29. Merkle, "Are the Qualification for Elders?," 183.

in the other three occurrences of this formula practically eliminates the notion that marriage is here proposed as a prerequisite for those who exercise the Christian ministries."[30]

Household Management

In 3:4, the shift from the style of the preceding adjectives to a participial phrase (οἴκου καλῶς προϊστάμενον, *oikou kalōs proistamenon,* "managing [his own] household well") "draws attention to the major quality of the overseer, his domestic governance," described both in terms of his care for his household and the related care for the divine household, God's church (3:4–5).[31]

That the church officer must be a good "manager" of his household (προϊστάμενος, 3:4–5) is also sounded in Titus 1:6 (and in 1 Tim 3:12 for deacons). The verb προΐστημι, *proistēmi,* is used eight times by Paul, six of them in the PE (1 Tim 3:4, 5, 12; 5:17; Titus 3:8, 14—all linked with καλῶς/καλός). Paul's regard of the church as an extension of the household explains the use of the metaphor for church leadership (Gal 6:10; Eph 2:19–22; 1 Tim 3:4–5, 15). The primary manifestation of such managerial leadership in the domestic household, at least one that was pertinent to the current discussion of leadership in the ecclesial household, was "keeping children in submission with all dignity" (1 Tim 3:4). How parental authority and leadership was exercised in the home determined the suitability of the candidate for the office-related authority and leadership of the church. The prepositional phrase μετὰ πάσης σεμνότητος, *meta pasēs semnotētos,* "with all dignity," likely refers to the managerial bearing of the father, rather than to the submissiveness of the children, since the cognate σεμνός (*semnos,* "dignified") also describes deacons (3:8), deaconesses (3:11), and older men (Titus 2:2), not to mention all believers (σεμνότης in 1 Tim 2:2; Titus 2:7). This authority is exercised not only with dignity but also with "care" (ἐπιμελέομαι, *epimeleomai,* 3:5); the verb is employed to describe the Good Samaritan's "care" of the victim of the highway robbery (Luke 10:34, 35). Using related words, Philo (*On the Virtues* 57) writes regarding Moses choosing his successor:

> And therefore, slow to trust in himself, he besought and entreated God, who surveys the invisible soul and to whom alone it is given to discern the secrets of the mind, to choose on his merits the man most fitted to command, who would care for his subjects as a father [ὃς οἷα πατὴρ ἐπιμελήσεται τῶν ὑπηκόων, *hos hoia patēr epimelēsetai tōn hypēkoōn*]. And stretching up to heaven his pure, and, as it might be put figuratively, his virgin hands he said, "Let the God of spirits and all flesh look to find a man to set over the multitude to guard and protect it [εἰς ἐπιμέλειαν καὶ προστασίαν, *eis epimeleian kai prostasian*], a shepherd [ποιμένα, *poimena*] who shall lead it blamelessly that the nation may not decay like a flock [ποίμνη, *poimnē*] scattered about without one to guide it.[32]

Thus even these household imperatives in Scripture had their parallels in Greco-Roman literature. Managing the household well was a recognized qualification for candidates who

---

30. Quinn, *Letter to Titus,* 85.
31. Malherbe, "Overseers as Household Managers," 565.
32. Philo, *On the Special Laws, Book 4, On the Virtues,* 198–99.

would manage a city.³³ The conjunction of the verb προΐστημι with οἶκος occurs in 2 Sam 13:17; Prov 23:5; Amos 6:10 LXX; and Paul employs προΐστημι of leadership characterized by liberality, diligence, mercy, and cheerfulness (Rom 12:8; 1 Thess 5:12). So much so, if one was not able to manage the domestic household, then one would be incapable of leading the ecclesial household (1 Tim 3:5). In sum, before the elder can be a steward of the divine household, he must demonstrably be a steward of his domestic household (οἰκονόμος, *oikonomos*, "steward"; this word and a cognate are found in 1 Tim 1:4 and Titus 1:7).

5.1.2 *Corporate conduct in the divine household is guided by deacons and deaconesses (ministers and servers) who are characterized by virtue, including being irreproachable to outsiders and capable caretakers of the domestic household, as they model exemplary traits for the faith and praxis of members of the divine household (3:8–13).*

As with the elder list (1 Tim 3:1–7), the deacon list in 3:8–13 also mainly deals with character rather than duties. Thus, there are considerable similarities between the two lists:

Elders (3:1–7)	Deacons (3:8–13)
"one-woman man"	"one-woman men"
"temperate"	"temperate"
"not addicted to *wine*"	"not given to much *wine*"
"*managing ... household* well [καλῶς] keeping *children* in submission"	"good [καλῶς] *managers* of *children* and ... *households*"
"dignity"	"dignified" (×2)
"free from the love of money"	"not covetous of sordid gain"
"irreproachable"	"blameless"

Both lists emphasize the irreproachability and blamelessness of the candidates for office (3:2, 10; also see Titus 1, 6; and both deal with what is "good" (καλός, 3:1, 7, 13) and what is to be done "well" (καλῶς, 3:4, 12, 13).

However the requirement for an ability to teach (3:2) is restricted to elders, as also is the explicit call to be managers of the divine household (3:4–5; though managerial capability in domestic households is required for deacons also, 3:12). Nonetheless, this does not rule out speaking roles for deacons: it is possible that παρρησία, *parrēsia*, "confidence," in 3:13 may refer to confidence or boldness of speech (as in 2 Cor 3:12; 7:4; Eph 6:19; Phlm 8; etc.). In any case the two lists, considered together, commence and conclude, respectively, with commendations of those seeking and serving in these offices: 3:1, 13.³⁴

Below, I will address the role of deaconesses, before dealing with some of the individual requirements of deacon candidates.

---

33. See Sophocles (fifth century BCE), *Antigone* 661–62; and Aeschines (fourth century BCE), *Timarchus* 30. Isocrates (fourth century BCE), *To Nicocles* 19, warned that "the man who has mismanaged his own household [οἶκος] will handle the affairs of the city in like manner" (*To Demonicus, To Nicocles*, 51).

34. Incidentally, there is nothing in this pericope on the relationship between elders and deacons, or about the scope of ministry of each office and how they may (or may not) intersect.

First Timothy 3:11 begins with γυναῖκας ὡσαύτως. Earlier, 2:9 had ὡσαύτως γυναῖκας—clearly not dealing with the wives of the praying males (2:8). One may safely assume wives of deacons are not being considered in 3:11 either. In the PE, one often finds ὡσαύτως introducing a new, but related, idea (2:9; 3:8; Titus 2:3, 6), suggesting that, here, the move is not to deacon spouses, but to deaconesses. If the character of officials' spouses were important enough to have deacons' wives discussed in this list, one would have expected the wives of elders to have been addressed in the elder list—but they are not.[35] And if wives of deacons were the subjects of discussion, 1 Tim 3:11 would have commenced with αἱ γυναῖκες αὐτῶν (*hai gynaikes autōn*, "their wives," or something similar). Thus, the current referents in 3:11 are likely to be female deacons, especially since the surrounding verses, 3:10 and 3:12, use διάκονος, suggesting that 3:11 deals with deacons, too, rather than being a parenthetical remark about deacons' wives.[36] Also, both 3:8 and 3:11 have σεμνός/σεμνάς (*semnos/semnas*, found only here in 1 Timothy); both deal with matters of speech—deacons are to be μὴ διλόγους (*mē dilogous*, "not double-tongued," 3:8), and deaconesses μὴ διαβόλους (*mē diabolous*, "not slanderous," 3:11); 3:8 and 3:11 ("temperate") deal with sobriety in alcohol consumption; and both 3:9 and 3:11 conclude with notes on faith/faithfulness (3:9, 13). In addition, both 3:8 and 3:11 have anarthrous nouns in an accusative plural (διακόνους/γυναῖκας), and both verses are verbless, the implied verb coming from 3:2 (δεῖ . . . εἶναι; the verb δεῖ is also present in 3:7). It is best to see 3:8–13 as having some requirements broadly for all deacons, as well as some others separately listed for deacons and deaconesses:

1 Tim 3:8–13	Requirements for ...
3:8–10	Both deacons and deaconesses
3:11	Deaconesses (specific for women)
3:12	Deacons (specific for men)
3:13	Both deacons and deaconesses

Deacons were not to be "given to" (προσέχω, *prosechō*) much wine (3:8), but they were to be "keeping" (ἔχω, *echō*, 3:9) the "mystery of the faith with a pure conscience." This is a further explication of their character: candidates were to live lives congruent with divine

---

35. Especially since elders, unlike deacons, were expressly called to be hospitable (3:2).

36. We find no feminine form of the word διάκονος in usage (in Rom 16:1, it is the masculine form that is used of Phoebe) until the Council of Nicaea in the fourth century (*Canon* 19): διακόνισσα (*diakonissa*; also later, in the *Apostolic Constitutions* 8.19.1–2 [ca. 375–380]). Köstenberger, *Commentary on 1–2 Timothy and Titus*, 134, notes that "since serving as a deacon doesn't involve [public/corporate] teaching or ruling, both men and women are eligible to function in this capacity." Phoebe, in Rom 16:1–2, is described as a "sister," a "servant" (διάκονος), and a "helper" (προστάτις, *prostatis*; also used in the LXX of officers of the court: 1 Chr 27:31; 29:6; 2 Chr 8:10; 24:11). Perry, in a review of non-biblical writings of that period, notes that προστάτις "referred in a specific sense to a woman (or goddess) who acted as a 'patron(ess)' providing material support to her beneficiaries." In fact, there was a woman at Corinth, Junia Theodora, who was famous for her "patronage" (προστασίαν, *prostasian*) (Perry, "Phoebe of Cenchreae," 15). It is possible, then, that Phoebe was not a deacon in the sense of an office-bearer, but more of a relatively wealthy benefactor who had "helped" and was a "servant" to many, including Paul himself (Rom 16:2). However, the firm linkage of her "diaconate" with a specific local church could conceivably indicate an official status.

revelation—i.e., "faith" as the content of what is believed.[37] The "keeping," the lived out subjective element (faithfulness) of the objective item (faith), is also noted for deaconesses (3:11): they were to be "faithful in all things." Thus, "it is not sufficient to have a grasp on the theological profession of the church; that knowledge must be accompanied with the appropriate behavior, in this case a conscience that is clear from any stain of sin."[38] In the deacon list, both 3:9 and 3:13 deal with "faith": in 3:9, they are called to keep the "mystery of the faith"; in 3:13, those deacons who serve well grow in "confidence in the faith." Faithfulness begets itself!

We do not know what kind of "testing" (from δοκιμάζω, *dokimazō*) was involved for deacon candidates (3:10). The elder list has no corresponding component; perhaps the prohibition of new converts as elders (3:6; 5:22) was a reasonable equivalent. Indeed, the καὶ οὗτοι δὲ of 3:10 (*kai houtoi de*, "but these men also") seems to imply that elders had to undergo testing of some sort, too. Or perhaps the diaconate was a probationary period for eldership, itself a test, if elders were chosen from the ranks of deacons. In any case, divine approval (2 Tim 2:15, using δόκιμον, *dokimon*) is perhaps implicit in the assent of the corporate body of Christ to the appointments of these elders and deacons (as well as other of other leaders: 1 Tim 1:18–19; 4:14; 2 Tim 1:8). This is suggested also by the "high standing" deacons achieve within the community of God's people (1 Tim 3:13). In other words, the selection is ultimately a matter of divine choice recognized and ratified by the saints.

As was noted earlier, almost all of these character requirements of elders and deacons were to be found in *all* believers. As go the leaders, so go the people, hence the emphasis that these qualities be demonstrated in elders and deacons, for leaders are models to the flock of what God would want of all of his children. In sum, 1 Tim 3:1–13 suggests a two-tiered leadership (as also in Phil 1:1), with elders primarily engaged in teaching; nonetheless, the character of those occupying both offices was to be marked by irreproachability.

5.2   1 Timothy 3:14–16

THEOLOGICAL FOCUS 5.2

5.2   The core truth of the work of Christ with regard to his Person (incarnation, resurrection, and ascension) and with regard to his people (proclamation, reception, and exaltation) initiates and sustains the godliness of believers (3:14–16).

TRANSLATION 5.2

3:14   *These things I am writing to you, hoping to come to you soon;*

---

37. The "mystery of faith" was hidden until now (Rom 16:25; 1 Cor 2:7; Eph 3:9), and only fully revealed in the current dispensation (1 Cor 4:1; 15:51–52; Eph 1:9; 3:3, 9; Col 1:25–27)—the consummation of all things in the cosmos in Christ (1 Cor 2:2, 7–8; Eph 1:9–10; 3:3–4, 8–9; Col 2:2; 4:3). The call here in 1 Tim 3:8 for this congruence of life and doctrine is absent in the elder list; perhaps it was taken for granted—note that "keeping [also ἔχω] faith and a good conscience" was recommended to Timothy himself in 1:19. Obviously, to teach the faith, as elders have to, would require them to keep the faith themselves.

38. Mounce, *Pastoral Epistles*, 200.

1 TIMOTHY

3:15   but if I am delayed, [I write] so that you may know how one must conduct oneself in the household of God, which is the church of the living God, a pillar and support of the truth.

3:16   By common confession, great is the mystery of godliness: He who was revealed in flesh, vindicated in spirit, seen by angels, proclaimed among nations, believed on in earth, taken up in glory.

NOTES 5.2

5.2   *The core truth of the work of Christ with regard to his Person (incarnation, resurrection, and ascension) and with regard to his people (proclamation, reception, and exaltation) initiates and sustains the godliness of believers* (3:14–16).

Several linguistic parallels indicate that 3:14–16 belongs with what preceded it in 1 Tim 3: the word δεῖ in 3:2, 7 (and implied in 3:8, 11) is repeated in 3:15; οἶκος is found in 3:4, 12 and 3:15; and μυστήριον in 3:9 and 3:16.

Paul's writing was apparently prompted by his travel delay and his inability to see the Ephesians in person soon (3:14), perhaps continuing his travel-related comment to Timothy in 1:3. But the issue of how one was to conduct oneself in the household of God—the guardian of truth, its "pillar and support" (3:15)—was of such crucial nature that, despite his postponed arrival, he decided to pen this Epistle to Timothy (assuming the congregation would be glancing over the recipient's shoulder).

The ταῦτά, *tauta*, "these things," in 3:14 likely points to all that had been written so far, 1 Tim 1–3: right handing of Scripture and faithfulness to calling (Pericopes 1 and 2), behavior in the public context of worship (Pericopes 3 and 4), and the character of potential church leaders (Pericope 5). We see again the pressing imperative, δεῖ, in 3:15: "how one *must* conduct oneself in the household of God." Not suggestions, these prescribe the way things *must* happen in the *ecclesia*. Indeed 3:4–5, 12 made it explicit that "God's οἶκος is his ἐκκλησία [*ekklēsia*, 'church']"[39] This "church of the living God," wherein dwells God in his Spirit, is "a pillar [στῦλος, *stylos*] and support of the truth" (perhaps an allusion to the temple of God: 1 Kgs 7:15; 2 Kgs 25:13; 2 Chr 3:15; 4:12 LXX—all have στῦλος).[40] But notice that in 1 Tim 3:15 it is the truth that is being supported and protected, not the church. While the epithet "living God" often focuses on God as the giver of life (as in 4:10), here, as in 2 Cor 6:16 (also Josh 3:10; and perhaps Heb 12:22 and Rev 7:2), it emphasizes the active presence of God in the community of his people, as they corporately reinforce the truth with their lives of godliness, thus furthering the divine economy.

The greatness (μέγα, *mega*) of the "mystery of godliness" sounds similar to the Ephesian acclamation of the goddess Artemis (Acts 19:28, 34: μεγάλη ἡ Ἄρτεμις Ἐφεσίων, *megalē hē Artemis Ephesiōn*). We see a similar echo in Xenophon of Ephesus (*Anthia and Habrocomes* 1.11.5): τῆς μεγάλης Ἐφεσίων Ἄρτεμις, *tēs megalēs Ephesiōn Artemis*. Athenaeus (*The Learned Banqueters* 13.571) refers to Zeus as "the greatest" (τὸ μέγιστος, *to*

---

39. Knight, *Pastoral Epistles*, 180. Also see 2 Tim 2:20.

40. The anarthrous expression "a pillar and support of the truth," suggests that the church is only one of these; Scripture would certainly be another.

megistos). It is not inconceivable that Paul is deliberately hijacking a pagan exclamation to make a theological point.

"Godliness" (εὐσέβεια) is found in the PE in 1 Tim 2:2; 3:16; 4:7, 8; 6:3, 5, 6, 11; 2 Tim 3:5; Titus 1:1.[41] It indicates "the wholeness of Christian existence as the integration of faith and behavior."[42] The use of "godliness" in 1 Tim 3:16 is perhaps to be expected, following as it does the exhortation to right behavior in the divine household, the church (3:15). That godliness is related to the truth is made clear in 3:15, truth that the church upholds and supports.[43] The phrase in 3:16a, μέγα ἐστὶν τὸ τῆς εὐσεβείας μυστήριον, *mega estin to tēs eusebeias mystērion*, literally reads "great is the godliness's mystery," the forward position of the genitive εὐσεβείας ahead of the noun μυστήριον giving it emphasis. It is best to see the "mystery of godliness" as the essential "truth" that the church upholds as a "pillar and support" thereof (3:15) and which is acknowledged "by common confession" (3:16a)—the entirety of the grand plan of the work of God in Christ, past, present, and future (not very different from the "mystery of the faith" in 3:9). And out of this core truth flows the kind of life lived in response to it: godliness. Thus 3:16b–g becomes the heartbeat that drives the faith and praxis of the church and the people of God, a creedal confession with a christological lens: the relative pronoun ὅς (3:16b) most likely refers to Christ, who becomes the subject of the verbs in each of the six subsequent lines.[44]

The six lines of 3:16b–g are parallel, each line beginning with an aorist passive third-person singular verb, followed by a prepositional phrase (ἐν . . . ; absent in 3:16d) and a dative noun. There are several rhetorical devices operating: homoioteleuton (words ending in -θη that echo in each line: ἐφανερώθη, ἐδικαιώθη, ὤφθη, ἐκηρύχθη, ἐπιστεύθη, and ἀνελήμφθη; *ephanerōthē, edikaiōthē, ōphthē, ekērychthē, episteuthē,* and *anelēmphthē*), and perhaps a chiasm: two singular nouns in 3:16b, c ("flesh," "spirit"); two plural nouns in 3:16d, e ("angels," "nations"); and two singular nouns again in 3:16f, g ("earth," "glory"). The absence of definite articles in the six lines (3:16b–g) indicates further that it was read as poetry, not as prose. All of these structural and syntactical idiosyncrasies suggest that 3:16b–g was part of a liturgical hymn.

> The liturgical and hymnic character of the following confession reminds the reader that it is not the creative synthesis of an individual theologian that one encounters here. Rather, one hears a community or an order within it singing out its belief in public worship. The noblest act of the church, its faith in and love of God, is cited here in the form in which it has been verbalized and chanted.[45]

The six-line hymn is best seen as comprising two three-line stanzas, the first concerning Christ's work in particular relation to his Person (each line dealing, respectively, with

---

41. And Titus 2:12 contrasts ἀσέβεια (*asebeia*, "ungodliness") with εὐσέβεια. The word is also employed in the LXX to translate "fear of the Lord" in Isa 11:2; 33:6 (Gen 20:11 and Job 28:28 have θεοσέβεια, *theosebeia*, as also does 1 Tim 2:10).

42. Towner, *Letters to Timothy and Titus,* 277.

43. 1 Tim 6:3 and Titus 1:1 also relate godliness to "teaching" and "truth," respectively.

44. How Christ and his work becomes the core truth of this confession is explained below, but the Savior's exemplary life is, in the PE, always a model for Timothy (1 Tim 4:12), for Titus (Titus 2:11–12), and, indeed, for every believer (2 Tim 1:14).

45. Quinn and Wacker, *First and Second Letters to Timothy,* 318.

his incarnation,[46] resurrection,[47] and ascension[48]), and Christ's work in particular relation to his people, the church (each line dealing respectively with his proclamation, reception, and exaltation[49]). No doubt, these two categories are not watertight and mutually exclusive, but such is the nature of poetry and utterances in the throes of heartfelt emotion!

Christ and his Person	3:16b	A	Incarnation ("revealed in flesh")	earth
	3:16c	A'	Resurrection ("vindicated in spirit")	earth
	3:16d	B	Ascension ("beheld by angels")	heaven
Christ and his People	3:16e	A''	Proclamation ("proclaimed among nations")	earth
	3:16f	A'''	Reception ("believed on in earth")	earth
	3:16g	B'	Exaltation ("taken up in glory")	heaven

In sum, it is this core "truth," of which the church is the "pillar and support," that drives godliness in its members, the body of Christ, the people of God. What God requires of mankind to be godly is the keeping of divine demand in God's law in all its representations. But that law can do nothing in and of itself to justify the sinner: it has no expiatory provision to wipe away sin, it exercises no forgiving grace to effect reconciliation with God, and it cannot empower obedience to its own requirements. But with Christ, all things have been made anew. Sinners have been justified, sin canceled, forgiveness freely offered, and reconciliation with God accomplished for those who believe in Jesus Christ—*incarnated,*

---

46. In light of the fact that φανερόω and σάρξ (*phaneroō* and *sarx*) are used elsewhere for the entire incarnate ministry of Jesus Christ (John 1:31; Heb 9:26; 1 Pet 1:20; 1 John 1:2; 3:5, 8; and John 1:14; 6:51; Rom 8:3; Col 1:22; Heb 5:7; 10:20; 1 Pet 3:18; 4:1; 1 John 4:2; 2 John 7, respectively), it is best to see 1 Tim 3:16b ("revealed in flesh") that way, as well.

47. The verb "vindicate" is the Greek word δικαιόω (*dikaioō*, 3:16c), elsewhere meaning "to declare righteous." This vindication is in the realm of the spirit—relating to the spiritual status of the body of resurrected Christ (1 Cor 15:44)—corresponding to the realm of the flesh in which Jesus was incarnated (3:16b). Leaning one towards seeing ἐν πνεύματι in 3:16c as locative (of sphere) is the fact that the dative noun, "spirit," lacks an article; thus, both "in flesh" and "in spirit" are locative and in parallel, indicating arenas of operation, as also are the datives in 3:16e and 3:16f ("among nations"; "in earth"). "The frequent antithesis of flesh and spirit in the NT with its OT background [Matt 26:41; Mark 14:38; John 3:6; 6:63; Rom 1:4; 8:4, 5, 6, 9, 13; 1 Cor 5:5; 2 Cor 7:1; Gal 3:3; 4:29; 5:16, 17 (×2), 19; 6:8; Col 2:5; Heb 12:9; 1 Pet 3:18], suggests that the contrast is between the human mode (or sphere) and the supernatural mode of Jesus' two-stage existence" (Marshall, *Pastoral Epistles*, 525–26). The spirit-flesh connection of 1 Tim 3:16b-c is also seen in 1 Pet 3:18, where Jesus is said to have been "put to death in the flesh, but made alive in the spirit" (vindicated?). Also see Rom 1:3-4, which links the resurrection with a vindicative declaration of Christ as the Son of God; and Rom 4:25, which connects the resurrection with "justification" (δικαίωσις, *dikaiōsis*), though the justification here is that of the believer.

48. "Angels" refers most likely to the witnesses of the ascension (Acts 1:10), though, of course, angelic presence at Christ's resurrection is also well attested. However, there is no explicit mention of the death of Jesus Christ or his atoning work in this hymn. In all likelihood, that aspect of the work of Christ is wrapped up in the notions of the incarnation, resurrection, and ascension.

49. Though Acts 1:2 (and the less authoritative Mark 16:19) employ ἀναλαμβάνω (*analambanō*, used here in 1 Tim 3:16g) for the ascension, it is still probably best to see the six lines as chronologically progressing, culminating in the exaltation of Jesus Christ, "the consummation of all things in Christ, things in the heavens and things on the earth" (Eph 1:10). The "glory" in 1 Tim 3:16g is the presence of God's glory, perhaps referring to the enthronement of Christ (2 Thess 1:10). This glorification has already commenced (John 12:16, 23; Phil 2:9; 3:21; 1 Pet 1:21) but will be consummated in the eschaton.

resurrected, ascended—as their only God and Savior: believers' *proclamation* and *reception* of him. There is yet another aspect of the work of Christ that is crucial for godliness: Christ's *exaltation* to God's right hand of glory made possible his sending of the Holy Spirit (John 14:16; 15:26; 16:7), and with the indwelling of the Holy Spirit joining believers to Christ, a new life is begun, and the Christian is enabled to fulfill the demand of God in all of Scripture (Rom 8:4, 12–16). And beyond this, there is also the exalted Christ's ongoing ministry before the Father on behalf of the ones he redeemed: intercession (Rom 8:34; Heb 7:25) and advocacy (Heb 9:24; 1 John 2:1). This is how God in Christ is glorified!

All that to say, there is no godliness without the core truths expressed in this hymn of 3:16b–g: Christ's incarnation, resurrection, ascension, and the resulting response of his people in their proclamation and reception. And by their godliness, Christ is exalted. In short, in everything pertaining to the godliness of the Christian, Christ is the initiating and sustaining agent, directly or indirectly, and from start to finish: his incarnation, resurrection, ascension, and his proclamation, reception, and exaltation. "Worthy is the Lamb who was slain, to receive power and riches and wisdom and strength and honor and glory and blessing," a rousing cheer echoed by "every creature which is in heaven and on the earth and under the earth and on the sea and all that is in them" (Rev 5:12–13).[50]

SERMON MAPS

THEOLOGICAL FOCUS OF PERICOPE 5 FOR PREACHING

5   Corporate conduct in the divine household is to be guided by leaders characterized by virtue, modeling exemplary traits for the faith and praxis of every member of the divine household (3:1–16).

Lists are always difficult to preach. While there may be a place for treating biblical texts as sources of information and systematization of doctrine by dissecting and atomizing pericopes, such operations only leave behind a corpse. For preaching purposes, the interpreter must approach such texts—indeed, *all* biblical texts—rhetorically, catching what the author is *doing* with what he is saying. And in the case of lists, they are intended to overwhelm the reader with a single thrust. In the current pericope, 1 Tim 3:1–16, the godliness of church leaders is paramount, and such irreproachable individuals are to serve as exemplars ("ideals" in the maps below) for the rest of the divine household. Besides, *all* God's people are called to be leaders to some extent, to some degree, in some fashion, in some arena. Therefore, in a sense, all the leadership qualities in this pericope are to be adopted by all God's people: these are marks of Christlikeness.

Possible Preaching Maps for Pericope 5

    I.   Leaders as Irreproachable
         Elders (3:1–7)
         Deacons and deaconesses (3:8–13)
         Move-to-Relevance: Leaders today—in society, in the church

---

50. Much in these last two paragraphs were modified from my discussion in Kuruvilla, *Vision for Preaching*, 142–43.

1 TIMOTHY

    II. Leaders as Ideals
        Leadership character traits called for in *all* believers
        The initiation and sustenance of godliness: Christ's work (3:14–16)
        Move-to-Relevance: How all God's people are leaders
    III. *Lead Irreproachably and Ideally!*
        Specifics on leadership that is irreproachable and exemplary[51]

Another way to structure a sermon on this pericope:

    I. Christ, the Ultimate Model
        The initiation and sustenance of godliness: Christ's work (3:14–16)
        Move-to-Relevance: Our failure to accomplish Christlikeness
    II. Leaders, the Proximal Models
        Elders (3:1–7)
        Deacons and deaconesses (3:8–13)
        Move-to-Relevance: All God's people as leaders
    III. *Lead Irreproachably and Ideally!*
        Specifics on leadership that is irreproachable and exemplary

---

51. Depending on the circumstances of the audience and their need, one of the many leadership qualities discussed in this pericope might be focused upon, for application.

PERICOPE 6

Devoted and Disciplined

1 Timothy 4:1–16

[False Teachers vs. Truth Teachers: Devotion and Discipline]

REVIEW, SUMMARY, PREVIEW

Review of Pericope 5: The fifth pericope (1 Tim 3:1–16) dealt with the offices of the church: eldership and diaconate, the members of which guide and model the communal and individual conduct of the people of God. Such exemplary behavior, by leaders and their followers, is grounded in the work of Jesus Christ that initiates and sustains the godliness of the people of God.

Summary of Pericope 6: This pericope (1 Tim 4:1–16) warns of a time when false teachers, in their focus on, and devotion to, doctrines demonic, will deceive many. To counter these nefarious tendencies, the people of God remain focused on Scripture and discipline themselves for godliness, based on truth and by the Spirit, being examples to others.

Preview of Pericope 7: The next pericope (1 Tim 5:1–16) focuses on the care of the needy, an extension of the godliness that is pleasing to God. The care of the deserving needy in both domestic and divine households is addressed, as well as reasons for not supporting the undeserving.

6   1 Timothy 4:1–16

> **THEOLOGICAL FOCUS OF PERICOPE 6**
>
> 6   In contrast to those advocating demonic teaching that denies the goodness of God, God's people, nourished on good teaching based in Scripture, engage intensely in spiritual discipline, persevering in modeling Spirit-directed godliness that ensures future reward (4:1–16).
>
> 6.1   In contrast to those advocating demonic teaching, often couched in a form of spiritual discipline that denies the goodness of God, God's people accept all his gifts with thanksgiving and prayer (4:1–5).
>
> 6.2   God's people, nourished on good teaching, engage intensely in spiritual discipline for godliness that promises benefits for this life and for the life to come (4:6–11).
>
> 6.3   God's leaders (and all his people), irrespective of age, persevere in modeling Spirit-directed godliness guided by Scripture, ensuring future reward for themselves (4:12–16).

OVERVIEW

There appears to be a more personal tone in the last three chapters of 1 Timothy, with the resounding of several second-person singular verbs and pronouns: 4:6–7, 11–16; 5:1–2, 7, 21–23; 6:2, 11–16, 20–21. These are interspersed with more general statements, exhortations, or criticisms. This is characteristic of *mandata principis* communiques—personal advice to the delegate alternating with instructions for the larger body of readers regarding public order.[1]

Pronouns derived from οὗτος, *houtos*, show up in 4:6a, 10, 11, 15a, 15b, and 16—all meaning "these things/them/this" (also αὐτοῖς, *autois*, in 4:16, "them"). "These things" in 4:6a likely indicates what was stated in 4:1–5; in 4:11, what was noted in 4:6b–10; in 4:15a, to what was exhorted in 4:12–13; and that in 4:16 summarizes the pericope (see the table below). Thus we could consider 4:1–16 as comprising three parallel sections that have a number of similarities, with 4:16 forming a conclusion. Each of the sections commences with a mention of "faith" and "teaching" (4:1, 6b, 12) and a verb describing ministry (or heresy) focus ("attend," 4:1; "follow closely," 4:6b; "attend," 4:13; and "attend closely," 4:16). And each section, as noted, concludes with an exhortation concerning "these [aforementioned] things" (4:6a, 11, 15).[2] The first section, of course, is negative, dealing with the apostates; the second and third deal with what, instead, should be happening in the church.

---

1. Johnson, *First and Second Letters to Timothy*, 244.
2. The statement in 4:6a and the summary in 4:16 are also unique in that they contain the only two second-person singular future verbs in 1 Timothy that are applied to the delegate, Timothy: "you will be" and "you will save." A third such verb, not applied explicitly to Timothy, is found in the OT quotation in 5:18. See Van Neste, *Cohesion and Structure*, 92. At any rate, I have structured the pericope by sentences in the text, rather than by these markers.

4:1–6a	4:6b–11	4:12–15	4:16
ταῦτα *tauta* (4:6a)	τοῦτο, ταῦτα *touto, tauta* (4:10, 11)	ταῦτα, τούτοις *tauta, toutois* (4:15)	αὐτοῖς, τοῦτο *autois, touto*
Point out (4:6a)	Prescribe, teach (4:11)	Take pains, be (4:15)	Persevere
Faith (4:1)	Faith (4:6b)	Faith (4:12)	Save
"teachings" (4:1)	"teachings" (4:6b)	"teach" (4:11) "teaching" (4:13)	"teaching"
Believers (4:3)	Believers (4:10)	Believers (4:12)	Hearers
προσέχω *prosechō* (4:1) "attend"	παρηκολουθέω *parēkoloutheō* (4:6b) "follow closely"	προσέχω *prosechō* (4:13) "attend"	ἔπεχε *epeche* "attend closely"

6.1 1 Timothy 4:1–5

THEOLOGICAL FOCUS 6.1

6.1 In contrast to those advocating demonic teaching, often couched in a form of spiritual discipline that denies the goodness of God, God's people accept all his gifts with thanksgiving and prayer (4:1–5).

TRANSLATION 6.1

4:1 But the Spirit explicitly says that in later times some will apostatize from the faith, attending to deceitful spirits and teachings of demons,

4:2 through the hypocrisy of liars cauterized in their own conscience,

4:3 forbidding marrying, abstaining from foods which God created to be received with thanksgiving by those who believe and know the truth.

4:4 Since everything created by God is good, and nothing is to be rejected when received with thanksgiving;

4:5 for it is made holy by the word of God and prayer.

NOTES 6.1

6.1 *In contrast to those advocating demonic teaching, often couched in a form of spiritual discipline that denies the goodness of God, God's people accept all his gifts with thanksgiving and prayer (4:1–5).*

The δέ in 4:1 signals a contrast to "mystery of godliness" (3:16), as Paul returns to the issue of false teaching in 4:1–5. Here he labels the deceit with an eschatological tag: such heterodoxy, with links to demonism, was an indicator of "later times" (4:1). Earlier in the letter, a couple of apostates had been "delivered over to Satan" (1:20), and elders had been warned not to partake of the "condemnation of the devil" (3:6–7); later, the falling away of certain younger widows is called a "turning aside to follow Satan" (5:15; also see 2 Tim 2:26). Those "later times," apparently, had arrived!

After providing requirements for godly leaders in Pericope 5: 1 Tim 3:1–16, this pericope contains both negative and positive exhortations to a leader: broadly, advice regarding false teaching (4:1–7a; how to avoid the negative) and advice for personal ministry (4:7b–16; how to follow the positive). There are stark contrasts between the teachers of falsehood and Timothy, representing teachers of truth:

Falsehood Teachers	Truth Teachers
Follow deceitful "spirits" (4:1)	Are warned by the "Spirit" (4:1)
	Are among those who have "faith" (4:3)
Fall away from the "faith" (4:1)	Are nourished by words of the "faith" (4:6)
	Are exemplars of "faith" (4:12)
Advocate "*teachings* of demons" (4:1)	Sponsor "good *teachings*" (4:6)
"Attend" (προσέχω) to evil (4:1)	"Attend" (προσέχω) to Scripture (4:13)
	"Attend closely" (ἐπέχω) to self/ministry (4:16)
Are "liars" (ψευδολόγοι, *pseudologoi*, 4:2)	Know the "truth" (4:3)
	Adhere to "word(s)" (λόγος, *logos*, 4:5, 6, [9])

The comparisons also draw from what has already been stated about teachers/leaders in prior pericopes, particularly with relation to "faith" and "conscience"[3]:

False Teachers (1 Timothy 4)	Truth Teachers (1 Timothy 1—3)
"apostatize from the **faith**" (4:1)	"unhypocritical **faith**" (1:5) "keeping **faith**" (1:19) "teacher … in **faith**" (2:7) "keeping the mystery of the **faith**" (3:9) "**faithful** in all things" (3:11) "much confidence in the **faith**" (3:13)
"cauterized … **conscience**" (4:2)	"good **conscience**" (1:5, 19) "a clear **conscience**" (3:9)

The "cauterized [or "desensitized"] consciences" of these purveyors of error (4:2), rendered them insensible to the overtures of God and his truth. "The implication … is probably that they did not respond to their consciences but sinned deliberately and consciously …, so that they themselves were by no means innocent victims of deception."[4] While the goal of Paul's teaching (and that of Timothy and of the church) was love from a "good *conscience* and an unhypocritical [ἀνυπόκριτος, *anypokritos*] *faith*" (1:5), the results of the heterodoxy here are a cauterized *conscience* and apostatizing from the *faith* (4:1, 2). Notice also that these proponents of heterodoxy operated "in the hypocrisy [ὑπόκρισις, *hypokrisis*] of liars" (4:2)—another label for intentional deception: "they were not who they said they were, and

---

3. Besides the descriptions of the "faith" of the truth teachers in 1 Timothy 1–3, there is also "pursue … faith" (6:11) and "fight the good fight of faith" (6:12).

4. Marshall, *Pastoral Epistles*, 540–41. Köstenberger, *Commentary on 1–2 Timothy and Titus*, 141, is right when he labels κεκαυστηριασμένων, *kekaustēriasmenōn*, "a diabolical passive," with Satan as the implicit agent of the cauterization.

their teaching was not what they claimed it to be."[5] And, given the importance of "truth" in 1 Timothy (and indeed, in all of the PE), it is particularly poignant that these false teachers are labeled "liars" (ψευδολόγοι, 4:2): God desires all to come to the "truth" (2:4); Paul was a teacher in "truth" (2:7); and the church was a pillar and support of the "truth" (3:15).[6] Thus, "what is demonic in origin [4:1] involves human duplicity in execution [4:2]; it is this collusion that makes heresy both appalling and perilous."[7] In sum, these fallen, then, were believers who ended up "attending" (προσέχω) to διδασκαλίαι δαιμονίων, *didaskaliai daimoniōn*, like the false teachers in 1:3–4 who were also "attending" (προσέχω) to falsehood and "teaching false doctrine" (ἑτεροδιδασκαλέω)—all part of the gang that rejected a "good *conscience*" and were "shipwrecked in *faith*" (1:19).[8]

All this shows that an impressive web of references links these false teachers in 4:1–3a to other equivalent descriptions of their abominable activities elsewhere in 1 Timothy. But, more importantly, they also create a stark contrast between what these heretics do and what truth teachers—elders, deacons, and leaders in every capacity, official or otherwise—do as managers of the divine household and shepherds of the flock, upholding truth and living out truth. Thus, this pericope, following one that talks about the character of church leaders, contrasts false teachers with true ones, and directs the latter on how they can maintain their godliness in the face of attacks by apostates.

The issue of "later times" (4:1) and their mayhem, Paul avers, should come as no surprise to those facing them: the Spirit had already warned the church about such eras. This increase in evil in the last days is a common theme in the NT; see Mark 13:1–27 and parallels; 1 Cor 7:26; 2 Thess 2:1–13; 2 Tim 3:1–9; 4:3–4; 2 Pet 3:3–7; 1 John 2:18; Jude 17–18.[9] The unsurprising (and diabolical) turn of "later times" notwithstanding, the mingling of issues in 4:3–5—the prohibition of marriage (abstinence from sex?) and the avoidance of certain foods—is difficult to unravel. It is possible the references are specific to what was being propounded and practiced by false teachers in Ephesus at that time.[10] The statement about sanctification in 4:5 also hints that in some sense the false teachers considered certain foods (and perhaps even marriage/sex) to be unclean. It is likely that they were concerned with asceticism of some sort, engaging in pseudo-spiritual disciplines. That interpretation

---

5. Towner, *Letters to Timothy and Titus*, 292.

6. Also see 4:3, 5, 6, 9 for knowing the "truth" and adhering to God's "word(s)."

7. Towner, *Letters to Timothy and Titus*, 291.

8. All false teaching ultimately has demonic roots, especially those that have devastating effects in the community; one imagines that the heterodoxy mentioned here may have created some havoc in the church.

9. Perhaps even more pertinent to the Ephesians in Paul's time was the latter's own warning to the Ephesian church elders in Acts 20:29–30.

10. It has been speculated that perhaps the false teachers espoused an "overrealized eschatology," an assumption that the resurrection had already occurred (see 2 Tim 2:18), so much so, marriage was forbidden in an eschatological kingdom that was not "eating [βρῶσις, *brōsis*] and drinking [πόσις, *posis*]" (Rom 14:17; note that 1 Tim 4:3 has βρῶμα, *brōma*, and that Timothy is later exhorted to "drink" wine, 5:23, using a cognate of ποτέω, *poteō*). The work of the false teachers, then, was an attempt "to enact the life of resurrection paradise" (Towner, *1–2 Timothy and Titus*, 103–4; also see Marshall, *Pastoral Epistles*, 535). Or perhaps this was a "denial of one's human earthly, material existence in favor of a mere spiritual, otherworldly one" (Köstenberger, *Commentary on 1–2 Timothy and Titus*, 143). That all of these are imaginative reconstructions is obvious; we just do not know the background of these deceitful, demonic doctrines, what exactly they entailed, and why they were gaining traction then.

makes sense: later in 4:8 there is a reference to "bodily discipline," and in contrast, Timothy is asked to discipline himself for godliness—*spiritual* discipline.

The parallels between 1 Tim 4:3 and 4:4 are significant, both verbal and conceptual[11]:

1 Timothy 4:3	1 Timothy 4:4–5
"... foods which *God created* [which false teachers apparently *reject*] to be *received* (μετάλημψις, *metalēmpsis*) with thanksgiving by those who believe and know the *truth*."	"Everything *created by God* is good, and nothing is to be *rejected* when *received* (λαμβάνω, *lambanō*) with thanksgiving, for it is made holy by *the word of God* and prayer."

The "word of God" in 4:5 is likely the divine utterance asserting the goodness of creation: LXX Gen 1:31 has καὶ εἶδεν ὁ θεὸς τὰ πάντα ὅσα ἐποίησεν ... καλά, *kai eiden ho theos ta panta hosa epoiēsen ... kala* ("and *God* saw *everything* he had made ... *good*"); 1 Tim 4:4a has ὅτι πᾶν κτίσμα θεοῦ καλόν, *hoti pan ktisma theou kalon* ("since *everything* created by *God* is *good*").[12]

The receiving/sharing of gifts in utter dependence upon the Gifter, the Creator God, evokes a double thanksgiving, in parallel to the double mention of God's creative activity (4:3, 4).[13] Mounce perspicaciously notes the two-dimensional nature of Paul's argument (God's work/word and mankind's work/word), stated thrice altogether, once in each of the verses in 4:3–5[14]:

	God's Work/Word	Mankind's Work/Word
4:3	"God created"	"received with thanksgiving"
4:4	"Everything created by God is good"	"received with thanksgiving"
4:5	"Made holy by the word of God"	"and prayer"

In other words, what the work (creation: 4:3a, 4a) and word (sanctifying utterance: 4:5a) of God have declared good is acknowledged by the work (thanksgiving: 4:3b, 4b) and word (prayer: 4:5b) of God's people who receive his gifts. Through thanksgiving and prayer, the divine household acknowledges and accepts what the divine Householder has created and gifted to his people.

Excursus on Food

The question of whether the consumption of certain foods was acceptable in the Christian community—that had only very recently emerged from, and perhaps still was immersed in, the Jewish milieu—resonated in the time of Paul. The issue of marriage, celibacy, and

---

11. From Liefeld, *1 and 2 Timothy, Titus*, 151. Note that μετάλημψις and λαμβάνω are cognates.

12. Also see LXX Gen 1:4, 10, 12, 18, 21, 25; Sir 39:33.

13. Giving thanks at the table is also noted in Rom 14:6; 1 Cor 10:16, 30; as well as in the Qumran *Rule of the Community* 6:4–6; 10:14–15.

14. Mounce, *Pastoral Epistles*, 240.

related matters had also been of some concern in local churches (see 1 Cor 7:1–40). The fact remains, however, that the versions of such heterodoxies, if one might label them that way, differed: in the Corinth of 1 Corinthians, celibacy was seemingly being promoted (1 Cor 7:1), but not food abstinence (1 Cor 6:13[15]); in the Ephesus of the PE, celibacy was viewed positively, but so also was food abstinence (1 Tim 4:3). Thus, it is almost impossible to reconstruct a "global" solution of heterodoxy that incorporates all these differences in outlook and praxis; even in the local case of Ephesus, we have far too little information to systematize the hermeneutics of the false teachers.[16]

The neuter plural relative pronoun ἅ, *ha*, in 4:3 indicates that it is "foods" (βρώματα, *brōmata*, neuter plural) that is being linked to that "which God created . . ." (not marriage: an infinitive verb is employed for this). It is best to see that Paul is, here, not making a particular statement about foods, kosher or otherwise. Even in the OT, while abiding by food restrictions, it was possible to assert that all things were good and given by the Creator to be enjoyed (Gen 1:31; 9:3; Deut 26:11; Eccl 3:12–13; 5:18; etc.). It is therefore likely that the abstention advocated by the false teachers in Ephesus was disconnected from the prohibitions of the Mosaic Law.[17]

In the OT, separation was the critical element of holiness. A "holy nation" meant separation unto Yahweh from other defiled peoples (Lev 18:2–5, 24–25; 20:23–26), in cuisine, in cult, in calendar.[18] Such issues furthered *ritual* purity rather than *moral* purity (unless, of course, these laws were disobeyed—that would then make it a moral matter). One might see the food laws, apparently based on the Creator's arbitrary distinction of what could and could not be consumed, as intended to underscore the profound truth of separation of God's people unto himself. "There is nothing intrinsically abominable or defiling [i.e., *moral*] about a pig. It is a creature like all creatures. But, says God in effect, I have forbidden it to you, and you are to consider it an abomination [i.e., *ritually*]; . . . it is alien and removed totally from you, and sacrally unfit."[19] The key phrase is טְמֵאָה הִוא לָכֶם (*tmeʾah hiʾ lakem*, "unclean to *you*," Lev 11:6, 7, 8, 10, 11, 12, 20, 23, 26, 27, 28, 29, 31). The only explicit rationale given for food restrictions was this: "For I am Yahweh who brought you up from the land of Egypt to be your God; thus you shall be holy, for I am holy" (Lev 11:45). Thus it was an uncleanness by divine decree, not by intrinsic essence—"an experiential mnemonic, confronted daily at the dining table, that Israel must separate itself from the nations"—a *ritual* separation of God's chosen people (positionally "holy") from those outside ("unholy").[20] There was to be a differing standard between Israelites and gentiles: the former, in the earlier dispensation, were a priestly nation with a dedicated *ritual* purity code that was applicable to outsiders only when they became, by choice, insiders—part of Israel.[21] "The whole purity code [i.e., the *ritual* purity code] found in the Torah and elabo-

---

15. Though not the same issue, food is dealt with in 1 Cor 8:1–13, too.

16. For the PE emphasis on marriage as acceptable, albeit indirect, see 1 Tim 2:15; 3:2, 4–5, 12; 5:14; Titus 2:4; and for acceptance of all foods, see 1 Tim 5:23; Titus 1:5 (besides Rom 14:6; 1 Cor 8:8; etc.).

17. And disassociated also from the restrictions/concessions imposed by the Jerusalem Council, in Acts 15:20, 29. Though ἀπέχω, *apechō*, "abstain," is used there and in 1 Tim 4:3, there is no indication that the foods prohibited in Acts were the objects of abstention in 1 Timothy.

18. Hartley, *Leviticus*, lix.

19. Feldman, *Biblical and Post-Biblical Defilement*, 51–52.

20. Milgrom, "Rationale for Cultic Law," 105.

21. However, these laws, though not "obeyable" in the current age, are still "applicable." One must

rated in the rabbinic literature is thus . . . a kind of palace protocol or etiquette, observed in the court of a monarch, but not required outside the confines of the palace."[22] However, in the NT age, the significant changes wrought in the divine-human relationship by the work of Jesus Christ rendered this distinction between ritual and moral impurity moot (with some concession to the former, in light of the sensibility of Jews in the early church; see Acts 15:1–20). Indeed, Jesus himself reaffirmed in Mark 7:18–19 that all foods are *morally clean*.[23] Things that go in from the outside cannot defile morally (7:18). And as those foods do not go into man's heart, they, being eliminated, are, for all practical purposes, "clean" *morally*, even if they were unclean *ritually* (7:19) in an earlier dispensation. Anatomically and physiologically, that makes sense, for the gastrointestinal tract is essentially "outside" the body. On the other hand, things that come out from the inside (the "heart") are what *morally* defile a person (7:20–21).[24]

All that to say, there is no conflict between Paul's exhortation to Timothy regarding the consumption of "everything" that was created by God (= *morally* "good"; 1 Tim 4:4), and what was demanded for *ritual* purity in the Mosaic Law in a prior dispensation. Indeed, Paul's conclusions are quite congruent with Jesus's prescriptions on the matter. And, therefore, there could be no countenancing of these pseudo-spiritual disciplines of food abstention being propagated by false teachers in Ephesus (4:3).

6.2   1 Timothy 4:6–11

THEOLOGICAL FOCUS 6.2

6.2   God's people, nourished on good teaching, engage intensely in spiritual discipline for godliness that promises benefits for this life and for the life to come (4:6–11).

TRANSLATION 6.2

4:6   *Pointing out these things to the brothers and sisters, you will be a good servant of Christ Jesus, nourishing [yourself] on the words of the faith and of the good teachings that you have followed closely.*

4:7   *But reject profane and old-women myths. And discipline yourself for godliness;*

4:8   *for bodily discipline is profitable for little, but godliness is profitable for all things, holding the promise of present life and of that to come.*

4:9   *The statement is trustworthy and deserving of full acceptance.*

4:10 *For it is for this we work hard and strive, because we have hoped in the living God, who is the Savior of all people, especially believers.*

4:11 *Command and teach these things.*

---

consider how Christians today can be separate from non-believers (without compromising their witness, of course).

22. Maccoby, *Ritual and Morality*, 9.

23. The last phrase of Mark 7:19, "cleansing all foods," is part of Jesus's question, as the punctuation in the Greek indicates (*Novum Testamentum Graece*, Nestle-Aland, 28th ed).

24. See Kuruvilla, *Mark*, 142–54; Marcus, *Mark*, 453; Rudolph, "Jesus and the Food Laws," 298.

PERICOPE 6: 1 TIMOTHY 4:1-16

NOTES 6.2

6.2 God's people, nourished on good teaching, engage intensely in spiritual discipline for godliness that promises benefits for this life and for the life to come (4:6–11).

It is notable that Paul calls Timothy a διάκονος in 4:6—his protégé is to model for the flock those attitudes and actions he had earlier required of διάκονοι (3:8–13). And such an intention is explicit in 4:12 where Timothy is prompted to become "an example" for believers. Paul is following a pattern here in 1 Timothy 4: the heresy (4:1–5) followed by a personal charge to his delegate, Timothy (4:6–16). That same sequence was also present in 1 Timothy 1 (3–17 and 18–20, respectively), and will reappear in 1 Timothy 6 (3–10 and 11–16, respectively). This juxtaposition keeps reminding believers that they must exercise care not to fall into the trap of false teaching.

There is a palpable sense of urgency in the cascade of twelve imperatives (the first such injunctions to Timothy in this Epistle), coming in six pairs, with all but one of the dozen being a second-person imperative:

> "reject" and "discipline yourself" (4:7)
> "charge" and "teach" (4:11)
> "let no one disdain" [*third person imperative*] and "be an example" (4:12)
> "attend" (4:13) and "do not neglect" (4:14)
> "take pains" and "be [absorbed]" (4:15)
> "attend closely" and "persevere" (4:16)

Paul makes a contrast between good teaching and bad, 4:6 vs. 4:7a. Timothy (and the rest of the church) is to "reject profane and old-women myths."[25] The phrase γραώδης μυθολογίας, *graōdēs mythologias*, was an accepted idiom, "old wives' fables."[26] "Together the two terms portray the heresy as pagan in its thrust and insignificant in its contribution."[27] Instead, believers undertake spiritual discipline (4:7b). As was noted earlier, the "discipline" prescribed in 4:7–8 was likely a contrast to the ascetical (demonic?) discipline with regard to food and marriage/sex forbidden by false teachers in 4:1–3: perhaps that is the "bodily discipline" disparaged in 4:8a. In any case, the athletic metaphor is introduced with the issue of "nourishment" on the "words of the faith and of the good teachings" (= truth; 4:6). Thus, the undernourishment—nay, the malnourishment!—of deceitful words and demonic doctrine (4:1–2) is to be repudiated and redressed. The contrast is clear: 4:1 has "on the words of faith and of the good teachings"; and 4:3 has "to deceitful spirits and teachings of demons."

And this proper intake of words of faith + good teachings (= truth) is to be accompanied by the proper output of praxis, for which practice is essential—"discipline . . . for *godliness*" (4:7). Perhaps Paul's hard work and striving (4:10) continues the athletic metaphor, linking his own exertions with spiritual disciplining—an intensive undertaking for

---

25. "Profane" was also used in 1:9, and "myths" in 1:4.

26. The Greek geographer and historian, Strabo [63/64 BCE—24 CE], employed it in *Geographica* 1.2.3; as also did Plato, in *Republic* 350e; and *Gorgias* 527a.

27. Towner, *Letters to Timothy and Titus*, 305.

1 TIMOTHY

godliness. In short, the discipline referred to here, including proper nourishment of truth (4:6), has godliness as its outcome (4:7b), towards which end God's people are to "work hard and strive," as did the apostle.

There is a complete parallelism between 4:8a and 4:8b:

4:8a	For	bodily discipline	for little	is profitable
4:8b	But	godliness	for all things	is profitable

This discipline for godliness is profitable not only for the present life, as might be expected to be the case for bodily discipline, but promises to be so also for eternity (4:8). This "promise of present life and of that to come" is life eternal and abundant, with its accompanying rewards for godliness.[28] In other words, bodily discipline has utility for developing physical health (or for a [demonic] spirituality, if one equates this discipline with the abstentions advocated by the false teachers in 4:3), with gains only temporary. On the other hand, discipline in godliness has utility for developing true spirituality, with gains eternal, benefits which begin to accrue even in the earthly phase of that everlasting life. The emphasis is explicit: godliness, and the discipline thereunto, has value for all things, for all time!

We also see the third of the five instances of "the statement is trustworthy" in the PE, here in 4:9 (the others are 1:15; 3:1; 2 Tim 2:11; and Titus 3:8). The personal comment of 1 Tim 4:10a, coming between 4:9 and 4:10b, seems to argue against the statement referring forward to 4:10b. Besides, 4:8 does reads like a gnomic saying, almost proverbial, with its rare vocabulary—γυμνασία, *gymnasia*, "discipline," is a *hapax,* and σωματικός, *somatikos,* "bodily," elsewhere in the NT is found only in Luke 3:22. In addition, εἰς τοῦτο γάρ, *eis touto gar,* "for it is for this," in 4:10a, appears to point back to the trustworthy statement of 4:8. Thus, in order to further the godliness that is profitable for temporal and eternal *life* (ζωή, *zōē,* 4:8) (the trustworthy statement), Paul works hard and strives, focused on the *living* (ζῶν, *zōn,* 4:10) God, the Savior.[29] Baugh has noted that in extrabiblical literature, and in the environs of the city of Ephesus, σωτήρ, *sōtēr,* "savior," was "the functional equivalent of 'patron' or 'benefactor,'" commonly employed of dead emperors.[30] And here we have Paul, labeling as σωτήρ no dead being, but "the living God," capable of keeping his promise of life abundant, now and forever, to all believers.

6.3 1 Timothy 4:12–16

THEOLOGICAL FOCUS 1

6.3 God's leaders (and all his people), irrespective of age, persevere in modeling Spirit-directed godliness guided by Scripture, ensuring future reward for themselves (4:12–16).

---

28. The genitive ζωῆς, *zōēs,* "of life," is best seen as epexegetical; thus: "promise *that is* the present life and the [life] to come" (4:8c), as also in 2 Tim 1:1 (and similarly with "promise" in Heb 9:15 and 2 Pet 3:4).

29. The description of God as "Savior of all people, *especially believers*" (4:10, and "who desires all people to be saved," 2:3–4), could be making a distinction between "all people" to whom salvation is offered, and believers who actually accept that offer. Another valid option is to see μάλιστα, *malista,* as simply particularizing or defining what was just stated, thus: "Savior of all men, i.e., believers" (as is likely with its use in 2 Tim 4:13 and Titus 1:10; see Skeat, "'Especially the Parchments,'" 174–75).

30. Baugh, "'Savior of All People,'" 336–37.

TRANSLATION 6.3

4:12   Let no one disdain your youth, but be an example to those who believe, in speech, in conduct, in love, in faith, in purity.

4:13   Until I come, attend to the [public] reading [of Scripture], to the exhortation, to the teaching.

4:14   Do not neglect the spiritual gift within you, which was given to you through prophecy with the laying on of hands by the council of elders.

4:15   Take pains with these things, be [absorbed] in them, so that your progress may be manifest to all.

4:16   Attend closely to yourself and to the teaching, persevere in them; for doing this you will save both yourself and those who hear you.

NOTES 6.3

6.3   God's leaders (and all his people), irrespective of age, persevere in modeling Spirit-directed godliness guided by Scripture, ensuring future reward for themselves (4:12–16).

Unlike in 2 Timothy, where Paul is the model for Timothy and others, here in 1 Timothy, and especially in 1 Timothy 4, it is Timothy himself who is to pattern behavior for others.

The focus of 4:12–16 is on Timothy's gift that links Paul's exhortations to Timothy with the Holy Spirit's work in the protégé's life. Being an example to others (4:12) by the power of the Spirit (4:14), as one takes pains with "these things" (4:15), is critical, because "you will save both yourself and those who hear you" (4:16; see below). In other words, "the personal life and the work of the church leader are closely related and cannot be separated from one another."[31]

No doubt, intergenerational conflict, as today, was prevalent in Paul's day.[32] In that context, the apostle's instruction to his young delegate in 4:12 is encouraging, even after he himself has just argued for appointing older elders, or at least not new converts (3:6): no matter what the age of the leader or of any believer, an exemplary lifestyle of godliness should silence any critic anywhere.[33]

Timothy's youth is suggested by the labels "son" and "child" in 1 Tim 1:2, 18; 2 Tim 1:2; 2:1; and by the exhortations in 1 Tim 5:1–2 and 2 Tim 2:22 (also see 1 Cor 4:17; Phil 2:22). Here he possesses νεότης (neotēs, "youth," 1 Tim 4:12). Polybius, the Greek historian of the second century, reported of Flamininus that "he was yet quite young [νέος, neos], not being over thirty" (18.12.5).[34] Apparently, "one would, in the ancient world have neotēs as long as he could bear arms . . . and thus into his mid-forties" (see 1 Macc 2:66; 16:2).[35]

---

31. Marshall, *Pastoral Epistles*, 558.
32. See Malherbe, "How to Treat Old Women," 268–69.
33. Titus is also called to be an example (Titus 2:7).
34. Polybius, *Histories*, 5:128–29. Philo, *On the Creation* 36.105, cited Hippocrates on the seven stages of the human life: the fourth stage, νεανίσκος, *neaniskos*, was described to be from 22–28 years of age. Irenaeus extended the upper limit of youth to forty (*Against Heresies* 2.22.5).
35. Quinn and Wacker, *First and Second Letters to Timothy*, 388.

The "purity" that Timothy is called to model (1 Tim 4:12) often referred to matters related to sexual behavior as in 5:2, perhaps related to Timothy's "youth."[36] Of course, the term νεότης here may simply be relative to the age of Paul, himself, and to that of the leaders of the Ephesian church.

Five prepositional ἐν (*en*)-phrases mark out the domains of Timothy's exemplary lifestyle: "in speech, in conduct, in love, in faith, in purity" (4:12). Lists, as I oft note, are not to be preached in sliced and atomized parts; they must be respected for what they convey with a unified, integrated, cohesive thrust. Here, Timothy's setting of a precedent in every aspect of his life is paramount.

Following upon generalities of the attitudes and actions that Timothy needed to exemplify, Paul moves on in 4:13–14 to some more specific items. "Until I come" (4:13) further emphasizes Timothy's role as the delegate of his mentor in a *mandata principis* epistle. The particular aspects of Timothy's ministry being exhorted are threefold, all related to Scripture: "the reading,"[37] "the exhortation,"[38] and "the teaching" (4:13), with the article before each noun indicating that they were familiar corporate activities. The asyndeton indicates the relatedness of the three undertakings.[39] The subsequent verse seems to assume that this transaction of reading-exhortation-teaching transaction of Scripture was a Spirit-directed ministry, by means of a χάρισμα (*charisma*, 4:14).[40] This may likely have been an attempt

---

36. And as, for example, in Philo, *On the Life of Abraham* 98; and *On the Contemplative Life* 68.

37. The call to read has often been taken as a requirement that Scripture must always be read in public. But one has to consider the context of this exhortation in those days: there were no multiple copies of the text; even if there were multiple copies, their price would have made it prohibitive for the vast majority to possess one; even if people owned their own copies of the text, literacy was not widespread; even if everyone could read, their free time to do so would have been limited to nights; even if they had the necessary leisure at night, reading by lamps would have made the activity quite difficult; and even if they had adequate lighting, the absence of reading aids easily obtainable today (spectacles, contacts, and so on) would have rendered these tomes inaccessible to most. All things considered, the public reading of Scripture encouraged here is most likely to have been conducted in the context of its exhortation and teaching. Besides, ἀνάγνωσις, *anagnōsis*, of the Law, translating the MT קָרָא, *qara'*, in LXX Neh 8:8, is closely linked to the translation of the text and "giving the sense so that the assembly understood" (also see 1 Esd 9:48). Thus, ἀνάγνωσις may rightly be considered the reading of Scripture + its explication: i.e., equivalent to preaching. Indeed, preaching (κηρύσσω, *kēryssō*) and reading (ἀναγινώσκω, *anaginōskō*) are paired together in Acts 15:21. "Reading" (again ἀναγινώσκω) for application is indicated in Deut 31:11–12 (also see Rev 1:3, where application is urged along with the reading of prophecy). A practical note: I rarely read my preaching text *en masse* in the beginning of a sermon, choosing rather to read parts as I preach those portions, thus leading my listeners through the text, rather than letting them encounter the text in one chunk without any mediation—it is almost impossible to catch authorial *doings* (pericopal theology) *sans* pastoral glossing. I remain unconvinced of the value of simply reading a pericope in our day when none of the contextual factors of the early times pertain. Even the argument that an unglossed reading might improve biblical literacy is unsustainable. Therefore, if a church I am preaching at insists on a public reading of Scripture, I either ask that it be separated from my sermon by a song or prayer or something else, or I offer a Psalm to be read that is topically and tangentially related to my preaching pericope. In fact, I would argue that the best time to read the preaching text in a large chunk in uninterrupted fashion is *after* the sermon, not before! Then will listeners be reminded of, and be impacted again by, the thrust (pericopal theology) and thereby motivated further to apply.

38. Exhortation (παράκλησις, *paraklēsis*) is related directly to Scripture in 1 Macc 12:9; 2 Macc 15:9; also see Acts 13:15; Heb 12:5; 13:22 for this co-location (and perhaps Titus 1:9 as well).

39. The three show up together in one of the earliest extrabiblical descriptions of a worship service: Justin Martyr, *1 Apology* 1.67.

40. This spiritual gifting of Timothy is also referred to in 2 Tim 1:6. The prophecy and the laying on of hands mentioned here in 1 Tim 4:14 is likely to have been an accompaniment, or a public recognition, of

to counter the heretical readings and interpretations of Scripture performed by the false teachers (1:3–4; 4:1–3, 7), under the influence of a different spirit (4:1).

A set of six more or less synonymous imperatives drives 4:13–16: πρόσεχω ("attend") in 4:13; μὴ ἀμελέω (mē ameleō, "do not neglect") in 4:14; μελετάω (meletaō, "take pains") in 4:15; εἰμί (eimi, "be [absorbed]")[41] in 4:15; ἐπέχω ("attend closely") in 4:16; and ἐπιμένω (epimenō, "persevere") in 4:16. In 4:15b, 16b, we are given the outcomes of all these activities: "that your progress may be manifest to all" and that "you will save both yourself and those who hear you."[42] While Paul asserts that "the living God . . . is the Savior of all men" in 4:10 (and 1:15; 2:3–4), in 4:15–16 he seems to be indicating some human responsibility for this "salvation." In light of the reference to godliness profiting this life *and the next* (4:8), it is best to see "salvation" here as that which will be consummated at the return of Christ, in particular indicating the attendant rewards for godly living (as in 1 Cor 9:27; 15:1–2; Phil 2:12; Col 1:22–23; Heb 3:6, 14).[43] Here, godliness of lifestyle, as modeled by Timothy and emulated by the flock at Ephesus, ensures "salvation"—i.e., rewards—in the future, for both modeler and emulators.

SERMON MAPS

THEOLOGICAL FOCUS OF PERICOPE 6 FOR PREACHING

6 God's people nourished on scriptural teaching engage intensely in spiritual discipline, persevering in modeling Spirit-directed, Scripture-based godliness, ensuring future reward for themselves (4:1–16).

The notion of modeling was encountered in the previous pericope (Pericope 5: 1 Tim 3:1–16), so that need not consume much sermonic space for this pericope. I have, instead, chosen to focus on spiritual disciplines related to Scripture. While teachers appear to be the focus in this pericope, it is obviously not about leaders alone: as in Pericope 5, all believers are called to be engaging in such pedagogical activities to some extent, to some degree, in some fashion, in some arena. What Timothy is called to do, here and elsewhere, is what God's people are called to do always.

Possible Preaching Maps for Pericope 6

    I.   False Teachers: Their Devotion[44] and Their "Disciplines"

Timothy's gifting, and an invocation of divine blessing upon him (as also in 1 Tim 1:18; 2 Tim 1:6—here it is Paul who is laying his hands on Timothy, not necessarily mutually exclusive with 1 Tim 4:14). On the necessity for ordination for a pastor-preacher, see Kuruvilla, *Vision for Preaching*, 36–42.

41. The imperative ἴσθι, *isthi*, can have this sense, as also in Prov 23:17 LXX.

42. The genitive pronoun σου in 4:15 is placed in a position of emphasis: "so that *your* progress may be manifest to all," stressing the importance of Timothy's own life being exemplary before the congregation. In other words, the Spirit has gifted, but every Christian has his/her responsibility to "do." And there needs to be manifest "progress" (4:15) in this "doing"—progress in spirituality, godliness, and maturity.

43. See Dillow, *Reign of the Servant Kings*. Another option might be to see "ensuring salvation" as pointing to the life and word of the people of God by which witness unbelievers are brought to salvation in Christ (as in Rom 11:14; 1 Cor 7:16; 9:22; Jas 5:20; Jude 23). I prefer the eschatological sense; such a future focus permeates this pericope.

44. By "devotion" I mean what these parties are focusing on, attending to.

False teachers and their devotion (4:1–2)
   Their "disciplines": unscriptural, ungodly (4:3–5)
   Move-to-Relevance: False teachers in our midst
II. Truth Teachers: Their Devotion and Their Disciplines
   Truth teachers and their devotion (4:6–7a)
   Their disciplines: scriptural, for godliness (4:7b–16)
   Move-to-Relevance: Our failure of discipline
III. *Be Disciplined for Godliness, through Scripture!*
   Specifics on disciplines related to Scripture

Another way to create a map on this pericope is by contrasting the devotion and discipline of false and truth teachers in each move:

I. Devotion
   False teachers and their devotion (4:1–2)
   Truth teachers and their devotion (4:6–7a)
   Move-to-Relevance: Our lack of focus on Scripture[45]
II. Discipline
   False teachers' "disciplines": unscriptural, ungodly (4:3–5)
   Truth teachers' disciplines: scriptural, for godliness (4:7b–16)
   Move-to-Relevance: What we discipline ourselves for (or with), instead
III. *Be Disciplined for Godliness, through Scripture!*
   Specifics on disciplines related to Scripture

---

45. One does not always have to point out failures in moves-to-relevance; if the preacher is convinced the congregation is doing well in whatever is being discussed, a public pat on the back and an encouragement to persevere is quite appropriate.

PERICOPE 7

Godly Care for the Needy

1 Timothy 5:1–16

[Care for the Needy; Deserving and Undeserving Recipients]

REVIEW, SUMMARY, PREVIEW

Review of Pericope 6: The sixth pericope (1 Tim 4:1–16) warned of a time when false teachers, in their focus on, and devotion to, doctrines demonic, would deceive many. To counter these nefarious tendencies, the people of God remain focused on Scripture and discipline themselves for godliness, based on truth and by the Spirit, being examples to others.

Summary of Pericope 7: This pericope (1 Tim 5:1–16) focuses on the care of the needy, an extension of godliness that is pleasing to God. The care of the deserving needy in both the domestic and the divine households is addressed, as well as reasons for not supporting the undeserving.

Preview of Pericope 8: The next pericope (1 Tim 5:17–25) deals with leaders who are discharging their responsibilities creditably (and are worthy of honor), as well as with those who are sinning (and are disciplined). Such incentives for godliness and disincentives for ungodliness are integral to the church's defense of its holiness. The appointment of leaders is therefore undertaken carefully.

1 TIMOTHY

7   1 Timothy 5:1–16

> **THEOLOGICAL FOCUS OF PERICOPE 7**
>
> 7   God's people, treating fellow believers as family members, care for the needy, both in their own households and in the divine household, focusing upon deserving ones who are believers, who have manifested godliness with a reputation for good works, and who are engaging in the community's worship, rather than focusing upon undeserving ones who, because of their ungodliness, incur divine condemnation as they follow after Satan, disregarding Christ (5:1–16).
>
> 7.1 God's people treat one another as family members, as befitting their joint membership in the divine household (5:1–2).
>
> 7.2 God's people aid the afflicted both in their own households and in the divine household, focusing upon deserving ones who are believers, who have manifested godliness with a reputation for good works in aiding the afflicted, and who are engaging in the community's worship, rather than focusing upon undeserving ones who, because of their ungodliness, incur divine condemnation as they follow after Satan, disregarding Christ (5:3–16).

OVERVIEW

Second-person imperatives continue from 1 Timothy 4 into this chapter in 5:1, 3, 7, 11, 19, 20, 22, 23 (and indirectly in 5:21 by means of an infinitive). Timothy is Paul's representative in Ephesus and to him are addressed these instructions in this *mandata principis*. This pericope should be interpreted in light of the instructions in Pericope 6: 1 Tim 4:1–16, how God's people, exercising discipline for godliness, should follow the truth—persevering in it, teaching it, and exemplifying it. In this chapter, that theme is continued as specific leadership issues gain prominence: the treatment of older and younger men and women (5:1–2); the care of widows (5:3–16); and how to deal with elders (5:17–25; see Pericope 8).

"Honor" shows up in 5:3, 17; and 6:1, suggesting a threefold division of 5:3—6:2 concerning, respectively, how Timothy should deal with widows (5:3–16); with elders (5:17–25); and how slaves should deal with their masters (6:1–2; see Pericope 9). And παρακαλέω, *parakaleō*, "exhort," in 5:1 and 6:2 begins and ends the whole section. Perhaps, then, 5:1–2, the instruction on treating older men and women (along with younger men and women, making the full complement of a household) is a prelude to these three sections: widows were older women, elders were older men (3:4–6), and slave-masters may well have been older men, too, hence the call to slaves not to be disrespectful of their masters. Indeed, one could connect 1 Tim 5:3—6:2 with 4:16: "those who hear you" (4:16) are the ones in 5:3—6:2, especially the older ones, who may have "looked down on [Timothy's] youthfulness" (4:12). Unlike these older ones disdaining Timothy, in 5:1–2 he is specifically asked to honor them, treating them as parents.

7.1   1 Timothy 5:1–2

> **THEOLOGICAL FOCUS 7.1**
>
> 7.1 God's people treat one another as family members, as befitting their joint membership in the divine household (5:1–2).

TRANSLATION 7.1

5:1 Do not harshly rebuke an older man, but exhort [him] as a father, younger men as brothers,

5:2 older women as mothers, younger women as sisters, in all purity.

NOTES 7.1

7.1 *God's people treat one another as family members, as befitting their joint membership in the divine household* (5:1–2).

As noted, it is best to see 5:1–2 as introducing the following two issues dealt with in this chapter: the treatment of widows and the treatment of church elders—both from a point of view of how they must be cared for and handled, and how those individuals may serve as models of behavior for the rest of the congregation. At the commencement of the pericope, while "old man" is in the singular (πρεσβύτερος, *presbyteros*), the others—"younger men," "older women," and "younger women"—are in the plural (5:1, 2, 11). Perhaps this is to distinguish the category of "older men" from that of church officers composed of elders (πρεσβύτεροι, *presbyteroi*, plural, is employed of them later in 5:17, 19); their cases of malfeasance or misbehavior are dealt with separately (see Pericope 8: 1 Tim 5:17–25).

Respect for the aged is a matter addressed in the OT: Lev 19:32; Deut 28:50; Prov 20:29 (all employing either πρεσβύτερος or πρεσβύτης [*presbytēs*] in the LXX). Jesus himself remarked on the household nature of the church: Mark 3:31–35; Luke 8:21; John 19:26–27 (also see elsewhere in Paul, for e.g., Rom 16:13). The notion of the church as a household (1 Tim 3:15) is reinforced with the exhortation to the leader, Timothy, to treat others as parents and siblings (5:1–2), emphasized with four instances of ὡς, *hōs*, "as" (5:1–2).[1] "On the whole, the impression is that the fellowship of Christians is to operate with the notions of respect and intimacy proper to a family."[2]

In any case, the call for respecting elders here is entirely congruent with the prevalent attitude that younger people were supposed to harbor toward older ones. Polybius (*Histories* 6.4.5) equated such respect with worship of deity: "In a community . . . it is traditional and customary to reverence the gods, to honor our parents, to respect our elders [πρεσβύτεροι]."[3] Hierocles (second century CE), exhorted: "And indeed, even if they [i.e., parents] should err in something . . . they should be corrected, to be sure, but not with a rebuke [οὐ μετ' ἐπιπλήξεως, *ou met' epiplēxeōs*], by Zeus, as it is customary to do with those who are our inferiors or equals, but rather with exhortation [μετὰ παρακλήσεως, *meta paraklēseōs*] . . . . The necessary cure for their oversights is with exhortation [μετὰ παρακλήσεως] and a kind of art." Both ἐπιπλήσσω (*epiplēssō*) and παρακαλέω are shared with 1 Tim 5:1.[4]

---

1. Neither was this a novel notion in Greco-Roman times: Plato (*Republic* 5.463c) declared that a person in the guardian class (i.e., city rulers) "will regard [everyone he encounters] as either his brother, or sister, or father, or mother, or son, or daughter, or the children or parents of these" (*Republic*, 1:500–501).

2. Towner, *Letters to Timothy and Titus*, 330.

3. Polybius, *Histories*, 3:298–99.

4. Ramelli, *Hierocles*, 84–85. The verb ἐπιπλήσσω, "harshly rebuke" (5:1), is a *hapax legomenon* in the NT; but it reminds the reader of πλήκτης, *plēktēs*, "pugnacious person," in 3:3 (and Titus 1:7)—what an elder ought not to be. In other words, Timothy is being exhorted: "Don't beat up on an older man." So

1 TIMOTHY

The issue of purity (in 5:2) was already exhorted of Timothy in 4:12—ἁγνεία, *hagneia*, occurs only in these two locations in the NT. It is likely that, in the context of purity towards younger women, and that of Timothy's own youthfulness (4:12), such purity involved chastity in matters sexual.

7.2   1 Timothy 5:3–16

THEOLOGICAL FOCUS 7.2

7.2   God's people aid the afflicted, both in their own households and in the divine household, focusing upon deserving ones who are believers, who have manifested godliness with a reputation for good works in aiding the afflicted, and who are engaging in the community's worship, rather than focusing upon undeserving ones who, because of their ungodliness, have incurred divine condemnation as they follow after Satan, disregarding Christ (5:3–16).

TRANSLATION 7.2

5:3   *Honor widows who are indeed widows;*

5:4   *but if any widow has children or grandchildren, let them first learn to practice godliness to their own household and to make some return to their parents; for this is pleasing before God.*

5:5   *But she who is indeed a widow and has been left alone has hoped in God and continues in the requests and the prayers night and day,*

5:6   *but the one being self-indulgent has died while living.*

5:7   *Charge these things also, so that that they may be irreproachable.*

5:8   *But if anyone does not provide for his own, and especially for [his] household, he has denied the faith and is worse than an unbeliever.*

5:9   *A widow is to be enrolled [if] she is not less than sixty years old, a one-man woman,*

5:10 *having a testimony for good works, if she has raised children, if she has practiced hospitality to strangers, if she has washed saints' feet, if she has aided the afflicted, if she has pursued every good work.*

5:11 *But reject [enrolling] younger widows, for when they indulge sensual appetites in opposition to Christ, they want to marry,*

5:12 *incurring judgment because they have set aside their first faith.*

5:13 *And at the same time they also learn [to be] idle, going around houses, and not merely idle, but also gossips and busybodies, speaking about things they should not.*

5:14 *Therefore, I want the younger to marry, bear children, keep house, to give the enemy no opportunity for reviling;*

5:15 *for some have already turned aside after Satan.*

---

also, Plato (*Laws* 879C): "Everyone shall reverence his elder both by deed and word; whosoever, man or woman, exceeds himself in age by twenty years he shall regard as a father or a mother, and he shall keep his hands off that person" (in a context that mentions "beating," πληγέντι, *plēgenti*, from πληγή, πλήσσω, *plēgē, plēssō*, "to beat") (Plato, *Laws*, 2:286–87).

5:16   *If any woman believer has widows [in her household], she must aid them and the church must not be burdened, so that it may aid those who are indeed widows.*

NOTES 7.2

7.2   *God's people aid the afflicted, both in their own households and in the divine household, focusing upon deserving ones who are believers, who have manifested godliness with a reputation for good works in aiding the afflicted, and who are engaging in the community's worship, rather than focusing upon undeserving ones who, because of their ungodliness, incur divine condemnation as they follow after Satan, disregarding Christ (5:3–16).*

The discourse on the treatment of widows (5:3–16) is the longest in 1 Timothy that is dedicated to a specific group of people. While there is uncertainty about whether there was an official order of widows in the Ephesian church, there is no doubt there was some sort of a list of eligible women (i.e., those who were "indeed widows," 5:3, 5, 16) to whom church monies would be disbursed. Enrollment of qualified widows is explicitly mentioned in 5:9; they included those who had raised a family (5:4, 8, 10), who were prayer warriors hoping in God (5:5), above reproach (5:7), who were of an appropriate age (5:9, 11–15), who had exhibited fidelity while married (5:9), and who had practiced good works (5:10). These are past reflections on activities determining character rather than a listing of future roles and responsibilities of an enrolled order of widows. Such qualifications are somewhat similar to those of church officers (3:1–13), but no official function is noted here.[5] In other words, even if recipients of church funds were not functioning in an official capacity, by virtue of the support they received, they were representatives of the body of Christ, and had to live up to that calling.

This section on widows in 5:3–16 depicts at least three groups: supporting family members of widows, widows deserving of church support, and widows not qualified for (or undeserving of) church funds. This sequence in 5:4–6 is repeated in 5:7–13 (and recapitulated in the closing section of 5:14–16); the three parties will be considered individually below. Obviously, this was a crucial issue, integral to the church's care for the needy. And so Paul is addressing the whole church through his delegate, Timothy: notice the plural verbs in 5:4, 7, and the indefinite "any/anyone" in 5:4, 8, 16a; also, "church" is mentioned in 5:16b.

Opening Instruction:		
Church's support for those "indeed widows" (5:3)		
Supporting Family	5:4	5:7–8
Deserving Widows	5:5	5:9–10
Undeserving Widows	5:6	5:11–13
Closing Instructions:		
Other support for those "indeed widows" (5:14–16) [family, deserving, and undeserving widows]		

---

5. Sexagenarians, considering these widows' age at enrollment (5:9), were not the best suited to engage in official ministries of the church, particularly in those days.

"Honor" was what was due to widows who were "indeed widows" (5:3); it indicated financial support, as also in 5:17-18—i.e., to "'provide the support that honor demands.' That is to say, the subtext of the 'honor' command is explicitly material."[6] This is particularly true in the context of 5:4, 8, 16, explicitly calling for families to take care of their own.[7] The goal of 5:3-16 is to establish "a formal relationship between the church and the widow so that she knows she will be cared for until death."[8] In sum, it is a preachment of care for the needy: "The woman whose husband has died was in antiquity a veritable paradigm for the helpless and oppressed."[9] Indeed, God himself was the defender of the defenseless (including widows): Exod 22:22-23; Deut 10:18; 24:17; Pss 68:5; 146:9; Prov 15:25 (also see Deut 14:29; 27:19; Ps 82:3; Isa 1:17; Zech 7:6; etc., for divine priorities regarding the care of such disenfranchised people in the community). Therefore, the people of God needed to follow in his footsteps. And so they did, in the early church (Acts 6:1; Jas 1:27; Ignatius, *Polycarp* 4.1; Hermas, *Similitudes* 1.7; etc.).

Supporting Family

Family support (5:4, 7-8, 16) was to be the first line of care for deserving widows (5:4, 7-8, 16), for "this is pleasing before God" and integral to the practice of godliness (εὐσεβέω, *eusebeō*, 5:4).[10] What is "pleasing" before God (ἀπόδεκτος, *apodektos*, 5:4; from ἀποδέχομαι, *apodechomai*) is the "return" to parents (ἀποδίδωμι, *apodidōmi*, 5:4); considering the relationship between these verbs, support of parents is equated to giving to God, himself. Plutarch (*On Brotherly Love* 479F) declared: "Both Nature and the Law, which upholds Nature, have assigned to parents, after gods, first and greatest honour; and there is nothing which men do that is more acceptable to gods than with goodwill and zeal to repay . . . those who bore them and brought them up . . . . Nor is there, again, a greater exhibition of an impious nature than neglect of parents or offences against them."[11] Therefore, the one not caring for dependent relatives receives a serious rebuke: "he has denied the faith and is worse than an unbeliever" (5:8), for this is antithetical to "godliness" (5:4). Usually ἀρνέομαι

---

6. Towner, *Letters to Timothy and Titus*, 337-38.

7. The verb τιμάω, *timaō*, "to honor" (and its cognate noun) includes the notion of financial dividends also in Sir 38:1 and Mark 7:9-13 (and parallels). Reflecting a similar connotation of "remuneration," Diogenes Laertius (third century CE; *Lives of Eminent Philosophers* 5.4.72) pointed to a philosopher's will that instructed his survivors to "remunerate [τιμησάτωσαν, *timēsatōsan*] the physicians Pasithemis and Medias who for their attention to me and their skill deserve far higher reward [τιμῆς, *timēs*]." See *Lives of Eminent Philosophers, Volume I*, 524-25. Likewise, Xenophon (fourth/fifth century BCE), *Hellenica*, 6.1.6, on a ruler's reward for soldiers: "He rewards [τιμᾷ, *tima*] [them], some with double pay, others with triple pay, others even with quadruple pay, and with gifts besides, . . . ; so that all the mercenaries in his service know that martial prowess assures to them a life of greatest honour [ἐντιμότατόν, *entimotaton*] and abundance" (*Hellenica*, 2:118-19).

8. Mounce, *Pastoral Epistles*, 276.

9. Quinn and Wacker, *First and Second Letters to Timothy*, 427.

10. The use of "children" and "grandchildren" in 5:4 indicates that the domestic household here is quite an expanded one.

11. Plutarch, *Moralia*, 6:256-57. And Philo noted (*On the Decalogue* 119-20): "For parents are the servants of God for the task of begetting children, and he who dishonours [ἀτιμάζων, *atimazōn*] the servant dishonours also [συνατιμάζει, *synatimazei*] the Lord. . . . How can reverence be rendered (εὐσεβεῖσθαι, *eusebeisthai*) to the invisible God by those who show irreverence (ἀσεβούντων, *asebountōn*) to the gods who are near at hand and seen by the eye?" (*On the Decalogue* 66-69).

(*arneomai*, "to deny," 5:8) is the antonym of confession (1 John 2:22–23): thus here we see how "practice can disconfirm profession"—actions of unsupportiveness belying confessions of faith. "Faith" thus involves more than doctrinal belief and encompasses its outworking in a lifestyle of godliness—in particular in this pericope, its outworking in the aid of the needy. Indeed, those who "deny the *faith* [πιστίς, *pistis*]" (1 Tim 5:8) are rendered equivalent to false teachers under the influence of demonic doctrine—those who have "fallen away from the *faith*" (4:1) and those who have "shipwrecked their *faith*" (1:19). In the exercise and expression of faith in godliness, according to this text care for needy kin was to be a "first priority" (πρῶτος, *prōtos,* 5:4). The failure of such a duty was considered scandalous: such a person was "worse than a *faithless person*" (ἄπιστος, *apistos,* or "unbeliever," 5:8). "For Paul, Christianity begins at home; and one's conduct in the microcosm of the home shows one's abilities, or lack of abilities, in the macrocosm of the church."[12] Of course, this had already shown up in the requirement that candidate leaders be good managers of their human households (3:4–5, 12; Titus 1:6). Therefore, οἰκεῖος, *oikeios,* "household," here in 1 Tim 5:8, may actually refer to the divine household, the fellowship of believers. This makes it even more imperative that *believing* relatives be aided: "especially" those of the "household."[13] These supportive activities would render those engaging in them irreproachable before outsiders (5:7) for, as was already noted, such care for elder relatives was an entrenched value in the surrounding culture.

Interestingly, in his closing instructions in 5:16, a new member of the family is introduced—women with widows in the family. Certainly, men with such dependents are not being excluded here (5:4; and "anyone" in 5:8), but after a section on the ungodly behavior of some women (the younger [undeserving] widows, 5:13–14; see below), Paul may have opted to highlight the godly behavior of role-modeling women capable and willing to care for widows in their families, thus reducing the burden upon churches. Such a ministry of "aiding" engaged in by these women (from the verb ἐπαρκέω [*eparkeō*; ×2 in 5:16]), was similar to that performed by deserving widows as they "aided" the afflicted themselves (also ἐπαρκέω, 5:10). So we have a picture of widows "aiding" others, family members "aiding" widows, and churches "aiding" the unattached deserving ones who were "indeed widows"—a truly remarkable portrait of the body of Christ in action, irreproachability and godliness manifest in Christian solicitude for the defenseless and disenfranchised!

Deserving Widows

Deserving widows are described in 5:5, 9–10, 16. These are the ones hoping in the "defender of the widows" (Ps 68:5). The perfect tense "has hoped" (1 Tim 5:5; from ἐλπίζω, *elpizō*) "depicts emblematically the unique Christian posture of confident anticipation of God's

---

12. Mounce, *Pastoral Epistles,* 280.

13. See 1 Tim 3:15; 2 Tim 2:20–21; etc. "It is a natural conclusion that Christians, as members of God's οἶκος, are his οἰκεῖοι [*oikeioi,* "household member"], just as the overseer is God's οἰκονόμος [*oikonomos,* "household steward"] (Titus 1:7)" (Campbell, "ΚΑΙ ΜΑΛΙΣΤΑ ΟΙΚΕΙΩΝ," 159). And see Gal 6:10 that also uses μάλιστα, *malista,* "especially," to emphasize the doing of good to fellow believers. This, of course, is not to deny that benevolence extended to those outside the church is a valid endeavor for the people of God. It is simply not a topic addressed in this pericope, which focuses on caring for the needy *within* the divine household.

1 TIMOTHY

intervention and provision."[14] This is to fix one's hope upon Yahweh (for e.g., LXX Pss 4:6; 5:12; 7:2; 9:11; 15:1; 17:3, etc., all using ἐλπίζω), an attitude of deep devotion and a facet of godliness.

The use of articles in "*the* requests and *the* prayers" (1 Tim 5:5) meant more than just the personal petitions of the widow. More likely in view is their participation in the liturgical activities of the body of Christ—*the* corporate transaction of prayer (as in 2:1), with "night and day" suggesting "a serious and enduring commitment to the prayer life of the community."[15]

As was mentioned in Pericope 5: 1 Tim 3:1–16, in connection with similarly structured phrases there (in 3:2, 12), here in 5:9 "one-man woman" indicates an individual, now widowed, who had "lived together prudently [chastely], either with one [husband] or afterwards with another," not necessarily that she had ever had only one husband: purity is the issue here.[16]

These women's reputation for good works are lauded in 5:10a; and they are spelled out in 5:10b, bracketed by ἔργοις καλοῖς (*ergois kalois*, "good works") and ἔργῳ ἀγαθῷ (*ergō agathō*, "good work"). They are ministrations of Christian service performed in faith: care of children, strangers, saints,[17] and the distressed—all visible acts by which one could gauge the godliness of the widow. Each of these four activities, along with their having "pursued every good work," is a conditional protasis beginning with εἰ and ending with an aorist active indicative third-person singular with the final -σεν/-ψεν, yielding an almost palpable assonance, with the sequence increasing in syllables from the first to the fifth, providing a sense of escalating intensity.

> εἰ ἐτεκνοτρόφησεν
> *ei eteknotrophēsen*
> "if she has raised children"
>
> εἰ ἐξενοδόχησεν
> *ei exenodochēsen*
> "if she has practiced hospitality"
>
> εἰ ἁγίων πόδας ἔνιψεν
> *ei hagiōn podas enipsen*
> "if she has washed saints' feet"
>
> εἰ θλιβομένοις ἐπήρκεσεν
> *ei thlibomenois epērkesen*
> "if she has aided the afflicted"
>
> εἰ παντὶ ἔργῳ ἀγαθῷ ἐπηκολούθησεν
> *ei panti ergō agathō epēkolouthēsen*
> "if she has pursued every good work"

Truly, these were deserving widows, indeed!

14. Towner, *Letters to Timothy and Titus*, 341.
15. Johnson, *First and Second Letters to Timothy*, 262.
16. Theodore of Mopsuestia, *Commentary on 1 Timothy* 5:9 (*Patrologia Graeca* 66:943–44; my translation from the Latin).
17. Washing feet is likely to have been symbolic of humble service rendered to fellow believers, exemplified by Jesus Christ (John 13:5, 12, 14).

Undeserving Widows

In contrast to the deserving widows engaging in the prayers of the community ceaselessly, undeserving (younger) widows (5:6, 11–13, 15) were being "self-indulgent," partaking of a riotous life of wanton pleasure (5:6; σπαταλάω, *spatalaō*; also used in Ezek 16:49 LXX of the lifestyle of Sodomites). This kind of prodigal luxury in a community lacking resources and amidst destitutes deserving of support in a community short on the resources to aid them was unconscionable, brazen, and iniquitous—"a death to that life by which the community claims to live by the one 'who gave himself as a ransom for all'" (1 Tim 2:6).[18] These were the ones entrapped by their "sensual desires in opposition to Christ" (5:11). The verb καταστρηνιάω, *katastrēniaō*, "indulge sensual appetites," in 5:11, is a *hapax*; a basic form of the verb, στρηνιάω, *strēniaō*, "live sensuously," occurs in Rev 18:7, 9, describing the behavior of the harlot, Babylon, and her consorts. That, and the intensification of this verbal form with the preposition κατά in our text may carry connotations of aberrant sexuality (perhaps promiscuity, see 1 Tim 5:13).

These younger widows' desire to remarry is deprecated in 5:11–12. Of course, remarriage was not the issue; that state was even recommended of these same individuals in 5:14. So here in 5:11–12, Paul's criticism is not of remarriage per se, but of the "sensual appetites in opposition to Christ" that are prompting it (5:11). This desire for remarriage, impelled by such unchaste longings, was an abandonment of their πρῶτος πίστις (*prōtos pistis*, "first faith"), equivalent to the denial of the faith by an unsupportive family member (5:8). While the reason for such a condemnation is not given, it is not much of a leap to adduce that a possible association with non-Christian spouses in remarriage must have been what resulted in Paul's unfavorable verdict. "The real problem is that the younger widows have given themselves over to a self-centered, self-indulgent lifestyle and have followed after Satan.... Their desire to remarry is symptomatic of their wantonness, and it is a wanton remarriage that Paul condemns."[19]

But the potential of an unmarried widow with a tendency towards idleness and gossip—all causing a stain on the church—was equally reprehensible (5:13). In fact, "idleness" occupies an emphatic position in 5:13a (literally: "and at the same time also, idleness they learn"); the word is repeated in 5:13b. We are in the dark about what it was these women were communicating—"speaking about things they should not" (5:13), though in the context of their sensual desires, it might have had something to do with scandalous and shameful sexual talk. So much so, Winter asserts that "when cognizance is taken of the immoral activities referred to (5:11) and the specific connecting particles 'at the same time also' (ἅμα δὲ καί [*hama de kai*]) (5:13), it is right to draw the conclusion that there was a connection between the promiscuous activities of the indolent widows and what they did in going from household to household."[20] Remarriage of the proper kind to the proper person was, therefore, recommended (5:14).

In any case, these undeserving widows, in their profligate lifestyles, were giving the "enemy" opportunity for vilification (5:14); some had already "turned aside to follow Satan" (5:15). "Whereas Paul had to 'hand over to Satan' Hymenaeus and Alexander (1:20),

---

18. Johnson, *First and Second Letters to Timothy*, 262–63.
19. Mounce, *Pastoral Epistles*, 290–91; also see Towner, *Letters to Timothy and Titus*, 352.
20. Winter, *Roman Wives, Roman Widows*, 133.

1 TIMOTHY

these women have gone willingly."[21] These undeserving widows therefore had already died a death of sorts (5:6), and divine judgment was only to be expected (5:12). Supporting such people and their reproachable conduct was a blot on the church, the truth it was supporting, and the God it followed, not to mention the consequential financial burden it was imposing on the divine household. These incontinent ones were, therefore, to remarry, raise children, and keep house (5:14). In short, Paul is recommending that young (here, undeserving) widows take on the responsibilities of the domestic sphere.[22]

SERMON MAPS

> **THEOLOGICAL FOCUS OF PERICOPE 7 FOR PREACHING**
>
> 7   God's people care for the needy, both personally within their own households, and also corporately within the divine household, focusing upon those deserving ones who are believers, who have lived godly lives with a reputation for good works, and who are engaging in the community's worship (5:1–16).

While this pericope does address care within the domestic household, it might be best in a sermon to focus upon corporate care and how that may specifically be accomplished, and how individuals may participate in that worthy, God-pleasing endeavor. This sermon might be a good opportunity to kick off a new corporate endeavor in the care of the needy within the body, or to promote and inaugurate other such ongoing activities.

Possible Preaching Maps for Pericope 7

    I. Domestic Household Care for the Needy
        Godliness in care of needy relatives (5:3–4, 7–8, 16)
        Move-to-Relevance: The deserving needy in our homes
    II. Divine Household Care for the Needy
        Godliness in the honor of fellow believers (5:1–2)
        Godliness in the care of the needy (5:9a)
        Deserving needy (5:5, 9b–10)
        Undeserving needy (5:6, 11–15)
        Move-to-Relevance: The deserving needy in our circumstances
    III. *Meet Needs, Be Godly!*[23]
        Specifics on caring for the needy

With more focus on the corporate care of the needy, this outline may be tweaked to produce another:

    I. Presence of the Needy
        Godliness in the honor of fellow believers (5:1–2)
        Move-to-Relevance: Our call to be godly towards needy believers

---

21. Johnson, *First and Second Letters to Timothy*, 268.
22. That sentiment was already seen in 1 Tim 2:13–15.
23. Considering that the pericope deals with financial support ("honor"), the application should probably also head in that general direction.

II. Probity of the Needy
   Deserving needy (5:5, 9b–10)
   Undeserving needy (5:6, 11–15)
   Move-to-Relevance: The deserving needy in our circumstances
III. Protection of the Needy
   First line of care: domestic household (5:3–4, 7–8, 16a)
   Second line of care: divine household (5:9a, 16b)[24]
IV. *Meet Needs, Be Godly!*
   Specifics on caring for the needy

---

[24]. I've skipped the move-to-relevance in the third move of this map. Since the next move, application (IV.) is all relevance, that is not a big detriment. One could conceivably add a move-to-relevance that details the failure of the church to care for the needy. The subsequent move to application then provides the corrective.

PERICOPE 8

Maintenance of Godliness

1 Timothy 5:17–25

[Discipline of Wayward Elders; Church's Defense of Holiness]

REVIEW, SUMMARY, PREVIEW

Review of Pericope 7: The seventh pericope (1 Tim 5:1–16) focused on the care of the needy, an extension of godliness that is pleasing to God. The care of the deserving needy in both domestic and divine households was addressed, as well as reasons for not supporting the undeserving.

Summary of Pericope 8: This pericope (1 Tim 5:17–25) deals with leaders who are discharging their responsibilities creditably (they are worthy of honor) and with those who are sinning (they are to be disciplined). Such incentives for godliness and disincentives for ungodliness are integral to the church's defense of its holiness.

Preview of Pericope 9: The next pericope (1 Tim 6:1–2) considers the responsibility of believing slaves to their masters: they honor them, and bestow service upon them, so that God's name and the teaching of the church are not brought into disrepute. Just as even slaves can be benefactors to their masters, all believers render honor and service to one another in the divine household of God.

8   1 Timothy 5:17–25

> **THEOLOGICAL FOCUS OF PERICOPE 8**
>
> 8   The treatment of elders in office is a paradigm for the church's defense of its holiness—a solemn responsibility—and elders who demonstrate godliness in their ministries, particularly with regard to Scripture, are amply rewarded, and they are impartially disciplined when they do not (5:17–25).
>
> 8.1   Good leaders, especially those engaged in the ministries of Scripture, are amply rewarded (5:17–18).
>
> 8.2   Bad leaders, especially those who continue in sin, are impartially disciplined—a solemn responsibility—but more importantly, preventive care is exercised and leaders are not carelessly installed (5:19–25).

OVERVIEW

It was noted in the previous pericope, Pericope 7: 1 Tim 5:1–16, that "honor" in 5:3, 17; 6:1 suggested a threefold division of 5:3—6:2: how Timothy should deal with widows (5:3–16); with elders (5:17–25); and how slaves should deal with their masters (6:1–2). It is likely that 5:1–2 is a preamble to these three sections, since widows were older women, elders were generally older men, and slave-masters were possibly older men, too. Also, a torrent of second-person imperatives flows from 1 Timothy 4 into this chapter: 5:1, 3, 7, 11, 19, 20, 22, 23 (and indirectly, 5:21, employing an infinitive). All, therefore, continue the instructions to Timothy in chapter 4 on how he, exercising discipline for godliness, should follow the truth—persevering in it, teaching it, and exemplifying it (see Pericope 5: 1 Tim 4:1–16).

This previous pericope (Pericope 7: 1 Tim 5:3–16) and this one (Pericope 8: 1 Tim 5:17–25) share a number of features: besides the numerous imperatives mentioned, both open with a plural noun labeling the group of people being discussed (5:3, 17); honor is to be granted to both parties (5:3, 17); both sections contain good and bad examples of each group; "judgment" for either group is noted (κρίμα, *krima*, 5:12; κρίσις, *krisis*, 5:24); both discussions warn of dangers the bad examples pose to the church (5:8, 11–15, 20, 24); "good works" shows up in 5:10 and 5:25; with a ἵνα (*hina*)-clause, a firm exhortation to Timothy to uphold what Paul has instructed is present in 5:7 and 5:21; these two verses also have the only instances of ταῦτα, *tauta*, "these things," in 5:3–25; also, "before God" is found in 5:4 and in 5:21.[1]

8.1   1 Timothy 5:17–18

> **THEOLOGICAL FOCUS 8.1**
>
> 8.1   Good leaders, especially those engaged in the ministries of Scripture, are amply rewarded (5:17–18).

---

1. See Van Neste, *Cohesion and Structure*, 95.

1 TIMOTHY

TRANSLATION 8.1

5:17 *The elders leading well are to be considered worthy of double honor, especially those working hard at instructing and teaching.*

5:18 *For the Scripture says, "You shall not muzzle the threshing ox," and "The worker is worthy of his wages."*

NOTES 8.1

8.1 Good leaders, especially those engaged in the ministries of Scripture, are to be amply rewarded (5:17–18).

"Honor," which began the previous section (τιμάω, verb, 5:3), recurs to mark a new section (τιμή, noun, 5:17; also in 6:1). As was noted in the previous pericope, the word clearly has the connotation of remuneration; especially here in 5:17, in light of the following verse.[2] It could also be that "double" honor means the honor of respect and the honor of remuneration.

The issue of whether there were two classes of elders, leading/ruling and instructing/teaching, has risen frequently in church history, based on how 1 Tim 5:17 is read.[3] It is unlikely that there ever were elders in those days who did not "lead" (or "rule/preside," προΐστημι, *proistēmi*). In fact, προΐστημι is used of the function of elders in 3:4, 5, 12; and προϊστάμενοι, *proistamenoi*, is often a synonym for "elder": Rom 12:8; 1 Thess 5:12–13; 1 Tim 3:4–5, 12; 5:17. "It is questionable whether—this early in the Church's history—there were any otiose presbyters who simply did not preside, i.e., exercise some form of leadership. Rather, 'presiding' is the very definition of what a presbyter is."[4] And 1 Tim 3:2 indicates that all elders also teach (also Titus 1:9). "Especially in light of the Ephesian problem, it seems somewhat contradictory to speak of leaders who did not teach. More likely the leaders of the church were able and active in refuting error and encouraging the truth of the gospel."[5] Meier sees "a college within a college," a distinction between those who took the primary responsibility of teaching and others who also taught, but not to the extent of "working hard" at doing so. In other words, this verse is not making a distinction between two exclusive, non-overlapping groups of leaders: ruling elders and teaching elders. Rather this verse honors elders who lead well, including (or especially) those in this group who may be "working hard at instructing and teaching" (i.e., preaching) by bearing the primary responsibility for the pedagogy of Scripture. This was likely a case of *primi inter pares* ("first [plural] among equals"), *all* elders leading and teaching, but *some* taking the greater share

---

2. The scope of "Scripture says" in 5:18 has been debated. Clearly it includes the citation of Deut 25:4 (also cited in 1 Cor 9:9, but with a different verb than that in Deut 25:4 LXX and in 1 Tim 5:18), but what about the rest, asserting that "the laborer is worthy of his wages?" That seems to come from Luke 10:7, lending that Gospel the status of "Scripture" (also see Matt 10:10). Or perhaps 1 Tim 5:18b is a paraphrase of the dominical statement in 1 Cor 9:14. Elsewhere, NT writers frequently link two citations of Scripture with καί: Matt 15:4; Mark 7:10; Acts 1:20; Heb 1:8–10; 1 Pet 2:6; 2 Pet 2:22.

3. In 5:17, "at instructing" is literally, "in the word [ἐν λόγῳ, *en logo*]." I take "instructing" and "teaching" as a hendiadys referring to preaching: scriptural exhortation with application. See my *Vision for Preaching*, as well as *Manual for Preaching*. However, to keep matters simple, for the most part I shall refer to this function as "teaching," though "preaching" is what is intended in the text.

4. Meier, "*Presbyteros*," 326.

5. Mounce, *Pastoral Epistles*, 307.

of the latter task, perhaps in the larger context of the corporate body.[6] The designation of individuals with a participle in 5:17b (οἱ κοπιῶντες, *hoi kopiōntes*, "those working hard") indicates that it is dealing with select members of the larger group of well-leading elders mentioned in 5:17a. Therefore, one could read 1 Tim 5:17 thus: "The elders leading well are to be considered worthy of double honor—especially [worthy of double honor are] those [who lead well by] working hard at instructing and teaching."[7] So, again, the distinction being made here is not between leading elders and teaching elders (two distinct groups of elders); rather the verse lauds leading elders (all of whom instruct/teach) who do well, especially those leading elders who toil hard in instructing/teaching (this second group of hard workers being part of the first).

All that being said, when one considers this pericope in its entirety, one realizes that the real distinction being made is between elders leading well (5:17–18), and elders *not* doing so (5:19–25; see below).

8.2 1 Timothy 5:19–25

THEOLOGICAL FOCUS 8.2

8.2 Bad leaders, especially those who continue in sin, are impartially disciplined—a solemn responsibility—but more importantly, preventive care is exercised and leaders are not carelessly installed (5:19–25).

TRANSLATION 8.2

5:19 *Do not accept an accusation against an elder except on the basis of two or three witnesses.*

5:20 *Those sinning, reprove before all, so that the rest also will have fear.*

5:21 *I solemnly charge you before God and Christ Jesus and chosen angels, that you may follow these things without partiality, doing nothing according to bias.*

5:22 *Lay hands upon no one hastily, nor share in the sins of others; keep yourself pure.*

5:23 *No longer drink water, but use a little wine for the stomach and for your frequent ailments.*

5:24 *The sins of some are evident, preceding [them] to judgment; for others, they follow after.*

5:25 *Likewise also, the good works are evident, and those that are otherwise cannot remain hidden.*

---

6. Other venues for instruction operated, no doubt, with all elders involved in such pedagogy.

7. Another option is to read μάλιστα, *malista*, "especially," as "namely" or "that is/i.e."—"elders leading well . . . namely, those working hard at instructing and teaching." Both options would maintain "the two-level structure [elders and deacons] evidenced elsewhere in the early church," without having to further divide elders into leaders-rulers and instructors-teachers (i.e., preachers)(Mounce, *Pastoral Epistles*, 308).

1 TIMOTHY

NOTES 8.2

8.2 *Bad leaders, especially those who continue in sin, are impartially disciplined—a solemn responsibility—but more importantly, preventive care is exercised and leaders are not carelessly installed (5:19–25).*

The articulated participle τοὺς ἁμαρτάνοντας (*tous hamartanontas*, "those sinning," 5:20) is better read as "those [individuals of the group mentioned above, i.e., elders] sinning." This is similar to 5:5–6 and 5:17a–b: in each case the following participle (σπαταλῶσα, *spatalōsa*, in 5:6; κοπιῶντες in 5:17b) is dealing with individuals of the group mentioned antecedently (widows in 5:3; elders in 5:17a). The laying on of hands mentioned in 5:22, likely some sort of ordination, also indicates that what is being considered in this discussion is an eldership issue. Besides, two participles have already described elders in 5:17a, b: οἱ ... προεστῶτες and οἱ κοπιῶντες (*hoi ... proestōtes* and *hoi kopiōntes*); we have a third now in 5:20, keeping the focus on the same subjects—elders. Also, note the bracketing of 5:17–25 with similar words: καλῶς (*kalōs*, "well," an adverb; 5:17) and καλά (*kala*, "good," an adjective; 5:25); this *inclusio* wraps the entire pericope into one neat package, dealing with one specific issue and one specific group of people. Meier describes the movement in this pericope from positive (dealing with good elders) to negative (dealing with bad elders), and returning to the positive (dealing with good elders again)[8]:

A Positive (good elders): **5:17–18**
      5:17   Character of good elders; καλῶς; "worthy"
      5:18   Proof: Scripture, "worthy"
B Negative (bad elders): **5:19–22**
      5:19   Private accusation of an elder: Scripture; 3 witnesses
      5:20   Public reproof; "those sinning"; "before all"
      5:21   Impartiality in judgment: 3 witnesses; "before God"
      5:22   Carefulness in appointment: "sins"
  C Digression: 5:23
      5:23   Exhortation to Timothy: purity
B′ Negative (bad elders): **5:24**
      5:24   Manifestation of sinners; "sins"; "evident"
A′ Positive (good elders): **5:25**
      5:25   Manifestation of good elders; καλά; "evident"

The multiple links tying the various parts of this argument together are clear: καλῶς/καλά (5:17, 25); adducing Scripture (5:18, 19); the trio of witnesses: one set in a private accusation, the other in a public reproof (5:19, 20); and "those sinning" and "sins" (5:20, 22, 24); etc.[9]

The pattern is a very natural one, arising spontaneously from the drift of thought. The thought begins with a positive observation, drifts into some negative

---

8. Modified from Meier, "*Presbyteros*," 335–36.

9. That Paul begins with the plural "elders" in 5:17 and proceeds to use a collective singular, "elder" (in 5:19), is not surprising; such singular-plural oscillations appear also in 1 Tim 2:9, 11; 5:1a, 1b; and 5:3, 4.

themes, wanders in v. 23, returns to the negative theme, and finally comes home to rest on a positive note. Precisely because the chiastic pattern is simple and unreflected, one cannot press individual elements for greater symmetry: B', for example, is much shorter than B.[10]

So there appears to be a "sliding ethical scale" in this pericope, based on the kind of elder and the response to their behavior[11]:

	Elder	Response
5:17–18	Good elder	Double honor
5:19	Suspected bad elder	Private accusation
5:20–21	Confirmed bad elder	Public reproof

And all of this is followed by warnings to Timothy (and other leaders, as well as the congregation) on how to avoid such incidents in the future (5:22–25)—all for the purpose of keeping the body of Christ functioning optimally, defending its holiness and maintaining its irreproachability.

The requirement of multiple witnesses in 1 Tim 5:19 reflects Deut 17:6 and 19:15 (also cited in Matt 18:16; John 8:17; 2 Cor 13:1; Heb 10:28). But there are some striking parallels between Deut 19:15 and 1 Tim 5:19–20: person accused of sinning (ἁμάρτημα, ἁμαρτίαν, ἁμάρτῃ, *hamartēma, hamartian, hamartē*, in Deut 19:15; ἁμαρτάνω, *hamartanō*, in 1 Tim 5:20); the sin being considered does not appear to be unduly serious, deserving no harsh penalty; "fear" is evoked in others by the judgment (φόβος, *phobos*, in Deut 19:20; φοβέω, *phobeō*, in 1 Tim 5:20); exhortation to impartiality (Deut 19:21; 1 Tim 5:21); two or three human witnesses (μαρτύρων, *martyrōn*, in Deut 19:15, 17; 1 Tim 5:19); and three other witnesses, including a heavenly being or two (Deut 19:17 has Yahweh, priests, and judges; 1 Tim 5:21 has God, Christ Jesus, and the chosen angels).[12] In this latter triad, "chosen angels" are included probably because of the OT understanding that angels were involved in judicial inquiries, particularly those of the heavenly council; in the NT era, they were understood to be involved in eschatological judgment (Matt 13:49–50; 16:27; Luke 9:26).[13]

It appears that the reception of accusation against elders in the presence of two or three witnesses (5:19) is a private confrontation (Matt 18:15–16); in that case, the reproof in the presence of all in 1 Tim 5:20 would indicate that "those sinning" are those who persist in such nefarious activities despite the private accusation and challenge (Matt 18:17). Thus "all" in 1 Tim 5:20 refers to the congregation before whom the public charge is brought, and "the rest" indicates the remaining elders (in contrast to "those sinning"), who are deterred from temptation to misbehave by the "fear" of public censure and shame before a human court. But there is also a divine court involved in the proceedings, with God, Christ, and

---

10. Meier, "*Presbyteros*," 336
11. See Fuller, "Of Elders and Triads," 261.
12. See Fuller, "Of Elders and Triads," 260.

13. The role of angels in the heavenly court is seen also in Dan 7:9–11; Matt 24:31; 25:31; Mark 8:38; 13:27; Luke 12:9; 15:10; 1 Cor 11:10 (?); 1 Thess 4:16; 2 Thess 1:7; Rev 3:5; 14:10 (and perhaps Job 1:6; 2:1; Ps 81:1). The trio of Father, Son, and angels are also found in: Matt 16:27; Mark 8:38; Luke 9:26; 2 Thess 1:6–7; Heb 12:22–24. "Angels" always refers to those who did not fall, so "chosen angels" must indicate those whom God elects for special undertakings.

the chosen angels (another set of three witnesses). Here it is Timothy himself who is being judged by this heavenly jury as to how he "follows these things" impartially (5:21).

> In both passages [1 Tim 5:19, 21] a fair examination can only be conducted on the basis of the testimony of "two or three witnesses." But no less a fair examination awaits the examiner, for he in turn has "three witnesses" to determine how well he has carried out his appointed task. Certainly having "God, Christ Jesus, and the elect angels" for witnesses at one's "trial" ought to have made Timothy, and ought to make a congregation and its pastor, careful about how they conduct disciplinary matters in the church![14]

Clearly, Paul is seeing these matters in an extremely serious light, given the solemnity of the charge in 5:21. It is the holiness of the church that is at stake, particularly in the behavior of its leaders, and Timothy and all believers are to safeguard the church's irreproachability.

After the digression of 5:23 (on which, see below), 5:24 returns to what was broached in 5:20 and 5:22, with a similar label for the felonies of the elders: αἱ ἁμαρτίαι (5:24) linking with τοὺς ἁμαρτάνοντας in 5:20 and with their "sins" (ἁμαρτίαις) in 5:22. The two verses, 5:24–25, picture a parade, sins leading the flagrantly bad elders, sins following other more secretive bad elders, but all headed to the same destination: judgment! Thus, neither sin nor righteousness ("good works," 5:25) can be hidden: they *will* become evident. At any event, Timothy was to exercise preventive care in the appointment of church leaders; prudence and caution are advised, lest he share the blame for poor choices (5:22a).[15] Of course, he had already been warned not to endorse new converts as elders (3:6), or install untested candidates as deacons (3:10). "If Timothy keeps people in office who are sinning (5:20) or does not pay attention to the moral quality of those on the board, then Paul implies that he colludes in the corruption of the institution," not to mention the deleterious "modeling" effect upon the congregation by condoning sin.[16] Leaders must also be careful in their investigations of potential elder candidates so as not to overlook good works that may not be very public.

Amidst this brouhaha, Timothy is urged to keep his own hands clean, maintaining his purity (5:22b; also see 4:12; 5:2). The logic of introducing 5:23 and Timothy's drinking habits (or lack thereof) into this discussion regarding elders is unclear. Perhaps the exhortation in 5:22b, that Timothy keep himself pure, sparked in Paul's mind some of the ascetic practices of those mentioned in 4:1–3. Were those false teachers also calling for abstention from alcohol in addition to certain foods? Towner notes that "'water drinking' was often indicative of asceticism" (Dan 1:12; Epictetus, *Discourses* 3.13.21; *Pirqe Abot* 6.4), a practice perhaps followed by the Ephesian false teachers.[17]

> Inasmuch as medicine and philosophy were closely related in antiquity, we should not be surprised to see a bit of medical advice tossed into a section of moral exhortation. If we understand Timothy's abstinence as an exercise in purity, then we can see that his drinking "a little wine," including drinking for

---

14. Fuller, "Of Elders and Triads," 262.

15. For laying on of hands indicating bestowal of the Holy Spirit and/or his gift(s), see Acts 8:17–19; 19:6; 1 Tim 4:14; 2 Tim 1:6. The process was linked to ordination, as seen in Hippolytus, *Apostolic Tradition* 2.1–4 (also see Acts 6:6; 13:3).

16. Johnson, *First and Second Letters to Timothy*, 281.

17. Towner, *Letters to Timothy and Titus*, 376.

medicinal purposes, could also function as part of his own exemplary behavior, in this case demonstrating appropriate use of wine. By his exemplary behavior, the youthful Timothy gains credibility in his administration of his duties toward older men.[18]

However, none of this is certain, so our speculations about Paul's reasons in penning 5:23 remain just that. In any case, the personal comment is to assure Timothy that purity does not exclude alcohol for issues of health. This was, apparently, standard medical advice of the day: Plutarch, *Advice About Keeping Well* 19, declared that "wine is the most beneficial of beverages."[19] Drunkenness, on the other hand, was *verboten*: what is prescribed in our text is οἶνος ὀλίγος (*oinos oligos*, "little wine," 1 Tim 5:23), as opposed to the proscription of οἶνος πολύς (*oinos polys*, "much wine," 3:8; Titus 2:3); in fact, both Timothy and Titus were warned against elder candidates who were susceptible to addiction to the libation (πάροινος, *paroinos*, in 1 Tim 3:3; Titus 1:7).

In sum, this pericope demonstrates how the treatment of elders in office forged a paradigm for the church's guard of its holiness.

SERMON MAPS

THEOLOGICAL FOCUS OF PERICOPE 8 FOR PREACHING

8   God's leaders who demonstrate godliness in their ministries, particularly with regard to Scripture, are to be amply rewarded, and impartially disciplined when they do not (5:17–25).

The idea of modeling shows up again, as it did in Pericope 5: 1 Tim 3:1–16 and Pericope 6: 1 Tim 4:1–16. That is understandable since this current pericope deals with leaders, as did 1 Tim 3:1–16. It is best to have a sermon on this text deal with discipline for non-godliness; after all, the treatment of God's leaders (and this goes beyond those in office) is paradigmatic of the church's defense of its holiness and maintenance of its irreproachability. Such a sermon may also need to spend some time on the particular congregation's criteria and processes for church discipline.

Possible Preaching Maps for Pericope 8

I. Dereliction[20]
    Ungodliness among leaders and among God's people
    Move-to-Relevance: Specific instances (positive or negative)
II. Discipline

18. Hutson, "'Little Wine,'" 91.

19. Plutarch, *Moralia*, 2:265. Also see Hippocrates, *On Ancient Medicine* 13; Dioscorides, *De Materia Medica* 5.7.1; Celsus, *On Medicine* 1.8.1–2; Pliny the Elder, *Natural History* 23:22; b. Berakhot 51a; b. Baba Batra 58b; etc.

20. This first move is the background for this pericope. No text curation is necessary (or possible), except to point out that the pericope points fingers at sinning elders. It is best to consider the importance of godliness among leaders of the divine household in this move, with some specific instances perhaps (positive or negative; local or otherwise) in the move-to-relevance. Briefly referring back to Pericope 5: 1 Tim 3:1–16 is also appropriate.

1 TIMOTHY

> Disincentives for ungodliness: discipline (5:19–20)
> Importance of church discipline: maintenance of holiness (5:21–25)
> Move-to-Relevance: The process of church discipline[21]
> III. *Celebrate Godliness!*
> Incentives for godliness: double honor (5:17–18)[22]
> Specifics on how the local body, as well as individuals, can honor godliness.

With more focus on the corporate care of the needy this outline may be tweaked to produce another:

I. Ungodliness
> Ungodliness among leaders and among God's people
> Disincentives for ungodliness: discipline (5:19–20)
> Importance of church discipline: maintenance of holiness (5:21–25)
> Move-to-Relevance: The process of church discipline

II. Godliness
> Incentives for godliness: double honor (5:17–18)
> Move-to-Relevance: Specific instances (positive)

III. *Celebrate Godliness!*
> Specifics on how the local body, as well as individuals, can honor godliness.

---

21. It may be appropriate to briefly discuss the types of sin that call for public discipline, and the private confrontation of a rebellious sinner prior to taking public action (Matt 18:15–20), though care must be taken not to overdo these items.

22. As a general rule, I avoid bringing in text into the application move; I prefer to restrict that move to telling-and-showing how application should be done (see Kuruvilla, *Manual for Preaching*, 57–86).

PERICOPE 9

Bestowal of Service

1 Timothy 6:1–2

[Slaves Benefit Masters; Believers Serve One Another]

REVIEW, SUMMARY, PREVIEW

Review of Pericope 8: The eighth pericope (1 Tim 5:17–25) dealt with leaders who were discharging their responsibilities creditably (they were worthy of honor), as well with those who were sinning (they were to be disciplined). Such incentives for godliness and disincentives for ungodliness are integral to the church's defense of its holiness. The appointment of leaders is therefore undertaken carefully.

Summary of Pericope 9: This pericope (1 Tim 6:1–2) considers the responsibility of believing slaves to their masters: they honor them, and bestow service upon them, so that God's name and the teaching of the church is not brought into repute. If even slaves can be benefactors to their masters, then all believers should render such honor and service to one another in the divine household of God.

Preview of Pericope 10: The next pericope (1 Tim 6:3–21) tackles the broader issue of contentment with the basic necessities of life and the tendencies of false teachers to yearn for wealth (and the resulting calamities they suffer). Instead, truth teachers, satisfied with what God has given, follow the model of Christ, growing in godliness by being generous (thus guaranteeing for themselves eternal rewards).

1 TIMOTHY

9   1 Timothy 6:1–2

THEOLOGICAL FOCUS OF PERICOPE 9

9   The service of believing slaves towards their masters—fellow believers and beloved—a benefaction bestowed by the former upon the latter, is paradigmatic of selflessness and godliness in the divine household, as believers serve one another with good works, an undertaking that doxologizes rather than disparages the reputation of God (6:1–2).

OVERVIEW

As was noted in Pericope 7: 1 Tim 5:1–16, "honor" is found in 5:3, 17, and 6:1, giving rise to three sections dealing with the treatment of widows (5:3–16), of elders (5:17–25), and masters (by slaves) (6:1–2). Similarities between the preceding pericope (Pericope 8: 1 Tim 5:17–25) and the current one, 6:1–2, include: "honor" (5:17 and 6:1); "worthy" (5:17 and 6:1); "teaching" (5:17 and 6:1); both 5:17 and 6:1 begin with nominative plurals labeling the particular group in consideration ("the elders ruling well" and "all who are under the yoke as slaves"). As well, a number of imperatives make up the finite verbs in 5:17–25 (seven out of ten) and in 6:1–2 (eight out of ten).[1] The repetition of παρακαλέω in 5:1 and 6:2 bookends this larger section, 5:1—6:2, that concludes with ταῦτα δίδασκε καὶ παρακάλει (*tauta didaske kai parakalei*, "these things teach and urge," 6:2). A similar injunction, ταῦτα λάλει καὶ παρακάλει, *tauta lalei kai parakalei*, "these things speak and urge," in Titus 2:15, concludes another larger section (Titus 2:1–15) that, like 1 Tim 5:1—6:2, contains exhortations dealing with older men, younger men, older women, younger women, and slaves.

Excursus on Slavery[2]

Though legally Roman law distinguished between slaves and the free in terms of power, in practice such distinctions were not sharp, and a smooth gradation of status existed between the two categories. For example, "slaves of Greek owners could own property, including their own slaves, and could obtain permission to take other employment in addition to their duties as slaves. . . . [I]n general slaves were treated reasonably well, if only because their masters recognized that this was the way to get the best out of them."[3] The institution of slavery was a fixture of Mediterranean economic life, part and parcel of the labor structure of that day, and often entered into voluntarily by slaves in exchange for the economic and social security that they would receive. Besides, "the change of legal status out of enslavement into liberty, by way of manumission, was as constant and as easy in Greco-Roman life as the reverse transition over the short passage from individual freedom of action into the constraints of nonfreedom; and the methods employed for making either transition were many."[4] That is quite unlike modern slavery in many parts of the world where movement from freedom to slavery is usually involuntary, and that from slavery to freedom almost impossible. In ancient days, "many slaves had talents and skills useful to their owners; they

---

1. Van Neste, *Cohesion and Structure*, 97.
2. This section is modified from Kuruvilla, *Ephesians*, 192–95.
3. Lincoln, *Ephesians*, 416–17.
4. Westermann, "Between Slavery and Freedom," 215.

might work at some craft in a business; while in larger households some did the 'dirty' work, others found openings as musicians, medical advisers, educators, stewards, mistresses, companions of the elderly. Sometimes owners hired them out to work for others and were paid for their work."[5] It has been estimated by some that up to a third of the population of the Roman Empire were slaves.[6]

That is not to say that the ancient institution was not deplorable, or that it needed no change. The reality was that slaves were looked upon as economic instruments, to satisfy the selfish desires of their masters. Aristotle noted that there is no need to consider justice in the relationship "between a craftsman and his tool, between the soul and body, or between master and slave"—"there can be no friendship, nor justice, towards inanimate things; indeed not even towards a horse or an ox, nor yet towards a slave as slave. For master and slave have nothing in common: a slave is a living tool, just as a tool is an inanimate slave" (*Nicomachean Ethics* 8.11.7).[7] He did not think the use of slaves and of animals very different: "bodily service for the necessities of life is forthcoming from both, from slaves and from domestic animals alike" (*Politics* 1.2.14).[8]

But this was not uniformly the case in Greco-Roman society. The first-century Stoic philosopher Seneca the Younger was far more humanitarian in his recommendations, as seen in a letter to a protégé (but intended for broader readership; *Epistle* 47.1, 10, 11, 13):

> I am glad to learn . . . that you live on friendly terms with your slaves. This befits a sensible and well-educated man like yourself. "They are slaves," people declare. Nay, rather they are men. "Slaves!" No, comrades. "Slaves!" No, they are unpretentious friends. "Slaves!" No, they are our fellow-slaves, if one reflects that Fortune has equal rights over slaves and free men alike. . . . Kindly remember that he whom you call your slave sprang from the same stock, is smiled upon by the same skies, and on equal terms with yourself breathes, lives, and dies. . . . This is the kernel of my advice: Treat your inferiors as you would be treated by your betters. . . . Associate with your slave on kindly, even on affable, terms; let him talk with you, plan with you, live with you.[9]

Likewise, Cicero, the first-century-BCE statesman, philosopher, and rhetorician (*On Duties* 1.13.41): "But let us remember that we must have regard for justice even towards the humblest. Now the humblest station and the poorest fortune are those of slaves; and they give us no bad rule who bid us treat our slaves as we should our employees: they must be required to work; they must be given their dues."[10]

For the most part, Hellenistic Judaism concurred: masters were not to abuse slaves. Philo (*On the Decalogue* 167) discusses various Mosaic commandments, including those "to servants on rendering an affectionate loyalty to their masters [φιλοδέσποτον, *philodespoton*], to masters on showing the gentleness and kindness by which inequality is equalized."[11]

---

5. Best, *Ephesians*, 574.

6. Scheidel, "Human Mobility in Roman Italy, I," 9; also see Scheidel, "Human Mobility in Roman Italy, II," 64-71.

7. Aristotle, *Nicomachean Ethics*, 497.

8. Aristotle, *Politics*, 23.

9. Seneca, *Epistles*, 1:301, 303, 307, 309.

10. Cicero, *On Duties*, 45.

11. Philo, *On the Decalogue*, 88-89. Also see Philo, *Special Laws* 2.66-68, 89-91; 3.137-43;

So while there is no direct condemnation of slavery in this pericope (1 Tim 6:1–2), or elsewhere in the NT (1 Cor 7:20–24; Eph 6:5–9; Col 3:22—4:1; Titus 2:9–10; Phlm 10–21; 1 Pet 2:18–25), one gets the sense that what is being exhorted of believing slaves, especially if their masters are also believers, erodes the "function" (the traditional conduct of slaves and masters) that makes the "form" (the very institution of slavery) harder to sustain. This is particularly true in those NT texts where the role of masters is also delineated (Eph 6:9; Col 4:1): the level of mutual respect between the two parties and the reciprocity of actions exhorted chip away at traditional and oppressive understandings of slavery. Hoehner declares: "The abolition of slavery is a modern phenomenon. Certainly Paul and the early Christian church did not advocate the abolition of slavery as an institution. Christianity's emphasis has always been on the transformation of individuals who will in turn influence society, not the transformation of society which will then transform individuals (1 Cor 1:18—2:16)."[12] And here in 1 Tim 6:1–2, the goal of the Pauline exhortation to slaves is clear: "so that the name of God and the teaching may not be blasphemed" (6:1). But I note, *pace* Hoehner, that the abolition of slavery—or at least attempts at abolition—are *not* modern. One of the first references in Christian literature—indeed, perhaps in *all* literature—calling for the abolition of slavery comes from Gregory of Nyssa in the fourth century CE (*Homilies on Ecclesiastes* 4 [on Eccl 2:7]):

> You condemn a human to slavery, whose nature is free and self-determining, and you legislate in competition with God, overturning his law for the human species. The one made on the specific terms that he should be the owner of the earth, and appointed to rulership by the Creator—him you bring under the yoke of slavery, as though defying and fighting against the divine decree. You have forgotten the limits of authority, and that your rule is confined to dominion over unreasoning animals. For it says *Let them rule over winged creatures and fishes and four-footed things and creeping things* [Gen 1:26]. Why do you go beyond what is enslaved to you and raise yourself up against the free species, counting your own kind [on a level] with four-footed things and even footless things? . . . I see no superiority over the subordinate accruing to you from the title [of master, δεσπότης, *despotēs*] other than the mere title. What does this power contribute to you as a person? Not longevity, nor beauty, nor good health, nor advantage in virtue. Your origin is from the same ancestors, your life is similar, sufferings of soul and body prevail alike over you who lord over [from κυριεύω, *kyrieuō*] and over the one who is under the yoke of your lordship—pains and pleasures, merriment and distress, sorrows and delights, rages and terrors, sickness and death. Is there any difference in these things between the slave and the lord? Do they not draw in the same air as they breathe? Do they not see the sun in the same way? Do they not alike sustain their nature by consuming food? Is not the arrangement of their guts the same? Are not the two one dust after death? Is there not one judgment [for all]—a common Kingdom, and a common Gehenna? If, then, you are equal in all these ways, therefore, in what respect have you some superiority, tell me, so that you, being human, think yourself the master of a human being, and say, *I got me slaves and slave-girls* [Eccl 2:7], like herds of goats or pigs?[13]

Pseudo-Phocylides, *Sentences* 223–27; and Sir 7:20, 21; 33:31.

12. Hoehner, *Ephesians*, 804.

13. Translation modified from Hall and Moriarty, "Gregory, Bishop of Nyssa," 73–75. My modification

So perhaps it is not surprising—though it is certainly countercultural—that slaves are appealed to here in 1 Tim 6:1-2 (and elsewhere in the NT) as those with the same standing in the body of Christ and before God as their owners had (1 Tim 6:2 calls masters and slaves "brothers"; in Phlm 7, 16, 20, both master and slave are called "brother"). Indeed, that slaves are directly addressed is remarkable, for it assumes at least some degree of self-determination, considering these workers capable of exercising volition to obey Paul's exhortations. As even the secular Seneca declared (*De Beneficiis* 3.18), "The path of virtue is closed to no one, it lies open to all; it admits and invites all, whether they be free-born men, slaves or freed-men, kings or exiles; it requires no qualifications of family or of property, it is satisfied with a mere man."[14] Here in Pericope 9: 1 Tim 6:1-2, slaves are asked to exercise their volition in order to submit; masters are never to demand such submission from them.[15] Such attitudes and behaviors of slaves were part of what it meant to do "good works" (usually ἔργα ἀγαθά or καλά ἔργα in the PE, but εὐεργεσία, *euergesia*, here in 1 Tim 6:1[16])—the mark of godliness.

Of note, some of these slaves might even have been leaders in the church. Pliny the Younger (61-113 CE), in a letter to the Emperor Trajan (*Epistle* 10.97.8), wrote of torturing two Christian female slaves who, he noted, were called "deaconesses" (from the Latin *ministra*, which is synonymous with *diāconus*, "deacon").[17] The PE, of course, do not list freedom as a qualification for holding church office. And while some domestic household hierarchies are carried over into the divine household, the slave–master ordering is not one of them. Besides, for the institution of marriage and conduct within domestic and divine households, God's creation order and hierarchy are appealed to, even in this very epistle in 1 Tim 2:9-15; 5:14-15 (also in the PE in Titus 2:3-5). And for the framework of relationships between parents and children, the Decalogue is cited in support (e.g., Eph 6:1-4). However, for slavery, no such appeal to creation order or divine mandate is adduced in any NT text; instead, if possible, slaves were to become free (1 Cor 7:21) and masters were to free slaves (Phlm 10-21). The issue in the NT for slaves (and masters) is always focused on godly conduct, and that is the case in 1 Tim 6:1-2 as well.[18]

> [Paul] has consistently expressed his desire that households respect the socially defined subordination of ranks. His administrative criterion for supervisors [elders] and deacons, we recall, is that they can manage children of their own household, keeping them in subordination (3:4, 12). His expectation of women is that they marry, govern their households, have children, and raise them in the faith (2:15; 5:14). Children are to care for their parents as an expression of godliness (5:4). The apostle's concern for the stability and order of households derives from both his appreciation of the Hellenistic *oikos* as part of the *oikonomia theou*

---

of this translation was based on Greek text of Gregory's homily from *Thesaurus Linguae Graecae* Digital Library (ed. Maria C. Pantelia; University of California, Irvine; http://www.tlg.uci.edu), 335.5-17; 337.19—338.17.

14. Seneca, *Moral Essays*, 3:161.

15. Indeed, the forcible abduction and trade of slaves would fall under the category of kidnapping, proscribed in no uncertain terms in 1 Tim 1:10.

16. "Good works" (ἔργα ἀγαθά) in the PE is found in 1 Tim 2:10; 5:10, 25; 2 Tim 2:21; 3:17; Titus 1:16; 2:7, 14; 3:1, 8, 14; καλά ἔργα is used in 1 Tim 3:1; 6:18b; and ἀγαθοεργέω, *agathoergeō*, in 6:18a.

17. Pliny the Younger, *Letters*, 2:289.

18. See Knight, *Pastoral Epistles*, 242.

1 TIMOTHY

> (1:4).... Without challenging the structure of the social system, Paul's language creates the possibility of envisaging the sort of reciprocity between master and slave that was at the heart of ancient *koinonia*.... Indeed, it is possible that the subtle use of language in 1 Tim 6:1–2a might well be more liberating, in the final analysis, than Paul's clever diplomacy in Philemon.[19]

Thus, relationships in the body of Christ are to demonstrate exemplary and irreproachable behavior, godliness marked by service one to another, that transcends that seen in similar institutions of secular society.

All that to say, slavery in the Greco-Roman times was not what modern-day slavery is. And with that in mind, the closest analogy to this ancient situation in our times is the employer–employee relationship, though there are significant differences, of course. In any case, this is the best focus of application for a sermon on this pericope (see below).

9 1 Timothy 6:1–2

THEOLOGICAL FOCUS 9

9   The service of believing slaves towards their masters—fellow believers and beloved—a benefaction bestowed by the former upon the latter, is paradigmatic of selflessness and godliness in the divine household, as believers serve one another with good works, an undertaking that doxologizes rather than disparages the reputation of God (6:1–2).

TRANSLATION 9

6:1   *All who are under the yoke as slaves are to consider their own masters as worthy of all honor, so that the name of God and the teaching may not be blasphemed.*

6:2   *And those who have believers as their masters must not disdain them, for they are brothers, but must serve them even more, because those who benefit from the good work are believers and beloved. These things teach and urge.*

NOTES 9

9   *The service of slaves towards their masters—fellow believers and beloved—a benefaction bestowed by the former upon the latter, is paradigmatic of selflessness and godliness in the divine household, as believers serve one another with good works, an undertaking that doxologizes rather than disparages the reputation of God (6:1–2).*

It is likely that since the behavior of masters is not addressed here in 1 Tim 6:1–2, these latter belonged to an older generation, bringing the discussion into line with the exhortations of 5:1–2 on dealing with the elderly: thus, this text on slaves and masters continues what was instructed there—the treatment of older men (here, masters).

In 6:2, it appears that that situation is of believing slaves working for believing masters; therefore, it seems that 6:1 deals with the case of believing slaves working for unbelieving masters. In the latter case, godly behavior that honors masters is called for "so that the

---

19. Johnson, *Letters to Timothy and Titus*, 290.

name of God and the teaching may not be blasphemed" (6:1). "The ever-present concern to evangelize these masters and not to set their minds against Christianity had to be taken into consideration by those Christians who were nearest to them"—these slaves were perhaps the only believers seen by these non-Christians.[20] Of course, a missiological concern is prevalent all throughout the PE and underlies many of its exhortations: 1 Tim 2:1-6; 3:7, 10; 4:10; 5:8, 14; 6:1; 2 Tim 2:8-10, 25-26; Titus 1:6; 2:8-10; 3:1-2, 8.

"Honor" in 1 Tim 6:1 cannot mean financial compensation as it does in 5:3 and 5:17; here it simply counters the "disdain" in 6:2. "*All* honor" (πᾶς τιμή, *pas timē*, 6:1) has the scope of "in *everything*" (ἐν πᾶσιν, *en pasin*) of the similar exhortation to slaves in Titus 2:10. And to "*consider* their own masters worthy of all honor" is to make a deliberate positive evaluation of masters, akin to the call to respect civil authorities and rulers, irrespective of whether such powers were intrinsically or essentially worthy (Rom 13:1-7; Titus 3:1; 1 Pet 2:13-17).

Personal freedom is apparently less of an important matter than the reputation of "the name of God and the teaching."[21] That "teaching" is involved reminds us that "the social tension being created by slaves might wrongly be attributed to the gospel by the unbelieving slave owners, or by outsiders observing the church through critical eyes."[22] In God's economy and in the divine household, the spiritual status of slave is no different from that of one who is free; in essence, in ontology, they stand equal before God (1 Cor 12:13; Gal 3:28; Col 3:11; Rev 13:16). But equality in Christian essence does not obviate the responsibility of attending to one's duties within a social hierarchy (again, the abuses that may have occurred in these relationships are not the express concern of the PE). "The success of the gospel is more significant than the lot of any one individual, and therefore slaves should behave in a way that does not bring reproach on the gospel."[23]

On the other hand, in the instance where both slave and master are believers, the former are to consider the latter as "beloved" (6:2)—either beloved by God (Rom 1:7; 11:28), or beloved by the slaves themselves (as, for e.g., in Exod 21:5; Deut 15:16). In either case, it behooves slaves (δοῦλοι, *douloi*) to "serve [δουλεύω, *douleuō*] them even more" (6:2)! As Chrysostom observed: "So do not suppose, because thou art a believer, that thou art therefore a free man: since thy freedom is to serve the more faithfully" (*Homilies on First Timothy* 16).[24]

The phrase οἱ τῆς εὐεργεσίας ἀντιλαμβανόμενοι, *hoi tēs euergesias antilambanomenoi*, "those who benefit from the good work" (6:2), likely points to (believing) masters who are recipients of the service (εὐεργεσία, "good work") of slaves, their fellow believers. This is quite a surprising statement, for it is usually the person higher in the hierarchy and the one in authority who is considered a benefactor (for εὐεργεσία relating to God, see Ps 77:11 LXX; Acts 4:9; 10:38; 2 Macc 6:13; and relating to rulers, see Luke 22:25; 2 Macc 9:26). "It is startling to see *euergesia* applied to any deed done by someone lower on the social scale for someone higher, most of all when it is a matter of a slave serving a master."[25] Thus

---

20. Knight, *Pastoral Epistles*, 243.
21. This, of course, is not an excuse for, or an approval of, the abuses of slavery.
22. Towner, *Letters to Timothy and Titus*, 382.
23. Mounce, *Pastoral Epistles*, 327.
24. *Nicene and Post-Nicene Fathers* 13:465.
25. Johnson, *Letters to Timothy and Titus*, 284-85. The verb ἀντιλαμβάνομαι, *antilambanomai*, can mean either "give" or "receive" a benefit; conceivably the phrase could be about slaves *receiving* benefits from their masters. In that case, the masters are to be beloved by their slaves for what benefits the former

Paul has, against the contemporary grain, depicted the unusual role of a slave as one who confers benefits upon, and does good works for, another—in this case for the slave's master, a fellow believer and a beloved one. This is nothing but a "stunning reversal" that makes slaves benefactors of their masters, and their services "rendered from a position of strength, nobility, and honor."[26] Slaves are being portrayed as equal, if not superior, to their masters.

> Paul has turned the tables. The slaves serve, but in God's surprising *oikonomia* they do so from a position of power; nobility and honor, the rewards of benefaction, are accorded here implicitly to the slaves. In all of this, the privileges of honor which that culture reserved for well-to-do patrons, benefactors, and slave owners are not denied; nor are the obligations of slaves to their masters trivialized. But the meaning and value of life lived at that level are relativized by the more fundamental reality of the universal Lordship of Christ within God's *oikonomia*.[27]

It might be worth noting Jesus's own words in Luke 22:25–27: "The kings of the gentiles lord over them, and those in authority over them are called 'benefactors' [εὐεργέται, *euergetai*, related to εὐεργεσία in 1 Tim 6:2]. But not so with you; instead the one who is the greatest among you must become as the youngest, and the leader as the servant.... I am among you—I am as the one who serves." This is essentially "to redefine genuine beneficent action in terms of an attitude of humility and its product—genuine service."[28] This notion of slaves benefitting their masters, though no doubt unusual, was not entirely absent in Greco-Roman culture. Seneca actually expounded on this at considerable length in *De Beneficiis* 18.2, 4; 19.1:

> He who denies that a slave can sometimes give a benefit [*beneficium*[29]] to his master is ignorant of the rights of man; for, not the status, but the intention, of the one who bestows is what counts. Virtue closes the door to no man; it is open to all, admits all, invites all, the freeborn and the freedman, the slave and the king.... A man can give a benefit to his king, a man can give a benefit to his general; therefore a slave also can give one to a master. It is possible for a slave to be just, it is possible for him to be brave, it is possible for him to be magnanimous; therefore it is possible also for him to give a benefit, for this also is one part of virtue.... There is no doubt that a slave is able to give a benefit to anyone he pleases; why not, therefore, also to his master?[30]

It is not the call of duty, but what is done over and above duty that converts duty/service into a benefit—which, of course, is exactly what Paul calls slaves to do: "serve them even more" (1 Tim 6:2). Here's Seneca again (*De Beneficiis* 21:1–2; 22:1–2):

> There are certain acts that the law neither enjoins nor forbids; it is in these that a slave finds opportunity to perform a benefit. So long as what he supplies is only that which is ordinarily required of a slave, it is a "service"; when he supplies more than a slave need do, it is a "benefit"; it ceases to be called a service when it passes

---

may extend to the latter. But this reading makes less sense contextually and renders the motivation of slaves' service to their benefactors somewhat suspect.

26. Köstenberger, *Commentary on 1–2 Timothy and Titus*, 179–80.
27. Towner, *Letters to Timothy and Titus*, 390.
28. Towner, *Letters to Timothy and Titus*, 388.
29. Lewis et al., "*Beneficium*," 231, lists εὐεργέτημα, *euergetēma*, as a synonym.
30. Seneca, *Moral Essays*, 3:161, 163.

over into the domain of friendly affection [*amici*]. . . . All that he does in excess of what is prescribed as the duty of a slave, what he supplies, not from obedience to authority, but from his own desire, will be a benefit. . . . When he [the slave] exceeds the bounds of his station in goodwill toward his master, and surpasses the expectation of his master by daring some lofty deed that would be an honour even to those more happily born, a benefit is found to exist inside the household.[31]

Notice that Seneca labels such acts of service/benefit as falling into "the domain of friendly affection"; the word *amici* can also indicate "love," paralleling Paul's nomenclature of masters as "beloved."

Even if one agrees that 1 Tim 6:1–2 fits the larger section of 5:1—6:2 that deals with particular relationships in the divine household, one wonders why the slave-master relationship—and it is one-sided here, since masters are not addressed—shows up in an epistle to Timothy majoring on pastoral issues. The reason must be that selfless service is of the essence in the community of believers in the οἶκος θεοῦ. And by pointing out that even slaves benefit their masters with good works, Paul makes an argument from that extreme to a norm. If slaves can thus be benefactors, how much more can others, free men and women, be benefactors serving one another in the body of Christ with good works?

Serving one's fellow believers—no matter what one's position in social hierarchies, no matter what the degree of authority being wielded (or lack thereof)—is equivalent to being a benefactor to them: the inferior (in whatever way) becomes a conduit of benefit to the superior via good works! And to masters there is a strong hint: "Just as the slave views his master as a fellow Christian and works all the more, so also the master must realize that the slave is not ultimately a slave but a fellow Christian whose labors are acts of kindness," good works in the model of all the other good works recommended in the PE.[32] In effect, then, Paul's exhortations here subvert the traditional order quite acutely, especially as he reverses the language of honor and shame: slavery as a good works-benefaction upon masters! If this was the case for slaves and masters—"believers," "brethren," and "beloved"—surely any kind of good works could be considered a benefaction of server upon "servee" in any arena within the local community of God's people, the divine household. In fact, Paul is asserting that such good works of benefaction are an honor and a privilege to engage in. And thereby, "the name of God and teaching" are not disparaged but doxologized. "These things," Paul exhorts Timothy, he is to "teach and urge" (6:2),[33] critical as they are for the proper functioning of the divine household.

SERMON MAPS

THEOLOGICAL FOCUS OF PERICOPE 9 FOR PREACHING

9 The service of believing slaves towards their masters, a benefaction bestowed by the former upon the latter, is paradigmatic of selflessness and godliness in the divine household, as believers serve one another with good works, thus enhancing the reputation of God (6:1–2).

---

31. Seneca, *Moral Essays*, 3:165, 167.
32. Mounce, *Pastoral Epistles*, 328.
33. Generally, in 1 Timothy, "these things" point backward to what has just been said: 3:14; 4:6, 11, 15; 5:7, 21; 6:2, 11.

1 TIMOTHY

In Pericope 7: 1 Tim 5:1–16, we saw godly care for the needy being addressed, focused upon the deserving ones, needy "indeed." Here the service is extended more generally to all believers, one to another.

In the first move-to-relevance in the maps below, I have suggested that a brief distinction be made between ancient and modern forms of slavery. This clarification is necessary, lest listeners, misunderstanding what Paul is advocating, get sidetracked and tune out the rest of the sermon. Also, I have focused one of the moves and the final application move on service to fellow believers; that, however, may be changed to service on behalf of outsiders, if there is a lack of that in the congregation. However, a better place for the latter application is in a sermon on Pericope 18: Titus 3:1–15.

Possible Preaching Maps for Pericope 9

   I. Slaves to Masters
      Honor (6:1)
      Benefaction (6:2)
      For the sake of God (6:1b)
      Move-to-Relevance: Slavery in Greco-Roman vs. modern times
  II. Believers to Believers[34]
      Honoring one another
      Serving one another
      For the glory of God
      Move-to-Relevance: Our failure to do so
 III. *Bestow Service!*
      Specifics on how the Christian can serve fellow believers

This map may be tweaked to produce another:

   I. Honor and Benefaction of others
      Slaves to masters (6:1a, 2)
      Move-to-Relevance: Slavery in Greco-Roman vs. modern times
      Believers to believers
  II. Brings glory to God
      Slaves to masters (6:1b)
      Believers to believers
      Move-to-Relevance: Our failure to do so
 III. *Bestow Service!*
      Specifics on how the Christian can serve fellow believers

---

34. Almost all of this move will find no explicit reference in the text. That is not a problem: Paul is simply arguing from the greater ("Even *slaves* benefit others!") to the lesser ("Well, then, so can we!").

PERICOPE 10

Giving to Get

1 Timothy 6:3–21

[Contentment; Godliness; Rewards]

REVIEW, SUMMARY[1]

Review of Pericope 9: The ninth pericope (1 Tim 6:1–2) considered the responsibility of believing slaves to their masters: they honor them, and bestow service upon them, so that God's name and the teaching of the church is not brought into disrepute. If slaves can be benefactors to their masters, then even believers should render such honor and service to one another in the divine household of God.

Summary of Pericope 10: This final pericope of 1 Timothy (1 Tim 6:3–21) tackles the broader issue of contentment with the basic necessities of life and the tendencies of false teachers to yearn for wealth (and its resulting calamities). On the other hand, truth teachers, content with what God has given, follow the model of Christ and grow in godliness by being generous, thus guaranteeing for themselves eternal reward.

---

1. Recognizing that 1 Timothy is a discrete Epistle, I will forego a "Preview" of the following pericope that commences 2 Timothy.

1 TIMOTHY

10   1 Timothy 6:3–21

> **THEOLOGICAL FOCUS OF PERICOPE 10**
>
> 10   The people of God are characterized by the relentless pursuit of godliness as modeled by Christ, marked by a God-dependent, humble contentment with basic needs and a richness of generosity that results in an amply rewarded eternity, while avoiding the desire for money that results in dangerous ruin (6:3–21).
>
>   10.1   Humble contentment with basic needs is a mark of godliness, resulting in great gain, whereas the desire for money leads to harmful lusts, much evil, and abandonment of the faith, culminating in dangerous ruin (6:3–10).
>
>   10.2   The people of God are characterized by the relentless pursuit of godliness as modeled by Christ, marked by God-dependence and a richness of generosity that results in an amply rewarded eternity (6:11–21).

OVERVIEW

Generally, "these things" in 1 Timothy points backwards to what preceded such a summary: 3:14; 4:6, 11, 15; 5:7, 21; 6:2, 11. Hence the inclusion of 6:2b ("teach and urge these things") with Pericope 9: 1 Tim 6:1–2. However, 6:2b is also linked to 6:3 to contrast what Paul asked Timothy to teach and preach ("these things") with what the false teachers were proclaiming (6:3). In opposition to ταῦτα δίδασκε in 6:2b ("these things teach"), we see ἑτεροδιδασκαλέω in 6:3a ("teach falsely"). The character and motivations of those propounding heterodoxy takes up most of this pericope, with a central exhortation to Timothy to persevere[2]:

> **A**   Heterodox teaching (6:3–5)
>   **B**   Wealth (6:6–10: contentment [6:6–8] *vs.* discontentment [6:9–10])
>   **C**   Flee, pursue, fight, take hold, keep the commandment (6:11–16)
>   **B'**   Wealth (6:17–19: wrong attitude [6:17a] *vs.* right attitude [6:17b–19])
> **A'**   Heterodox teaching (6:20–21)

10.1   1 Timothy 6:3–10

> **THEOLOGICAL FOCUS 10.1**
>
>   10.1   Humble contentment with basic needs is a mark of godliness, resulting in great gain, whereas the desire for money leads to harmful lusts, much evil, and abandonment of the faith, culminating in dangerous ruin (6:3–10).

TRANSLATION 10.1

6:3   *If anyone teaches falsely and does not agree with sound words, those of our Lord Jesus Christ, and with the teaching that is according to godliness,*

---

2. Modified from Gourgues, "Jesus's Testimony," 641.

6:4   *he is conceited, understands nothing, but has a morbid craving for controversies and word-quarrels, out of which come envy, strife, blasphemies, evil conjectures,*

6:5   *constant friction among people who have been depraved of mind and deprived of truth, presuming godliness to be a means of gain.*

6:6   *But it is a means of great gain—godliness with contentment.*

6:7   *For we have brought nothing into the world, so we are not able to take anything out either;*

6:8   *and having sustenance and shelter, with these we shall be content.*

6:9   *But those who want to be rich fall into temptation and a snare and [into] many foolish and harmful lusts that plunge people into ruin and destruction.*

6:10 *For a root of all evil is the love of money, longing for which some have wandered away from the faith and have pierced themselves with many pains.*

NOTES 10.1

10.1 *Humble contentment with basic needs is a mark of godliness, resulting in great gain, whereas the desire for money leads to harmful lusts, much evil, and abandonment of the faith, culminating in dangerous ruin (6:3–10).*

While 6:3 does link to 6:2b, it also connects with 6:4 in the positive/negative contrasts it makes between ἑτεροδιδασκαλέω and κατ' εὐσέβειαν διδασκαλία (*kat' eusebeian didaskalia*, "teaching that is according to godliness," 6:3), and between ὑγιαίνοντες λόγοι (*hygiainontes logoi*, "sound words," 6:3) and λογομαχία (*logomachia*, "word-quarrels," 6:4): thus, heterodoxy *vs.* orthodoxy, word-quarrels *vs.* sound words. In fact, Paul is returning to an issue with which he had commenced this Epistle: ἑτεροδιδασκαλέω shows up only here in 6:3 and in 1:3; likewise, ὑγιαίνοντες λόγοι is found in 6:3, and ὑγιαινούσα διδασκαλία in 1:10, the only two instances of ὑγιαίνω, *hygiainō*, "to be sound," in 1 Timothy. But excoriation of falsehood and its advocates is not all that Paul is about here: εὐσέβεια, *eusebeia*, "godliness," is repeated in 6:3, 5, 6, and 11, emphasizing that doctrine is never divorced from practicality, but is thoroughly integrated with it: "teaching that is according to godliness" (6:3), teaching that is expected to result in godliness.[3]

The complicated sentence of 6:3–5 is unusually characterized by a cascade of doublets linked by conjunctions: "if anyone teaches falsely *and* does not agree with sound words" (6:3); "with sound words . . . *and* with the teaching that is according to godliness" (6:2–3); "understands nothing, *but* has a morbid craving" (6:4); "controversies *and* word-quarrels"(6:4); "depraved of mind *and* deprived of truth" (6:5).[4] Besides, the mounting complexity of the predicate as 6:4–5 progresses, including these doublets and those five asyndetic vices (in 6:4b–5a)—"five moral defects that affect human relationships and threaten unity"[5]—is a good indication that this list (like most, if not all, biblical lists) is rhetorical in intent, not

---

3. The noun εὐσέβεια and its cognates are found in the PE in 1 Tim 1:9; 2:2; 3:16; 4:7, 8; 5:4; 6:3, 5, 6, 11; 2 Tim 2:12, 16; 3:5.

4. The participles διεφθαρμένων, *diephtharmenōn*, "depraved," and ἀπεστερημένων, *apesterēmenōn*, "deprived," are in the perfect tense, suggesting "the established and seemingly permanent condition of the opponents' condition," resulting from past rejections of right teaching (Mounce, *Pastoral Epistles*, 338).

5. Towner, *Letters to Timothy and Titus*, 396.

1 TIMOTHY

offered by the chef to be sliced and diced into their individual components by consumers.[6] The sentence in 6:3–5 is intended to overwhelm readers with the character and motivation of these "heterodoxers": these conceited ones know nothing and are mercenary in intent. Completely ignorant and depraved, they think that godliness is a means to make money and "gain"—πορισμός, *porismos* (6:5–6). Instead what they fall into is "temptation"—πειρασμός, *peirasmos* (6:9).

One notices immediately that these purveyors of false teaching were demonstrating character traits that were prohibited in the church's leaders and, therefore, in the church's congregation. A leader was not to be "conceited" (from τυφόω, *typhoō*, 3:6; used here in 6:4, 17), but "irreproachable, . . . temperate, self-controlled, honorable" (3:2). Leaders are not to be those who "understand nothing" (6:4), but knowledgeable enough to be "able to teach" (3:3); they are not to be interested in controversies and disputes that generate all kinds of quarrels (6:4), and therefore are "not . . . pugnacious, but gentle, uncontentious" (3:3). These false teachers were also operating out of pecuniary motives, having a "love of money" (6:10); church leaders, on the other hand were explicitly required to be "free from the love of money" (3:3; also 3:8; Titus 1:7).[7]

No doubt there were believers in the Ephesian church who were "rich in the present world" (1 Tim 6:17), holding slaves (6:1–2), able to support widowed women in their families (5:4, 8, 16), and possessed of fancy clothing and jewelry (2:9). Perhaps all this flaunted wealth created allures for teachers, especially those already "depraved of mind" and "deprived of truth" (6:5). It is made clear in 6:9 that the problem was not the wealth of the false teachers; rather, it was their desire to *become* wealthy: they were wanting to be rich, afflicted as they were with "the love of money" (6:10). Thus, for the false teachers, religion had become a livelihood, not a life.[8] These wretched folks were trying to make godliness a business enterprise, ministry a mercenary undertaking, and, as a result, harboring "many foolish and harmful lusts that plunge people into ruin and destruction" (6:9). Indeed, some of these seekers of wealth had even "wandered away from the faith" in the process of sating their avaricious tendencies (6:10). "Acquisitiveness is the vice that never says 'enough.' . . . The deceptiveness is found in the claim of possessions to ensure life and security and worth; the danger lies in the fact that a life lived in pursuit of such false security can end up in utter destruction."[9]

The sentence in 6:10 begins with ῥίζα, *rhiza*; since it is inarticular, "a root" is the best reading. Thus "the love of money" is "a root of all evil"—a hyperbolic expression no doubt, but emphasizing the pervasive deceptiveness of the uncontrolled pursuit of wealth.[10] There was

---

6. Which also affirms that grammar is *never* the final arbiter of meaning; rather, what the author is *doing* is the ultimate referee. That is not to say grammar is irrelevant: it is just not the supreme judge of the *doings* of utterances, whether spoken or scripted, sacred or secular (for e.g., irony).

7. Or as the KJV puts the phrase in 1 Tim 3:8 with panache, "not greedy of filthy lucre!"

8. Modified from Quinn and Wacker, *First and Second Letters to Timothy*, 495.

9. Johnson, *First and Second Letters to Timothy*, 303. First Timothy 6:9a has a cascade of alliterative π's: οἱ δὲ βουλόμενοι πλουτεῖν ἐμπίπτουσιν εἰς πειρασμὸν καὶ παγίδα καὶ ἐπιθυμίας πολλάς (*oi de boulomenoi ploutein empiptousin eis peirasmon kai pagida kai epithymias pollas*). I took up the challenge and created this substitute: "Those who want possessions plummet into predispositions to evil and a pitfall and plenty of sinful propensities." Such rhetorical devices emphasize the dangers of discontentment. And there is yet another word play: πειρασμός and περιπείρω (*peripeirō*, "impale"; 6:10): the pain becomes a bane!

10. Witherington, *Letters and Homilies*, 287, suggests that "the love of money (not money itself) is *a* root, not *the* root, of every kind or all sorts of evil (not all evil)." While that is, no doubt, true, "of all evils"

precedent for Paul's sentiment. According to the third-century biographer, Diogenes Laertius (*Lives* 6.50), quoting the Cynic, Diogenes of Sinope, "The love of money [φιλαργυρίαν, *philargyrian* (also in 1 Tim 6:10)] he declared to be mother-city [μητρόπολιν, *mētropolin*] of all evils."[11] *Testament of Judah* 19:1, warned that "the love of money [φιλαργυρία] leads to idolatry," and noted that people are "led astray through money" causing them to "fall [ἐμπίπτω, *empiptō* (also in 1 Tim 6:9)] into madness."[12] Chrysostom (*Homilies on First Timothy* 17) put it well:

> For what evil is not caused by wealth, or rather not by wealth, but by the wicked will of those who know not how to use it? . . . What evils then does it not cause! What fraudulent practices, what robberies! What miseries, enmities, contentions, battles! . . . Do not they who are possessed by this passion violate the laws of nature, and the commandments of God? In short everything? . . . Take away therefore the love of money, and you put an end to war, to battle, to enmity, to strife and contention. . . . It is a plague that so seizes all, some more, some less, but all in a degree. Like a fire catching a wood, that desolates and destroys all around, this passion has laid waste the world.[13]

In light of the use of both ἐμπίπτω and παγίς in 1 Tim 3:7, where they referred to the snare of the devil that Paul wanted elders to avoid, it is likely that a similar demonic snare is also implied in 6:9—the same two words are repeated here (also see 2 Tim 2:26, where "snare" is again satanic). Yet, the greedy, we are told, "*have pierced themselves* with many a pang" (1 Tim 6:10).[14] So, while there are demonic temptations and satanic snares involved, the wound of these wealth-seekers is largely self-inflicted!

Countering such dangerous tendencies and to preclude such calamitous outcomes, Paul argues for "contentment" (6:6), based on the understanding that one comes into this world naked and departs from it equally bereft (6:7).[15] For the Greek philosophers αὐτάρκεια (*autarkeia*, 6:6; the verb ἀρκέω, *arkeō*, is found in 6:8[16]) meant self-sufficiency (see Plato, *Timaeus*, 33D), but for Paul it is *God*-sufficiency—the difference between conceit (6:4) and contentment that confesses one's own insufficiency but acknowledges an all-powerful and loving God's utter sufficiency for everything: security in God, not in self, or the self's possessions (6:8). Such a philosophy of contentment with simplicity was not entirely new in that age. In the first century CE, Epictetus (*Encheiridion* 33.7) recommended that one "take only as much as your bare need requires, I mean such things as food, drink, clothing, shelter, and

---

(πάντων τῶν κακῶν, *pantōn tōn kakōn*) does not easily lend itself to being read generically as "of every kind/all sorts of evil." For other warnings against riches in the NT, see Matt 6:25–34; 13:22 (and parallels); 19:16–30 (and parallels); Luke 1:53; 12:13–21; 16:14–15; Jas 1:10–11; 2:6–7; 5:3–5; Rev 3:17–18. And, likewise, in the OT: Pss 39:6; 49:6–10; 52:7; Prov 11:4, 16, 28; 23:4–5; Eccl 5:12–13.

11. *Lives of Eminent Philosophers*, 2:52–53.

12. *Patrologia Graeca* 2:1080 (my translation).

13. *Nicene and Post-Nicene Fathers* 13:469–70.

14. "Many . . . lusts" (6:9), "all evil," and "many pains" (6:10) are likely synonymous.

15. The theme of departing the world as one entered it was commonly employed in antiquity: Job 1:21; Eccl 5:15; Ps 49:17; Wis 7:6; Seneca, *Epistles* 102.24–25; etc. The bringing in and taking out in 1 Tim 6:7, εἰσφέρω and ἐκφέρω (*eispherō* and *ekpherō*), respectively, are derived from the same root verb.

16. That verb is what God used to declare to the apostle in 2 Cor 12:9: "My grace is sufficient [ἀρκέω] for you!"

1 TIMOTHY

household slaves; but cut down everything which is for outward show or luxury."[17] The call for godliness in this section recognizes God as ultimate gifter, God as total provider, and service unto this God as a powerful proclamation of these raw truths:

> Such simplicity is a dimension of freedom. . . . Embedded in this simple yet profoundly true observation are three theological corollaries. The first is that true "godliness" (*eusebeia*) must begin with precisely this recognition, that human existence is itself a gift from God that cannot in any significant fashion be improved by material possessions. The second is that the insensate pursuit of possessions is a flight from the truth of creation, which is that humans are at every moment dependent on the God who makes all things good and to be received with thanksgiving (4:3). The third is that to make religious profession itself a means of gaining wealth is a peculiarly twisted perversion of the proper order of creation and of the human relationship with God.[18]

Thus, in a real sense, godliness with contentment *is* in fact a means of great gain—*spiritual* gain (6:6). In 6:6, the verb begins the sentence in a position of emphasis: "*It is* a means of great gain—godliness with contentment." Notice the progression of tenses in 6:7–8 from aorist (εἰσηνέγκαμεν, *eisēnenkamen*, "we have brought nothing") to present (οὐδὲ . . . δυνάμεθα, *oude . . . dynametha*, "we are not able") to future (ἀρκεσθησόμεθα, *arkesthēsometha*, "we shall be content"). Thus the future has an imperative tone to its utterance, a call to be content. Contentment with basic needs leads to godliness, resulting in great gain (6:6–8); but the desire for money leads to harmful lusts, all kinds of evil, and a wandering away from the faith, resulting in ruin and destruction (6:9–10).

6:6–8	Contentment with basic needs	Godliness	Great gain
6:9–10	Love/longing for money	Temptation/lusts All evil Abandon faith	Ruin/destruction

Mounce is right: "The topic is not wealth but the love of wealth, the pursuit of wealth at all costs," and the dire consequences thereof.[19]

10.2 1 Timothy 6:11–21

THEOLOGICAL FOCUS 10.2

10.2 The people of God are characterized by the relentless pursuit of godliness as modeled by Christ, marked by God-dependence and a richness of generosity that results in an amply rewarded eternity (6:11–21).

---

17. Epictetus, *Discourses*, 519. Or in contemporary parlance, "Look for the Bare Necessities" (*The Jungle Book*, directed by Wolfgang Reitherman [1967; Burbank, CA: Walt Disney Pictures]) or, if you prefer, "*Hakuna Matata*" (*The Lion King*, directed by Roger Allers and Rob Minkoff [1994; Burbank, CA: Walt Disney Pictures]).

18. Johnson, *First and Second Letters to Timothy*, 304.

19. Mounce, *Pastoral Epistles*, 346.

Pericope 10: 1 Timothy 6:3–21

TRANSLATION 10.2

6:11 *But you, O man of God, flee from these things; and pursue righteousness, godliness, faith, love, steadfastness, gentleness.*

6:12 *Fight the good fight of faith, take hold of the eternal life to which you were called and you confessed the good confession before many witnesses.*

6:13 *I charge you before God who gives life to all things, and Christ Jesus who bore witness to the good confession before Pontius Pilate,*

6:14 *to keep the commandment unblemished, irreproachable, until the appearing of our Lord Jesus Christ,*

6:15 *which He will reveal at the proper time—the blessed and only Sovereign, the King of kings and Lord of lords,*

6:16 *who alone possesses immortality, dwells in unapproachable light, whom no person has seen or is able to see; to whom [be] honor and eternal power! Amen.*

6:17 *Charge the ones rich in the present world not to be haughty or to hope in the insecurity of riches, but in God, who provides us all things richly for enjoyment,*

6:18 *to do good works, to be rich in good works, to be generous, sharing,*

6:19 *storing up a treasure for themselves, a good foundation for the future, so that they may take hold of that which is indeed life.*

6:20 *O Timothy, guard the deposit, turning aside from profane, empty talk and contradictions of what is falsely called "knowledge,"*

6:21 *which some professing, have gone astray from the faith. Grace be with you [all].*

NOTES 10.2

10.2 *The people of God are characterized by the relentless pursuit of godliness as modeled by Christ, marked by God-dependence and a richness of generosity that results in an amply rewarded eternity (6:11–21).*

There seems to be a pattern to Paul's polemic in 1 Timothy; often those passages critical of the opposition (1 Tim 1:3–7; 4:1–5; and 6:3–10) are followed by an exhortation to Timothy that also adduces the latter's initiation as a point of encouragement and a motivation to commitment:

Criticism of opponents	1:3–7	4:1–5	6:3–10
Exhortation of Timothy	1:18–20	4:6–16	6:11–15
Reference to Timothy's initiation	1:18	4:14	6:12

While 6:3–10 flayed the false teachers and their financial ambitions and the resulting perils (in contrast to the gains of contentment), 6:11 turns to address Timothy: "But you . . . ." The former band of mercenaries pursue wealth, but the latter is to pursue virtue (and a list of virtues is provided, 6:11; see below), including the right kind of godliness, as opposed to the wrong kind that linked it with monetary gain (εὐσέβεια is seen in 6:3, 5, 6, 11). The false teachers had "wandered from the *faith*" (6:10), but Timothy is urged to

"pursue . . . *faith*" (6:11) and to "fight the good fight of *faith*" (6:12). And, in parallel to the asyndetic *vices* in 6:4–5 from which Timothy is exhorted to flee (6:11a refers back to that list with "these things"), we have in 6:11b asyndetic *virtues* that Timothy is recommended to pursue. Notice that there is "love" in this list (likely towards God and his people), in opposition to the wrongly directed "love" in 6:10 (towards money). Of course the "man of God" in 6:11 includes every believer: this person of God is one who pursues godliness.

In the PE, the theme of the "fight" (ἀγωνίζομαι, *agōnizomai*), either martial or athletic, shows up in 1 Tim 1:18; 4:10; 6:12; and 2 Tim 4:7. The present imperative form of the verb in 6:12 indicates an ongoing, perhaps ceaseless, campaign: Timothy is in it for life! It is a fight conducted *with* the attitude of faith (6:12; as the instance of "faith" in the previous verse implies), rather than a fight *because of* Timothy's faith and Christian stance. The firm grasp on eternal life (6:12 and also in 6:19—the only other occurrence of ἐπιλαμβάνω, *epilambanō*, in the PE) is the major reason for the faith-filled warfare that Timothy and all believers can confidently conduct.[20] This "taking hold" includes the faith exercised at conversion, as well as the ongoing faith that is integral to the Christian life in its entirety. Thus, it is by "taking hold of the eternal life" that one can engage in the "good fight of faith."

The "good confession" in 6:12 is likely related to a personal pledge by Timothy during his ordination. Notice the parallel in 6:12, 13: Timothy "confessed the good confession before many witnesses" (6:12), and Jesus "bore witness to the good confession before Pontius Pilate" (6:13). The element added in Jesus's case, that is missing in Timothy's, is the hostile audience of the former.[21] Clearly the one who made the "good confession" even before his enemies was to be the model for Timothy's own "good confession" in his encounter with opposition. In other words, if one, called by God, is to "fight the good fight," then one is going to have to "confess a good confession" before enemies. God calls, and a "good fight" and a "good confession" ensue! And as he engages that battle, Timothy is to "keep the commandment" (6:14; likely inclusive of all that Paul has urged Timothy in this letter with regard to his life and ministry; perhaps focusing on 6:11). By "keeping the commandment" God's leader remains unblemished and irreproachable.[22] Timothy's ministry is thus bounded on one side by its initiation (6:12) and on the other by its consummation upon the "appearing of our Lord Jesus Christ" (6:14). Within these boundary markers of past and future lies the present. And in this current space and time, Timothy is urged to "flee" and to "pursue": "In a very real sense the present experience of Christian life is a continual process of flight from and pursuit toward."[23]

But "agonizing" (a pun on ἀγωνίζομαι and ἀγών, *agōnizomai* and *agōn*, "fight," 6:12) is not all that the believer has to look forward to. Even as Paul issues a solemn charge to his protégé "before God . . . and Christ Jesus" (6:13) that Timothy keep the "commandment . . . *until the appearing of . . . Christ*" (6:14), we are being reminded of how the fights, struggles,

---

20. Both 1 Tim 6:12–14 and 2 Tim 4:6–8 have "fight the good fight"; "keep" (τηρέω, *tēreō*) the commandment/faith; the promise of a reward—eternal life/crown of righteousness; and the anticipation of the eschaton with the "appearing" (ἐπιφάνεια, *epiphaneia*) of Christ. In addition, 1 Tim 1:19 also has "fight the good fight" and "keeping [ἔχω, *echō*] faith."

21. Incidentally, outside the Gospels and Acts, 1 Tim 6:13 is the only place in the NT that names the procurator of Judea during 26–36 CE.

22. Two alpha-privatives, ἄσπιλος and ἀνεπίλημπτος, *aspilos* and *anepilēmptos*, are employed in 6:14. The root of the former, σπίλος, "spotted," is a medical term with poignant relevance for a dermatologist: a nevus spilus is a special kind of a spotted mole, not uncommonly found on the skin.

23. Towner, *Letters to Timothy and Titus*, 406.

and campaigns will end: Jesus is coming![24] God, at the "proper time" will bring about the end (6:15), with the appearing of Christ Jesus. So fervent are Paul's own emotions as he utters those words and expresses that hope, even as the grains of his own life slowly slip down the hourglass, that he cannot hold back a magnificent doxology (6:15).[25] The following august and liturgical emphasis on God's attributes in connection with Timothy's commission and charge would, no doubt, enable Timothy and those co-reading the Epistle with him (and after him) to recognize the gravity of their individual commissions to "fight the good fight," and to "take hold of the eternal life to which [they] were called" (6:12).[26] The "eternal *life*" of 6:12, that which is "indeed *life*" (6:19), sourced in a "*living* God" (3:15; 4:10), who gives *life* to all things (6:13), must be a sharing of the life of God himself![27] And it is going to happen soon!

One would have thought the Epistle would conclude after 6:15–16, with this majestic finale, but Paul continues the Epistle for several verses more—not uncommon for the apostle: see 1 Tim 1:17; as well as Eph 3:20–21. It is likely that with the note on how the good fights and good confessions would end (1 Tim 6:14–16), Paul was prompted to add a coda describing what this might mean for wealthy Christians, as they look for an eternal future. After all, much of this pericope had been dealing with issues of money.

The exhortations to Timothy in 6:17–19 regarding the rich are thematically parallel to that in 6:11–15a: both come in the form of charges (παραγγέλλω, *parangellō*, "charge," is used in 6:13 and 6:17); both urge eschewing the pursuit of wealth, and instead advocate righteousness—richness of a different kind that yields rewards in the eschaton ("good" occurs in 6:12 [καλός ×2] and 6:18 [also twice: a compound of ἀγαθός, and καλός]). This kind of godliness is to "take hold of that which is indeed life" (6:19), for rewards are guaranteed![28]

The motif of "riches" resounds in these three verses, 6:17–19, employing πλουσίοις, πλούτου, πλουσίως, πλουτεῖν, as well as ἀποθησαυρίζοντας (*plousiois*, "the ones rich"; *ploutou*, "riches"; *plousiōs*, "richly"; *ploutein*, "to be rich"; and *apothēsaurizontas*, "storing up a treasure"). The contrast, of course, is between the riches of "the present age" (τῷ νῦν αἰῶνι, *tō nyn aiōni*, 6:17) and that of the future (6:19), granted by a Sovereign with "eternal power" (κράτος αἰώνιον, *kratos aiōnion*, 6:16). Wealth in the current time is characterized by "insecurity" (6:17), but the riches of eternity are solid—a "good foundation" (6:19). While an earlier warning was directed to "those [false teachers] who want to get rich" (6:9), this section pointedly addresses those who *already* are rich, and therefore perhaps conceited (6:4),

---

24. In the PE, the appearing or epiphany (ἐπιφάνεια in 6:14) of Christ may refer to his incarnation, as in 2 Tim 1:10, or to his eschatological return, the Second Advent, as here and in 2 Tim 4:1, 8; Titus 2:13. The verbal cognate, ἐπιφαίνω, *epiphainō*, deals with a more comprehensive span of Christ's ministry as in Titus 2:11 and 3:4.

25. The doxology of 6:15–16 is quite similar to that in 1:17, together with which an *inclusio* to the whole Epistle is created: both occur in mid-discussion; they share "king/King of kings," "immortal," "only God/Sovereign"; "honor"; "forever"; and one has "invisible," while the other has "whom no person has seen or is able to see."

26. Just as there were two alpha-privatives describing the kind of life Timothy was to lead (6:14), now there are two more describing the life of God (6:16): ἀθανασίαν, *athanasian*, and, with regard to the light in which he dwells, ἀπρόσιτον, *aprositon*—immortal and unapproachable.

27. Johnson, *First and Second Letters to Timothy*, 311.

28. Divine promises for the future of an eternity with God should not make us forget that he also does "provide us all things richly for enjoyment" (6:17)—his beneficences in *this* age (4:4).

tending to fix their hope on their earthly riches (6:17), as is often the wont of those with plenty.²⁹ Rather, one's hopes must be fixed on God, not upon transitory riches.

This exhortation of 6:17 is explicated in three infinitives in 6:18 (but offering four equivalent exhortations in those three clauses), each the expression of God-dependence, rather than wealth-dependence: "to do good works [ἀγαθοεργέω, *agathoergeō*]," "to be rich in good works [καλὰ ἔργα, *kala erga*]," and "to be generous" and "sharing."³⁰ Indeed, one might say that one enjoys God's rich providence (6:17b) by generously doling out those provisions as richly to others as God gave them to their first possessors. "One aspect of *autarkeia* [αὐτάρκεια, "contentment," in 6:6; ἀρκέω, "be content," in 6:8] was the freedom it gave from the enticement and entrapment of material possessions. But within Paul's theological understanding of creation, freedom is seen as the capacity to give away possessions to others with no diminishment to the self. Paul could scarcely be more emphatic in his desire that the rich use their possessions in just this way."³¹ And what a remarkable "return-on-investment": treasure for the future (6:19)! The obtaining of such rewards in the afterlife is what it means to "take hold of that which is indeed life," the consummation of the abundant life Jesus promises (John 10:10).

The Epistle finally concludes (1 Tim 6:20–21). Timothy is named in 1:2, 18 at the beginning of the Epistle, and now again at its end, here in 6:20. Appropriate for a letter to the delegate no doubt, but this is, in reality, a private discourse intended to be overheard by the church and taken to heart by every believer living in every age of this dispensation.

As Towner observes, the combination of "guard" with "deposit" "alludes to the process (in Greco-Roman and Jewish cultures) of entrusting some commodity with a person who is to ensure its safekeeping (and, in this context, [its] proper use) and eventually return it to its owner. Assumed in the process are the ownership of the commodity and the obligation of faithfulness on the part of the trustee."³² Of course, God is the ultimate Trustee, with Paul doing the honors of handing over the trust to his delegate, Timothy. That deposit/entrustment, passed down through generations of God's people, is each believer's spiritual call and stewardship in ministry.³³

The "knowledge" referred to (γνῶσις, *gnōsis*, 6:20, the only instance of the word in the PE) simply categorizes the "profane, empty talk and contradictions" that Timothy was to turn aside from. Whereas false teachers "turned away" (ἐκτρέπω, *ektrepō*) from true doctrine and instruction (1:5–6), and wayward widows likewise, to follow after Satan (ἐκτρέπω in 5:15), here Timothy is urged to "turn away" from falsehood (ἐκτρέπω again in 6:20).

The descriptions, in 6:10 and 6:21, of those who have abandoned "the faith" are almost identical:

---

29. This is not a screed against wealth. Riches, after all, are relative. And *everyone* is prone to the faults of conceit and the sins of overly relying on worldly goods and resources.

30. The double emphasis on "good works" here is remarkable, but perhaps not surprising in a trio of letters frequently punctuated by "good works": ἔργα ἀγαθά is found in 1 Tim 2:10; 5:10, 25; 2 Tim 2:21; 3:17; Titus 1:16; 2:7, 14; 3:1, 8, 14 (and ἀγαθοεργέω in 6:18a); καλὰ ἔργα is used in 1 Tim 3:1; 6:18b.

31. Johnson, *First and Second Letters to Timothy*, 315.

32. Towner, *Letters to Timothy and Titus*, 430.

33. See 2 Tim 1:12, 14; and also 1 Cor 11:2; 2 Thess 2:15; 3:6.

	6:10	6:21
Negative element	"love of money"	"'knowledge'"
Relative pronoun	"which"	"which"
Indefinite pronoun	"some"	"some"
Participle of behavior	"longing for"	"professing"
Verb of rejection	"wandered away"	"gone astray"
Prepositional phrase	"from the faith"	"from the faith"

In each, there is a negative element, a pair of pronouns, a participle denoting behavior, a verb of rejection, and a prepositional phrase (ἀπὸ, *apo* . . ./περὶ, *peri* . . .) dealing with "faith."[34] Thus the section is tightly packaged and focused on the evils prone to beset those with wealth or seeking for it.

The letter that began with "grace" (1:2) now ends with it, too (6:21). And of course, the concluding benediction is directed to "you" (plural, thus "you [all]"), since the Epistle was intended to be read by the whole church.[35]

SERMON MAPS

THEOLOGICAL FOCUS OF PERICOPE 10 FOR PREACHING

10 The people of God relentlessly pursue godliness as modeled by Christ, marked by a God-dependent, humble contentment with basic needs, manifesting a richness of generosity that results in an amply rewarded eternity (6:3–21).

As I have mentioned earlier, there ought to be no constraint on the preacher to follow the sequence of the text: a spoken sermon and a scripted pericope are two different modes of communication. The former, in any case, is not trying to duplicate the latter: the sermon is only facilitating the audience's reading of the pericope and their experiencing of its thrust as its author intended. While there is something to be said for paralleling the text's sequence in a sermon—ease of following on the part of listeners—the driving order of the sermon ought to be what makes it "narratival," or storylike, with a smooth flow.

Possible Preaching Maps for Pericope 10

I. False Teachers
   Characteristics (6:3a, 4, 5a)
   Relationship to money (6:5b, 9–10)
   Move-to-Relevance: False teachers today; perhaps even ourselves
II. Truth Teachers
   Characteristics (6:3b, 11)
   Relationship to money (6:6–8)
   Generosity: alternative to seeking/hoarding money (6:17–18, 20–21)
   Rewards (6:19)

---

34. Van Neste, *Cohesion and Structure*, 129.
35. Only Colossians and 1 Timothy conclude without personal greetings from the apostle.

1 TIMOTHY

      Following Christ's model (6:12–16)

      Move-to-Relevance: Our wrong attitudes to money

  III. *Give to Get!*

      Specifics on how the Christian can be generous[36]

This map may be reconstructed with a closer focus on the contrast between false and truth teachers within each move:

  I. Characteristics

      False teachers (6:3a, 4, 5a)

      Truth teachers (6:3b, 11)

      Move-to-Relevance: Godliness, a call for all believers

  II. Contentment

      False teachers (6:5b, 9–10)

      Truth teachers (6:6–8)

      Move-to-Relevance: Our own discontentment

  III. Cause

      Rewards (6:19)

      Following Christ's model (6:12–16)

  III. Challenge: *Give to Get!*

      Generosity: alternative to seeking/hoarding money (6:17–18, 20–21)

      Specifics on how the Christian can be generous

---

[36]. And I'd focus on something related to finances for this application.

2 TIMOTHY

Completing the Course

PERICOPE 11

Suffering with Confidence

2 Timothy 1:1–18

[Following Exemplars; Inheriting Suffering; Empowered by God]

SUMMARY, PREVIEW[1]

Summary of Pericope 11: This first pericope of 2 Timothy (2 Tim 1:1–18) calls on believers to endure suffering confidently on behalf of the gospel, empowered by God and entrusting their mission to him, encouraged by exemplars, entrenched in the faith handed down—the legacies of those who have gone on before—and expecting future rewards.

Preview of Pericope 12: The next pericope (2 Tim 2:1–13) continues the theme of suffering, but focuses upon the undistractedness, uprightness, and industriousness of believers engaging in faithful ministry—including their entrustment of the future work of God to other faithful people—thus garnering for themselves eternal rewards of glory.

11   2 Timothy 1:1–18

THEOLOGICAL FOCUS OF PERICOPE 11

11 God's authoritative call on his people involves their faithful, legacy-preserving, unashamed endurance of inevitable suffering as they successfully undertake their divine commission—empowered graciously by God's Spirit, confident of his seeing their work through, and anticipating rewards (1:1–18).

---

1. Recognizing that 2 Timothy is a discrete Epistle, I will forego a "Review" of the previous pericope that concludes 1 Timothy.

2 Timothy

11.1   God's authoritative call of his people involves continuance in faith that keeps intact the legacy of one's God-fearing forbears and brings thankfulness to one's mentors (1:1–5).

11.2   The people of God, called and gifted by him, endure suffering—unashamedly and empowered by God's Spirit—for the sake of the cause, the gospel, and the causative agent, God, the giver of grace and the conqueror of death (1:6–10).

11.3   Believers, confident that God, who appointed them, will take responsibility for their successful undertaking of the divine appointment, are driven by faith, love, and self-control, and are empowered by the Holy Spirit, as they follow the model of those who have gone before them (1:11–14).

11.4   Faithfulness to the mission of God (by direct involvement) also involves faithfulness to those carrying out the mission (by indirect involvement), even risking danger, but ensuring mercy and rewards on the day of reckoning (1:15–18).

OVERVIEW

While all three PE mention Timothy's kinship with Paul—"true child in faith" (1 Tim 1:2); "beloved son" (2 Tim 1:2); "genuine child in a common faith" (Titus 1:4)—and are composed with a personal touch, 2 Timothy is far more direct and heartfelt, scripted almost exclusively for Paul's "beloved son." Besides the specific content addressed to Timothy, this Epistle also uses fourteen verses for introspective and autobiographical comments as it concludes (4:9–22).[2] Nonetheless, the closing second-person plural pronoun "you [all]" in 4:22 (as in 1 Tim 6:21) indicates that the Epistle was to be read not only by Timothy, but by the entire congregation.

Though all of the PE emphasize eternal life (1 Tim 1:16–17; 4:8; 6:12, 13, 16, 19; 2 Tim 1:1, 10, 12; 2:10, 11; 4:8, 18; Titus 1:2; 3:7), in 2 Timothy the references are even more poignant, as the apostle is on the threshold of his entry into that phase of existence. Indeed, in light of approaching eternity, exhortations to endure suffering for the faith occur throughout the letter: 1:8, 12; 2:3–13; 3:10–12; 4:5–8.[3] It is this need to remind Timothy of the inevitability of suffering in the life of God's leader that causes Paul to draw upon his apostolic authority at the outset, even in this very personal missive (1:1).

11.1 2 Timothy 1:1–5

THEOLOGICAL FOCUS 11.1

11.1   God's authoritative call of his people involves continuance in faith that keeps intact the legacy of one's God-fearing forbears and brings thankfulness to one's mentors (1:1–5).

TRANSLATION 11.1

1:1   *Paul, an apostle of Christ Jesus by the will of God, according to the promise of life that is in Christ Jesus,*

---

2. Titus has four verses dedicated to a personal conclusion; 1 Timothy, perhaps the least personal of the three, has no concluding references to coworkers.

3. Cognates of the παθ (*path*)-root are employed in 1:8, 12; 2:3, 9; 3:11; 4:5.

1:2 *To Timothy, beloved son: Grace, mercy, peace from God the Father and Christ Jesus our Lord.*

1:3 *I give thanks to God, whom I serve with a pure conscience as [did] the forefathers, as I have unceasing remembrance of you in my prayers night and day,*

1:4 *longing to see you—having remembered your tears—so that that I may be filled with joy,*

1:5 *for, receiving a reminder of the unhypocritical faith in you, that first dwelt in your grandmother Lois and your mother Eunice, I have been convinced that [it is] in you also.*

NOTES 11.1

11.1 *God's authoritative call of his people involves continuance in faith that keeps intact the legacy of one's God-fearing forbears and brings thankfulness to one's mentors (1:1–5).*

The opening salutation is quite similar to that in 1 Timothy (1:1–2), Paul's apostleship being defined in relation to Christ Jesus "by the will of God" (2 Tim 1:1; "commandment" in 1 Tim 1:1). 2 Tim 1:1 also qualifies the apostle's call as being "according to the promise of life that is in Christ Jesus" (1 Tim 1:1 labeled God "our Savior").[4] One reason for remaining faithful amidst tribulation is the authority of the one who calls his servant into this risky business of Christian ministry. Another reason, also adduced here, is "the promise of life in Christ Jesus" (2 Tim 1:1). This phrase likely means the *telos*, the sure end-point, of all ministry—"according to [for the sake of/in virtue of/anticipating] the promise of life that is in Christ Jesus." This is equivalent to "gospel," considered in its broadest sense of all that God is accomplishing in his economy which, of course, includes eternal life with its abundance of rewards for the faithful. Keeping one's eyes on the goal of life eternal is essential for faithfulness unto God.

Both the letters to Timothy add "mercy" (1 Tim 1:2; 2 Tim 1:2) to the standard epistolary greeting of "grace and peace." "Mercy" in 1 Tim 1:2 is immediately related to Paul himself, the prototypical recipient of divine mercy (1:13, 16). But here in 2 Timothy, we find the salutation of "mercy" (1:2) linked later in this pericope to Onesiphorus (and his household: 2 Tim 1:16, 18), for whom Paul asks God for "mercy"—the one who, in spite of potential danger, unashamedly and generously served the captive Paul (1:15–18; see below). Thus in 2 Timothy, Onesiphorus becomes the prototypical recipient of divine mercy. So the employment of "mercy" in Paul's greeting here is to encourage Timothy not to be ashamed or to retreat in fear of suffering, but to undertake, with boldness and confidence, his responsibility to God and to the people of God.

A single sentence makes up 1:3–5: Paul begins with his thanks to God in 1:3, but the reason for his gratitude is given only in 1:5 ("for . . . I have been convinced . . .").[5] This sentence is bookended by the mention of ancestors: "forefathers" show up in 1:3, and

---

4. Paul's more personal letters, such as the ones to the Philippians (Phil 1:1), the Thessalonians (1 Thess 1:1; 2 Thess 1:1), and Philemon (Phlm 1), omit his official title of "apostle."

5. Second Timothy is the only one of the PE that commences with a standard thanksgiving.

Timothy's grandmother and mother in 1:5.[6] Mentioning "forefathers" is simply Paul's nod to his Jewish ancestry and his general affiliation to the God of the patriarchs and the prophets, his spiritual heritage, along with whom the apostle had served with a "pure conscience." This, Paul's faithfulness, in concord with the godly legacy left for him by the "forefathers," is therefore also to be reflected in Timothy's own faithfulness, consistent with the spiritual heritage he acquired through his own ancestors.[7] As Paul's ministry is imminently concluding, this makes for a poignant exhortation to Timothy: he, too, must continue faithfully. Indeed, Paul is confident about Timothy's future undertakings: twice in the thanksgiving of 1:3–5, he mentions Timothy's sincere faith ("unhypocritical faith . . . in you," and again "in you"; 1:5a, 5c), the engine and dynamo of a believer's life and ministry.[8] This "faith" is clearly not the salvific faith exercised at the point of conversion, but rather

> an ongoing response toward God—a quality of character, indeed—that can be implanted and nurtured by human relationships and passed down from parent to child; thus the fidelity shown by parents and teachers toward the young, and emulated by the young in the formation of their own character, is a critical part of the formation of the theological virtue. Faith [here] is not a momentary decision that occurs at a moment of crisis or conversion. It is a virtue that can grow through the stages of a person's life.[9]

Tears and joy show up together in 1:4, evidencing the deeply emotional tenor of this pericope (and the entire Epistle).[10] Paul's desire to be reunited with his protégé concludes the letter, too (4:9, 21). The number of second-person pronouns—seven times in the single sentence of 1:3–5—attests to this tenderness: Paul is constantly mindful "of you" (1:3), longing "to see you" (1:4), remembering "your tears," and being reminded of the sincere faith that is "in you," as it was in "your" grandmother and "your" mother (1:5) and, Paul is sure, is "in you" as well (1:5).[11]

Of note is the recurrence of remembrance as a theme in this first pericope of 2 Timothy: a whole set of μν (*mn*)-root words is found in its opening section: μνείαν (*mneian*, "remembrance," 1:3); μεμνημένος (*memnēmenos*, "having remembered," 1:4); ὑπόμνησιν (*hypomnēsin*, "reminder," 1:5); and ἀναμιμνήσκω (*anamimnēskō*, "remind," 1:6).[12] Other

---

6. Acts 16:1–3 tells us that Timothy's mother was Jewish, and his father Greek.

7. Marshall hits the nail on the head, as he describes Paul's *doing* in this thanksgiving report: "The purpose of a thanksgiving in the Pauline correspondence is not to offer an actual prayer to God but rather to *report* what Paul says in his prayers as a means of encouragement and exhortation to the readers. Here the intent of the 'prayer-report' is not simply to give news of Paul's concern for him to Timothy but rather to give him strong encouragement" (*Pastoral Epistles*, 689 [emphasis original]).

8. Perhaps it was Onesiphorus who had personally jogged Paul's memory about Timothy's "unhypocritical faith" (1:5). Elsewhere in this letter, Timothy is called upon to pass on what he has heard from Paul to the "faithful" (2:2); and he is to pursue "faith" (2:22), unlike those who are upsetting the "faith" of some (2:18), and who are rejected with regard to "faith" (3:8).

9. Johnson, *First and Second Letters to Timothy*, 342. Here "faith" overlaps considerably in notion with "faithfulness."

10. Perhaps the grief was exhibited at the parting of Paul and Timothy as recounted in Acts 20:37 (or in 1 Tim 1:3).

11. The personal pronoun "you" (σε) shows up in the next sentence, too (1:6).

12. And also ὑπομίμνησκε, *hypomimnēske*, "remind," in 2:14.

PERICOPE 11: 2 TIMOTHY 1:1–18

parallels and repetitions are also found in this pericope, mostly between Paul's actions and those exhorted of Timothy, all of which enable one to discern the theology of this pericope.

	Paul	Timothy
Remembrance (μν-root)	1:3, 4, 5 (by Paul)	1:6 (by Timothy)
Godly heritage	1:3	1:5 (also 3:15)
Attitude	1:3 ("pure conscience")	1:5 ("sincere faith")
Paul is "convinced"	1:12 (re: God)	1:5 (re: Timothy)
δυν (*dyn*)-root words	1:12 (δυνατός, *dynatos*, "able")	1:7, 12 (δυνάμις, *dynamis*, "power")
Suffering (to be shared)	1:8, 12 (also 2:9–10)	1:8 (also 2:3)
"Not ashamed"	1:12	1:8 (also 1:16)
Trust in God	1:12 (πιστεύω, *pisteuō*, "believe")	1:5, 13 (πίστις, *pistis*, "faith")
"Guard"	1:12 (by God)	1:14 (by Timothy)
"Deposit"	1:12 (to Paul)	1:14 (to Timothy)

This intertwining of apostle and delegate continues throughout this Epistle: 2:1–13; 3:10–17; 4:6–8, 18. Paul is the model that Timothy—and, indeed, all God's people—must follow in their devotion to God and their dedication to his service.[13]

11.2 2 Timothy 1:6–10

THEOLOGICAL FOCUS 11.2

11.2 The people of God, called and gifted by him, endure suffering—unashamedly and empowered by God's Spirit—for the sake of the cause, the gospel, and the causative agent, God, the giver of grace and the conqueror of death (1:6–10).

TRANSLATION 11.2

1:6 *For which reason I remind you to rekindle the gift of God which is in you through the laying on of my hands.*

1:7 *For God has not granted us a Spirit of timidity, but of power and love and self-control.*

1:8 *Therefore do not be ashamed of the testimony of our Lord or of me His prisoner, but co-suffer affliction [with us] for the gospel according to the power of God,*

1:9 *who saved us and called us with a holy calling, not according to our works, but according to His own purpose and grace which was granted us in Christ Jesus from the time of eternity,*

---

13. A number of first-person pronouns and verb suffixes also punctuate the pericope: 1:3 (×3), 4, 5, 6 (×2), 8, 11, 12 (×6), 13, 15, 16 (×2), 17. But along with that personal emphasis, there is also Paul's inclusive language employing first-person plurals to register Timothy with himself for a common cause: "granted *us*" (1:7); "*our* Lord" (1:8); "saved *us*" (1:9); "*our* works" (1:9); "granted *us*" (1:9); "*our* Savior" (1:10); and "in *us*" (1:14). As with Paul, so it ought to be with Timothy—a theme this pericope will dilate on. Note also the συν-prefixed word in 1:8: συγκακοπαθέω, *synkakopatheō*, "co-suffer affliction."

1:10 but now has been made apparent by the appearing of our Savior Christ Jesus, who abolished death but brought to light life and immortality through the gospel,

NOTES 11.2

11.2   The people of God, called and gifted by him, endure suffering—unashamedly and empowered by God's Spirit—for the sake of the cause, the gospel, and the causative agent, God, the giver of grace and the conqueror of death (1:6–10).

The layout of 1:6–14 is quite precise[14]:

A	ἐν σοί (*en soi*, "in you"); "Spirit"; δύναμις (*dynamis*, "power"); "love"	1:6–7
B	Not "ashamed"	1:8a
C	"Suffering" for the gospel (συγκακοπαθέω)	1:8b
D	The "gospel"	1:9–10
C'	"Suffering" for the gospel (πάσχω, *paschō*)	1:11–12a
B'	Not "ashamed"	1:12b
A'	δυνατός (*dynatos*, "able"); "love"; "Spirit"; ἐν ἡμῖν (*en hemin*, "in us")	1:12c–14

This section underscores that Timothy is not to be "ashamed" (1:8a) of the situation, of his ministry, or of Paul. Instead he is to "co-suffer affliction" with Paul and Jesus (1:8b[15]). But Paul is not "ashamed" (1:12b)—his was a "determined mind-set": "I am not ashamed." For Timothy, it was an exhortation to be fulfilled: "Do not be ashamed."[16] Of course, humanly speaking, there was much to be ashamed of in the gospel:

> It was the message of a failed prophet, rejected by his people, executed by the world's power, and preached by a collection of fishermen and other undesirables. The message they proclaimed was foolishness in the world's eyes (1 Cor 1:23), based on assumptions that ran counter to the generally accepted norms of Greek philosophy (Acts 17:32). And there was, on the surface, much to the ashamed about in reference to Paul, a man who met constant opposition (2 Cor 11:23–27) and was imprisoned in Rome.[17]

Yet Paul is confident that Timothy can be unashamed: his faith is creditable enough to be noted twice in 2 Tim 1:5, and he has the empowerment of God (1:7, 8, 14). In light of the parallelism and equivalence of πνεῦμα . . . δυνάμεως (*pneuma . . . dynameōs*, "Spirit . . . of power," 1:7) and δύναμις θεοῦ (*dynamis theou*, "power of God," 1:8), this "gift of God" (1:6)

---

14. Modified from Couser, "'Testimony about the Lord," 315.

15. The translation "*co-suffer affliction*" is somewhat redundantly employed to bring out the prepositional suffix συν and κακος in συγκακοπαθέω. The text does not specify with whom Timothy must co-suffer, but in context, it must be with both Paul and Jesus.

16. Towner, *Letters to Timothy and Titus*, 475.

17. Mounce, *Pastoral Epistles*, 480.

is obviously related to the Holy Spirit, himself granted by God (1:7). The mention of πνεῦμα in 1:14, explicitly referring to the Holy Spirit, also makes this the best reading, considering that A and A' (in the table above) are parallel elements in the structure of this pericope (there is also the parallel between ἐν σοί (1:6) and ἐν ἡμῖν (1:14).[18] Thus the event described in 2 Tim 1:6 may be akin to the donation of a gift of God's Spirit concurrent with the laying of hands upon the conferee (as in Acts 8:17–18; 9:12, 17; 19:6), perhaps linked to the act of the delegate's commissioning (as in Acts 13:1–3). In any case, it is not the indwelling of the Spirit upon conversion/justification that is being noted here[19]; rather, it is a particular (and peculiar) sending of the Spirit, a formal acknowledgment (and a public demonstration, perhaps) of Timothy's gifting.[20] This also helps makes sense of the rekindling exhorted in 2 Tim 1:6: this refreshing of a spiritual gift required a *re*kindling (whereas the Spirit's indwelling is a one-time, permanent occurrence).[21] This kind of spiritual gifting would be accompanied by "power," "love" (ἀγάπη, 1:7; also in 1:13), and "self-control" (σωφρονισμός, *sōphronismos*, 1:7). Only such power, love, and self-control would enable one to be unashamed in suffering and to remain steadfast to Jesus Christ and to his prisoner, Paul (1:8).

Second Timothy 1:8–12 is one long sentence.[22] As we've seen, it is bracketed by the twin motifs of the "shame" and "suffering" undergone by Paul and Jesus who gave his "testimony" (1:8b, 10c–12a).[23] If suffering happened to Paul and to Jesus (and, as we will see, to Onesiphorus as well), then it should come as no surprise that Timothy, too, would have to face suffering (as also will all of God's children: 3:12). The (suffering) mission of the apostle is being handed over to his protégé: it is his turn now . . . to suffer unashamedly for Christ.

But the good news is that this suffering is not to be endured on one's own strength, but "according to the power of God" (1:8), the same Spirit-derived power referred to in 1:7. And the magnificent outworking of this "power of God" is depicted in the content of the gospel in 1:9–10. Its contrasting phrases emphasize this divine might: "not according to *our* works, but according to *His* . . ."; "granted to us . . . from the time of *eternity*, but *now* has been revealed";

---

18. The Holy Spirit and χάρισμα, *charisma*, "gift," are also found together in 1 Cor 12:5, 7 (as in 2 Tim 1:6–7); and Holy Spirit and δίδωμι, *didōmi*, "grant," in Rom 5:5; 1 Cor 12:7; 2 Cor 1:22; 5:5; 1 Thess 4:8 (as here in 2 Tim 1:7). In addition, Rom 8:15 and 1 Cor 2:12, both dealing with the Holy Spirit, have a "not . . . but . . ." construction, as also does 2 Tim 1:7. Of course, the co-location of "power," "love," and "self-control" with the Holy Spirit (as in 2 Tim 1:7) is quite Pauline in style: see Rom 5:5; 15:13, 19, 30; 1 Cor 2:4; Gal 5:22, 23; Eph 3:16; Col 1:8; 1 Thess 1:5 (also see Luke 4:14; Acts 1:8; 6:5, 8).

19. However, in 1:14, it is that justification-related indwelling of the Holy Spirit that is referred to.

20. Elsewhere in the PE, χάρισμα (1:6) is found only in 1 Tim 4:14, also describing the *charisma* bestowed upon Timothy. In that earlier text it was the Ephesian elders who were officiating at the event of Timothy's initiation; prophetic utterance was involved (as also in 1 Tim 1:18). Here, in 2 Tim 1:6, however, Paul is said to have officiated himself, and no prophecy is noted as having occurred. These descriptions are not necessarily contradictory.

21. "I *remind* you to *re*kindle" employs two verbs with the same ανα (*ana*)- prefix, yielding an alliteration: ἀναμιμνήσκω and ἀναζωπυρέω (*anamimnēskō* and *anazōpyreo*, 1:6). Whether Timothy was actually guilty of "timidity" is impossible to determine, though 1 Cor 16:10 may suggest he was fearful. Then again, even Paul was fearful at times: 1 Cor 2:1–3. On the other hand, this protégé's intrepidity is evident in Acts 16:2–3; 17:14–15; 19:22; Rom 16:21; 1 Cor 4:16–17; 2 Cor 1:19; Phil 2:19–24; 1 Thess 3:2–3, 6. Most likely, the reference to timidity in 2 Tim 1:7 is simply warning against potential future diffidence, a rhetorical flourish rather than a shaming accusation.

22. I have broken it up to create the section 1:6–10 for the sake of clarity and unity of theme.

23. Elsewhere in the PE μαρτύριον, *martyrion*, is used only in 1 Tim 2:6. Also see 1 Tim 6:13.

"abolished *death*[24] but brought to light *life* and *immortality*"; and "*made apparent* [from φανερόω, *phaneroō*] by the *appearing* [ἐπιφάνεια, *epiphaneia*] of our Savior Jesus Christ . . . brought life and immortality to *light*." Likewise, the contrasts in each of the three verses, 1:7, 8, 9, with a negative statement ("not granted us . . ."; "do not be ashamed . . ."; "not according to our works," respectively) in each case followed by ἀλλά, *alla*, "but," and a positive statement ("but of power . . ."; "but co-suffer affliction . . ."; "but according to His own purpose and grace," respectively).[25] Divine power was clearly operating in the lives of those called to suffer for and with Christ. Marshall notes that 1:9–10 "has a balanced rhythmical form and could be part of a hymn . . . or other existing form of words."[26] That is quite appropriate for a doxological utterance, as is Paul's wont whenever "gospel" (or its content) is mentioned (see 1 Tim 1:17; 6:15–16 in the PE; also Rom 11:33–36). What God has done, and is continuing to do through his people, even when it involves suffering, is cause for praise![27]

In the middle of the parallelisms in 2 Tim 1:6–14 (*D* in the table above) stands the cause for which Paul and Timothy (and Onesiphorus; see below) were striving and suffering (and for which all believers are to strive and suffer)—"the gospel," God's grand, eternal plan "from the time of eternity" (1:9).[28] It must be noted that this is not merely a description of the atoning work of Christ; rather, it is the delineation of God's grand plan (his "purpose," 1:9) stretching from eternity to eternity. But it is the cause's originator who is given full billing in 1:8b–10: God, the Savior, who called his people by grace in Jesus Christ, the death abolisher who brought to light life and immortality. If even death has been abolished, surely Timothy can suffer with glee! And so the apostle's experience of suffering becomes paradigmatic for his delegate, Timothy, and through him to the entire church at Ephesus, and through this canonical Epistle to all of God's people everywhere. Service for God and his gospel is inextricably intertwined with suffering in this age.

11.3 2 Timothy 1:11–14

THEOLOGICAL FOCUS 11.3

> 11.3 Believers, confident that God, who appointed them, will take responsibility for their successful undertaking of the divine appointment, are driven by faith, love, and self-control, and are empowered by the Holy Spirit, as they follow the model of those who have gone before them (1:11–14).

24. This is the only instance of "death" in the PE; elsewhere in Paul it occurs over forty times.

25. Both the participles, δοθεῖσαν, *dotheisan*, "granted," and φανερωθεῖσαν, *phanerōtheisan*, "made apparent" (1:9, 10), are feminine singular, relating to χάριν, *charin*, "grace," the immediate antecedent, a feminine singular noun: divine grace *granted* to God's people was *made apparent* in the Savior, Jesus Christ.

26. Marshall, *Pastoral Epistles*, 700. The structure of 1:9–10 has as its backbone six aorist participle phrases (six "vertebrae") in three pairs, some occasionally branching out into "ribs" of κατά (*kata*)-clauses and prepositional phrases.

27. It is in the context of the power of *God* (1:8), the deeds of *God* (1:9–10), and the saving and the calling of *God* (1:9), and the appointment of *God* (1:11), that the text introduces the inevitable suffering involved (1:8, 12). In all likelihood, the "holy calling" (1:9) is the divine appointment to eternal life, as in 1 Tim 6:12; the call is "holy" because of the Holy One who made the call.

28. A plan for the entirety of the cosmos: see Eph 1:8–10 (and Kuruvilla, *Ephesians*, 20–35). Notice also the equation of "God, who *saved* us" (σῴζω; 2 Tim 1:8b–9a) and "our *Savior* Christ Jesus" (σωτήρ; 1:10). The Spirit, of course, was mentioned in 1:7 and will show up again in 1:14. Even if it involves suffering, we are powerfully reminded that this business of the gospel is a Trinitarian undertaking!

TRANSLATION 11.3

1:11   for which I was appointed proclaimer and apostle and teacher,

1:12   for which reason I also suffer these things; but I am not ashamed, for I know in whom I have believed and I am convinced that He is able to guard my deposit until that day.

1:13   Hold on to the example of words that are sound which you have heard from me, with faith and love which are in Christ Jesus;

1:14   guard the good deposit through the Holy Spirit who dwells in us.

NOTES 11.3

11.3 Believers, confident that God, who appointed them, will take responsibility for their successful undertaking of the divine appointment, are driven by faith, love, and self-control, and are empowered by the Holy Spirit, as they follow the model of those who have gone before them (1:11–14).

Paul's confidence in God's carrying through his divine purpose in his, Paul's, role as proclaimer, apostle, and teacher (1:11) is emphasized by two alliterated perfect-tense verbs: πεπίστευκα and πέπεισμαι (*pepisteuka* and *pepeismai*, 1:12).[29] Paul's belief is settled ("I have believed"—who God is) and his confidence is unshakeable ("I am convinced"—what God is doing). And therefore he can suffer unashamed (1:12). But what exactly is he trusting God with when he mentions παραθήκη, *parathēkē*, "deposit," in 1:12? In light of the parallel with 1:14 that has the same word, it is best to see this as a "deposit" from God to Paul. This is also evident in that παραθήκη (from παρατίθημι, *paratithēmi*, "to commit/entrust"), is related to τίθημι, *tithēmi*, "to appoint," (1:11). In other words, God's call and appointment to ministry is what is being discussed. Since God is the one who empowers his people to undertake their divine commissioning/appointment—the working out of his divine "deposit" to them—Paul is confident that God will "guard" (i.e., carry through, implement) what he has entrusted to his people, the divine "deposit" (φυλάσσω, *phylassō*; παραθήκη; 1:12). But at the same time, he urges Timothy himself to "guard" the "good deposit" (again φυλάσσω, παραθήκη; 1:14).[30] Divine and human responsibility seem to be working (guarding) in tandem. We are quickly reminded that the implementation of the divine commission is not an exclusively human responsibility, as the prepositional phrase "through the Holy Spirit who dwells in us" emphasizes (1:14): he "guards" *and* we "guard. "God will achieve that success [of the mission] in and through the cooperation of human agents."[31] And, undoubtedly,

---

29. In Paul's trio of portfolios, "proclaimer and apostle and teacher" (1:11), I take "teacher" (διδάσκαλος, *didaskalos*) to include preaching as we see it today, for the edification of believers; "proclaimer" (κῆρυξ, *kēryx*) refers to the role of heralding the good news to unbelievers; and "apostle" gives Paul the requisite authority as one sent by Jesus. At least in this text, it is best to see the distinctions between these terms this way.

30. The word παραθήκη is found only thrice in the NT and always with φυλάσσω: 1 Tim 6:20; 2 Tim 1:12, 14. The verb παρατίθημι is found in 1 Tim 1:18 and 2 Tim 2:2; here the "depositing/entrusting" appears to be of specific words (of life)—"instruction" in the former and "what you heard" in the latter.

31. Towner, *Letters to Timothy and Titus*, 479.

there is also the reward that accompanies such faithful "guarding" by God's people of their deposit (i.e., their call, their appointment to ministry), on "that day" (2:12).[32]

Paul's utterances in this his last Epistle, from his ignominious and deplorable circumstances in prison, is a remarkable witness to his faith and endurance. No wonder he pushes himself as a model for Timothy, for the Ephesian church, and for all God's people everywhere, who are in equally injurious situations of suffering for God and his gospel (1:13; and also 3:10). And in his prototype status, Paul exhorts his protégé to "hold on [or 'maintain'/'keep,' ἔχω]," in the entirety of his life, to "the example of sound words" delivered to Timothy by the apostle (1:13). "Example" begins the sentence for emphasis: "To the example of words that are sound [you] hold on." That is not to say that Timothy is to regurgitate the same kind of words that Paul uttered/wrote. Rather, this "holding on" includes a demonstration in life (and no doubt, in speech) of the soundness of words he had heard from his mentor.[33]

And this kind of life is to be conducted "with faith and love which are in Christ Jesus." Both faith and love have shown up before in this pericope (1:5, 7, 12). Without faith, and without love, one can only be ashamed "of the testimony of our Lord [and] of . . . His prisoner" (1:8). But with faith and love, and empowered by the Spirit (1:7), and engraced by God (1:9), one can unashamedly endure for the cause, for the cause's agent (God), and for the agent's representatives—our fellow believers, particularly those in ministry (see below). From Paul's point of view, this is the preparation of a successor to carry on the mission.

11.4 2 Timothy 1:15–18

THEOLOGICAL FOCUS 11.4

11.4 Faithfulness to the mission of God (by direct involvement) also involves faithfulness to those carrying out the mission (by indirect involvement), even risking danger, but ensuring mercy and rewards on the day of reckoning (1:15–18).

TRANSLATION 11.4

1:15 *This you know, that all in Asia turned away from me, among whom are Phygelus and Hermogenes.*

1:16 *The Lord grant mercy to the household of Onesiphorus, for often he revived me and he was not ashamed of my chains;*

1:17 *but when he was in Rome, he diligently sought me and found me;*

1:18 *the Lord grant to him to find mercy from the Lord on that day. And you are well aware how much he served in Ephesus.*

---

32. The eschatological "that day" (1:12) refers to the day of judgment, whether of believers or of others, also anticipated with "that day" in 1:18; 4:8; also see Matt 7:22; Luke 10:12; 21:34; 2 Thess 1:10 (as well, 1 Cor 3:13; 2 Tim 2:12).

33. The verb ἔχω is used in this sense of application in 1 Tim 1:19; 3:4, 7, 9; 2 Tim 3:5. Also see 1 Cor 14:37; 1 Thess 2:13; 2 Thess 2:15; 3:6–7 for Paul's teaching tradition that is inseparable from lived life.

NOTES 11.4

11.4 Faithfulness to the mission of God (by direct involvement) also involves faithfulness to those carrying out the mission (by indirect involvement), even risking danger, but ensuring mercy and rewards on the day of reckoning (1:15–18).

"You know" and "you are well aware" bracket 1:15–18. Telling Timothy what he knows and is well aware of is a means of reminding him. The abandonment of Paul by practically "all in Asia" in his hour of crisis—his arrest and trial in Rome—is mentioned here in the first chapter of this Epistle (1:15) and also in the last (4:10–18). The contrast between the abandonment of Paul by Asian believers (1:15) and the commitment to Paul by Onesiphorus (1:16–18) is the thrust of 1:15–18. All of this is, no doubt, spurring the writer's urgency to deputize a protégé to co-suffer with him (and with Jesus) and to carry on the baton.

The modeling undertaken by Paul now shifts to the modeling by Onesiphorus for Timothy. This servant of God (who "served," διακονέω, *diakoneō*, in Ephesus, 1:18) was exemplifying ministerial life for Timothy and others, unashamed of Paul's chains (1:16, also in 1:8, 12).

> It was no light thing for a person to be associated with a criminal. In doing so, one ran the risk of being regarded by the authorities (as well as by family members, friends, neighbors, and business associates) as a sympathizer and possibly an accomplice and, therefore, deserving imprisonment or punishment.... Onesiphorus's wholehearted solidarity with Paul in his circumstances demonstrated the same refusal to categorize imprisonment for the cause of Christ as a social stigma.[34]

That this manifestation of unashamed service to a prisoner was not a one-time occurrence is emphasized in 1:16 (Onesiphorus revived and refreshed Paul "often") and again in 1:17 (he sought out Paul "eagerly"). The double plea that God would grant Onesiphorus and his household mercy (1:16, 18) suggests that he, too, suffered in some fashion as a result of his faithfulness. Paul's prayer here is that the one who "found" Paul (εὗρεν, *heuren*, 1:17) may, in turn, "find" mercy from the Lord (εὑρεῖν, *heurein*, 1:18). The focus is on the fact that this worthy one, Onesiphorus, was unashamed of Paul and his imprisonment. Therefore, even as Paul entrusted his life's course and the conduct of his divine appointment to God "unto that day" (εἰς ἐκείνην τὴν ἡμέραν, *eis ekeinēn tēn hēmeran*, 1:12), so also Paul, entrusting Onesiphorus to God and his mercy, is sure of the latter obtaining rewards "on that day" (ἐν ἐκείνῃ τῇ ἡμέρᾳ, *en ekeinē tē hēmera*, 1:18).[35] All of this echoes themes and motifs previously seen, a strong incentive for believers to follow in the footsteps of this relatively unknown "deacon" (1:18).[36] With the request that Timothy hasten to come to Paul in Rome

---

34. Towner, *Letters to Timothy and Titus*, 483.

35. This theme of future rewards "on that day" will show up one more time in 2 Timothy, in 4:8 (ἐν ἐκείνῃ τῇ ἡμέρᾳ). Some (for instance, Quinn and Wacker, *First and Second Letters to Timothy*, 614) speculate that Onesiphorus had died unexpectedly and hence the double wish for divine mercy upon him and on his household, especially in light of the mention specifically of his household in 4:19, with no naming of the man there, and the rather broken construction of 1:16–18 in the Greek. But it is unclear whether Paul would have prayed for a deceased person as he does here, employing the optative mood of δίδωμι, *didōmi*, "grant" (1:16, 18).

36. Unknown to humans, perhaps, but not unknown to God (Heb 6:10).

(4:9, 21), the former is thereby being asked to follow in the footsteps of Onesiphorus, who did exactly that, unashamed and suffering (unlike the deserters who abandoned Paul: 1:15; also 4:10, 14–16). No wonder the very next words from the quill of the apostle in this Epistle are "You therefore, my son . . ." (2:1).

Without a doubt, faithfulness to God entails faithfulness to God's gospel mission (direct involvement of the people of God in the mission) and to all who conduct it (indirect involvement of the people of God in the mission, through "missionaries").

SERMON MAPS

> **THEOLOGICAL FOCUS OF PERICOPE 11 FOR PREACHING**
> 11 God's call on his people involves a faithful, unashamed endurance of inevitable suffering as they undertake their divine commission, empowered graciously by God's Spirit, confident of his seeing their work through, and anticipating rewards (1:1–18).

Lots of things are going on in this pericope, which reminds me to remind my readers (following the linguistic predilection of this pericope!) to keep things simple. I follow, advise, and strongly recommend the dictum *Keep it simple!* I will confess that, in the interests of comprehensiveness, the maps in this work (and in others within the same series) are often not simple and tend to include more than what is necessary. Do your hard work in the interpretation (with this commentary as a guide), but when it comes to your sermon, let the thrust and import and force of the pericope and what its author is *doing*, shape and mold your sermons as you exercise your pastoral wisdom in the pursuit of simplicity, and your pastoral love in the pursuit of the spiritual formation of your flock.

Possible Preaching Maps for Pericope 11

I. Examples of Suffering
    Paul (1:8a, 12a)
    Jesus (1:8b, 10b)
    Onesiphorus (1:15–18)
    For the cause and agent of cause, God (1:9–10a)
    Move-to-Relevance: Examples in the congregation
II. Endurance in Suffering
    Empowerment (1:7, 8d, 14)
    Move-to-Relevance: How this empowerment looks in our lives
III. Encouragement for Suffering
    Entrustment (1:8c, 11, 13–14)
    Expectation of rewards (1:12, 18)
    Entrenched in the faith handed down (1:1–6, 13)
    Move-to-Relevance: Legacies in our lives
IV. *Inherit the Suffering!*
    What the Christian can do in suffering, or in preparation to suffer

While I think the map above creates a "narratival" sequence in the sermon, another option is shown below, employing the same moves, but in a different order that utilizes four questions: Who? What? How (the application)? and Why?

I. Who? Examples of Suffering
    Paul (1:8a, 12a)
    Jesus (1:8b, 10b)
    Onesiphorus (1:15–18)
    For the cause and agent of cause, God (1:9–10a)
    Move-to-Relevance: Examples in the congregation
II. What? Endurance in Suffering
    Empowerment (1:7, 8d, 14)
    Move-to-Relevance: How this empowerment looks in our lives
III. How? *Inherit the Suffering!*
    What the Christian can do in suffering, or in preparation to suffer
IV. Why? Encouragement for Suffering
    Entrustment (1:8c, 11, 13–14)
    Expectation of rewards (1:12, 18)
    Entrenched in the faith handed down (1:1–6, 13)
    Move-to-Relevance: Legacies in our lives

PERICOPE 12

Working Hard, Pleasing God

2 Timothy 2:1–13

[Faithful Ministry; Undistracted, Upright, Industrious; Rewards]

REVIEW, SUMMARY, PREVIEW

Review of Pericope 11: The first pericope of 2 Timothy (Pericope 11: 2 Tim 1:1–18) called on believers to endure suffering on behalf of the gospel, empowered by God and entrusting their mission to him, encouraged by exemplars, entrenched in the faith handed down—the legacies of those who have gone on before—and expecting future rewards.

Summary of Pericope 12: This pericope (2 Tim 2:1–13) continues the theme of suffering, but focuses upon the undistractedness, uprightness, and industriousness of believers in faithful ministry—including their entrustment of the future work of God to other faithful people—thus garnering for themselves eternal rewards of glory.

Preview of Pericope 13: The next pericope (2 Tim 2:14–26) contrasts the speech and deeds of false teachers and truth teachers. The latter, beneficial for God, and prepared for every good work, including that of rehabilitating the erring, wins approval and honor from God.

12   2 Timothy 2:1–13

THEOLOGICAL FOCUS OF PERICOPE 12

12   The servants of God, strengthened by God's grace, and entrusting the future work of God to faithful people of God, face potential suffering, but are undistracted, upright, and industrious, seeking only to please their faithful God and to further his cause, thus gaining great eternal rewards (2:1–13).

12.1   The servants of God, continually strengthened by God's grace, and entrusting the future work of God to other faithful people of God, face potential suffering, but are undistracted, upright, and industrious, seeking only to please God, thus gaining eternal rewards (2:1–7).

12.2   Remembering God and his grand plan, believers are willing to suffer for God's cause, for the consummation of their own salvation and that of those to whom they minister, even eternal glory, for great rewards are promised to such believers (as well as discipline for those who fail) from the hand of a God who ever remains faithful to his people (2:8–13).

OVERVIEW

This pericope continues Paul's appeal to Timothy that he be willing to suffer for God and for the gospel, expanding that theme with three metaphors, martial, athletic, and agrarian, and the citation of a hymn that assures the faithful believer of rewards. That it is a continuation of what preceded is evident in the similarities between 1:6–14 and 2:1–13, both containing personal exhortations to Timothy with several second-person imperatives[1]:

2 Timothy 1:6–14	2 Timothy 2:1–13
χάρισμα (*charisma*; 1:6); χάρις (*charis*; 1:9)	χάρις (2:1)
δύναμις (*dynamis*; 1:7, 8)	ἐνδυναμόω (*endynamoō*; 2:1)
"which you have heard from me" (1:13)	"what you have heard from me" (2:2)
παραθήκη (*parathēkē*; 1:12, 14)	παρατίθημι (*paratithēmi*; 2:2)
Eschatological focus (1:10, 12, 16, 18)	Eschatological focus (2:5–6, 10)
Suffering (συγκακοπαθέω, 1:8; πάσχω, *paschō*; 1:12)	Suffering (συγκακοπαθέω, 2:3; κακοπαθέω, *kakopatheō*; 2:9)
for the "gospel" (1:8, 10)	for the "gospel" (2:8)
Paul's experience (1:6, 8, 11–12)	Paul's experience (2:9–10)
δέσμιος (*desmios*, "prisoner"; 1:8)	δεσμός (*desmos*, "bonds"; 2:9)
Christ's work (1:9–10)	Christ's work (2:8)
Named individuals (1:15–18)	Named individuals (1:14–18)

---

1. The intervening section, 1:15–18, has no such imperatives. Also, there are only two instances of συγκακοπαθέω, *synkakopatheō*, in the NT, in 2 Tim 1:8 and 2:3.

12.1 2 Timothy 2:1–7

> **THEOLOGICAL FOCUS 12.1**
>
> 12.1 The servants of God, continually strengthened by God's grace, and entrusting the future work of God to other faithful people of God, face potential suffering, but are undistracted, upright, and industrious, seeking only to please God, thus gaining eternal rewards (2:1–7).

TRANSLATION 12.1

2:1   You therefore, my son, be strengthened in the grace that is in Christ Jesus.

2:2   And what you have heard from me in the presence of many witnesses, these things entrust to faithful people who will be competent to teach others also.

2:3   Co-suffer affliction [with us], as a good soldier of Christ Jesus.

2:4   No one soldiering gets entangled in the things of [daily] life, so that that he may please the soldier-recruiter.

2:5   Also, if anyone competes as an athlete, he is not crowned [victor] unless he competes as an athlete by the rules.

2:6   The hard-working farmer ought to be the first to receive his share of the crops.

2:7   Consider what I am saying; for the Lord will give you understanding in everything.

NOTES 12.1

12.1 *The servants of God, continually strengthened by God's grace, and entrusting the future work of God to other faithful people of God, face potential suffering, but are undistracted, upright, and industrious, seeking only to please God, thus gaining eternal rewards* (2:1–7).

Here, after unloading three imperatives ("be strengthened"; "entrust"; and "co-suffer affliction"; 2:1, 2, 3, respectively), Paul unleashes three illustrations that are typical of Greco-Roman models of instruction: that of the soldier (2:3–4), the athlete (2:5), and the farmer (2:6).

As noted in the table above, elements and motifs revealed in the previous pericope echo in this one. And right after the positive example of Onesiphorus in 1:15–18 come the words: "You therefore, my son . . ." (2:1). The coordinating conjunction "therefore" is a deliberate link to what preceded. Timothy is enjoined to "be strengthened" in the "grace" of Christ Jesus so that he may be faithful, as Onesiphorus was. While ἐνδυναμοῦ, *endynamou*, is likely a middle-voice verb, the context and the already noted δυν (*dyn*)-root verbs in Pericope 11: 2 Tim 1:1–18 suggest that it refers to divine strengthening. The present tense of the verb points to an ongoing strengthening that is essential to the rest of Paul's exhortations to Timothy. "Recognizing and accessing spiritual power is preparatory to other activities Timothy is to carry out. . . . The sense of the imperative [in 2 Tim 2:1] is really 'yield yourself to divine empowerment.'"[2] And that was how Timothy would be like Onesiphorus (1:16–18; and like Paul, 1:12), but unlike Phygelus and Hermogenes (1:15).

---

2. Towner, *Letters to Timothy and Titus*, 488–89. While it is *divine* strengthening, the imperative

What Timothy has "heard" publicly from Paul, "in the presence of many witnesses" (2:2), he is to convey to others who are "faithful." While 2:2 seems to be dealing mostly with the verbal component of pedagogy, this is not to divorce sound words from sound living—the "pattern" of life lived according to those "words that are sound" (1:13).[3] The ability to teach, required of these "faithful people" who would thereby be able to pass it on to others, is no doubt connected to 1 Tim 3:2; 5:17; and Titus 1:9—a requirement for elders. The primary, though not exclusive, audience for Timothy's teaching may well have been such officers of the church. In any case, Timothy's "faithful" hearers needed to be "competent to teach others." Thus we have a series of concentric circles of teaching being developed: apostle to delegate to elders to others. In context, this might well be an aside from Paul, exhorting Timothy of the importance of passing on what he was going to say next: "Co-suffer affliction [with us]" as soldier, athlete, and farmer.[4]

How is one to go through this suffering? By means of three metaphors, that of the soldier, athlete, and farmer—all common occupations of that age—the yoke of pain borne by the co-suffering disciple is described, along with the wreath of gain[5]:

2 Timothy 2:3–6			
Metaphor	Soldier	Athlete	Farmer
Suffer by ...	Singlemindedness	Rule-keeping	Hard work
Outcome	Pleasure of recruiter	Winning the prize	Receiving a share

While the manner of suffering and the burden thereof are different for each metaphor (and for each child of God in any age), there is a focus in each on the positive outcome, no doubt linked to the eschatological reward of "eternal glory" (2:10), primarily for those on behalf of whom the sufferers undergo affliction, but also for themselves, as 2:11–12 will establish.[6]

The motif of soldiering is found in 2:3–4: we have a noun, στρατιώτης (*stratiōtēs*, "soldier"); and two participles, στρατευόμενος (*strateuomenos*, "soldiering," from στρατεύω, *strateuō*, "to soldier"), and στρατολογήσαντι (*stratologēsanti*, "soldier-recruiting," from στρατολογέω, *stratologeō*, "to recruit as soldier"). It is the singlemindedness of the soldier that is critical here, an undistracted devotion to duty that precludes entanglement in "the things of [daily] life" (2:4).[7] Whether or not such entanglements are sinful is not the issue here; it is simply that such an embrace of the world ought not to be a priority for the recruited

---

assumes some *human* responsibility, whether yielding to the strengthening or being receptive to it.

3. Also see 1 Cor 14:37; 1 Thess 2:13; 2 Thess 2:15; 3:6–7. Because of this integral and inseparable link between work and life, I tend to see all the διδασκ-root words (διδάσκω, *didaskō*, occurs in 2:2) as relating primarily to preaching (= teaching-for-application; see Kuruvilla, *Vision for Preaching*, 71–129).

4. As in 2 Tim 1:8, I believe the call is to "co-suffer affliction *with us*," i.e., with Paul and Jesus (especially in light of the rest of 2:3), and perhaps with Onesiphorus, as well. This is the only recurrence of συγκακοπαθέω in the NT (after 1:8). For related terms, see 1:12 (πάσχω); and 2:9; 4:5 (κακοπαθέω). We also see "deposit/entrustment" language repeated in 2:2 (παρατίθημι; also in 1 Tim 1:18; and cognates in 6:20; and 2 Tim 1:12, 14).

5. Modified from Mounce, *Pastoral Epistles*, 507.

6. Timothy's own imprisonment and release are mentioned in Heb 13:23.

7. The only other use of the verb ἐμπλέκω, *emplekō*, in the NT has the same notion (2 Pet 2:20). Hermas, *Similitudes* 6.2.6–7, utilizes the verb twice to describe sheep "entangled" in "thorns and thistles" (my translation).

soldier, for it is a distraction for a single-minded warrior. Perhaps one could say that what is being criticized here is not involvement, but entanglement—undue and overwhelming liaisons with the world that drain one's time, resources, energies, and focus. That such undistractedness is recommended not only for Paul and for Timothy but for *all* is signified by the indefinite pronoun οὐδεὶς, *oudeis,* "no one," in 2:4.

The athletic metaphor was already reflected in the notion of the "fight" (wrestling) and the training in gymnasiums for that undertaking: 1 Tim 1:18; 4:7; 6:12; 2 Tim 4:7. The verb ἀθλέω, *athleō,* occurring twice in 2 Tim 2:5, is found only here in the NT. "Competing . . . by the rules" (νομίμως, *nomimōs,* "lawfully") cannot be restricted to the actual regulations and statutes of the contest per se; rather, these "rules" of the games likely included principles and norms of training, as the gymnasium references in 1 Tim 4:7 already indicated. There it was with regard to the development of godliness, the outcome of good nourishment upon Scripture, towards which God's people were to "work hard and strive" (4:7–10). That may not be far from view here, too. Pausanias, the second-century geographer, observed (*Description of Greece,* II: 5.24.9):

> Beside this image [of Zeus] it is the custom for athletes, their fathers and their brothers, as well as their trainers, to swear an oath upon slices of boar's flesh that in nothing will they sin against the Olympic games. The athletes take this further oath also, that for ten successive months they have strictly followed the regulations for training [τὰ πάντα ἐς ἄσκησιν, *ta panta es askēsin*].[8]

For the athlete that Timothy (and each believer) is called to be, such lawful competition "by the rules," Paul intimates here, is to exhibit a life marked by uprightness in every facet, and in every situation, i.e., the consistent manifestation of godliness (a recurring theme in the PE). That, no doubt involves pain and suffering, as does any strict athletic training regimen (see 2 Tim 3:12).

The metaphor of the farmer primarily emphasizes the eschatological outcome of suffering.[9] The industrious agriculturist has a right to the produce of the field on a future day (Deut 20:6; Prov 20:4; 27:18; 1 Cor 9:7)—the anticipation of rewards then, for all the effort expended now. The striving (from κοπιάω, *kopiaō*) of this laborer was reflected in Paul's own life in the PE in 1 Tim 4:10 (the verb is also used of the elder in 5:17).

All that to say, no matter what the intensity of the struggle, no matter what the shape of the strife, no matter what the scope of the battle, there will be rewards for the undistracted, upright, and industrious servant of God, one who is willing to endure to the end. "The metaphors, when duly pondered, suggest that beyond warfare is victory, beyond athletic effort a prize, and beyond agricultural labor a crop. In the same way, Timothy's share of hardship will be followed by reward."[10] The exhortation is intensified with Paul's νόει ὃ λέγω (*noei ho legō;* "Consider what I am saying") in 2 Tim 2:7.[11]

---

8. Pausanias, *Description of Greece,* 2:529.

9. The reward motif is present in the metaphors of the soldier and athlete, too: the former receives the pleasure of the commanding officer, and the latter is crowned victor with a wreath.

10. Barrett, *Pastoral Epistles,* 102.

11. Plato, *Epistle VIII* 352C has νοήσατε δὲ ἃ λέγω νῦν (*noēsate de ha legō nun;* "So consider what I am saying now"; my translation).

12.2 2 Timothy 2:8-13

> **THEOLOGICAL FOCUS 12.2**
>
> 12.2 Remembering God and his grand plan, believers are willing to suffer for God's cause, for the consummation of their own salvation and that of those to whom they minister, even eternal glory, for great rewards are promised to such believers (as well as discipline for those who fail) from the hand of a God who ever remains faithful to his people (2:8–13).

TRANSLATION 12.2

2:8 *Remember Jesus Christ, who has been raised from the dead, of the seed of David, according to my gospel,*

2:9 *for which I suffer affliction, even bonds as an evil-worker; but the word of God is not bound;*

2:10 *for this reason I endure all things for the sake of the elect, so that that they also may find the salvation which is in Christ Jesus with eternal glory.*

2:11 *This statement is trustworthy: For if we co-died [with Him], we will also co-live [with Him];*

2:12 *if we endure, we will also co-reign [with Him]; if we will deny [Him], He also will deny us;*

2:13 *if we are faithless, He remains faithful, for He is not able to deny Himself.*

NOTES 12.2

12.2 *Remembering God and his grand plan, believers are willing to suffer for God's cause, for the consummation of their own salvation and that of those to whom they minister, even eternal glory, for great rewards are promised to such believers (as well as discipline for those who fail) from the hand of a God who ever remains faithful to his people (2:8–13).*

Second Timothy 2:8–13 appears to be a section bracketed by μν-root words: μνημόνευε, *mnēmoneue*, "remember," in 2:8, and ὑπομίμνῃσκε, *hypomimnēske*, "remind," in 2:14, that commences the next pericope.[12] Here the theological basis for the appeal to Timothy to be an undistracted soldier, an upright athlete, and an industrious farmer (2:1–7) is provided in 2:8–13.

The pattern of Paul following Christ for the sake of the cause, the gospel, and its causative agent, God in Christ, is found here in the single sentence of 2:8–10 (as it was also in 1:8–12). The "seed of David" reference here (2:8), following the mention of Jesus's resurrection, is messianic and eschatological, pointing to the Lord's coming reign (also reflected in 2:12). The absence of any explicit mention of Christ's atoning work, while certainly implied in his resurrection, simply serves to focus Timothy's attention upon enduring for God and his cause, the gospel, just as Paul did, with the endpoint of the coming glory in sight (2:10).

---

12. The μν-root words show up in this Epistle in 2 Tim 1:3, 4, 5, 6; 2:8, 14; 3:8, 14.

The human representative of the cause, the servant of its divine agent, the apostle Paul, affirms that he "suffered affliction" (κακοπαθέω) as an "evil-worker" (κακοῦργος, *kakourgos*) and endured so that the ones he ministered to, "the elect," may also be saved for future glory (2:9–10). Their salvation and future glory likely refer to the same complex of events: "salvation" here meaning the consummation thereof in the final day with its attendant glories (rewards).[13] Thus we have the messianic model of Jesus, who died for others for the sake of God's grand plan (the gospel) but was resurrected to reign as the seed of David (2:8). And this is the pattern Paul is following—suffering now, but expecting glory later. As well, this is the road that Timothy and all believers should anticipate treading: suffering now, glory later (2:12). The irony is that even though in his suffering Paul is in "bonds" (δεσμῶν, *desmōn*, a cognate of δέω, *deō*, "to bind"), the word of God is not "bound" (δέδεται, *dedetai*, from δέω, 2:9). "The body they may kill; God's truth abideth still; His kingdom is forever!"[14] In sum, because of the unstoppable word of God proclaimed by Paul in the service of God and his gospel (2:8c–9), the apostle could endure all kinds of hardships ("all things," 2:10), for the consummation of salvation of others (as well as of himself: "that they *also* may find . . . salvation").

After dealing with his own endurance and suffering of evil—while remembering the risen Jesus and his cause, the gospel (2:8–10)—Paul again exhorts Timothy (and the rest of the readers of this Epistle) to sustained endurance. He does so by means of a four-line hymnic/creedal piece (2:11b–13), primarily dealing with the outcome of such endurance. It is a motivational section marked by both encouragement (Lines 1 and 2—2:11b; 2:12a) and warning (Lines 3 and 4—2:12b; 2:13). But it is introduced by one of Paul's favorite declarations in the PE: πιστὸς ὁ λόγος, *pistos ho logos*, "this statement is trustworthy" (2:11a; also in 1 Tim 1:15; 3:1; 4:9; Titus 3:8). Obviously, the antecedent mention of ὁ λόγος τοῦ θεοῦ, *ho logos tou theou*, "the word of God," that is not bound (2:9), is clearly in the writer's mind. The thrust of 2:11b–13 is that this trustworthy word (of God) promises a positive outcome despite all the κακ (*kak*)-prefixed words (2:9) and the negative connotations they conjure.

The "set piece" nature of 2:11b–13 is evident in its careful structure: each line comprises a conditional clause (with a protasis and an apodosis), the presence of συν-words without objects (translated with the prefix "co-"), and the unidentified third person implied by the verbs ἀρνήσεται, *arnēsetai*, in 2:12b ("if we will deny [whom?]") and μένει, *menei*, in 2:13 ("He remains faithful [to whom?]), and the unspecified referent of the pronouns ἐκεῖνος, *ekeinos*, "he," in 2:12b and 2:13[15]:

---

13. Also see Rom 5:2; 8:18, 30; 2 Cor 3:18; 4:17; 1 Thess 2:12; 2 Thess 2:14 for this glorious aspect of salvation future.

14. From Luther's *Ein feste Burg ist unser Gott*, translated by Frederic Henry Hedge.

15. Modified from Mounce, *Pastoral Epistles*, 502.

	Line 1 (2:11b) Positive	Line 2 (2:12a) Positive	Line 3 (2:12b) Negative	Line 4 (2:13) Negative
PROTASIS ("if ...")				
Introduction	εἰ γάρ, *ei gar* "For if ..."	εἰ "If ..."	εἰ "If ..."	εἰ "If ..."
Tense	Aorist "we co-died"	Present "we endure"	Future "we will deny"	Present "we are faithless"
Object	"Him" implied (συν-verb)	—	—	—
Issue	Conversion	Endurance	Denial	Faithlessness
APODOSIS ("then ...")				
Introduction	καί, *kai* "[we] also ..."	καί "[we] also ..."	καί + ἐκεῖνος "He also ..."	ἐκεῖνος "He ..."
Tense	Future "will co-live"	Future "will co-reign"	Future "will deny"	Present "remains"
Object	"Him" implied (συν-verb)	"Him" implied (συν-verb)	"us" ἡμᾶς, *hēmas*	—
Coda	—	—	—	"for He ..."

While this is no doubt an extant hymn or creed (or a fragment thereof), there appears to be some conscious shaping of this preexisting statement by Paul: a συν-verb was already introduced in 1:8 and 2:3 (συγκακοπαθέω), and we have a few more in 2:11b, 12a (συναπεθάνομεν, *synapethanomen*, "we co-died," συζήσομεν, *syzēsomen*, "we will co-live," and συμβασιλεύσομεν, *symbasileusomen*, "we will co-reign"); vocabulary in 2:11–13 is shared by the rest of the PE (ὑπομένω, *hypomenō*, "endure," in 2 Tim 2:10, 12, and the noun, ὑπομονή, *hypomonē*, "steadfastness," in 1 Tim 6:11; 2 Tim 3:10; and Titus 2:2; ἀρνέομαι, *arneomai*, "deny," in 2 Tim 2:12, 13; Titus 1:16; 2:12; ἀπιστέω, *apisteō*, "be faithless," in 1 Tim 1:13; 5:8; 2 Tim 2:13; Titus 1:15); and the connections between this section and what preceded it in 2:8–10 are made explicit with the coordinating conjunction that begins Line 1 (2:11b), γάρ, *gar*, "for."[16]

Obviously, Lines 1 and 2 describe believers' "co-actions" with/in Christ—these lines are positive and serve as encouragements (as was noted). Lines 3 and 4 explain Christ's actions toward believers—these lines are more negative and serve as warnings. Thus the correlation in each line is between "we" in the protasis and "He" (Christ) in the apodosis; even in 2:11b and 2:12a, the clearly implied focus is on Christ.

There might be a progression of the tenses in the protases from Line 1 to Line 4: past (aorist: dealing with prior conversion) to present (dealing with ongoing endurance) to future (dealing with potential denial), returning to a deliberate present (dealing with faithlessness now). The recurrence of the present (Line 4, 2:13) with regard to deprecated faithlessness indicates that this is an ever-present danger for the believer. Just as afflictions and trials are a constant accompaniment of the godly life (2 Tim 3:12), so are the dangers of lapsing into faithlessness. The future, however, is the motivational engine for this section (and pericope: eschatological aspects were already evident even in 2:8–10), and that future

---

16. See Towner, *Letters to Timothy and Titus*, 507. Death and resurrection are present in 2:8, of Jesus; and in 2:11b, of believers.

outcome, Paul tells us, is contingent upon a present response of faithful endurance by believers to those tumults and tribulations.

These four lines further dilate on what Timothy and the rest were to "remember" (2:8; and pass on to others, 2:2). While the call to suffer was clear in what preceded, "this insertion of theological affirmations makes the obligation to join in suffering impossible to miss and too serious to dismiss."[17] Particularly, the motivations for enduring suffering are underscored in 2:11–13: eschatological life with Christ; sharing in Christ's reign;[18] and the blessing of Christ's ultimate faithfulness to his people. On the other hand is the disincentive: the denial by Christ of his people who have failed to remain faithful (a loss of rewards obviously, not of salvation). This mutual denial—by people of Christ before others, and by Christ of people before the Father—was explicitly noted by Jesus himself (Matt 10:33 and parallels).

While the denial may be mutual (Line 3, 1 Tim 2:12b), faithlessness certainly is not—it remains unilaterally human-sided. As far as God is concerned, "He remains faithful" (Line 4, 2:13; also see Rom 3:3), in keeping with his divine character. This trait is so important that Paul adds a coda—"for He is not able to deny Himself"—upsetting the symmetry established in Lines 1–3. It is best to see the entirety of Line 4, 2:13, with its overturning of patterns established in Lines 1–3, as a needed explication of Line 3, 2:12b, a qualification or limitation of Christ's denial: If we deny him, he might deny us (loss of rewards), but he, in the end, is faithful no matter what (as far as salvation is concerned), for he cannot deny himself.

SERMON MAPS

THEOLOGICAL FOCUS OF PERICOPE 12 FOR PREACHING

12   The servants of God, strengthened by God's grace and entrusting the work of God to faithful people of God, face potential suffering, but seek only to please their faithful God and to further his cause—undistracted, upright, and industrious—thus gaining great eternal rewards (2:1–13).

Suffering has shown up in previous pericopes of the PE, even in the pericope preceding this one—and they will show up again in this Epistle. Therefore, the focus in a sermon on 2 Tim 2:1–13 is best placed upon faithfulness in soldiering, competing, farming: undistracted, upright, and industrious—pleasing God.

---

17. Towner, *Letters to Timothy and Titus*, 506.
18. This notion is also found in Matt 7:23; 19:28; Luke 12:9; 22:30; Mark 8:38; 2 Tim 2:12; Rev 1:6; 3:21; 4:4; 5:10; 11:16; 20:4, 6; 22:5.

Possible Preaching Maps for Pericope 12

I. Call
   In the strength of Christ (2:1, 7–8)
   Sharing of suffering (2:3a, 9)
   Entrustment of mission (2:2)
   Move-to-Relevance: Our passing on of the mission
II. Character
   Undistracted, upright, industrious—pleasing God (2:3b–6a)
   Move-to-Relevance: Our pleasing of the One who called us
III. Compensation
   Rewards (6b, 10–13)
IV. *Plod to Glory!*
   How to "plod," undistracted, upright, and industrious[19]

Another option, this one attending to the work of the protagonists in this drama, Christ, Paul, and ourselves:

I. Christ's Work
   His strength (2:1)
   His victory (2:7–8)
   His faithfulness in rewarding (2:11–13)
   Move-to-Relevance: Rewards for our faithfulness to Christ
II. Paul's Work
   Ministry: entrustment of mission (2:2a)
   Suffering (2:9–10)
   Move-to-Relevance: Our passing on of the mission
III. Our Work
   Sharing of suffering (2:3)
   Entrustment of mission (2:2b)
   Undistracted, upright, industrious—pleasing God (2:4–6)
   Move-to-Relevance: Our pleasing of the One who called us
IV. *Plod to Glory!*
   How to "plod," undistracted, upright, and industrious

---

19. One of these three may be chosen for emphasis in application. It will also work to have the application as move III., and "Compensation" as move IV., if one desires.

PERICOPE 13

Beneficial to God, Useful for Good Work

2 Timothy 2:14–26

[False Teachers vs. Truth Teachers; Right Speech; Approved and Honored by God]

REVIEW, SUMMARY, PREVIEW

Review of Pericope 12: The second pericope of 2 Timothy (Pericope 12: 2 Tim 2:1–13) continued the theme of suffering, but focused upon the undistractedness, uprightness, and industriousness of believers in faithful ministry—including their entrustment of the future work of God to other faithful people—thus garnering for themselves eternal rewards of glory.

Summary of Pericope 13: This pericope (2 Tim 2:14–26) contrasts the speech of false teachers and truth teachers (all believers). The latter win approval and honor from God and become beneficial for him, prepared as they are for every good work, including that of rehabilitating the erring.

Preview of Pericope 14: The next pericope (2 Tim 3:1–17) continues the contrasts made in the current pericope: the faithless and faithful are compared with regard to their character and relationship to truth. It is grounding in Scripture that enables the latter to follow after godly models, trusting in God's deliverance in times of suffering, and becoming capable persons of God, equipped for godliness.

13   2 Timothy 2:14–26

THEOLOGICAL FOCUS OF PERICOPE 13

13 God's people, his possession, obtain honor by pursuing righteousness and being beneficial for God, ready for good works, and they help opponents escape the captivity of Satan by clearly and graciously expounding the word (2:14–26).

> 13.1 God's people, known to God and sealed as his possession—clearly expounding the word, and therefore approved by God and unashamed—guard against word-quarreling that is unprofitable, that spreads dangerously, and that, by leading to further ungodliness, upsets others' faith to their ruin (2:14–19).
>
> 13.2 Those obtain honor who have purified themselves from unrighteousness—fleeing lusts and pursuing righteousness—and who are thereby made holy, beneficial for God, and ready for good works, including the correction of opponents with grace, so that the latter may be granted repentance by God, and helped to escape the captivity of Satan (2:20–26).

OVERVIEW

Second Timothy 2:14—4:8 may be considered the second major part of the Epistle. The first "half," so to speak (1:1—2:13), dealt with the endurance of the servant of God in ministry. In the second "half," at least until 4:6, the authorial first person is missing, but we see over a dozen second-person imperatives, directing the delegate, Timothy (and all the children of God), on matters of faith and praxis.

There are several similarities between Pericope 12: 2 Tim 2:1–13 and Pericope 13: 2 Tim 2:14–26. The closing hymn/creed of 2:12b–13 introduced the possibility of failure, and 2:14–26 (the entirety of this pericope) deals essentially with false teachers (apostates, i.e., failed teachers); 2:2 mentioned the ability to teach (ἱκανοὶ ἔσονται . . . διδάξαι, *hikanoi esontai . . . didaxai*, "be competent to teach"), and so does 2:24 (διδακτικός, *didaktikos*, "able to teach"); both 2:8 and 2:14 have an μν (*mn*)-root word; and 2:3–4 notes the pleasing of Christ, and 2:15 the approval of God.

The pericope may be seen as having two panels: 2:14–18 and 2:22–23 (in addition to an intervening section, 2:19–21, comparing teachers/leaders to vessels in a house, and a closing section, 2:24–26). Each of these two panels has a trio of imperatives in a negative-positive-negative sequence[1]:

	Imperatives	
2:14	"Remind ... not to ..."	−
2:15	"Make every effort ..."	+
2:16	"But avoid ..."	−
2:22a	"But flee ..."	−
2:22b	"And pursue ..."	+
2:23	"But reject ..."	−

---

1. Marshall, *Pastoral Epistles*, 743.

The closing section, 2:24–26, again compares teachers/leaders: "not be . . . but be" (2:24). Such contrasts between vice and virtue, as are seen throughout this pericope (and, indeed, throughout the PE), were common pedagogical tools of the time, as was also the drawing upon medical imagery in these discussions: 2:17 has "gangrene" and "eat away/spread"; one might add ὀρθοτομέω, *orthotomeō*, literally "to straight-cut" (i.e., "clearly expound"), in 2:15, perhaps a surgical allusion (see below). So while 1:13 described Paul's words as sound (ὑγιαινόντων λόγων, *hygiainontōn logōn*), in 2:17 the words of the false teachers are labeled gangrenous—ὁ λόγος αὐτῶν ὡς γάγγραινα, *ho logos autōn hōs gangraina*. "Its application is particularly suggestive when the 'surgeon' Timothy [2:15] is facing false teaching that is 'gangrenous and spreading' [2:17]!"[2]

The pericope, while dealing with the immediate need to counter false teachers, is an explication of the Christian leader's character in the face of opposition, particularly with regard to doctrine and grounding in Scripture. Yet there is hope for those apostates, for Timothy is to "remind them," "solemnly charging [them]" (2:14) with patience and gentleness (2:24–25) to change, "if perhaps God may give them repentance . . . and they may come to their senses [and escape] from the snare of the devil" (2:25–26). In striving for this goal, not only must Timothy be "able to teach" with attitudes evidencing humility (2:24), his life also must reflect what he teaches (2:15–16, 22–23).

That Timothy's pedagogical responsibilities were serious is indicated by the adjuration formula he was to employ, involving a solemn charge invoking the presence of God (2:14). One who was himself solemnly charged (1 Tim 5:21; 6:13; and 2 Tim 4:1) is to engage in some solemn charging himself. Again, the context of a leader passing a baton to a delegate is obvious.

13.1 2 Timothy 2:14–19

THEOLOGICAL FOCUS 13.1

13.1 God's people, known to God and sealed as his possession—clearly expounding the word, and therefore approved by God and unashamed—guard against word-quarrelling that is unprofitable, that spreads dangerously, and that, by leading to further ungodliness, upsets others' faith to their ruin (2:14–19).

TRANSLATION 13.1

2:14 *Remind [people] of these things, solemnly charging [them] before God not to word-quarrel, [which is] beneficial for nothing, [but] for the ruin of those who hear.*

2:15 *Make every effort to present yourself approved to God, a worker who does not need to be ashamed, clearly expounding the word of truth.*

2:16 *But avoid profane empty chatter; for it will progress to more ungodliness,*

2:17 *and their word will eat away like gangrene. Among whom are Hymenaeus and Philetus,*

---

2. Johnson, *First and Second Letters to Timothy*, 394. Medical imagery in the PE (mostly employing ὑγιαίνω, *hygiainō*, and cognates) is found in 1 Tim 1:10; 6:3; 2 Tim 1:13; 2:15, 17; 4:3; Titus 1:9, 13; 2:1, 2, 8.

2:18   *who have gone astray from the truth, saying the resurrection has already occurred, and they upset the faith of some.*

2:19   *Nevertheless, the firm foundation of God has stood, having this seal, "The Lord knows those who are His," and, "Everyone naming the name of the Lord is to abstain from unrighteousness."*

NOTES 13.1

13.1   *God's people, known to God and sealed as his possession—clearly expounding the word, and therefore approved by God and unashamed—guard against word-quarrelling that is unprofitable, that spreads dangerously, and that, by leading to further ungodliness, upsets others' faith to their ruin (2:14–19).*

It was Timothy who was reminded in 2:8; now in 2:14, Timothy is the one to do the reminding. Likewise, ἀκούω, *akouō*, in 1:13 and 2:2 were used of Timothy "hearing" Paul; here in 2:14, it is others "hearing." We are not told whom Timothy is to remind (2:14). The nearest antecedent might be "faithful people" in 2:2, but it is unlikely they would be considered "faithful" if they were engaged in word-quarreling, thus ruining others. In all likelihood, from the context, the ones to be reminded by Timothy are the false teachers, or those inclined to teach falsely (and for whom some hope of rehabilitation is retained; see below). The hearers in 2:14 then would be those who listened to these false teachers. As to the content of "these things" (2:14), it must refer to the encouragements and warnings of the four-line hymn (2:12b–13) that immediately preceded Paul's exhortation to Timothy here. All of the nefarious activities in 2:14, one would imagine, fall into the purview of denying Christ and being unfaithful to him (2:13).[3]

"Word-quarrel" is λογομαχέω (*logomacheō*; 2:14)[4]; two more μαχ (*mach*)-root words occur in this pericope: a noun, μάχη (*machē*; "quarrel," 2:23), and a verb, μάχομαι (*machomai*; "be quarrelsome," 2:24). And these false teachers' quarreling operations are dangerous—bringing "ruin!" The only other use of καταστροφή (*katastrophē*, "ruin") in the NT is in 2 Pet 2:6, where it describes the fate of Sodom and Gomorrah. This is one of several consequences of the vile ways of false teachers; the others are: "progressing to more ungodliness" (2 Tim 2:16); words "eating away like gangrene" (2:17); "upsetting the faith of some" (2:18); as well as "breeding quarrels" (2:23).

A number of contrasts punctuate this pericope, mostly between Timothy (and those on his side) and the band of opponents[5]:

---

3. So this is certainly something all God's people must avoid.

4. These wranglings also show up in the description of the opponents' heretical endeavors in 1 Tim 1:4; 6:4; 2 Tim 2:23.

5. Also see Van Neste, *Cohesion and Structure*, 169.

Timothy & Co.	Opponents
Those with a "clean" heart (2:22)	Vessel to "be cleansed" (2:21)
"Beneficial" for God (2:21)	"Beneficial" for nothing (2:14)
Approved to *God* (2:15) Known to *God* (2:19) Calling on *God* (2:22) The bondservant of *God* (2:24)	Captive to the *devil* (2:26)
Pursuing "faith" (2:22)	Upsetting people's "faith" (2:18)
"Clearly expounding" the "word" (λόγος, 2:15)	"Word-quarrelling" (λογομαχέω, 2:14) "Word" (λόγος) is gangrenous (2:17) False doctrine being "said" (λέγω, 2:18)
Handling the word of "truth" (2:15)	Going astray from the "truth" (2:18) May return to the "truth" (2:25)
Not "quarrelsome" (μάχομαι, 2:24)	"Word-quarrelling" (λογομαχέω, 2:14) Produce "quarrels" (μάχη, 2:23)

As depicted, Timothy's handling of the "*word* of *truth*" (2:15) is in marked contrast to the opponents' "*word*-quarrelling" (2:14) and the gangrenous spreading of the false "word" (2:17) by those who have gone astray from the "*truth*" (2:18). The "word of truth" points to the OT and the apostolic deposit handed down via Paul to Timothy (Ps 118:43 LXX; Eph 1:13; Col 1:5); of course, in this dispensation it includes Scripture in both its Testaments.

Paul's intent in employing ὀρθοτομέω in 2 Tim 2:15 is not entirely certain, though we can make some good guesses. Notice that "word of God" (in 2:9) and "word of truth" (in 2:15) are contrasted with "their [gangrenous] word" in 2:17 (and their "*word*-quarrelling" in 2:14). So it is mostly the speech acts of the opponents that are to be countered by Timothy undertaking ὀρθοτομέω. The verb is thus likely to deal with Timothy's speech acts, too.[6] The only other occurrences of the verb in Scripture are in LXX Prov 3:6 and 11:5. Both are linked to ὁδός, *hodos,* "way," and its straightening out (etymologically, "straight-cutting"). In Prov 3:6, this straightening is performed by God for the faithful; in 11:5, the righteousness of the faithful straightens out their own way (while the wickedness of the unfaithful trips them up). Outside the Bible, the root verb τέμνω ("to cut") is linked with ὁδός; together they are used both non-metaphorically for cutting an actual (straight) road,[7] and metaphorically for blazing a new (and direct, straight) path.[8] So the metaphorical use of ὀρθοτομέω in 2 Tim 2:15 ("straight cutting") applied to the "word of truth" likely has the sense of one who, as a

---

6. That is not to diminish the focus on right living in this pericope, of course.

7. For e.g., Thucydides (fifth century BCE), *The Peloponnesian War* 2.100: ὁδοὺς εὐθείας ἔτεμε, *odous eutheias eteme,* "cutting straight paths," is used of a Macedonian king improving infrastructure (my translation); here εὐθεῖα is a synonym for ὀρθός, *orthos*. Also see Isa 26:7: ὁδὸς εὐσεβῶν εὐθεῖα ἐγένετο, *hodos eusebōn eutheia egeneto,* "The way of the godly is straight/smooth."

8. For e.g., Lucian (second century CE), *Pro imaginibus* 24: οὐδὲ ἐγὼ πρῶτος ταύτην ἐτεμόμην τὴν ὁδόν, *oude egō prōtos tautēn etemomēn tēn hodon,* "this would be no new track that I was pioneering" (my translation). Such a metaphorical sense of "straight-cutting" to get to the destination is also seen in Plato, *Laws* 7.810E: τὴν νῦν ἐκ τῶν παρόντων λόγων τετμημένην ὁδὸν τῆς νομοθεσίας πορεύεσθαι, *tēn nun ek tōn parontōn logōn tetmēmenēn hodon tēs nomothesias poreuesthai* ("now to proceed boldly along the path of legislation cut out/cleared/marked out by our current words/discourse") (my translation). As well, Philo, *The Worse Attacks the Better* 110, advises that a vice that spreads is to be "excised [cut] by reason's knife [cutter]" (λόγῳ τομεῖ . . . τέμνεται, *logō tomei . . . temnetai*) (my translation).

leader, is cutting (clearing a straight path), i.e., "clearly expounding" God's word through all obstacles—"*word*-quarrelling" (2:14), "profane empty chatter" (2:16), "foolish and ignorant controversies" (2:23), and opponents' "word" that eats away gangrenously (2:17), all of which further ungodliness (2:16), cause straying from the truth, upset the faith of God's people (2:18), and produce more quarrels. That's quite a lot of roadblocks and logjams for a godly leader to undertake "straight cutting" through![9]

In sum, we have Paul's recommendation that Timothy "clearly expound" ("straight cut") the "word of truth" in the midst of, and through, all the misinformation propagated by opponents. This gains the approval of God; not doing so, or doing otherwise, garners only shame (2:15)! The motif of "shame was already seen in 1:8, 12, 16. In those earlier instances, it was unwarranted shame arising from the deplorable situation of Paul and of suffering for God. Here it is appropriate shame arising from a poor handling of the "word of truth." And "clearly expounding" God's word includes avoiding "profane empty chatter": it is not so much that Timothy is himself being discouraged from engaging in such profane and gangrenous talk as described in 2:16–17, as much as that he is not to allow such activities within the body, for they only promote ungodliness.

The background and details of the perversion of the doctrine of resurrection noted in 2:18 is not very clear, but it seems similar to what was mentioned in 1 Cor 15:12 and 2 Thess 2:1–2. Perhaps this heresy was in Paul's mind when he explicitly mentioned the resurrection of Jesus in 2 Tim 2:8, and that of both Jesus and believers in 2:11. The false view deprecated in 2:18 was that the resurrection had, in some sense, already occurred. In any case, this could not have been *the* major heresy circulating in Ephesus: Paul mentions a number of heretics in the PE, but only two of that lot ("among whom are . . .," 2:17), Hymenaeus and Philetus, appear to have been spreading the resurrection error.[10] Besides causing "the deflation of hope in a substantial resurrection," and thereby rendering salvation as only spiritual, it is uncertain how this heterodoxy fits the general contour of Paul's argument in this pericope.[11] Perhaps the implication is that since the resurrection had already occurred, no judgment would be forthcoming for sinful lifestyles (resurrection and judgment were found together in 2:12b–13; also see Luke 14:14; Acts 17:31; Rev 20:5–6). Then again, the reference to this denial might simply be a single, throw-away illustration of an extreme "word of *un*truth" being broadcast by false teachers—a rejection of the core Christian truth of the resurrection! In any case, these falsities could potentially sink the faith of believers and promote ungodliness (2 Tim 2:18). Notice λέγω in 2:18 (the [heretical] "saying" of the false teachers), continuing the gangrenous λογός of 2:17, and the λογομαχέω of 2:14. But it is the λόγος τῆς ἀληθείας, *logos tēs alētheias*, "word of truth," of 2:15 that moves the people of God towards godliness.

While "foundation" and "has stood" and "[the one] having [this seal]" in 2:19 are all singular, "everyone naming the name of the Lord" signifies a plurality of persons. Thus the "foundation" must indicate the group of "individuals who are firmly elect, not being swayed by the heresy," but who are aligned to the word of truth and who manifest godliness.[12] The

---

9. Marshall, *Pastoral Epistles*, 749, likewise sees the metaphor functioning this way: "to guide the word of truth along a straight path without being turned aside by wordy debates or impious talk."

10. Hymenaeus is mentioned 1 Tim 1:20, too. Apparently, efforts there to discipline him had failed—it wasn't easy to get rid of this guy!

11. Towner, *Letters to Timothy and Titus*, 529.

12. Mounce, *Pastoral Epistles*, 529. This is congruent to the divine household, "the church of the living God," being the "pillar and support of the truth" (1 Tim 3:15).

"seal" that is involved in 2:19 is the marking out by God of his property under his protection and provision. This marker is described by two gnomic statements.[13] The first, "the Lord knows those who are His," is a slightly changed version of "God knows those who are His," from Num 16:5. The context of the latter is Korah's rebellion and Moses' assurance that God knows who are his own (and who are not), a setting not very different from that in our pericope, in the light of false teachers infiltrating the body. The second statement, "everyone naming the name of the Lord is to abstain from unrighteousness," has a less precise parallel in Isa 26:13: "Lord, our God, possess us; Lord, except You, another we have not known; we name Your name." This, too, is uttered in the context of the wicked who do not know or see God whose fire will destroy his enemies (Isa 26:10–11, 14). If the church is to "stand" (from ἵστημι, *histēmi*; 2 Tim 2:19), it must "abstain" (ἀφίστημι, *aphistēmi*, a related verb; 2:19) from evil. In sum, 2 Tim 2:19 assures the people of God, aligned to his word of truth, that they are known to him and are to continue living righteously, manifesting godliness, even in the face of heresy and heterodoxy.

13.2 2 Timothy 2:20–26

> **THEOLOGICAL FOCUS 13.2**
>
> 13.2 Those obtain honor who have purified themselves from unrighteousness—fleeing lusts and pursuing righteousness—and who are thereby made holy, beneficial for God, and ready for good works, including the correction of opponents with grace, so that the latter may be granted repentance by God and helped to escape the captivity of Satan (2:20–26).

TRANSLATION 13.2

2:20   Now in a large house there are not only vessels of gold and silver, but also of wood and clay, that is, some for honor and some for dishonor;

2:21   therefore, if anyone purifies himself from these things, he will be a vessel for honor, being made holy, beneficial for the Master, prepared for every good work.

2:22   But flee youthful lusts and pursue righteousness, faith, love, peace, with those calling on the Lord from a pure heart.

2:23   But reject foolish and ignorant controversies, knowing that they breed quarrels.

2:24   The Lord's bondservant must not be quarrelsome, but be kind to all, able to teach, patient when afflicted

2:25   with gentleness correcting those who are opposing, if perhaps God may give them repentance [leading] to the knowledge of truth,

2:26   and they may come to their senses [and escape] the snare of the devil, having been captured by him to [do] his will.

---

13. "The metaphor is based on the practice of inscribing a seal on the foundation of a building in order to indicate ownership and sometimes the function of the building," as with inscription of the names of the twelve apostles on the twelve foundation stones of the New Jerusalem (Rev 21:14) (Mounce, *Pastoral Epistles*, 529).

NOTES 13.2

13.2 Those obtain honor who have purified themselves from unrighteousness—fleeing lusts and pursuing righteousness—and who are thereby made holy, beneficial for God, and ready for good works, including the correction of opponents with grace, so that the latter may be granted repentance by God and helped to escape the captivity of Satan (2:20–26).

After the metaphor of a "foundation" in 2:19, we now have the metaphor of a "house" (with "vessels") in 2:20–21.[14] The use of "made holy" (ἁγιάζω, *hagiazō*) in 2:21 "turns the notion of cleansing toward the ritual language associated with Temple worship and enables the reader to draw the conclusion that this 'great house' is, in fact, the *oikos theou* that is the community and the living Temple of God."[15] After a list of different materials of which those vessels are made, the καί that follows is best read as an epexegetical "that is": "not only gold and silver vessels, but also of wood and of clay, *that is*, some for honor and some for dishonor" (2:20). The picture of vessels of honor and dishonor deals with people who, in the context of this pericope, hold to truth/godliness and falsity/ungodliness, respectively. The "honor" and "dishonor" must include the rewards/punishments these "vessels" can expect on the day of judgment. Therefore, God's people are to "purify themselves from [ἀπό, *apo*] these things" (2:21)—the errors and misdeeds listed in 2:14, 16–19. In effect this "cleansing" is the "abstaining from [ἀπό] unrighteousness" exhorted in 2:19, thereby being "prepared for every good work" (2:21). Note, as well, the paronomasia: deeds "beneficial" (χρήσιμον, *chrēsimon*) for nothing (2:14) vs. deeds "beneficial" (εὔχρηστον, *euchrēston*) for the Master (2:21); and the similar words, "purify" (ἐκκαθαίρω, *ekkathairō*, 2:21) and "pure" (καθαρός, *katharos*) of heart, i.e., those who call on the Lord (2:22).[16] This purification includes "fleeing youthful lusts," "pursuing righteousness, faith, love, peace," and "rejecting" heresies (2:22–23).

What is of interest is that "anyone" (2:21) can move from the category of dishonor to that of honor, by "purifying themselves," thus becoming "beneficial for the Master" (2:21). That is to say, there is hope for those who have "gone astray," even Hymenaeus and Philetus (2:17–18; this is made explicit in 2:25). "Paul underlines more than anything the goal of producing changed lives so that people within the 'household' might be transformed from opposing to serving Christ."[17] With the contrast between vessels of honor and those of dishonor is a parallel contrast between fleeing and pursuing (2:22) forming a chiastic structure:

> **A** "But from youthful lusts" (2:22a)
> **B** "flee" (2:22b)
> **B'** "and pursue" (2:22c)
> **A'** "righteousness, faith, love, peace" (2:22d)

---

14. For notions related to the church as God's household, see also 1 Tim 3:4–5, 12, 15; 5:1–2; and also 1 Cor 4:1; Gal 6:10; Eph 2:10; etc.

15. Johnson, *First and Second Letters to Timothy*, 388.

16. Akin to those who "name the name of the Lord" (2:19).

17. Towner, *Letters to Timothy and Titus*, 543.

And while the heretical transactions of the dishonorable produce "quarrels" (μάχαι, 2:23), the "Lord's bondservant" (2:24) is exhorted not to be "quarrelsome" (μάχομαι, 2:24). With the right attitudes and actions (kindness, patience, gentleness) this one must be "able to teach,"[18] "instructing" opponents (2:24–25). In fact, this committed person hopes to rescue those "captured" by the devil (2:26). While the former does the "will" of God (1:1), the latter is ensnared in the "will" of Satan (2:26). Note that it is the "foolish" (ἀπαίδευτος, *apaideutos*, 2:23) undertakings of the opponents that need instruction by "correcting" (παιδεύω, *paideuō*, 2:25). All of this is focused on one goal: transformation. Perhaps in God's mercy, he may grant that those antagonists repent and come to the knowledge of the "truth" (2:25), from which "truth" they have gone astray (2:18), unlike Timothy and his cohort who "clearly expound" the "word of truth" (2:15).[19] Hopefully these straying dissenters will come to their senses and turn to God, i.e., "purify" themselves and be transformed from vessels of dishonor to those of honor, "made holy, beneficial for the Master, prepared for every good work" (2:21). "The point is not cutting off a sick member. The point is making the community well."[20]

SERMON MAPS

THEOLOGICAL FOCUS OF PERICOPE 13 FOR PREACHING

13 God's people, his possession, obtain honor by pursuing righteousness and being beneficial for God, ready for good works, even correcting opponents by clearly and graciously expounding the word (2:14–26).

This pericope also has some micro-lists, collections of types of speech and kinds of acts Again, employing our dictum—*Keep it simple!*—I'd recommend sticking with the overall thrust of each list, rather than atomizing them into impracticality and non-existence. While righteous deeds are mentioned in 2:14–26, I've kept the focus here on righteous speech (including the correction of opponents[21]) as a way of being beneficial to God and useful for good works, since that takes up the bulk of the space in this pericope. While 2:22 appears to deal with attitudes rather than speech, those characteristics, in this context, give rise to certain kinds of speech appropriate to godliness (2:24–26)—rejection of controversies, but correction of opponents, etc. However, "right speech" (here a more general and wider umbrella of communication) must be distinguished from "preaching the word" in Pericope 15: 2 Tim 4:1–22—engaging in the formal exposition of God's word everywhere and all the time (a more specific form of communication).

---

18. Echoed in 1 Tim 3:2 and Titus 1:9.

19. Ultimately it is God who grants the repentance, though his agents are called to work towards that end.

20. Johnson, *First and Second Letters to Timothy*, 415.

21. To be distinguished from the reproof of false teachers in Pericope 16: Titus 1:1–16, a more final rejection of the unrepentant than the gracious correction of the potentially teachable in this pericope.

Possible Preaching Maps for Pericope 13

I. Worthless for the Master
   Speech of the false teachers (2:14a, 16a, 18a, 22a, 23, 24a)
   Consequences: ruin of believers; dishonor (2:14b, 16b–17, 18b, 20b)
   Move-to-Relevance: Our dishonorable speech
II. Beneficial for the Master
   Speech of truth teachers (2:15b, 22b, 24–26)[22]
   Consequences: possession by God; honor (2:15a, 19, 20a, 21)
   Move-to-Relevance: What honorable speech looks like
III. *Win Honor!*
   Specifics for the current audience

The following map rearranges the preceding one, organizing it by speech and consequences in moves I and II, respectively:

I. Speech: dishonorable and honorable
   Speech of the false teachers (2:14a, 16a, 18a, 22a, 23, 24a)
   Speech of truth teachers (2:15b, 22b, 24–26)
   Move-to-Relevance: Our dishonorable speech[23]
II. Consequences: dishonorable and honorable
   Consequences: ruin of believers; dishonor (2:14b, 16b–17, 18b, 20b)
   Consequences: possession by God; honor (2:15a, 19, 20a, 21)
   Move-to-Relevance: Consequence of our dishonorable speech
III. *Win Honor!*
   Specifics for the current audience

---

22. "Truth teachers," of course, includes every believer.

23. I've chosen "our dishonorable speech" in the moves-to-relevance in these maps. There is no doubt we have all failed to be fully honorable in speech and we can all use some correction; unless we are convinced (and convicted) of our sickness, we are not necessarily going to take the medicine of application. But that does not rule out the possibility of applauding the congregation for their honorable speech, if seen fit.

PERICOPE 14

Continuing in Scripture

2 Timothy 3:1–17

[Faithless vs. Faithful; Following Godly Models; Equipped by Scripture]

REVIEW, SUMMARY, PREVIEW

Review of Pericope 13: The third pericope of 2 Timothy (2 Tim 2:14–26) contrasted the speech of false teachers and truth teachers (all believers). The latter win approval and honor from God, being beneficial for him, prepared as they are for every good work, including that of rehabilitating the erring.

Summary of Pericope 14: This pericope (2 Tim 3:1–17) continues the contrasts made in the previous pericope: here the faithless and faithful are compared with regard to their character and relationship to truth. It is grounding in Scripture that enables the former to follow godly models, trusting in God's deliverance in times of suffering, and being capable persons of God, fully equipped for a life of godliness.

Preview of Pericope 15: The final pericope of 2 Timothy (4:1–22) furthers the theme relating to Scripture from the two preceding pericopes. Believers are charged to communicate Scripture, to commit to their ministries, and to have the confidence of ultimate deliverance from God and of future rewards.

14   2 Timothy 3:1–17

THEOLOGICAL FOCUS OF PERICOPE 14

14   In contrast to those who are self-lovers rather than God-lovers, professing a false godliness and propagating all manner of evil that leads believers astray, the people of God follow godly models, trusting in divine deliverance from inevitable persecution and suffering, and continuing in Scripture that edifies, making them capable and fully equipped for good works (3:1–17).

14.1   God's people beware of perilous times in the last days because those who are self-lovers, rather than God-lovers—whose deviances are obvious to all as they, professing a false godliness, propagate all manner of evil—are liable to lead believers astray with demonic wiles (3:1–9).

14.2   God's people follow godly models, trusting in divine deliverance from inevitable persecution and suffering, and continuing in Scripture that edifies, making them capable and fully equipped for good works (3:10–17).

OVERVIEW

In this pericope, a slight shift in approach to opponents is visible. In the previous one, there was hope for their repentance, and the people of God were exhorted to teach and correct these heretics with grace (Pericope 13: 2 Tim 2:14–26); here it is assumed that the "last days" will have its share of those who will not, or will refuse to, change. In such a situation, the people of God are instructed to follow godly models and, above all, the divine word. Therefore in this pericope, one sees three main deployments of the conjunction δε, *de*, "but": in 3:1 to contrast the sense of hope of the previous pericope with the sense of inevitability of "last days"-error in this one; and in 3:10, 14 (each with σὺ δέ, *su de*, "but you") to contrast the experiences and behavior of the erring ones with that of the godly.

The linguistic links with the previous pericope include: ἀσέβεια, *asebeia*, "ungodliness," in 2:16, and εὐσέβεια, *eusebeia*, "godliness," in 3:5; "lusts," in 2:22 and 3:6; "truth" in 2:18, 25, and 3:7, 8 (with "the knowledge of the truth" in both 2:25 and 3:7); ἀντιδιατίθημι, *antidiatithēmi*, "oppose," in 2:25, and ἀνθίστημι, *anthistēmi*, "oppose," in 3:8; "progress" in 2:16 and 3:9; and διάβολος, *diabolos*, "devil," in 2:26, and διάβολοι, *diaboloi*, "slanderers," in 3:3. Interestingly, 3:1–9 focuses on opponents (3:1–5a, 6–9) with one reference to Timothy in the middle (3:5b); and 3:10–17 focuses on Timothy (3:10–12, 14–17) with one reference to opponents in the middle (3:13), creating a double chiasm:

2 Timothy 3:1–9
Opponents (3:1–5a)
    Timothy (3:5b)
Opponents (3:6–9)

2 Timothy 3:10–17
    Timothy (3:10–12)
Opponents (3:13)
    Timothy (3:14–17)

14.1 2 Timothy 3:1–9

THEOLOGICAL FOCUS 14.1

14.1 God's people beware of perilous times in the last days because those who are self-lovers, rather than God-lovers—whose deviances are obvious to all as they, professing a false godliness, propagate all manner of evil—are liable to lead believers astray with demonic wiles (3:1–9).

TRANSLATION 14.1

3:1   But know this, that in the last days perilous times will come;

3:2   for people will be self-lovers, money-lovers, boastful, arrogant, blasphemers, disobedient to parents, ungrateful, unholy,

3:3   unaffectionate, unforgiving, slanderers, without self-control, savage, not loving good,

3:4   treacherous, reckless, conceited, pleasure-lovers rather than God-lovers,

3:5   having a form of godliness, while denying its power; and avoid such [people].

3:6   For among them are those who infiltrate households and captivate weak women who have been weighed down with sins, led away by various lusts,

3:7   always learning and never able to come to the knowledge of truth.

3:8   Just as Jannes and Jambres opposed Moses, so these also oppose the truth, people corrupted of mind, rejected with regard to faith.

3:9   But they will not progress further; for their folly will be evident to all, as also theirs [Jannes's and Jambres's] was.

NOTES 14.1

14.1   God's people beware of perilous times in the last days because those who are self-lovers, rather than God-lovers—whose deviances are obvious to all as they, professing a false godliness, propagate all manner of evil—are liable to lead believers astray with demonic wiles (3:1–9).

The "last days" seem to have a variety of starting points in the NT: the pouring forth of God's Spirit at Pentecost (Acts 2:17); the sending of God's Son (Heb 1:2; 1 Pet 1:20); the eschatological judgment period (Jas 5:3); the Second Advent and the commencement of Christ's reign (LXX Isa 2:2; Micah 4:1). Perhaps Towner's assessment is best: "The phrase was understood to imply that with Jesus' appearance, the End, marked by divine interventions, had been inaugurated and would culminate in God's final intervention (in the Parousia of Christ) to complete salvation and execute judgment."[1] In any case, Paul, Timothy, and the Ephesians were, and those of us in the current dispensation are, in the "last days" conceived broadly.

In 3:1–5, Paul creates a worst-case scenario of the "last days" with the eighteen vices listed, making it one of the longest such lists in the NT (second only to Rom 1:29–31, with

---

1. Towner, *Letters to Timothy and Titus*, 553.

twenty-one items). The items run together in a conjunction-free asyndeton, many of them assonant (see below). Of course, not every conceivable vice is included, but a general picture of evil in the future is effectively painted. Then the camera swings back to the present.[2] Future "history" is thus repeating itself in the current last days!

There seems to be a pattern to the list in 3:1–5a, since it begins and ends with a pair of compound words formed from φίλος, *philos* (φίλαυτοι and φιλάργυροι in 3:2; φιλήδονοι and φιλόθεοι in 3:4; *philautoi*, "self-lovers"; *philargyroi*, "money-lovers"; *philēdonoi*, "pleasure-lovers"; and *philotheoi*, "God-lovers"; respectively)[3]; fourteen of the words end with -οι[4]; and eight begin with α (α-privatives). If there is a theme to the list, it appears to be one of pro-self and anti-other, as the φιλ-words attest: "self-lovers" and "money-lovers" at the beginning (3:2); "pleasure-lovers" and [non] "God-lovers" at the end (3:4); somewhere in the middle is also ἀφιλάγαθοι, *aphilagathoi*, "not loving good."[5] A "misdirection of love" appears to be the fundamental affliction of these individuals: "other vices flow from this misdirection."[6] Also in the center of the list, and surrounded by five α-privatives on one side and three on the other, stands διάβολοι (3:3); the link with διάβολος in 2:26, the one who holds these heretics captive to do his will, is not accidental. Pointedly, ἄνθρωποι in 3:2, 8, 13 refers to evildoers, in stark contrast to ὁ τοῦ θεοῦ ἄνθρωπος, *ho tou theou anthrōpos*, "the person of God," in 3:17, exemplified by Timothy and all of God's people. "The list as a whole isn't meant to serve as a comprehensive description of depraved humanity. Rather, the desired rhetorical effect is moral outrage."[7] And, perhaps, a searing caricature of opponents. In any case, the oral nature of the writing must be appreciated in its wordplays, with Timothy probably having read it out loud himself (and to others, as well).

Employing μόρφωσις (*morphōsis*, "form") of godliness in 2 Tim 3:5, Paul emphasizes the façade of piety and insubstantiality of the devotion of false teachers: theirs was a "counterfeit spirituality."[8] And, of course, these pretenders knew nothing of the "power" of godli-

---

2. Also evident in the perfect participle σεσωρευμένα, *sesōreumena*, "have been weighed down," in 3:6, indicating events proximal to Timothy's time. In fact, it appears that Paul is conflating future "last days" events with the present, without making too much of a distinction between the two.

3. The φιλ-prefixed words are *hapaxes*, with the exception of φιλάργυροι, found also in Luke 16:14. There is also ἀφιλάγαθοι in 2 Tim 3:3 (another *hapax*). If one additionally tallies ὑπερήφανοι, βλάσφημοι, and τετυφωμένοι (*hyperēphanoi*, "arrogant"; *blasphēmoi*, "blasphemers"; and *tetyphōmenoi*, "conceited") the number of words using φ (*ph*) increase. Also note the προ (*pro*)-prefixes on the first two items in 3:4: προδόται and προπετεῖς (*prodotai* and *propeteis*, "treacherous" and "reckless") adding to the alliteration and rhythmic feel of the whole. "In fact, 'accumulation' is the name of the rhetorical device being used here.... It has a rhetorical design, meaning that it is arranged so as to maximize the aural and rhetorical effect" (Witherington, *Letters and Homilies*, 349).

4. The occurrence of ἄνθρωποι, *anthrōpoi*, "people," in 3:2, accompanies the other -οι (-*oi*) words.

5. "It is reasonable to assume that the first item in the list sets the tone for what follows, and that the closing one(s) will wrap it up. On this assumption the dominant motif is that people will be self-centred rather than God-centred, and this affects their relationships with other people so that they think only of their own interests and behave violently to gain their own ends" (Marshall, *Pastoral Epistles*, 772). Philo, *On Husbandry* 19.88, makes a similar contrast: φιλήδονον καὶ φιλοπαθῆ μᾶλλον ἢ φιλάρετον καὶ φιλόθεον, *philēdonon kai philopathē mallon ē philareton kai philotheon* ("*a lover of pleasure* and a lover of passion *rather than* a lover of virtue and *a lover of God*" [my translation; italics indicate words shared with 2 Tim 3:2, 4]).

6. Knight, *Pastoral Epistles*, 430.

7. Köstenberger, *Commentary on 1–2 Timothy and Titus*, 256.

8. Towner, *Letters to Timothy and Titus*, 560.

ness, i.e., of God—in fact, they "deny" it (ἀρνέομαι, *arneomai*; 3:5). A couple of pericopes earlier, Paul had warned of what would happen to those who "deny" Christ (also ἀρνέομαι; 2:12–13). These denials are all, no doubt, equivalent.

At first sight, the recommendation to "avoid" such heretics (3:5b) seems counter to the more pastoral and gracious approach advocated in 2:23–26. This is best explained by seeing Paul dealing with a more hardened, implacable, and recalcitrant species of apostates, kin to those of the "last days." The avoidance recommended to Timothy is likely excommunication from the community, not necessarily an absolute apartheid or ghettoization. The reason for this disjoining from fellowship is given in 3:6: they were leading others astray.

The word γυναικάριον, *gynaikarion*, a *hapax* in the NT, is a dimunitive of γύνη, *gynē*, "woman"—so, "womanette." It has a pejorative tinge to it, particularly in the polemical context of our pericope; thus, the ones in question in 3:6 are "weak women." Their failing, ἐπιθυμία (*epithymia*, "lust"), has raised the suspicion that "there was some sexual involvement between the false teachers and these women."[9] In light of the "youthful lusts" (also ἐπιθυμία) that Timothy was warned against (2:22), this suspicion may not be far from the truth. In any case, these "weak women" are described by four back-to-back participles: σεσωρευμένα, ἀγόμενα, μανθάνοντα, and δυνάμενα (*sesōreumena, agomena, manthanonta,* and *dynamena*; 3:6–7; "weighed down," "led away," "learning," and "able"), giving the sequence a cascading sense of inevitability and despair. Why exactly some Ephesian women were susceptible to this misdirection is unclear, but an inkling of this tendency is evident also in 1 Tim 2:9–15; 5:11–15. "The problem is obviously not the natural defects of women, but the artificial and culturally induced deficiencies of a society that systematically keeps certain categories of persons in a chronically undereducated and disempowered position, and therefore chronically in the posture of victims of unscrupulous manipulators of desperate human need."[10] In any case, these women are "*always* learning, but *never* able to come to the knowledge of the truth" (2 Tim 3:7). That is an ironic summation of the activities of these inclining themselves to the seductions of false teachers, who were, themselves, far from the "knowledge of truth" (2:25). And like their mentors who were denying the "power" (δύναμις, *dynamis*) of godliness (3:5), these, their devotees, were not "able" (δύναμαι, *dynamai*) to learn the truth (3:7). Later, these futile exercises in learning will be contrasted with the *non pareil* ability (also δύναμαι, "able") of the "sacred writings" to give "wisdom" (3:15).

Jannes and Jambres, apparently Pharaoh's magicians in the days of the exodus, are not mentioned elsewhere in Scripture (or in the Apostolic Fathers, Philo, or Josephus). The duo, יָינִיס וְיִמְבְּרֵס, *yenis wyimbres*, are found in *Targum Pseudo-Jonathan*, where they are described as "the chief of the magicians" (1:3 on Exod 1:15), "the magicians of Egypt" (7:2 on Exod 7:11), and as Balaam's "two young men" (40:6 on Num 22:22).[11] Most, like Paul in 2 Tim 3:7, considered them enemies of Moses (and thus of God), working magic in the

---

9. Fee, *1 and 2 Timothy, Titus*, 272.

10. Johnson, *First and Second Letters to Timothy*, 412, 413. It is hardly misogyny from the pen of the apostle who does not hesitate to laud Timothy's female progenitors in this letter (1:5; 3:14–15). Then there are Paul's own female coworkers who are complimented later in the Epistle: Prisca and Claudia (4:19, 21). Obviously, not all the women in Timothy's precinct were partaking of these deceits described in 3:6–7.

11. Other rabbinic documents where they appear include *b. Menahot* 85a and *Exodus Rabbah* on Exod 9:7. "Jannes and his brother" are also found in the Qumran-Essene *Damascus Document*, apparently set up by Belial to oppose Moses (Cairo Genizah *Damascus Document* 5:17–18); and Jannes has a solo showing in Pliny the Elder, *Natural History* 30.2.

power of the evil one.¹² Their malevolence is reflected in the use of ἀνθίστημι twice in 3:8, and an implicit equivalence is created between them and the false teachers. Likewise, there is an implied association and parity between the early leader, Moses, and the current one, Paul (and his delegates). At any rate, the opposition of this crop of false teachers in contemporary Ephesus was to the truth. Note that "word of truth" was what Timothy was to propagate (2:15), and the false teachers' relation to the "truth" was described in 2:18; some hope was entertained that these who had "gone astray" would return to the "truth" (2:25). But their followers—and they too, presumably—are never able to come to the knowledge of the "truth" (3:7); instead, they turn away from the "truth" (4:4). The prepositional phrase, περὶ τὴν πίστιν, *peri tēn pistin*, "with regard to the faith" (3:8) is also found in 1 Tim 1:19; there it clearly refers to the personal (un)faith of the heretics. It is more than likely that the referent is the same here in 2 Tim 3:8: these nefarious characters are rejected by God because their personal faith is non-existent (which also makes their "faith," as in "doctrine"—the objective aspect of "faith"—equally tenuous). And, we are assured, these impious persons will not "progress" (προκόπτω, *prokoptō*) in their deceits in secrecy, but their folly will be public, just as was the folly of the two magicians in Moses' time (3:9). Indeed, their "progress" (also προκόπτω, 3:13)—ironically speaking—will be from bad to worse (see below)!¹³ These are the ones "rejected" by God (ἀδόκιμοι, *adokimoi*, 3:8), in contrast to the one "approved" by him (δόκιμος, *dokimos*, 2:15).

14.2 2 Timothy 3:10–17

> **THEOLOGICAL FOCUS 14.2**
>
> 14.2 God's people follow godly models, trusting in divine deliverance from inevitable persecution and suffering, and continuing in Scripture that edifies, making them capable and fully equipped for good works (3:10–17).

TRANSLATION 14.2

3:10   *But you followed my teaching, my conduct, my purpose, my faith, my patience, my love, my steadfastness,*

3:11   *my persecutions, my sufferings, such as happened to me in Antioch, in Iconium, in Lystra; what persecutions I endured, and out of them all the Lord rescued me!*

3:12   *And, indeed, all who want to live godly in Christ Jesus will be persecuted.*

3:13   *But evil people and sorcerers will progress [from bad] to worse, deceiving and being deceived.*

3:14   *But you should continue in the things you learned and are confident of, knowing from whom you learned [them],*

---

12. The word γόητες, *goētes* (in 3:13), best translated "sorcerers," likely indicates dabblers in the black arts. It is a *hapax* in the NT, but present in ancient non-biblical literature from the fifth century BCE to the second century CE; "whenever the context involves magic or wonder-working of some kind, the appropriate translation [of γόης, *goēs*] is magician/sorcerer" (Pietersen, "Women as Gossips," 29). The link between Ephesus and magic was noted in the introduction.

13. This sarcastic use of "progress" was also seen in 2:16.

3:15 *and that from childhood you have known the sacred writings that are able to make you wise unto salvation through faith that is in Christ Jesus.*

3:16 *Every [text of] Scripture [is] God-breathed and profitable for teaching, for reproof, for correction, for training in righteousness*

3:17 *so that that the person of God may be capable, fully equipped for every good work.*

NOTES 14.2

14.2 God's people follow godly models, trusting in divine deliverance from inevitable persecution and suffering, and continuing in Scripture that edifies, making them capable and fully equipped for good works (3:10–17).

As was noted, Timothy is directly addressed almost throughout this section (3:10–12, 14–17; each of these parts begins with σὺ δέ, and each gets one of the two instances of διδασκαλία, *didaskalia*, "teaching," in 2 Timothy); the opponents get a single verse in the middle (3:13). The whole section contains several teaching- and knowledge-related words: "followed" (3:10); "teaching" (3:10); "the things you learned and are confident of" (3:14a); "learned" (3:14b); "sacred writings"(3:15); "you have known" (3:15); "every [text of] Scripture"(3:16); "teaching" (3:16); "reproof" (3:16); "correction" (3:16); and "training" (3:16).

The "purpose" of Paul (3:10) is, no doubt, the same divine "purpose" that was mentioned in 1:9, the goal of God for his cosmos, capsulated in the gospel in its broadest sense: "the consummation of all things in Christ, both in the heavens and on earth" (Eph 1:9). Again we see Paul portraying himself as a model of faithfulness to God, one whom Timothy and all of God's people can "follow" (2 Tim 3:10; also see 1:13; 2:22). The possessive (genitive) μου, *mou*, is in the emphatic position in 3:10 to make an even starker contrast with what preceded—"But you followed *my* . . . ." Nine character traits and experiences of Paul—all articular and all datives—form a sort of "virtue" list in 3:10–11, corresponding to the "vice" list of 3:2–4: it is a Pauline autobiography in a nutshell.[14] The final two items, "persecutions" and "sufferings" are the only plurals, and they stand apart receiving more explication and application in 3:11b–12.

Reference to suffering thus becomes an important motif in this section (and the entire Epistle), perhaps the consequence of standing firm against the depredations of false teachers. It is interesting that Paul mentions his διωγμοί, *diōgmoi*, "persecutions," in 3:11—he himself was a self-confessed διώκτης (*diōktēs*, "persecutor," 1 Tim 1:13; related word); no wonder he can assure his readers that they will certainly "be persecuted" (διωχθήσομαι, *diōkthēsomai*, 2 Tim 3:12): the "all" is emphatic, placed between two conjunctions: καὶ πάντες δέ, *kai pantes de*, "and, indeed, all." In a clever wordplay, Paul had just urged Timothy to "pursue" (διώκω, *diōkō*) righteousness, faith, love, and peace (2:22). Now it is Timothy who is being pursued, i.e., "persecuted" (3:12), just as Paul himself was "persecuted" (3:11 [×2]). Mounce is right: "The gospel does not proclaim the cessation of pain as the highest good. Christ suffered, Paul suffered, Timothy suffered, and all believers who seek to live godly lives will suffer. . . . The absence of suffering is a sign that there is something wrong in a believer's

---

14. See Acts 13:14–52; 14:1–5, 6–20; 16:1–3. The named trio of cities in 2 Tim 3:11 occurs in the same order in Acts 13.

life."¹⁵ But God is sufficient, for he delivers: "Timothy, I suffered and God supported. You do the same, and he'll be there for you, too!"¹⁶

The godliness of these faithful sufferers (εὐσεβῶς, *eusebōs*, "live godly"; 3:12) is true godliness, in contrast to the "form of godliness" (3:5)—false godliness, evil, duplicitous, hollow, and hypocritical. And these ungodly ones' "progress" (3:9, 13), as was noted above, is actually a retrogression: their evildoing only increases, as they move "to worse" (3:13). Notice the direct contrast: "they will not progress further" (3:9) and "will progress [from bad] to worse" (3:13): they may not make progress in a forward direction, but they will, in a backward one! Considering that among the roster of these evil people are sorcerers (3:13), it is no wonder that these deceptive characters are themselves "being deceived" (3:13)—they have been "captured by him [the devil] to [do] his will" (2:26).

It is back to Timothy again in 3:14–17, with another σὺ δέ (3:14). While those following false teachers were "always learning" in futility (μανθάνω, *manthanō*, 3:7), Timothy, in contrast, is exhorted to continue in the things he had "learned" (μανθάνω [×2], 3:14) from his godly forbears ("whom," τίνων, *tinōn*, is plural; see 1:5), and perhaps from Paul, as well (3:10; also see 2:20), as opposed to the evil ones and sorcerers, deceivers and the deceived (3:13).

While "salvation" and the wisdom thereof (3:15) includes the barebones of the gospel message and Christ's atoning work (salvation as justification), most certainly there is more to "salvation" here: it also includes salvation as sanctification, for Scripture is profitable to make the person of God "capable, equipped for every good work" (3:17). So, yes, the sacred writ is able to give one the "wisdom unto salvation"—including *both* justification and sanctification, with the emphasis here on the latter, in light of the "good work" (a major motif in the PE).¹⁷

The word γραφή, *graphē*, in the NT is used only of Scripture. The anarthrous use of the phrase πᾶσα γραφή in 3:16, in light of the reference to ἱερὰ γράμματα, *hiera grammata*, "sacred writings," in 3:15,¹⁸ suggests that the entire collection of what is called Scripture is encompassed in the phrase. The inclusion of NT writings is implicit both in the label and in the context of the writing, which mentions "salvation through faith that is in Jesus Christ" (3:16).¹⁹ As well, note the other synonyms in the verses that immediately follow this

---

15. Mounce, *Pastoral Epistles*, 584.

16. The kind of deliverance God effects for his people is not necessarily liberation from oppression: it might certainly be that, or it might be a strengthening for suffering, or an inward peace. And, one must also add that removal from this earth is also a divine "deliverance" from evil, as Paul explicitly affirms in the next chapter (4:18).

17. The motif is found as ἔργον ἀγαθόν (or a variant) in 1 Tim 2:10; 2 Tim 2:21; 3:17; Titus 1:16; 3:1; and as ἔργον καλόν (or a variant) in 1 Tim 5:10, 25; 6:18; Titus 2:7, 14; 3:8, 14.

18. This phrase, though a *hapax* in the NT, was often a technical designation for the OT in non-biblical Jewish literature: see Philo, *On the Contemplative Life* 75, 78; *On the Embassy to Gaius* 195; *On Moses* 51.290, 292; and *On the Special Laws* 27.159; 43.238; as well as Josephus, *Against Apion* 1.54; and *Jewish Antiquities* 10.210; 13.168.

19. The debate as to whether "through faith that is in Christ Jesus" (3:15) deals with faith *in*-Christ (objective genitive) or the faith *of*-Christ (subjective genitive) has consumed reams of paper. Of the seven instances of πίστις, *pistis*, in 2 Timothy, five clearly deal with the faith of the believer *in* Christ (1:5, 13; 2:18, 22; 3:10); of the remaining two, one (3:8) is also likely dealing with the faith of the persons involved, because of the similar use of περὶ τὴν πίστιν in 1 Tim 1:19. That leaves our verse, 2 Tim 3:15. In light of the contextual use of the cognate verb πιστόω, *pistoō*, in 3:14, referring to Timothy's faith/conviction, it is fair to see 3:15 also dealing with the aspect of the believer's faith *in*-Christ (objective genitive).

pericope: "the word," in 4:2, "sound teaching," in 4:3, and "truth," in 4:4—certainly including NT truth.

> This understanding . . . fits well in this context. It provides a reason for Paul's use of πᾶσα and for his change from ἱερά γράμματα, an OT designation, to πᾶσα γραφή, a possibly more inclusive term. It would gather together Paul's concern for the preservation and communication of the gospel and the apostolic understanding and application of that gospel and place it on a par with the OT, as 2 Pet 3:16–17 clearly does. And it would provide a clearer background for and transition to his demand that Timothy "preach the word" (4:2).[20]

Does πᾶσα γραφή mean "the whole Scripture" or "every part/text of Scripture?" Practically, it does not make much of a difference since, undoubtedly, Paul considered all of the sacred text inspired, including every part of it. However, I am inclined, though not by much, in the latter direction: "Every [text of] Scripture [is] God-breathed and profitable." Paul has already alluded to particular OT texts and characters in this Epistle (2 Tim 2:7, 19; 3:8–9, 11; and will do so again: 4:14, 17–18) as the bases for godliness. Besides, normally, γραφή in the singular refers to specific passages: Mark 12:10; Luke 4:21; John 7:38; Rom 4:3; 9:17; 10:11; 11:2; Gal 3:8; 4:30; Jas 2:23; 1 Tim 5:18; etc.[21] In addition, John 19:38 and 1 Pet 2:6 have anarthrous uses of γραφή to refer to individual texts (γραφή in 2 Tim 3:16 is also anarthrous). Thus Paul, here in 3:16, is likely giving every text of Scripture equal importance—unlimited value, pericope by pericope, for edification: "The scope is extensive, leaving no text of 'Scripture' unaccounted for. . . . Consequently, he [Paul] conceives of it as 'useful' text by text, as it were, which is precisely the way in which it is employed in this letter and elsewhere."[22]

The word θεόπνευστος, *theopneustos,* is also a *hapax,* not found in the NT, LXX, or the Apostolic Fathers. The notion of inspired Scripture would not be foreign to Paul's readers. So "the main thrust of the sentence [3:16] lies in the second adjective ['profitable']. The writer declares that the Scriptures are inspired, as a datum with which his readers would agree, and uses this as a basis for the point that he wants to stress: whatever is divinely inspired is therefore useful."[23] Then follows four asyndetic components regarding the profitability of Scripture, each with the preposition πρός, *pros,* "for": "for teaching, for reproof, for correction, for training in righteousness" (3:16). The first two deal with truth and falsehood, respectively (*A* and *B,* "+" and "–"); the last two with improper behavior and proper behavior, respectively (*B'* and *A',* "–" and "+")[24]: thus, a chiasm is created.

---

20. Knight, *Pastoral Epistles,* 448.

21. While γραφή in Gal 3:22 may include all of Scripture, "in view of Paul's technique in Galatians (and elsewhere), and in view of his normal tendency (along with other NT writers) to distinguish between the singular and the plural, he is more likely to be referring to the implications of the texts he has employed than to the whole body of the OT Scriptures" (Towner, *Letters to Timothy and Titus,* 586).

22. Towner, *Letters to Timothy and Titus,* 587.

23. Marshall, *Pastoral Epistles,* 795. Whether 3:16 is asserting that "every [text of] God-breathed Scripture [is] profitable" or that "every [text of] Scripture [is] God-breathed and profitable" is irrelevant; while *semantically* distinct in each formulation, the utterance is *pragmatically* identical. Paul could hardly have been distinguishing between God-breathed Scripture and S/scripture that is *not* God-breathed. In other words, to keep the utterance unambiguous, it is best translated "every [text of] Scripture [is] God-breathed and profitable."

24. The word ἐπανόρθωσις (*epanorthōsis,* "straightening"/"correction," 3:16), a *hapax* in the NT, has

A	"Teaching" (of truth)	+
B	"Reproof" (of falsehood)	−
B'	"Correction" (of wrong behavior)	−
A'	"Training in righteousness" (right behavior)	+

This may also reflect, in the same order, the four major imperatives of 4:2: "preach" truth, "reprove" falsehood (ἐλέγχω, *elencho* [ἐλεγμός in 3:16]), "rebuke" wrong behavior, and "exhort" right behavior. The goal is that the person of God would be ἄρτιος (*artios*, 3:17), in the sense of being exactly fitted, well suited, prepared, ready: "capable." The verb ἐξαρτίζω, *exartizō*, also in 3:17, in a wordplay with ἄρτιος, complements it by adding the sense of "fully equipped."[25] The capability and equipage of the person of God is for "every good work"—this is the "profitability" of Scripture, for edification and the manifestation of godliness.

SERMON MAPS

THEOLOGICAL FOCUS OF PERICOPE 14 FOR PREACHING

14 The people of God follow godly models, trusting in divine deliverance from inevitable persecution, and continuing in Scripture that edifies, making them capable and fully equipped for good works (3:1–17).

Since the contrasts between the faithless and faithful appear to resemble the contrasts being made in the previous pericope (2 Tim 2:14–26, emphasizing speech), the focus in a sermon on the current text is best kept upon truth and Scripture for edification, in order that one might become a capable person of God (i.e., a godly individual, ready for good works[26]). In a sense, then, this pericope is an extension of the previous: beyond speech, here character and relationship to truth take prominence.

---

the sense of correction of wrong behavior that includes restoration (1 Esd 8:52; 1 Macc 14:34). Philo, *On the Life of Moses* 2.6.36, explained the reason for God answering the prayers of the translators of the LXX (αἱ ἱεραί βίβλοι, *hai hierai bibloi*, "the holy books") thus: that "the human race may be profited [ὠφεληθῇ] by employing [such] wise [φιλοσόφοις]... ordinances for a straightened [ἐπανόρθωσιν, corrected/improved] life" (my translation). The links with 2 Tim 3:16–17 are obvious. While παιδεία can include corrective measures (see Heb 12:5, 7, 8), παιδεία τὴν ἐν δικαιοσύνῃ, *paidei tēn en diakaiosynē*, is more precisely "training in righteousness," i.e., in right behavior/godliness.

25. Quinn and Wacker, *First and Second Letters to Timothy*, 752.

26. Being prepared for good works was emphasized in the sermon on the previous pericope (3:21); it need not receive undue attention here.

2 Timothy

Possible Preaching Maps for Pericope 14

I. Condemnation of the Faithless
   Character: self-lovers vs. God-lovers (3:1–5a)
   Rejection of truth (3:5a, 6–9, 13)
   Move-to-Relevance: False teaching in our day
II. Commendation of the Faithful
   Character: trust God's deliverance, follow godly models (3:5b, 10–12)
   Acceptance of Scripture (3:14–17)
   Move-to-Relevance: True, scriptural teaching in our church
III. *Be a Faithful Person of God!*
   Specifics for the current audience, regarding Scripture[27]

The following map rearranges the preceding one, organizing it by character and relation to truth in moves I and II, respectively:

I. Character: Faithless vs. Faithful
   Faithless: self-lovers vs. God-lovers (3:1–5a)
   Move-to-Relevance: False teaching in our day
   Faithful: trust God's deliverance, follow godly models (3:5b, 10–12)
II. Relation to truth: Rejection vs. Acceptance
   Faithless: Rejection of truth (3:5a, 6–9, 13)
   Faithful: Acceptance of Scripture (3:14–17)
   Move-to-Relevance: True, scriptural teaching in our church
III. *Be a Faithful Person of God!*
   Specifics for the current audience, regarding Scripture

---

27. Since Scripture gets a prominent place in this pericope, focusing application on some aspect of our encounter with the sacred writ is appropriate.

PERICOPE 15

Preach the Word

2 Timothy 4:1–22

[Confidence in God; Commitment to Ministry; Communication of Scripture]

REVIEW, SUMMARY[1]

Review of Pericope 14: The fourth pericope of 2 Timothy (Pericope 14: 2 Tim 3:1–17) continued the contrasts made in the previous pericope: the faithless and faithful were compared with regard to their character and relationship to truth. It is grounding in Scripture that enables the faithful to follow after godly models, trusting in God's deliverance in times of suffering, and being capable persons of God, fully equipped for godliness.

Summary of Pericope 15: This final pericope of 2 Timothy (4:1–22) furthers the Scripture-related theme from the two preceding pericopes. Believers are charged to communicate the Scriptures, to commit to their ministries, and to be confident of ultimate deliverance and eternal reward from God.

15   2 Timothy 4:1-22

THEOLOGICAL FOCUS OF PERICOPE 15

15   The people of God solemnly undertake their charge to preach God's word at every opportunity, despite opposition and through suffering, as they follow the example of godly leaders, asserting their lifelong faithfulness to God and to their ministries, confident of ultimate deliverance and eternal rewards from the hand of the righteous Judge (4:1–22).

---

1. Since 2 Timothy is a discrete Epistle, I will forego a "Preview" of the next pericope that commences Titus.

15.1 The people of God undertake their charge before an all-powerful God and Christ, the soon-coming Judge, preaching God's word at every opportunity, even in the face of rejection of truth, thus fulfilling their ministries (4:1–5).

15.2 God's people remain faithful to God throughout their lives, and are secure in the knowledge of eternal rewards that await them (4:6–8).

15.3 God's people persevere faithfully without deserting the cause, the gospel, and its Agent, God, even if they are suffering now, for they are confident of ultimate deliverance and eternal reward from the hand of the righteous Judge (4:9–22).

OVERVIEW

The break at 4:1 may be artificial: 3:10—4:8 seems to be of a piece, directed to Timothy, with Paul's autobiographical reflections flanking this larger section (3:10–11 and 4:6–8). Besides, σὺ δέ (*su de*, "but you") appears to designate three discrete sections in 3:10 (3:10–13); 3:14 (3:14—4:4); and 4:5 (4:5–8); also, διδασκαλία shows up in 3:10, 16; and 4:3, as well as διδαχή, *didachē*, "teaching," in 4:2, and διδάσκαλος, *didaskalos*, "teacher," in 4:3, further uniting all of these verses. Other links between the prior pericope and the current one include: σωρεύω, *sōreuō*, "weigh down" (3:6), and ἐπισωρεύω, *episōreuō*, "accumulate" (4:3); "lust" (3:10 and 4:3); "patience" (3:10 and 4:2); and "work" (3:17 and 4:5, 14, 18). Nevertheless, even though 2 Timothy 4 continues from Pericope 14: 2 Tim 3:1–17, a fresh start is implied in the "solemn charge" to Timothy in 4:1, as well in the cascade of imperatives in 4:2, 5. Also note the eschatological references in 4:1–2 and in 4:17–18 (that also share "His kingdom," 4:1 and 4:18; and κηρύσσω, *kēryssō*, "preach," in 4:2 and κήρυγμα, *kērygma*, "proclamation" in 4:17) forming an *inclusio* for this section.

Within this pericope, 4:1–8 stands separate from the rest of the chapter: the first and last verses of this section also forming an *inclusio*:

2 Timothy 4:1	2 Timothy 4:8
"God," "Christ Jesus" (4:1)	"Lord" (4:8)
"appearing" (4:1)	"appearing" (4:8; also 4:18)
κρίνω, *krinō*, "judge" (4:1)	κριτής, *kritēs*, "judge" (4:8)

It is apparent that the entire pericope is written with much emotion, expressing the characteristics of a "'last will and testament.'"[2]

15.1 2 Timothy 4:1–5

THEOLOGICAL FOCUS 15.1

15.1 The people of God undertake their charge before an all-powerful God and Christ, the soon-coming Judge, preaching God's word at every opportunity, even in the face of rejection of truth, thus fulfilling their ministries (4:1–5).

---

2. Marshall, *Pastoral Epistles*, 797.

TRANSLATION 15.1

4:1 I solemnly charge [you] before God and Christ Jesus who is going to judge the living and the dead, and by His appearing and His kingdom:

4:2 preach the word; be ready in favorable time, in unfavorable time; reprove, rebuke, exhort, with all patience and teaching.

4:3 For the time will come when they will not accept sound teaching; but, according to their own lusts, they will accumulate teachers for themselves, having itching ears;

4:4 and they will turn away their ears from the truth, but will turn aside to myths.

4:5 But you, be sober in all things, suffer affliction, do the work of an evangelist, fulfill your service.

NOTES 15.1

15.1 *The people of God undertake their charge before an all-powerful God and Christ, the soon-coming Judge, preaching God's word at every opportunity, even in the face of rejection of truth, thus fulfilling their ministries* (4:1–5).

While there are five second-person imperatives in 4:2—"preach," "be ready," "reprove," "rebuke," and "exhort"—the second ("be ready," accompanied by two adverbs, "in favorable time, in unfavorable time") is related to the first, together exhorting Timothy to "be ready and preach the word" at any and every opportunity.[3] That makes the force of all these imperatives relate to the preaching endeavor.[4] Thus these four particular imperatives ("[readily] preach," "reprove [ἐλέγχω, *elenchō*]," "rebuke," and "exhort") can be paralleled with the four avenues of the profitability of Scripture (in 3:16: for "teaching," "reproof [ἐλεγμός, *elegmos*]," "for correction," "for training in righteousness").[5] The solemnity of these charges is escalated by reference, not only to the presence of "God and of Christ Jesus," but also to the imminence of the latter's Second Advent, his judgment, and the establishment of his millennial kingdom.[6] All of these, collectively, impose a notion of the absolute and illimitable power of the divine Judge, whom the people of God serve, to whom they are committed,

---

3. This auxiliary use of ἐφίστημι, *ephistēmi*, "be ready," is repeated in 4:6 ("is at hand"), also in conjunction with καιρός, *kairos*, "time."

4. While κηρύσσω undoubtedly includes proclamation for evangelism, here it primarily indicates preaching for edification, where the subjects are false teachers, heretics departing from the faith (lapsed believers), and the goal is correction (not redemption). Even in 4:5, Timothy's mandate "to do the work of an evangelist" is broad and deals with the promotion of the "gospel," in its comprehensive sense; this is likely the case with the use of κήρυγμα in 4:17 also; see below). See my *Vision for Preaching*, as well as my contributions in Gibson and Kim, *Homiletics and Hermeneutics*, 30–34, 43–70, 111–12, 150–53, for the distinctions I make between "preaching" (for edification) and "proclamation" (for evangelism).

5. The prepositional phrase ἐν πάσῃ (*en pasē*, "with all," 4:2), distributed to both "patience" and "teaching," indicates the greatness of patience and carefulness of teaching with which Timothy is to operate. These methodological features likely qualify all the four main imperatives that preceded, relating to preaching.

6. This setting up of Christ's thousand-year earthly reign is not to rule out that βασιλεία αὐτοῦ, *basileia autou*, "His kingdom," refers to a more extensive kingdom theology—the full, final, and forever reign of God (1 Cor 15:24; even including its present inchoate state: Col 1:13), as all things in the cosmos are consummated in Jesus Christ (Eph 1:9–10). Note the employment of ἐπιφάνεια, *epiphaneia*, "appearing," for both the First (2 Tim 1:10) and Second Advents (4:1, 8).

and whose flock must be pastored.[7] The eschatological dangers posed by heretics is given in 4:3 as the reason for this stance on preaching.

There is a great deal of symmetry in the construction of 4:3–4. Two pairs of contrasting phrases are found in 4:3b–c and 4:4a–b. Each pair has a positive term ("teaching" in 4:3b; "the truth" in 4:4a) and a negative one ("[false] teachers" in 4:3c; "the myths" in 4:4b). The members of the first pair are linked by ἀλλά, *alla*, "but," and those of the second by μέν/δέ, *men/de*:

2 Timothy 4:3–4					
4:3b	"not accept"	"teaching"	+		ἀλλά
4:3c	"accumulate"	"teachers"	–	"ears"	
4:4a	μέν	"the truth"	+	"ears"	"turn away"
4:4b	δέ	"myths"	–		"turn aside"

Notice as well repetitions of "teach(ing/ers)" and "ears" (highlighted in light gray, above), the contrast between "the truth" and "myths" (highlighted in dark gray), and the quasi-synonymous future-tense verbs "turn away" and "turn aside" (derived from ἀποστρέφω, *apostrephō,* and ἐκτρέπω, *ektrepō,* in 4:4a and 4:4b).[8] And just as the disciples of the heretics (the "weak women") were "weighed down" with sins and "lusts" (σωρεύω and ἐπιθυμία, 3:6), now those listeners are "weighed down" with heretics (i.e., they "accumulate" such heresiarchs) in accordance with their "lusts" (ἐπισωρεύω and ἐπιθυμία, 4:3)—a stockpiling of false teachers in keeping with their devious desires.[9]

While Timothy was urged to be ready to preach εὐκαίρως and ἀκαίρως (*eukairōs* and *akairōs;* "in favorable time" and "in unfavorable time," 4:2), in 4:3 we have a warning about a future καιρός, *kairos,* one of disinterest and intolerance to "sound teaching" manifested by devotees of false teachers. This is, no doubt, exactly the ἀκαίρως Timothy is to beware of (4:2), and the καιρὸς χαλεπός, *kairos chalepos,* "perilous time," he was to be aware of (3:1).[10] Who knows, but that in the grace of God, preaching might avert the apostasy. In other words, such proclamation should be considered analogous to the practice of a preventive medicine clinic, not of an emergency room.[11]

Another set of imperatives to Timothy follows in 4:5, all of them urging him to persist in his "service" (διακονία, *diakonia;* also in 4:11)—soberly, suffering affliction, promoting

---

7. "Pastored," i.e., shepherded—a duty owed to the Chief Shepherd, to care for his flock, whatever its size, extent, scope, and context, whether at home, in the office, on the playground, or in the church.

8. The verbs, στρέφω, *strephō* (the root of ἀποστρέφω) and τρέπω, *trepō* (that of ἐκτρέπω) had, at least in Classical Greek, a partial semantic overlap. Homer uses one and the other almost interchangeably (*Iliad* 8.432 and 8.168, respectively) of horses being turned in direction by their riders. See Delgado, "Mycenaean Words," 43.

9. Towner, *Letters to Timothy and Titus,* 604.

10. And, in the horizon of another future but more proximal καιρός, Paul could see his own demise (4:6).

11. The latter is what I call "reactive preaching," a response to whatever is going on in the immediate surroundings and times; the former is "proactive preaching," preempting dangerous tendencies, counteracting potential risks, stifling wrong teaching, circumventing hidden traps, immunizing for future threats. Such "proactive preaching" should predominate in the church, furthering God's goal of conforming his children into the "image" (εἰκών) of his Son, Christ (Rom 8:29)—the christiconic hermeneutic. See Kuruvilla, *Privilege the Text!,* 238–69.

the "gospel" (εὐαγγέλιον, *euangelion,* in its broadest sense) as an εὐαγγελιστής, *euangelistēs,* "evangelist,"[12] and fulfilling his ministry.

15.2 2 Timothy 4:6–8

> **THEOLOGICAL FOCUS 15.2**
>
> 15.2 God's people remain faithful to God throughout their lives, and are secure in the knowledge of eternal rewards that await them (4:6–8).

TRANSLATION 15.2

4:6 For I myself am already being poured out as an offering, and the time of my departure is at hand.

4:7 I have fought the good fight, I have completed the course, I have kept the faith;

4:8 in the future there is laid up for me the crown of righteousness, which the Lord, the righteous Judge, will award to me on that day; and not only to me, but also to all who have loved His appearing.

NOTES 15.2

15.2 *God's people remain faithful to God throughout their lives, and are secure in the knowledge of eternal rewards that await them (4:6–8).*

After Timothy is addressed in 4:1–5 (σὺ δέ in 4:5), Paul turns the spotlight on himself (ἐγώ, *ego,* "I," in 4:6) with an autobiographical note (4:6–8). We are given Paul's reason for bombarding Timothy with imperatives: "for" (4:6) his time is running out—stated with the emphatic first-person pronoun, ἐγώ, at the head of the sentence: "For I myself . . . ." The relative frequencies of the first-person singular pronouns in the PE are illuminating: out of a total of forty-three, 1 Timothy has six, Titus four, and 2 Timothy thirty-three![13] And in this very personal Epistle, 4:6–8 is probably the most personal of all its paragraphs.

The metaphor of a drink offering being poured out on the altar to God is poignant.[14] The Moffat translation of 4:6 appropriately has: "The last drops of my own sacrifice are

---

12. Carson makes a strong case that "gospel ministry includes but is not restricted to what we commonly call evangelistic ministry . . . Gospel ministry is ministry that is faithful to the gospel, that announces the gospel and applies the gospel and encourages people to believe the gospel and thus live out the gospel" ("Do the Work of an Evangelist," 3). Indeed, "there is inscriptional evidence of εὐαγγελιστής used in a pagan setting to refer to certain kinds of pagan priests, without any thought that such priests were trying to win converts" ("Do the Work of an Evangelist," 3). In any case, "gospel" is the "good news" of all that God is doing, and its promotion involves *both* evangelistic proclamation to unbelievers (a justification-oriented address) *and* edifying preaching to believers (a sanctification-oriented address). Nevertheless, it must be admitted that Paul appears to make a distinction between "evangelists" and "pastors and teachers" (Eph 4:11).

13. Quinn and Wacker, *First and Second Letters to Timothy,* 784–85.

14. "Drink offering," σπονδή, *spondē,* is employed in Num 28 (×9), and elsewhere in the OT. The cognate verb σπένδω, *spendō,* "pour out," is used here in 2 Tim 4:6.

falling; the time to go has come."¹⁵ The present tense, "being poured out," informs readers that the process has commenced, and the passive voice that "God, not Rome, is still in control, despite appearances."¹⁶ Death is, therefore, not a defeat, only a "departure" (ἀνάλυσις, *analysis*, 4:6).

Besides this pressing personal and emotional reason, Paul is also encouraging his delegate with the assurance of eternal rewards for those who have been faithful in the Lord's service (4:7–8; a strong hint of that was already caught in 4:1, with the announcement of the "appearing" of the One "going to judge" [κρίνω]; the "Judge" [κριτής] shows up again in 4:8). Thus we have the present tense in 4:6 (Paul's imminent passing), the past in 4:7 (his irreproachable performance), and the future in 4:8 (his inevitable prize).

There is also a sense of urgency in Paul's final remarks: "already," "time," "is at hand" (4:6), "future," "that day" (4:8), and "soon" (4:9). Notice also the three perfect-tense verbs in 4:7, literally: "The good fight *I have fought*,¹⁷ the course *I have completed*, the faith *I have kept*¹⁸"—all likely to be athletic metaphors, in light of the στέφανος, *stephanos*, "crown" (or "wreath"), presented to victors (4:8). The emphatic location of the nouns ("fight," "course," and "faith") at the heads of their respective phrases emphasizes the august responsibility apportioned to the child of God—"life lived responsibly."¹⁹ Chrysostom (*Homilies on Second Timothy* 9), declared: "'The good fight'! There is no worthier than this contest. The crown is without end. This is not of olive trees. It has not a human umpire. It has not men for spectators. The theater is crowded with Angels."²⁰

Though victory is implied in the crown Paul expects, the intended focus for his readers in 4:7 is on the importance of persistence and perseverance in the ministry allotted to them. Unlike in athletics, the crowning reward for this race is for *all* who have persisted and persevered: they are *all* winners!²¹ While the rest of God's people may have a ways to go until that crowning day, "for Paul, the contest is all but over. What remains is receiving the prize."²² May Timothy (and all of God's people) do likewise, grasping the baton from Paul and continuing the race!

"The crown of righteousness," ὁ τῆς δικαιοσύνης στέφανος, *ho tēs dikaiosynēs stephanos* (4:8), could be a crown for those who were righteous, or a crown that is righteousness itself; the construction is compatible with either sense. The latter is more likely: "the crown, i.e., righteousness," particularly in light of the other instances of ὁ στέφανος with nouns in the genitive: "crown of exultation" (1 Thess 2:19); "crown of life" (Jas 1:12); "crown of glory" (1 Pet 5:4); and "crown of life" (Rev 2:10).²³ It is appropriate here that Paul and all the faithful will be "awarded" (ἀποδίδωμι, *apodidōmi*) "righteousness" from the "*righteous*

---

15. Moffat, *New Testament*, 521.

16. Mounce, *Pastoral Epistles*, 577.

17. Also in 1 Tim 1:18; 6:12.

18. "Keeping the faith" may be analogous to "competing according to the rules" in 2:7 (see Pericope 12: 2 Tim 2:1–13)—the maintenance of uprightness—a lifelong, Spirit-empowered, sanctified endeavor of righteousness, undertaken in faithfulness to the One who called the believer into his service.

19. Towner, *Letters to Timothy and Titus*, 612.

20. *Nicene and Post-Nicene Fathers* 13:511.

21. Needless to say, such persistence and perseverance (and the anticipated victory) is made possibly only by the grace of God (1 Tim 1:12–14; 2 Tim 2:1; 4:17).

22. Köstenberger, *Commentary on 1–2 Timothy and Titus*, 277.

23. Nevertheless, it is impossible to ascertain with precision what exactly these rewards in Scripture are.

Judge"—the ultimate vindication of their faithfulness to him. On the other hand, the Lord will "recompense" (also ἀποδίδωμι) unfaithful ones like Alexander the coppersmith "according to his [evil] deeds" (4:14): just deserts for all! And we are assured that the reward is for those who "love" (ἀγαπάω, *agapaō*) the Lord's appearing (4:8),[24] in stark contrast to the unfaithful Demas who "loved" (also ἀγαπάω) the present age and will no doubt get what is due him (4:10).

15.3 2 Timothy 4:9–22

THEOLOGICAL FOCUS 15.3

15.3 God's people persevere faithfully without deserting the cause, the gospel, and its Agent, God, even if they are suffering now, for they are confident of ultimate deliverance and eternal reward from the hand of the righteous Judge (4:9–22).

TRANSLATION 15.3

4:9   *Make every effort to come to me soon;*

4:10 *for Demas, having loved the present age, deserted me and went to Thessalonica, Crescens to Galatia, Titus to Dalmatia;*

4:11 *Luke alone is with me. Pick up Mark and bring him with you, for he is beneficial to me for service.*

4:12 *But Tychicus I have sent to Ephesus.*

4:13 *When you come, bring the cloak which I left in Troas with Carpus, and the scrolls, especially the parchments.*

4:14 *Alexander the coppersmith perpetrated much evil against me; the Lord will recompense him according to his work;*

4:15 *be on guard against him yourself, for he opposed our words.*

4:16 *At my first defense no one supported me, but all deserted me; may it not be counted against them.*

4:17 *But the Lord stood with me and strengthened me, so that through me the proclamation might be fulfilled and all the gentiles might hear; and I was delivered from the lion's mouth.*

4:18 *The Lord will deliver me from every evil work and will save [me] into His heavenly kingdom; to whom [be] the glory from eternity to eternity! Amen.*

4:19 *Greet Prisca and Aquila, and the household of Onesiphorus.*

4:20 *Erastus remained in Corinth, but Trophimus, being ill, I left in Miletus.*

4:21 *Make every effort to come before winter. Eubulus greets you and Pudens and Linus and Claudia and all the brothers and sisters.*

4:22 *The Lord be with your spirit. Grace be with you [all].*

---

24. The rapture is close enough in time to be included, without particular distinction, to the complex of events relating to the Second Advent.

NOTES 15.3

15.3 God's people persevere faithfully without deserting the cause, the gospel, and its agent, God, even if they are suffering now, for they are confident of ultimate deliverance and eternal reward from the hand of the righteous Judge (4:9–22).

In 4:9 and 4:21 we have "make every effort to come" bracketing the final section of the Epistle, 4:9–22.[25] It was with an expression of his desire to see and fellowship with Timothy that Paul also began this letter (1:4). The urgency is understandable: Paul doesn't think he has much time left in the earthly phase of his life, and he who is so focused on the "appearing" of his Lord and Savior, wants to greet the appearing of his "beloved son" (1:1) one last time: "Make every effort to come to me soon" (4:9)!

Unlike 1 Timothy, 2 Timothy proceeds to a close with a cluster of personal names and references, autobiographical snippets and plaints, and final instructions and warnings. Here, too, there are first-person forms in abundance: such pronouns and verb suffixes are found in every verse from 4:9–18, and all are singular, except for "our" in 4:15.

Demas's "moral and geographical" movements mark 4:10[26]: morally, he had loved the world, abandoning a "love for [Christ's] appearing" (4:8); geographically he had abandoned Rome (and Paul) for Thessalonica. This must have been grievous for the apostle, for Demas had earlier been considered by Paul to be part of his team (συνεργοί, *synergoi*, "co-workers," Phlm 24; also see Col 4:14). A "deserting" (ἐγκαταλείπω, *enkataleipō*) is also mentioned in relation to Paul's trials, in 2 Tim 4:16, suggesting that Demas's absconding (also ἐγκαταλείπω) in 4:10 refers to the same event; perhaps it resulted from a fear of being associated with a criminal under a life sentence.[27] Luke, though, remained faithful to Paul and the ministry (4:11; also see Acts 28:16; Col 4:14).[28] And Mark appears to have been rehabilitated (2 Tim 4:11; also see Col 4:10–11; Phlm 24) after the earlier separation from Paul (Acts 15:37–39). He is now considered εὔχρηστος, *euchrēstos*, by Paul (2 Tim 4:11), like "a vessel for honor, sanctified, *beneficial* [εὔχρηστος] to the Master" (2:21). Tychicus, who was sent to Ephesus (4:12), may have been the bearer of this Epistle, as he apparently was for other Pauline letters (see Eph 6:21; Col 4:7).

Paul makes a specific request of Timothy: besides his cloak,[29] Paul wants "the scrolls, especially the parchments" (2 Tim 4:13)—likely copies of Scripture[30] and other writings of

---

25. This phrase is also present in Titus 3:12.

26. Towner, *Letters to Timothy and Titus*, 621.

27. The modality and timing of Paul's trial(s) are unclear: scholars are divided on whether there were two parts to the proceedings. Attempts to decipher such historical circumstances to render clarity to timelines and sequences of events, though creditable, rarely yield much fruit, especially of the homiletical kind. In any case, those historical data *behind* the text do not affect the text's thrust or the world *in front of* the text, the pericopal theology.

28. "Only" (μόνος, 2 Tim 4:11) may be hyperbolic; 4:21 indicates others who remained with Paul. Perhaps Luke was the "only" one of the inner circle to be with Paul on a day-to-day basis (and serve as his amanuensis?).

29. "This garment was a heavy circular-shaped cape, made from goat hair, hide, or coarse wool, for outer wear, and especially important in the winter months. It was not a garment one took lightly, for it would have been relatively expensive, most men owning only one such piece of clothing, and it doubled as an outer protective covering for sleeping" (Towner, *Letters to Timothy and Titus*, 628–29).

30. As in Deut 28:58; Josh 1:8; 1 Chr 27:24; Dan 9:2 (all LXX); Luke 4:17; Gal 3:10; Heb 9:19; 10:7.

his and/or of others. Thus we have a final glimpse of Paul as one who, even in his last days, is focused on Scripture.

Alexander (4:14–15; also referred to in 1 Tim 1:20) apparently was one who opposed "our words," and perpetrated "great evil." This malefactor's antagonism is described with the verb ἀνθίστημι, *anthistēmi*, "oppose" (2 Tim 4:15), which was also used of the opposition of the magicians, Jannes and Jambres, to Moses (3:8). Though Paul is awaiting trial by an earthly court, it will be a heavenly court with a "righteous Judge" that actually judges him (4:8) as well as his antagonists (4:14), "awarding"/"recompensing" (ἀποδίδωμι, *apodidōmi*, in 4:8, 14) them all what is rightly their due.

The divine purpose for which Paul had been "strengthened" (ἐνδυναμόω, *endynamoō*, 4:17; also in 2:1) was for the "fulfillment" of the κήρυγμα through Paul,[31] explained here as the hearing of the proclamation by all the gentiles. Again, here, κήρυγμα need not be restricted to the gospel message of salvation (justification), since even the PE to Paul's delegates in gentile-dominated churches—clearly edifying in nature—furthered the κήρυγμα among them.

The links between Psalm 21 LXX (Psalm 22 English) and this closing section of our pericope (2 Tim 4:9–22) are several and substantial:

Psalm 21 LXX (Psalm 22 English)	2 Timothy 4
ἐγκαταλείπω, *enkataleipō* "forsake" 21:2 LXX (22:1)	ἐγκαταλείπω "desert" 4:10, 16
πᾶσαι αἱ πατριαὶ τῶν ἐθνῶν *pasai hai patriai tōn ethnōn* "all the families of the nations" 21:28 LXX (22:27)	πάντα τὰ ἔθνη *panta ta ethnē* "all the Gentiles" 4:17
ῥύομαι/σῴζω, *rhuomai/sōzō*, "deliver"/"save" 21:5/6, 9a/9b, 21/22 LXX (22:4/5, 8a/8b, 20/21)	ῥύομαι/σῴζω 4:17b, 18a/18b
"lion's mouth" 21:22 LXX (22:21)	"lion's mouth" 4:17
τοῦ κυρίου ἡ βασιλεία *tou kyriou hē basileia* "the kingdom is the Lord's" 21:29 LXX (22:28)	ἡ βασιλεία αὐτός *hē basileia autos* "His kingdom" 4:18

"Paul's behavior, as well as his circumstances, presents a rather dramatic parallel with that of Jesus in his last hours—betrayal (Alexander?), abandonment (the Asian team, Demas, 'everyone'), trial, prayer for mercy . . . — a parallel that . . . Paul encourages by additional allusions to the Messianic Psalm."[32]

While no human supported Paul (οὐδείς μοι παρεγένετο, *oudeis moi paregeneto*, 4:16), he was confident that the Lord had stood with him (ὁ δὲ κύριός μοι παρέστη, *ho de kyrios moi parestē*, 4:17). The "deliverance" in 4:17 was temporary and earthly; that in 4:18 would be permanent and heavenly. In any case, they were both the work of God (indicated by the

---

31. "Fulfillment" was also used in 2 Tim 4:5, where Paul urged Timothy to "fulfill" his service/ministry.

32. Towner, *Letters to Timothy and Titus*, 640. A side note: Here is the case of a Psalm that has a theological thrust applicable 1) to its original readers; 2) to Christ; 3) to Paul; and, of course, 4) to Timothy and every other reader. The christological maneuver is not to assert that that notion was the Psalm's referent, but only that Christology is a valid mode of *application* of this text.

"divine" passives).³³ Paul's "deliverance" (4:18a, ῥύομαι, also in 4:17) from a negative situation: "from every evil work," becomes a "salvation" (4:18b, σῴζω) into a positive situation: to God's heavenly kingdom, the consummation of salvation. And with that confident assertion of the Lord's deliverance in every facet and on every side, a doxology is evoked upon God, "to whom [be] the glory from eternity to eternity! Amen" (4:18).

A final set of names and a greeting concludes the pathos-filled pericope and the very personal letter (4:19–22)—the final recorded words of Paul in Scripture.³⁴ According to tradition, Paul was beheaded at Aquae Salviae near the third milestone on the Ostian Way, about three miles south of Rome, around 65 CE.³⁵

SERMON MAPS

THEOLOGICAL FOCUS OF PERICOPE 15 FOR PREACHING

15 The people of God solemnly preach God's word at every opportunity, despite opposition and suffering, as they follow the example of godly leaders, asserting their lifelong faithfulness to God and to their ministries, confident of ultimate deliverance and eternal rewards (4:1–22).

Thematically Pericope 13: 2 Tim 2:14–26, Pericope 14: 2 Tim 3:1–17, and the current pericope (2 Tim 4:1–22) are linked. All of them have a focus on Scripture, directly or indirectly. In Pericope 13, the focus was on the speech of the false teachers contrasted with that of believers (a more general and wider umbrella of communication); in Pericope 14, the grounding of believers upon Scripture was in view—continuance in Scripture for all of life. Here, in Pericope 15, we have the charge to "preach the word" (a more specific form of communication³⁶). Nuancing the differences between these three pericopes is essential.³⁷

Possible Preaching Maps for Pericope 15

I. Communication
   Priority of preaching (4:1–5)
   Move-to-Relevance: The need for this priority today
II. Commitment

---

33. Paul's anticipated rescue from "every evil *work*" (πᾶς ἔργον πονηρός, *pas ergon ponēros*, 4:18) no doubt includes the "works" of Alexander (ἔργα, 4:14).

34. Prisca (Priscilla) and Aquila are also mentioned in Acts 18:2–3, 18–19, 26; Rom 16:3–4; 1 Cor 16:19; Onesiphorus in 2 Tim 1:16–18; Erastus in Acts 19:22; Rom 16:23; and Trophimus in Acts 20:4; 21:29. About the rest, Scripture is silent.

35. Bruce, *Paul*, 450–51.

36. By "preaching," I am not restricting the activity to any person, place, or occasion; as long as it is the communication of Scripture for application, the act will qualify as "preaching." However, I do see preaching in the context of the corporate gathering of the local body of Christ as the primary example of this endeavor, restricted to the elders of the church.

37. Which also means that one should have a birds-eye view of the entire biblical book one is preaching, before one embarks on the sermonic journey. And on that note, somewhere in your travels through the PE, make sure you hit on eternal rewards: this is one of several pericopes that touches on them—pick one of those to deal with this important facet of the Christian's future hope.

Perseverance in ministry (4:6–7)[38]
   Move-to-Relevance: Why we falter
III. Confidence
   Faith in the rewards and deliverance of God (4:8–22)
   Move-to-Relevance: Advantage of being unshakeable in ministry
IV. *Commit to Confident Communication!*
   First steps on how one might do that

We can retell the "story" (the narratival nature of the sermon) with a rearrangement: "Here is Paul's *commitment*, because he was *confident*; so here is the ministry—*communication*—that we, like Paul, should engage in." This has the advantage of placing "Communication" right next to the application.

I. Commitment
   Perseverance in ministry (4:6–7)
   Move-to-Relevance: Why we falter
II. Confidence
   Faith in the rewards and deliverance of God (4:8–22)
   Move-to-Relevance: Advantage of being unshakeable in ministry
III. Communication
   Priority of preaching (4:1–5)
   Move-to-Relevance: The need for this priority today
IV. *Commit to Confident Communication!*
   First steps on how one might do that

---

38. "Ministry" is also best focused upon preaching; otherwise a single sermonic thrust is difficult to sustain.

TITUS

Exemplifying the Excellent

PERICOPE 16

Charitable Correction

Titus 1:1–16

[False Teachers vs. Truth Teachers; Reproof of False Teachers]

SUMMARY, PREVIEW[1]

Summary of Pericope 16: This first pericope of Titus (Pericope 16: Titus 1:1–16) once again creates a contrast between false teachers and truth teachers. The correction of the former by the latter is a serious responsibility of both leaders and laypeople, and they must be irreproachable in all these undertakings—reproof of error and exhortation of truth.

Preview of Pericope 17: The second pericope of Titus (Pericope 17: Titus 2:1–15) deals for the most part with behavior within community. All believers are to engage in good works and thus enhance God's reputation, grounded in the divine work that effectuates those human works.

16 Titus 1:1–16

> **THEOLOGICAL FOCUS OF PERICOPE 16**
>
> 16 Godly, blameless stewards of the church, who hold firmly the word of a deceitless God in their lives and their teaching, exhort and reprove rebellious, defiled false teachers in the church who, with their unruly lives, attend to unbiblical myths and human commands, engage in deceptive teaching with mercenary motives upsetting households, and are detestable in God's eyes (1:1–16).

---

1. Since 2 Timothy is a discrete Epistle, I will forego a "Review" of the prior pericope that concluded that letter.

TITUS

> 16.1 The people of God are enjoined to promote faith, truth for godliness, and hope that consummates in eternal life grounded in the promise of a deceitless God (1:1–4).
>
> 16.2 Godly and blameless stewards of the church hold firmly to God's word in their lives and their teaching, exhorting God's people and reproving false teachers (1:5–9).
>
> 16.3 Rebellious, defiled opponents in the church who, with their unruly lives, attend to unbiblical myths and human commands, engage in deceptive teaching with mercenary motives upsetting households, are detestable in God's eyes, and are reproved (1:10–16).

OVERVIEW

There is no thanksgiving section in the Epistle to Titus, unlike in those to Timothy (1 Tim 1:12; 2 Tim 1:3). Directly launching into Paul's exhortations to his delegate Titus, Pericope 16: Titus 1–16 "reads much more like a dispatch to a lieutenant with telegraphic instruction of how to proceed than a full-blown Pauline argument."[2]

16.1 Titus 1:1–4

> **THEOLOGICAL FOCUS 16.1**
>
> 16.1 The people of God are enjoined to promote faith, truth for godliness, and hope that consummates in eternal life grounded in the promise of a deceitless God (1:1–4).

TRANSLATION 16.1

1:1 *Paul, a bondservant of God and an apostle of Jesus Christ, for the faith of the elect of God and [for] the knowledge of the truth that is according to godliness,*

1:2 *unto the hope of eternal life, which the deceitless God promised before times eternal,*

1:3 *but at the proper time manifested His word, in the proclamation with which I myself was entrusted, according to the command of God our Savior,*

1:4 *to Titus, genuine child in a common faith: Grace and peace from God the Father and Christ Jesus our Savior.*

NOTES 16.1

16.1 *The people of God are enjoined to promote faith, truth for godliness, and hope that consummates in eternal life grounded in the promise of a deceitless God (1:1–4).*

Titus 1:1–4 is a single sentence; it constitutes the third-longest opening of all the Pauline letters with sixty-five words in the Greek text.[3] "Faith" and "truth [for godliness]" seem to be the focus of this salutation, appropriate for a letter to Cretan Christians who are going to be

---

2. Witherington, *Letters and Homilies*, 92.
3. Rom 1:1–7 has ninety-three words; Gal 1:1–5 has seventy-five.

warned against drifting from these key aspects of the Christian life (1:1).[4] Paul establishes his apostolic authority—designated and entrusted by divine commandment (1:1, 3), thus giving Titus's own ministry credibility.[5] Thus there is an implicit urging that false teachers ought not to be allowed to gain any ground in their community, while Titus is being credentialed as the authorized teacher in Paul's absence. This contrast between truth teachers and false teachers is shared between Titus and 1 Timothy, reflected in a number of similarities between the commencing chapters of those two letters[6]:

Titus 1	1 Timothy 1
διδαχή, διδασκαλία (1:9) *didachē, didaskalia*, "teaching"	διδασκαλία (1:10) *didaskalia*, "teaching"
διδάσκοντες ἃ μὴ δεῖ (1:11) *didaskontes ha mē dei* "teaching things they should not"	ἑτεροδιδασκαλέω (1:3) *heterodidaskaleō* "teaching falsely"
ματαιολόγοι, *mataiologoi* (1:10) "empty talkers"	ματαιολογία, *mataiologia* (1:6) "fruitless discussion"
"not attending to ... myths" (1:14)	"nor to attend to myths" (1:4)
"pure" (×2; 1:15)	"pure" (1:5)
"conscience" (1:15)	"conscience" (1:5)

The rather complex construction of 1:1–4 may be clarified by diagramming the sentence to reveal three parallel prepositional clauses (1:1b [with κατά, *kata*]; 1:1c [with an implied κατά]; and 1:2a [with ἐπί, *epi*]—all three are highlighted in light gray, below), each qualifying Paul's bondservant status and apostleship: his portfolio was to further both the faith of God's people (1:1b) and their knowledge of the truth (1:1c)—all in anticipation of the consummation of the hope of a God-promised eternal life (1:2a).[7]

1:1a	"Paul, a bond-servant of God and an apostle of Jesus Christ,
1:1b	*for/to further* [κατά] the **faith** of the elect of God and
1:1c	*[for/to further* (κατά)*]* the knowledge of the **truth** that
1:1d	is according to/leads to [κατά] **godliness**,
1:2a	*unto/for the consummation of* [ἐπί] the hope of eternal life,
1:2b–3	which the deceitless God promised ...,
1:4	to Titus, genuine child in [κατά] the common faith: ...."

---

4. "Faith" and related terms are found in this Epistle in 1:1, 3, 4, 13; 2:2, 10; 3:8, 15; and "truth" in 1:1, 13, 14.

5. Titus 1:1 is the only instance of Paul labeling himself as δοῦλος θεοῦ, *doulos theou*, "bondservant of God." The mention of the "elect of God" (1:1) clearly demarcates this letter as one written for the church at Crete, albeit directly addressed to Paul's delegate there, Titus. Also note that the "grace" extended in the final verse, 3:15, is to "you all" (plural), in anticipation of the entire church perusing this Epistle.

6. See Van Neste, *Cohesion and Structure*, 254; Mounce, *Pastoral Epistles*, 15.

7. I don't believe there is value in diagramming every sentence of a preaching pericope; I rarely ever do it, except for convoluted sentences such as the one that makes up 1:1–4. Even here, it is only minimally performed, just enough to throw some light on what qualifies what.

TITUS

Thus in 1:1–2 we have a trio of the critical aspects of Christian living: faith, truth leading to godliness, and hope (in bold, above).[8] All three elements, faith, truth, and hope—thus encompassing salvation past (faith), present (truth leading to godliness), and future (hope of eternal life)—were the aim of Paul's service to God.[9] Indeed, that is the implied call for Titus and all believers, too—the promotion of these critical aspects of Christian faith and praxis.

The consummation of believers' hope in eternal life (with its attendant rewards) had been promised by a God who never lies (1:2). The description of God as "deceitless" (ἀψευδὴς, *apseudēs*, 1:2) would have made a poignant description of deity to Paul's readers, for Zeus, the Greek entity, often lied to gain advantage over others, once even assuming the form of a husband to take sexual advantage of that one's wife, Alcmene.[10] Besides, "Cretans regarded lying as culturally acceptable, and hence the use of the term 'to speak like a Cretan' [κρητίζω, *krētizō*] came to mean 'to lie'" (more below, on Cretans being liars themselves; 1:12).[11] The divine promise made before "times eternal" (χρόνοι αἰώνιοι, *chronoi aiōnioi*, 1:2) was manifested in/by God's word at the "proper time" (καιρός ἴδιος, *kairos idios*, "his own time," 1:3).

The letter is primarily addressed to Titus, Paul's "genuine child" in "a common faith" (1:4)—referring to the shared commitment of both of them (one Jew, the other Greek[12]), i.e., "in a common/shared [response of] faith" towards Jesus Christ.

16.2 Titus 1:5–9

> **THEOLOGICAL FOCUS 16.2**
>
> 16.2 Godly and blameless stewards of the church hold firmly to God's word in their lives and their teaching, exhorting God's people and reproving false teachers (1:5–9).

TRANSLATION 16.2

1:5 *For this reason I left you in Crete, so that you would set straight what is left and appoint elders in each city as I myself directed you:*

1:6 *if one is blameless, a one-woman man, having believing children not accused of dissipation or [who are] rebellious.*

1:7 *For the overseer must be blameless as God's steward, not self-willed, not quick-tempered, not addicted to wine, not pugnacious, not fond of sordid gain,*

---

8. The prepositional clause in 1:1d (with κατά) qualifies "truth." Another in 1:3a (not shown above; also with κατά) qualifies Paul's entrustment: "according to the command of God"; yet another in 1:4 (and again with κατά) qualifies "genuine child": "in/according to the common faith." This yields a total of four κατά-clauses in 1:1b, 1d, 3a, 4, and an implied fifth in 1:1c.

9. The phrase ὃ ἐπιστεύθην ἐγώ, *ho episteuthēn egō*, "with which I myself was entrusted" (1:3), expresses Paul's sense of wonder at his own appointment (also in 1 Tim 1:11).

10. Apollodorus, *Library* 2.4.8.

11. Winter, *Roman Wives, Roman Widows*, 150. See Plutarch, *Aemilius Paulus* 23.6; and *Lysander* 20.2 for the use of κρητίζω.

12. While Timothy had Jewish blood in him (on his mother's side), Titus was fully gentile (Gal 2:3). Nonetheless, he is Paul's "genuine child" (Titus 1:4; converted by Paul?), his "brother" (2 Cor 2:13), and his "partner" and "coworker" (2 Cor 8:23).

1:8   *but hospitable, loving good, self-controlled, righteous, holy, disciplined,*

1:9   *holding firmly to the faithful word that is in accordance with the teaching, so that he will be able both to exhort in sound teaching and to reprove those contradicting.*

NOTES 16.2

16.2   *Godly and blameless stewards of the church hold firmly to God's word in their lives and their teaching, exhorting God's people and reproving false teachers (1:5–9).*

This section, 1:5–9, also has κατά-clauses, one at each end: κατὰ πόλιν, *kata polin* ("in each city," 1:5) and κατὰ τὴν διδαχὴν πιστοῦ λόγου, *kata tēn didachēn pistou logou* ("the faithful word that is in accordance with the teaching," 1:9).

Titus's immediate commission is set out in 1:5: "to set straight" and "to appoint elders in each city."[13] Subsequently, the second injunction is described first (in 1:6–9), followed by an expansion of the first mandate (in 1:10–16). Not that the two are unconnected of course; the disorder implied likely resulted from the lack of appropriate leadership in the Cretan church. Thus, Titus was "left" (from ἀπολείπω, *apoleipō*) in Crete, so that he might put in order what was "left" (from λείπω, *leipō*; 1:5). "The man and his task are seen as indissolubly linked in the apostolic commission."[14]

The mention of appointing elders (1:5) suggests that these were new elders who were being installed; on the other hand, in 1 Timothy, the church appears to have been one with already-functioning elders. The situation in Crete may therefore well have been that of a church plant, or at least of a younger church than the one at Ephesus (1 Tim 5:19–25 even mentions the discipline of established elders). The absence of any mention of deacons or deaconesses also substantiates the relative newness of this community. Besides, the assignment of Titus to appoint elders apparently unilaterally, without any community input, seems to validate the church as being of recent vintage.

But much has also been made of an absence of any indication that new converts would be forbidden from the office (as found in 1 Tim 3:6 and 5:22); and there is no explicit instruction that potential candidates maintain good reputations without the church (as we see in 1 Tim 3:7; also see 3:2, 10, 13). But to tie these seeming lacunae to the relative youth of the church is, I believe, erroneous, and reflects a "slice-and-dice" approach to lists that analyzes them as if they are scientific data. While there is no proscription of new converts in Titus 1, there are requirements that elders' children be faithful (1:6; see below); that elders be "righteous," "holy," and "disciplined" (1:8); and capable of teaching—"holding firmly" to Scripture, "exhorting" sound doctrine, and "reproving" those in opposition (1:9). It is highly unlikely that new converts would demonstrate such character traits. Besides, while an explicit need to have a good reputation is also missing from the Titus 1 list, we do have a repeated call here for elders to be "blameless" (1:6, 7). All that to say, lists such as these should not be hunted to capture their individual items, or atomized as scientifically precise

---

13. Apparently, there was more than one church on the island of Crete, 160 miles long and 8–37 miles wide (3,219 square miles in area). Homer labeled the island "Crete of a hundred cities" (Κρήτη ἑκατόμπολις, *Krētē hekatompolis*, *Iliad* 2.649; my translation).

14. Quinn, *Letter to Titus*, 83.

character qualifications that are mutually exclusive. Rather the whole mélange of qualities, their harmonious blending, is what is to be taken into account, for lists are rhetorically intended to overwhelm the reader, with the overall force and import of their components considered unitedly and integrally. Here the contrast is between the character and pedagogical habits of teachers of truth (elders; 1:5-9) and those of teachers of falsehood (1:10-16).

> In this format, they were not regarded as so many individual qualifications to be checked off; together they formed an ideal pattern of, for the most part, a life capable of outward, visible assessment. And in extolling an ideal life of virtue, philosophers held forth such lists of virtues to idealize the value of public respectability, and required the leaders in society to be measured against the ideal.... The individual items work together to point in some directions, but they are not to be slavishly exegeted in the hope that they will give up their mysterious secrets to "leadership."[15]

Irreproachability begins the list (ἀνέγκλητος, *anenklētos*, "blameless," 1:6) and presumably, that is what is spelled out and expanded upon in the remaining verses, 1:5-9, with the adjective repeated in 1:7. "Thus, in a general sense, the qualification for holding a leadership position is 'blamelessness.' The specific qualities explore this measurement of character within a concrete framework that includes a person's domestic, personal (and interpersonal), and ecclesiastical (ministry) spheres."[16]

The second item in both Titus 1 and 1 Timothy 3 is faithfulness in marriage (if married): μιᾶς γυναικὸς ἀνήρ, *mias gynaikos anēr*, "one-woman man."[17] Titus 1:6 also calls for children of elders to be believers.[18] We find out later that the false teachers were "rebellious" (ἀνυπότακτος, *anypotaktos*, 1:10); here even the elders' children were not to be tainted with such an accusation (ἀνυπότακτος in 1:6). "One is encountering here not the willfulness of mere youngsters but the rebelliousness of young adults in public opposition to the social and political orders," the flagrant violations of those still living under the authority of a father, and in his home.[19] Of course, τέκνα, *tekna*, can mean progeny irrespective of age; and "dissipation," involving a spectrum of concupiscent activities from illegitimate sexuality to excessive consumption of food or drink, would not likely apply to younger, non-adult children.

The notion of the church as the "household of God" (οἶκος θεοῦ, *oikos theou*, 1 Tim 3:15) is established further with the labeling of the elder here as "God's steward" (θεοῦ οἰκονόμος, *theou oikonomos*, Titus 1:7) who facilitates the "economy of God" (οἰκονομία θεοῦ, *oikonomia theou*, 1 Tim 1:4).[20] Such a one is faithful to the householder, God himself, as well as to the task, caretaking, and to the objects of the task, the members of the household.[21]

---

15. Towner, *Letters to Timothy and Titus*, 684.
16. Towner, *Letters to Timothy and Titus*, 681.
17. See on 1 Tim 3:2 in Pericope 5: 1 Tim 3:1-16.
18. The adjective πιστά, *pista*, in Titus 1:6 could also be translated "faithful," as in 1 Tim 1:12; 3:11; 2 Tim 2:2, 13; Titus 1:9; but see 1 Tim 6:2 (and Acts 16:1) for the sense of "believing" or "of faith." In structure, too, τέκνα ἔχων πιστά, *tekna echōn pista*, in Titus 1:6 is similar to πιστοὺς ἔχοντες δεσπότας, *pistous echontes despotas*, in 1 Tim 6:2, "having believing masters." Hence: "having believing children."
19. Quinn, *Letter to Titus*, 88.
20. For notions related to the church as God's household, also see 1 Tim 3:4-5, 12; 5:1-2; and 2 Tim 2:20 (and 1 Cor 4:1; Gal 6:10; Eph 2:10; etc.).
21. "Self-control" seems to be a key character trait of all God's people; σωφρον (*sōphron*)-related

The same "word" that was manifested for proclamation (1:3) is the "word" that elders were to hold fast to (1:9). That that "word" is described as πιστός, *pistos,* "faithful," makes a strong contrast to the lying words of the Cretans which will later be excoriated (1:10–16). "The candidate for becoming a Pauline presbyter-bishop is himself to be completely attached to God's message, that is, to the *logos* of 1:3 that was entrusted to Paul and proclaimed by him. An original and creative teaching is not the aim of the PE."[22] As was noted in Pericope 1: 1 Tim 1:1–11, nouns with the διδασκ-root occur in both plural (1 Tim 1:7; 4:1) and singular forms (1 Tim 1:10; 2:7; 4:6, 13, 16; 5:17; 6:1, 3; 2 Tim 1:11; 3:10, 16; 4:2, 3; Titus 1:9 [×2]; 2:1, 7, 10). Notably, the former instances all deal with false teaching (with the exception of Titus 2:3 that has a prefix giving it an unambiguously positive connotation: καλοδιδάσκαλοι, *kalodidaskaloi*); the latter, singular nouns, as in 1:9, are concerned with sound doctrine.

16.3 Titus 1:10–16

> **THEOLOGICAL FOCUS 16.3**
>
> 16.3 Rebellious, defiled opponents in the church who, with their unruly lives, attend to unbiblical myths and human commands, engage in deceptive teaching with mercenary motives upsetting households, are detestable in God's eyes, and are reproved (1:10–16).

TRANSLATION 16.3

1:10   *For there are many rebellious, empty talkers and deceivers, especially those of the circumcision,*

1:11   *who must be silenced—they who are indeed upsetting whole families, teaching things they should not for the sake of sordid gain.*

1:12   *One of themselves, their own prophet, said, "Cretans are always liars, evil beasts, lazy gluttons."*

1:13   *This testimony is true. For this reason reprove them sharply so that they may be sound in the faith,*

1:14   *not attending to Jewish myths and commandments of people who turn away from the truth.*

1:15   *To the pure, all things are pure; but to those who are defiled and unbelieving, nothing is pure, but both their mind and their conscience are defiled.*

1:16   *They profess to know God, but by works they deny [Him], being detestable and disobedient and rejected for every good work.*

---

words are found in 1:8; 2:2, 4, 5, 6, 12. This reminds us that elders were meant to serve as role models to their congregants.

22. Quinn, *Letter to Titus,* 92.

NOTES 16.3

16.3 Rebellious, defiled opponents in the church who, with their unruly lives, attend to unbiblical myths and human commands, engage in deceptive teaching with mercenary motives upsetting households, are detestable in God's eyes, and are reproved (1:10–16).

The γάρ in 1:10 explicates the reason for Paul's starting out with elder appointments and candidate qualifications—"for there are many" that needed to be "silenced" and "reproved" (1:9, 11, 13) by the teaching of the "faithful word" (1:9).[23]

In a sense, 1:10–16 is the "vice" list corresponding to the "virtue" list (for elders) of 1:5–9: one set of teachers "teaching [διδάσκοντες, *didaskontes*] things they should not" (1:11) is being contrasted with another set that is "holding firmly to the faithful word which is in accordance with the teaching" (διδασκαλία, 1:9)[24]:

Titus 1:5–9 (Elders)	Titus 1:10–16 (Opponents)
"Not rebellious" (1:6)	"rebellious" (1:10)
House manager (1:6)	House upsetters (1:11)
"Blameless" (1:6, 7)	"Abominable" (1:16)
πιστός, *pistos*, "believing" (1:6)	ἄπιστος, *apistos*, "unbelieving" (1:15)
Not quick-tempered (1:7)	Beastlike (1:12)
Not covetous (αἰσχροκερδής, *aischrokerdēs*, 1:7)	Covetous (αἰσχρός κέρδος, *aischros kerdos*, 1:11)
"loving *good*" (1:8)	"*good* work" (1:16)
ἀντεχόμενον, *antechomenon* "holding firmly" to truth (1:9)	προσέχοντες, *prosechontes* "attending" to falsehood (1:14)
Right teaching (διδασκαλία, 1:9)	False teaching (διδάσκω, 1:11)
"sound" (1:9)	"sound" (1:13)

Again, this list, like the "virtue" list in 1:5–9, is an amalgam, a composite of symptoms that points to a singular syndrome, not intended to be dissected out and analyzed individually.

The heterodox teaching and teachers in Crete appear to have been similar to those in Ephesus. "Those of the circumcision" are certainly Jews (1:10); here they are likely to be Jewish Christians (see Acts 10:45; 11:2; Gal 2:12; Col 4:11) who were adulterating sound doctrine with false teaching. Other hints of the Jewish nature of the false teaching are seen in Titus 1:14 ("Jewish myths") and 3:9 ("quarrels about the law").[25] Titus, being a gentile, could well have been a prime target for these heterodoxy propagators. The reference to purity (1:15) may also have been related to a Jewish take on dietary practices (also see 1 Tim 4:3–5). These are labeled "commandments of people" (ἐντολαί ἀνθρώπων, *entolai*

---

23. This pair of verbs, "exhort" and "reprove," also shows up in 2:15.
24. See Van Neste, *Cohesion and Structure*, 254; Witherington, *Letters and Homilies*, 127.
25. Also see 1 Tim 1:4, 7–8; 4:1–3, 7; 2 Tim 3:8–9; 4:5; Titus 3:9. Whatever "Jewish myths and commandments of people" means (1:14)—perhaps they related to embellishments of the Pentateuch stories or idiosyncratic takes on the oral law and midrash—"there is no escaping the contemptuous dismissal of these techniques and their products as merely human regulations and myths" (Quinn, *Letter to Titus*, 109).

anthrōpōn, 1:14) as opposed to those of God.[26] All this notwithstanding, what specifically the circumstances in Crete were that necessitated Paul's commissioning of Titus to counter this false teaching is unclear—it probably does not make much difference to the thrust of the text anyway.

The section, Titus 1:10–16, begins with a number of sonic echoes: "The artful rhetoric of this passage appears in the plosive consonants as they erupt in the stream of οι/αι (*oi/ai*) assonance [πολλοὶ καὶ ἀνυπότακτοι, ματαιολόγοι καὶ φρεναπάται, *polloi anypotaktoi, mataiologoi kai phrenapatai*, "many rebellious, empty talkers and deceivers"], which runs through the exotic terminology translated as 'spouting nonsense and seducing minds.'"[27] Elders were called to be μὴ αἰσχροκερδῆ, *mē aischrokerdē*, "not fond of sordid gain" (1:7), but these false teachers were purveying their perfidious pedagogy for αἰσχροῦ κέρδους, *aischrou kerdous*, "sordid gain" (1:11).[28] The notion of financial gain sought by the opponents implies at least some level of pecuniary support from those within the church. "From the perspective of church health, if Christians were not only listening to the nonsense (which was dangerous enough) but also endorsing and embracing it by their practical support of these teachers, then the defection of whole households from the apostolic faith could not have been far behind."[29] And that is exactly what we see: These who had "turned away" from the truth (ἀποστρέπω, *apostrepō*, 1:14) were "upsetting" whole households in the church (ἀνατρέπω, *anatrepō*, 1:11). While these false teachers were influential among women in Ephesus (1 Tim 5:14–16; 2 Tim 3:6), here in Titus it is entire families that were being upturned. In response, church leaders were to "exhort" and "reprove" (1:9, 13; 2:15) with the hope of correction; if that failed, they were to "avoid/reject" such rebellious ones (3:10).

Then follows a deprecation of Cretans and their lying tendencies (1:12). Apparently, Cretans claimed that Zeus's tomb was on their island. Such an assertion was labeled by the poet Callimachus (third century BCE) as false: Κρῆτες ἀεὶ ψεῦσται, *Krētes aei pseustai* ("Cretans are always liars," *Hymns 1, To Zeus*, 6.1.8–9)[30]; the exact sentence was cited by Paul in Titus 1:12. "The currency of such terms [in Greek literature] as κρητίζειν [*krētizein*], to lie, κρητισμός [*krētismos*], falsehood, and the expression, πρὸς Κρῆτα κρητίζειν [*pros Krēta krētizein*], 'to meet craft with craft,' suggest a widespread perception" and universal concurrence with Callimachus's epigram.[31] And, to add to the irony (and compound a paradox), Paul asserts that "this testimony is *true*" (1:12; notice "truth" also in 1:1, 14). Of course, the apostle and his delegate, Titus, and all God's people and their communities, serve a God

---

26. See Isa 29:13 LXX that has ἐντάλματα ἀνθρώπων, *entalmata anthrōpōn*, and the NT citations and allusions thereof, in Matt 15:9; Mark 7:7; Col 2:22.

27. Quinn, *Letter to Titus*, 106.

28. Magnificently rendered in the KJV as "filthy lucre!" Curiously enough, the phrase shows up in relation to Cretans in Polybius, *Histories* 6.46.3: "So much in fact do sordid love of gain [αἰσχροκέρδεια, *aischrokerdeia*] and lust for wealth prevail among them, that the Cretans are the only people in the world in whose eyes no gain is disgraceful [μηδὲν αἰσχρὸν νομίζεσθαι κέρδος, *mēden aischron nomizesthai kerdos*]" (Polybius, *Histories*, 3:412–13). The Cretans must have had quite a reputation for loathsome avarice.

29. Towner, *Letters to Timothy and Titus*, 698.

30. *Hymns and Epigrams*, 36–37. However, the poet is, here, apparently quoting a recognized statement, the source of which is unclear, though some, Clement of Alexandria and Jerome among them, have suggested it came from Epimenides (a sixth- or seventh-century BCE poet). With like sentiment, Cicero (*On the Republic* 3.9.15) remarked that "men's principles of life are so different that the Cretans... consider piracy and brigandage honourable" (*On the Republic*, 197).

31. Wieland, "Roman Crete," 345.

who is ἀψευδής, "deceitless" (or "unfalse/unlying," 1:2; ψεῦσται, "liars," is used in 1:14). The deprecation of the Cretans continues: While "good works" (ἔργα ἀγαθοί, *erga agathoi*) are later exhorted in 1:16, the Cretan opponents of Paul/Titus are described as ἀργαί, *argai* (likely from an α-privative of ἔργον, *ergon*; thus, "un-working," i.e., lazy) in 1:12; they are also likened to "evil beasts," brutish and wild.[32] The sum of it is that these false teachers need to be "reproved sharply" that they may be "sound in the faith" (1:13).[33]

The chiastic structure of 1:15 (below) has elements A and A' dealing with ritual purity (+) and ritual impurity (–) respectively; and B and B' dealing with moral purity (+) and moral impurity (–), respectively. The chiasm focuses on the central elements, B and B':

A	"All things are pure		Ritually	+
	B to those pure,		Morally	+
	B' but to those defiled and unbelieving,		Morally	–
A	nothing is pure, but … defiled."		Ritually	–

The utterance of 1:15 essentially portrays those who are morally pure as being also ritually pure (for they obey divine mandates, not the "commandments of people," 1:14). But those who are morally impure are also ritually impure (no matter what ritual they may engage in: "nothing is pure"), for their moral impurity, stemming from their defiled "mind" and "conscience," sullies every aspect of their lives.[34] In other words, if one is morally impure, like those Cretan opponents, no manmade imperative will help eliminate that defilement. The context here is likely to be of dietary restrictions. These false teachers "profess [and pretend] to know God, but by works they deny [Him]"—they are "rejected for every good work" (1:16). Whether "unbelieving" in 1:15 denies their salvation is doubtful: it points more to their lack of faith in the mandates of God, as they put their trust in the "commandments of people."

> Paul's evaluation of these false teachers corresponds with what he says elsewhere in the PE about the false teachers in the church [1 Tim 4:1–2; 6:3–5, 10; 2 Tim 2:17–18, 25–26; 3:5] … and to his indictment of false teachers in the Galatian

---

32. The invective use of θηρίον, *thērion*, "evil beast," to designate barbarous people was common in that day; see Josephus, *Jewish War* 1.624, 62; *Jewish Antiquities* 17.117, 120; etc. In the PE, "good works" employing καλός is found in 1 Tim 3:1; 5:10, 25; 6:18; Titus 2:7, 14; 3:8, 14; and using ἀγαθός in 1 Tim 2:10; 2 Tim 2:21; 3:17; Titus 1:16; 3:1. Notice that "good works" is found in every chapter of Titus, and almost every chapter of both Epistles to Timothy.

33. In the PE, "soundness" is usually related to teaching or doctrine: 1 Tim 1:10; 6:3; 2 Tim 1:13; 4:3; Titus 1:9; but here in Titus 1:13 (and in 2:2), it is "soundness" of faith that is urged. Here the context indicates that "faith" is objective, that which is believed (but in 2:2, it is likely subjective, that attitude of the person to God, as "faith" occurs in association with "love" and "perseverance" there).

34. Note that this does not abolish the ritual aspects of the Mosaic Law, but only relativizes it, while emphasizing the importance of the moral aspect (see 1 Tim 4:3–5). It "depreciates rather than abrogates" the issue of rituals dealt with (Holmén, *Jesus and Jewish Covenant Thinking*, 240–41), such as the food laws that rendered certain items impure simply by divine designation; they were intended to symbolize the greater reality (and emphasize the necessity) of separation from pagan custom and praxis. In Jesus's dialogue with a scribe in Mark 12:28–34, he declared that keeping the foremost commandments (the moral aspect of the Mosaic Law) was "greater" than all the offerings and sacrifices (the ritual aspect of the Mosaic Law). Not that one can be neglected for the other (for even the ritual law has moral overtones, coming as it does from a moral Lawgiver), but there are differences in degrees of importance between them. It must be emphasized that Jesus *did* agree with the need for offerings, a facet of ritual purity (Mark 1:44). Also see "Excursus on Food" in Pericope 6: 1 Tim 4:1–16.

Christian community (e.g., Gal 1:9). Being "of the circumcision" they do have some views that come from the Jewish community ("myths and endless genealogies"), but their views go beyond Judaism. It is unnecessary, therefore, to say Paul has shifted from the false teachers within the Christian community to those outside. In accordance with his normal practice, Paul deals with false teachers in the church; he rarely, if ever, deals with those outside the Christian community, and there is no reason to suggest that he does otherwise here.[35]

In any case, these who "turn away from the truth" (1:14) are morally impure, and nothing they attempt will help; all their "works" only renounce God, and so those "works" are "worthless," displeasing to God—they are "detestable" (βδελυκτοί, bdelyktoi).[36]

SERMON MAPS

THEOLOGICAL FOCUS OF PERICOPE 16 FOR PREACHING

16 Godly, blameless stewards of the church, who hold firmly the word God in their lives and their teaching, exhort and reprove rebellious false teachers in the church who, engaging in deceptive teaching and upsetting households, are detestable in God's eyes (1:1–16).

As was noted, this pericope and Pericope 1: 1 Tim 1:1–11 share the theme of truth teachers vs. false teachers. In the latter the focus was more on the correct use of Scripture in instruction (to further the divine economy); here the focus is on reproving the error-prone pedagogues, particularly in light of the appointment of elders noted in this text.

Possible Preaching Maps for Pericope 16

I. False Teachers
   Content (1:14)
   Character (1:10–13, 15–16)
   Move-to-Relevance: False teachers today
II. Truth Teachers
   Content (1:1–4)
   Character (1:5–9)
   Correction (1:9, 11)
   Move-to-Relevance: Nature of correction[37]
III. *Charitably Correct Charlatans!*
   Specific steps on undertaking such correction

One could go back and forth between false and truth teachers in each move:

---

35. Knight, *Pastoral Epistles*, 304.

36. In the LXX, this word is found in Prov 17:15 and 2 Macc 1:27. Its cognate, βδέλυγμα, *bdelygma*, is frequently employed in the LXX in the cultic sense of "abomination" to God, for instance, with regard to prohibited foods: in Lev 10, 11, 12, 13, 23, 41, 42 (and numerous times in Proverbs: 11:1, 20; 12:22; 15:8, 9, 26; 16:12; 20:23; 21:27; 29:27).

37. The character qualities of the truth-teacher come into play here: if that one is "blameless . . . , not self-willed, not-quick-tempered," but "loving good, self-controlled, righteous, holy, disciplined," this correction will never be an aggressive confrontation.

TITUS

I. Content
   False teachers (1:14)
   Truth teachers (1:1–4)
   Move-to-Relevance: False teachers today
II. Character
   False Teachers (1:10–13, 15–16)
   Truth Teachers (1:5–9)
   Move-to-Relevance: Nature of correction
III. *Charitably Correct Charlatans!*
   Correction (1:9, 11)
   Specific steps on undertaking such correction

PERICOPE 17

Being God's Own: Godliness in Community

Titus 2:1–15

[Godliness of God's People in Community; Being the People of God]

REVIEW, SUMMARY, PREVIEW

Review of Pericope 16: The first pericope of Titus (Pericope 16: Titus 1:1–16) created a contrast between false teachers and truth teachers. The correction of the former by the latter is a serious responsibility of both leaders and laypeople, conducted irreproachably—reproof of error and exhortation of truth.

Summary of Pericope 17: This second pericope of Titus (Pericope 17: Titus 2:1–15) deals for the most part with behavior within community. All believers engage in godliness, grounded in the divine work that effectuates those human works, and thus enhance God's reputation and further his economy.

Preview of Pericope 18: The third and final pericope of Titus (Pericope 18: Titus 3:1–15) parallels the structure and logic of the previous pericope, except that it deals with behavior in society. Because a gracious and merciful God saved his people who were sinful for the purpose of good works, believers engage fruitfully in these good works towards all, extending the grace and mercy of God to those without the community.

17 Titus 2:1–15

THEOLOGICAL FOCUS OF PERICOPE 17

17 God's people, irrespective of age, gender, and social standing, demonstrate exemplary godliness within community in word and in deed—a lifestyle grounded in the work of God in Christ that redeemed them for his own: salvation begun and to be consummated with Christ's Advent—for the enhancement of the reputation of God and the furtherance of his economy (2:1–15).

17.1 God's people, irrespective of age, gender, and social standing, demonstrate exemplary godliness within community in word and in deed, for the enhancement of the reputation of God and the furtherance of his economy (2:1–10).

17.2 The ground of Christian behavior—abandonment of ungodliness and the adoption of godliness—is the work of God in Christ that redeemed people for his own possession: salvation already begun and to be consummated with Christ's Advent (2:11–15).

OVERVIEW

The bulk of each of the remaining chapters of the Epistle are instructions for Titus to pass on to the church regarding behavior in community (2:1–15: towards older men [2:1], older women [2:2–5], younger men, including Titus himself [2:6–8], and slaves [2:9–10]) and behavior in society (3:1–11).

Titus 2:1–15	Titus 3:1–11
***Exhortations** (2:1–10)*	***Exhortations** (3:1–2)*
(regarding behavior in community)	*(regarding behavior in society)*
"speak" (2:1); good works (2:7)	"remind" (3:1); good deeds (3:1, 8)
"be subject" (2:5, 9)	"be subject" (3:1)
***Theological Bases** (2:11–14)*	***Theological Bases** (3:3–7)*
"for" (2:11); "appeared" (2:11)	"for" (3:3); "appeared" (3:4)
"grace" (2:11); "hope" (2:13)	"grace" (3:7); "hope" (3:7)
σωτηρ (*sōter*)-root (2:11, 13)	σωτηρ-root (3:4, 5, 6)
***Exhortations** (2:15)*	***Exhortations** (3:8–11)*
(regarding false teachers)	*(regarding false teachers)*
"these things" (2:15)	"these things" (3:8 [×2])
"speak," "urge," "reprove" (2:15)	"assert," "shun," "reject" (3:8–10)

Indeed, this signals a careful arrangement of the entire Epistle, with a number of elements shared, even between the introduction and conclusion[1]:

---

1. Modified from Fee, *1 and 2 Timothy, Titus*, 210; and Quinn, *Letter to Titus*, 260.

Introduction	"faith," 1:4; "grace," 1:4; ἀπέλιπόν, *apelipon,* "left"; τὰ λείποντα, *ta leiponta,* "what is left," 1:5	1:1–9
A	Warnings against false teachers	1:10–16
B	"Good works" in community	2:1–14
C	Warnings against false teachers	2:15
B'	"Good works" in society	3:1–7
A'	Warnings against false teachers	3:8–11
Conclusion	λείπω, *leipō,* "lack," 3:13; "faith," 3:15; "grace," 3:15	3:12–15

17.1 Titus 2:1–10

THEOLOGICAL FOCUS 17.1

17.1 God's people, irrespective of age, gender, and social standing, demonstrate exemplary godliness within community in word and in deed, for the enhancement of the reputation of God and the furtherance of his economy (2:1–10).

TRANSLATION 17.1

2:1 But you, speak the things that are proper to sound teaching.

2:2 Older men are to be temperate, dignified, self-controlled, sound in faith, in love, in perseverance;

2:3 older women likewise are to be reverent in behavior, not slanderers, not enslaved to much wine, teaching what is good,

2:4 so that they may encourage the young women to be husband-lovers, children-lovers,

2:5 self-controlled, pure, good home-workers, being subject to their own husbands, so that the word of God may not be blasphemed.

2:6 Likewise urge the younger men to be self-controlled

2:7 in all things, showing yourself to be an example of good works, pure in teaching, dignified,

2:8 above criticism in sound word[s], so that one who is opposed will be shamed, having nothing evil to say about us.

2:9 [Urge] slaves to be subject to their own masters in all things, to be well-pleasing, not argumentative,

2:10 not stealing, but demonstrating all good faith so that they may adorn the teaching of God our Savior in all things.

TITUS

NOTES 17.1

17.1 God's people, irrespective of age, gender, and social standing, demonstrate exemplary godliness within community in word and in deed, for the enhancement of the reputation of God and the furtherance of his economy (2:1–10).

The first two sections of this pericope, 2:1–10 (exhortations regarding behavior in community) and 2:11–14 (theological bases), share καλὰ ἔργα, *kala erga*, "good works" (2:7, 14) and a description of God as "Savior" (2:10,13); the third and final section, 2:15 (exhortations regarding false teachers) shares "speak" with the first section (2:1, 15).

Titus 2:1–10 resembles 1 Tim 5:1–2 with a breakdown of addressees by gender and age.[2] Thrice the reason for such behavior by older men and women, by younger men and women, and by slaves are stated: that the members of the divine household may be irreproachable and not bring dishonor to God and his word—Titus 2:5, 8, 10; all three are in the form of ἵνα (*hina*)-clauses. This emphasizes the missionary and for-the-world role of the church, a critical part of the furtherance of God's economy. Hence, it is not surprising that Titus 2:1–10 has διδασκαλία, *didaskalia*, "teaching," in 2:1 and 2:10, forming an *inclusio*.

"But you" (2:1)—an emphatic construction—signals a contrast between what the false teachers have been doing (1:10–16) and what Titus is to do (2:1–10, 15). After labeling the former as "rejected for every good work" (1:16), it is appropriate that Paul focuses on individual groups within the community in 2:1–10, instructing them on how to be worthy for "good works."

Titus 1:10–16 (Opponents)	Titus 2:1–10 (Community)
ἀνυπότακτος, *anypotaktos*, "rebellious" (1:10)	ὑποτάσσω, *hypotassō*, "be subject" (2:5, 9)
διδάσκοντες ἃ μὴ δεῖ (1:11) *didaskontes ha mē dei* "teaching things they should not"	διδασκαλία, καλοδιδάσκαλοι (2:1, 3, 7, 10) *didaskalia, kalodidaskaloi* "teaching," "teaching what is good"
"sound in the faith" (1:13)	"sound in faith" (2:2; "sound" in 2:1, 8)
Impurity (1:15)	Purity (2:5)
Detestable (1:16)	Well-pleasing (2:9)
"deny" God (1:16)	"deny" ungodliness (2:12)
Rejected for every "good work" (1:16)	Exemplars of "good works" (2:7)

Many of the qualities of the older men (2:2), older and younger women (2:3–5), and younger men (2:6–8) are replicated elsewhere in the PE: "temperate" (Titus 2:2) in 1 Tim 3:2, 11; "dignified" (Titus 2:2, 7) in 1 Tim 3:8, 11; "self-controlled" (Titus 2:2, 5, 6; and also in 2:12) in 1 Tim 2:9; 3:2; Titus 1:8[3]; "sound in the faith" (2:2) in 1:13; and the triad

---

2. Philo, *On the Creation* 36.105, cites Hippocrates on the seven stages of the human life, the sixth of which, πρεσβύτης, *presbytēs*, "elderly man," described those from 50–56 years of age (after which came γέρων, *gerōn*, "old man"). However, in his *On the Special Laws* 2.8.33, the elderly are said to be over 60, the same number mentioned in 1 Tim 5:9. Philo's fourth stage, νεανίσκος, *neaniskos*, "young man," was from 22–28 years of age (*On the Creation* 36.105). But the label used in Titus 2:6 is νεώτεροι, *neōteroi* (a comparative noun: "younger men").

3. In 2:4 it is the verb form, σωφρονίζω, *sōphronizō*, "to encourage." Ten of the sixteen NT uses of the

"faith"—"love"—"perseverance" (2:2) in 1 Tim 6:11; 2 Tim 3:10.⁴ While "reverence in behavior" (2:3) is unique, μὴ διάβολοι, *mē diaboloi*, "not slanderers" (2:3) is seen in 1 Tim 3:11, and the exhortation against drunkenness (Titus 2:3) in 1 Tim 3:8. The requirement to teach (Titus 2:1, 3, 7, 10) is, of course, a characteristic of elders (1 Tim 3:2; 5:17; 2 Tim 2:2; Titus 1:9), as is irreproachability (2:8), found also in 1 Tim 3:2, 7, 10; 5:7, 14; 6:14; Titus 1:6, 7. Thus most of the character traits in Titus 2:1–10 are desirable for all of God's people, irrespective of office, gender, age, or social standing (notice the linkages within the list with ὡσαύτως, *hōsautos*, "likewise," 2:3, 6, suggesting a widespread applicability of these dispositions and doings).⁵

Young women are not directly addressed, but only via instructions to the older women to teach them (2:4–5), thus entrusting the older women with "a very significant educative responsibility within the context of the *oikos*."⁶ A unique portfolio is designated for these younger women: they were to be "husband-lovers" (φιλάνδροι, *philandroi*),⁷ "children-lovers" (φιλότεκνοι, *philoteknoi*, 2:4), "good home-workers," and to be "subject to their own husbands" (2:5).⁸ The mention of "husbands" commences and concludes the list for these younger women (2:4–5). "The household was the chief theater of Paul's campaign," with the primary role of women being in that arena.⁹ There appears to be some indication that, in comparison to Athenian women, their sisters in Crete were "in a more privileged legal position concerning rights and matters relating to their inheritance."¹⁰ That relative sense of emancipation may have resulted in a lesser interest in matters relating to the household and its management; usually, that was the domain of women. In turn, that might explain Paul's indirect exhortations to the younger women in the Cretan church.

σωφρον (*sōphron*)-related words are in the PE, five of them here in Titus 2 (another in 1:8).

4. This triad also necessitates seeing "faith" here in 2:2 as subjective, the attitude of the individual to God, rather than as objective, referring to the body of doctrine that is to be believed.

5. Of course, "good works," exhorted of young men and Titus (2:7), show up in the PE elsewhere in 1 Tim 2:10; 2 Tim 2:21; 3:17; Titus 1:16; 3:1 (with the adjective ἀγαθός; there is also οἰκουργοί ἀγαθαί, "good home-workers," in 2:5); and in 1 Tim 3:1; 5:10, 25; 6:18; Titus 2:14; 3:8, 14 (using καλός, as in 2:7).

6. Towner, *Letters to Timothy and Titus*, 724.

7. Interestingly enough, nowhere else in the NT are wives expected to love their husbands; even here in 2:4, it is not a direct command. Perhaps it is assumed that that feeling will naturally arise when husbands love their wives as Christ loved the church (Eph 5:25–29).

8. The middle voice of the verb ὑποτάσσω, *hypotassō*, "be subject" (2:5; cognate of ἀνυπότακτος in 1:10) indicates that what is called for is the submission of a free agent (as also, surprisingly enough, for slaves, 2:9). As Eph 5:22–33 makes clear, just as the church is never forced to submit to its head, Christ, so also the wife is never to be forced to do so to her husband, even though it is a divine demand. The same verb is used of Christ's submission to the Father (1 Cor 15:28), thus demonstrating that subordination in economy (i.e., functional subordination) does not equal inferiority in essence (i.e., ontological subordination). On the other hand, Josephus (*Against Apion* 2.201) considered women to be inferior to men. Indeed, the mental capacity of that gender was supposed to be defective according to the first-century-BCE philosopher, Arius Didymus (cited in Stobaeus, *Anthology* 2.7.26; 2.149.5); so also Aristotle (*Politics* 1.1254b13–14, 1.1259b1–2; 1.1260a9–14). Thus this exhortation by Paul to wives is countercultural, giving them the responsibility to submit voluntarily, not to mention their being treated equally with their husbands as both parties are addressed and assigned responsibilities in this household code. See Kuruvilla, *Ephesians*, 167–83.

9. Towner, *Letters to Timothy and Titus*, 726.

10. Winter, *Roman Wives, Roman Widows*, 141. Perhaps related to this prevalent attitude towards that gender, Cretans called their island the "motherland" (μητρίς, *mētris*) (Plutarch, *Whether an Old Man Should Engage in Public Affairs* 792E).

In 2:7, Titus himself is directly addressed in conjunction with the exhortations to "younger men," thus putting this leader in that same category (so also Timothy: 1 Tim 4:12; 5:1; 2 Tim 2:22). Purity of teaching is urged in Titus 2:7: they are also to be "sound in word[s]/speech" (2:8).[11] In sum, Titus is exhorted to be exemplary (2:7)—as is presumably required of all younger men, not to mention all of God's people. Chrysostom (*Homilies on Titus* 4) noted: "Let the luster of thy life be a common school of instruction, a pattern of virtue to all, publicly exhibited . . . affording examples whence those who are willing may easily imprint upon themselves any of its excellences."[12]

Quinn notes that "there was a ratio of five slaves to one free person throughout the Roman Empire, perhaps three to one in Rome."[13] That made it imperative that Paul include them in any discussion on behavior within the community of God's people, for it was quite possible that several of them were believers. But the inclusion of slaves, generally the non-persons of ancient society, is remarkable, for they, too, are understood to have considerable self-determination, as Titus is to urge them to choose behavior of a certain kind. The verb used for slaves in relation to their masters is ὑποτάσσεσθαι, *hypotassesthai*, which was already encountered in 2:5. This "submission" is not just a matter for slaves: see its use in Eph 5:21 (for all believers to one another), 22, 24; Col 3:18; Titus 2:5; and 1 Pet 3:1, 5 (for wives to husbands); 1 Tim 3:4 (children to fathers); 1 Cor 16:16 (for all believers to leaders); 1 Cor 14:34; 1 Tim 2:11 (women to leaders); Rom 13:1; Titus 3:1; and 1 Pet 2:13 (for all citizens to civic authorities), not to mention the submission of the Son to the Father as noted earlier. "What Paul asks for is not unique to the slave situation but is a response that those under authority can appropriately be asked to render as part of their duty and responsibility to the one in authority."[14]

"In all things" (ἐν πᾶσιν, *en pasin*) is repeated in 2:9, 10, and thus πᾶς occurs thrice in these two verses. The scope of "all" does not mean that slaves submit even to evil, of course: it is simply a call to demonstrate "*all* good faith" (2:10; likely "faithfulness," reliability with respect to all that is good) in "all things" (2:9) so as not to bring discredit to God and the teaching in "all things" (2:10). Being in subjection to masters, "well-pleasing" to them, and not being argumentative, would further the reputation of the God whose δοῦλοι, *douloi* ("bondslaves") these slaves truly were.[15] The "adorning" of divine doctrine/teaching by slaves is striking—they are the only ones in this list explicitly noted to have that capacity.

---

11. Words with the διδασκ (*didask*)-root show up twenty-five times in the PE (indicating both the act of teaching and the content thereof, those who engage in it, and their ability to do so): 1 Tim 1:3, 7, 10; 2:7, 12; 4:1, 6, 11, 13, 16; 5:17; 6:1, 2, 3; 2 Tim 1:11; 2:2; 3:10, 16; 4:2, 3; Titus 1:9 (×2), 11; 2:1, 7, 10. Elsewhere, Paul uses the root twenty-two times in six other letters. The theme of "soundness," whether of teaching or of words, also echoes throughout the PE (and only in the PE): 1 Tim 1:10; 6:3; 2 Tim 1:13; 4:3; Titus 1:9; 2:1, 8 (the verb "to be sound" also occurs in Titus 1:13; 2:2). Being sound in "word" (λόγος) renders opponents devoid of any word to "say" (from λέγω; 2:8).

12. *Nicene and Post-Nicene Fathers* 13:533. Timothy, too, was exhorted to be an "example" (1 Tim 4:12). Modeling was essential for shepherding and discipling, with Paul (Phil 3:17; 1 Thess 1:6; 2 Thess 3:9; 1 Tim 1:16; 2 Tim 1:13), Timothy (1 Tim 4:12), Titus (Titus 2:7), church leaders (1 Pet 5:3), and all the people of God (1 Thess 1:7) becoming exemplars of godliness.

13. Quinn, *Letter to Titus*, 146. See "Excursus on Slavery" in Pericope 9: 1 Tim 6:1–2.

14. Knight, *Pastoral Epistles*, 314.

15. Slaves were warned in Eph 6:6–7; Col 3:22 not to be merely "men-pleasers" (ἀνθρωπάρεσκος, *anthrōpareskos*, from ἄρεσκος, *areskos*, "pleasing"), but also God-fearers. One remembers that the soldier of Christ Jesus is to be "pleasing" (ἀρέσκω, *areskō*) to the One who recruited him (2 Tim 2:4).

"Ordinarily, it was the well-to-do benefactors, not slaves or the masses, who gave 'adornments' to cities and leaders in return for public recognition. But life in Christ involved many reversals."[16] Indeed!

The reasons for the exhortations in this section are indicated by purpose clauses (ἵνα [*hina*]-clauses): the one in 2:5 seeks to protect the word of God from dishonor; in 2:8, the good reputation of the community is upheld; and in 2:10, the doctrine of God in every respect is adorned. In sum, there is a "missiological thrust" to godly conduct. "Life itself—and here it is life lived in very ordinary circumstances with regard to the expectations of secular society—augments, supports, endorses, and illustrates 'the teaching about God our Savior'" and the promotion of the divine economy.[17] The lives of individual believers, whether old or young or even enslaved, *does* matter to the reputation of God, his word, his church, and his grand and glorious plan for the cosmos.

17.2 Titus 2:11–15

> **THEOLOGICAL FOCUS 17.2**
>
> 17.2 The ground of Christian behavior—abandonment of ungodliness and the adoption of godliness—is the work of God in Christ that redeemed people for his own possession: salvation already begun and yet to be consummated with Christ's Advent (2:11–15).

TRANSLATION 17.2

2:11   *For the grace of God has appeared—salvation to all people,*

2:12   *instructing us, so that we, denying ungodliness and worldly lusts, may live self-controlled and righteous and godly in the present age,*

2:13   *awaiting the blessed hope and the glorious appearance of our great God and Savior, Jesus Christ,*

2:14   *who gave Himself for us so that He may redeem us from all lawlessness and purify for Himself a people for His very own, zealous for good works.*

2:15   *These things speak and urge and reprove with all authority. Let no one disregard you.*

NOTES 17.2

17.2   *The ground of Christian behavior—abandonment of ungodliness and the adoption of godliness—is the work of God in Christ that redeemed people for his own possession: salvation already begun and yet to be consummated with Christ's Advent (2:11–15).*

Titus 2:11–14 is a single sentence that deals with the christological bases for the exhortations that preceded (2:1–10; 2:11 begins with γάρ) and the one that follows (2:15). The links between 2:1–10 and 2:11–15 include: "speak," in 2:1 and 2:15; πᾶς, "all," in 2:7, 9, 10 (×2)

---

16. Towner, *Letters to Timothy and Titus*, 739.
17. Towner, *Letters to Timothy and Titus*, 738, 739.

and 2:11, 14, 15; "our"/"us" in 2:10 and 2:12, 13, 14; "God" in 2:10 and 2:11, 13; and σωτηρ (*sōtēr*)-root words in 2:10 and 2:11, 13.

Notice the *ABCC'* pattern repeated in 2:11–12 and 2:13–14 (below). Both 2:11 and 2:13 have "appeared"/"appearance" (ἐπιφαίνω/ἐπιφάνεια, *epiphainō/epiphaneia*)—the first referring to salvific divine grace (in Christ), the second to Christ's glorious personal revealing[18]—and words relating to salvation (σωτήριος[19]/σωτήρ, *sōterios/sōtēr*, "salvation"/"Savior"), as well as "God" (*A*; all in italics below). The effect of the appearance of divine grace and of Christ is salvation (2:11)[20]; the one doing the saving is God (2:10) and Christ Jesus (2:13; both are labeled "Savior"[21]) who gave himself for his people and whose appearing in glory will consummate salvation. Thus the notion of salvation in these verses encompasses Christ's incarnation, atonement, and Second Advent—the entirety of the salvific undertaking of the Savior, "a massive incursion of the invisible, divine into visible human history."[22] And its consequence is godliness in the Christian's life. Both 2:12a and 2:14a (*B*) have ἵνα-clauses ("so that . . ."). Then, in both 2:12bc and 2:14bc (*CC'*; in dark gray, below), we find imperatival forces resulting from the appearing of divine grace/Christ and the salvation wrought by God/Christ: the lifestyle to abandon ("–" in the table below) and the lifestyle to adopt ("+")[23]:

---

18. The "blessed hope" is the "appearance," the Second Advent of Christ in his glory (2:13; also see Col 1:27; and Mark 13:26; 1 Pet 4:13). This need not necessarily exclude the rapture that is proximal to the complex of events surrounding the Second Advent. The phrase ἐπιφάνειαν τῆς δόξης, *epiphaneian tēs doxēs*, likely is a Hebraism meaning "the glorious appearance," taking the genitive as attributive. The genitive τῆς δόξης is used in this fashion in Rom 8:21; 9:23; 1 Cor 2:8; 2 Cor 4:4, 6; Eph 1:17, 18; 3:16; Phil 3:21; Col 1:11, 27; 1 Tim 1:11; etc.—constituting at least two-thirds of the uses of this construction in Paul (Bowman, "Jesus Christ, God Manifest," 736). The parallelism of 2:13a and 2:13b also suggests the attributive use of τῆς δόξης: article + adjective + noun + καί + noun + genitive (see Bowman, "Jesus Christ, God Manifest," 740).

19. This is the only instance of σωτήριος in the canonical Scriptures.

20. "Salvation to all people" is not universalism; rather, it indicates the divine desire that "all people" be saved (1 Tim 2:4)—it has been offered to "all people" (Titus 2:11).

21. The phrase τοῦ μεγάλου θεοῦ καὶ σωτῆρος ἡμῶν Ἰησοῦ Χριστοῦ, *tou megalou theou kai sōtēros hēmōn Iēsou Christou*, "of our great God and Savior, Jesus Christ," in 2:13 is one of the clearest texts in the NT that point to the deity of Jesus Christ. Granville Sharp's rule asserts that in a construction with the syntax: article + noun[A] + καί + noun[B] (as here: τοῦ . . . θεοῦ[A] καὶ σωτῆρος[B]), where the two nouns are singular, personal, and common (i.e., that can be pluralized; not proper names), noun[A] and noun[B] will have the same referent. So in 2:13, "God"[A] = "Savior"[B] (Christ Jesus). See Wallace, *Greek Grammar*, 276. With the focus on the Second Person in the following verse, 2:14, this is congruent with the flow of the text. Besides, ἐπιφάνεια in Paul almost always refers to the Advent of Christ (usually to the Second in the PE; see 1 Tim 6:14; 2 Tim 4:1, 8; and Titus 2:13; but see 2 Tim 1:10 for a reference to the First). The verb form, ἐπιφαίνω, is used of the appearance of divine grace (Titus 2:11) and of divine kindness (3:4); of course, metonymically both again indicate salvation through Jesus Christ (σωτήριος in 2:11; σῴζω, "save," in 3:5).

22. Towner, *Letters to Timothy and Titus*, 745.

23. In stark contrast to the "denial" of God by opponents in Crete (1:16), we see in 2:12 the "denial" of ungodliness by the people of God (both employing ἀρνέομαι). Also, 2:12c resounds with seven ως—σωφρόνως καὶ δικαίως καὶ εὐσεβῶς ζήσωμεν ἐν τῷ νῦν αἰῶνι (*sōphronōs kai dikaiōs kai eusebōs zēsōmen en tō nun aiōni*, "that we . . . may live self-controlled and righteous and godly in the present age")—alliteratively emphasizing the godly Christian life. Notice, also, ἀσέβεια, *asebeia*, "ungodliness," contrasted with εὐσεβῶς, *eusebōs*, "godly" (2:12b, 12c).

A	"For the grace of *God appeared*, —*salvation* to all people [**2:11**],
B	instructing us, so that we, [**2:12a**]
C	denying ungodliness and worldly lusts [**2:12b**] —
C'	may live self-controlled and righteous and godly ... [**2:12c**], +
A	awaiting the blessed hope and the glorious *appearance* of our great *God* and *Savior*, Christ Jesus [**2:13**],
B	who gave Himself for us, so that He may [**2:14a**]
C	redeem us from all lawlessness and [**2:14b**] —
C'	purify for Himself a people ... zealous for good works [**2:14c**]." +

The negative elements in each pair (*C*: 2:12b; 2:14b) are equivalent; likewise, the positive elements in each pair (*C'*: 2:12c; 2:14c). The focus is clearly on virtuous living (the two pairs *CC'*: 2:12b, 12c and 2:14b, 14c). Such a life is marked by abandonment of ungodliness, worldly lusts, and lawlessness, and the adoption of a self-controlled, righteous, godly lifestyle manifesting good works.

All that to say, "not only has God's grace saved believers, but it has the ongoing task of teaching them to live righteously. . . . This verse [2:12, and 2:14 as well] deals a death blow to any theology that separates salvation from the demands of obedience to the Lordship of Christ."[24] After all, sanctification, in addition to justification (and glorification—also alluded to here), is an integral part of salvation. "The Christian commitment . . . is both an expectation and an obligation: an expectation of seeing the Lord and an implied obligation to stay true to one's commitment until that day" when judgment for rewards occurs.[25] Eschatology encourages endurance!

The use of περιούσιος, *periousios*, "his very own" (2:14; a *hapax* in the NT) reflects the LXX Exod 19:5; 23:22; Deut 7:6 (and 7:8 has λυτρόω, *lytroō*, "redeem"; also in Titus 2:14); Deut 14:2; 26:18. All of them, like Titus 2:14, have λαὸς περιούσιος.[26] Thus, at least for preaching purposes (i.e., for application), the church is the NT continuation of the OT people of God, notwithstanding the distinction in eschatological destinies of these groups. I emphasize "preaching purposes," recognizing that the specific commands to, and demands made of, Israel in the OT are not directly "obeyable," but are *all* theologically (i.e., via pericopal theology) "applicable." In fact, even what was written in the NT, to an idiosyncratic group of, say, Romans or Corinthians, or to unique individuals like Timothy or Titus, is, indeed, only "applicable" to the joint and unified community of *all* God's people of *all* time in *all* places (and not "obeyable" by them).[27] In the power of the Holy Spirit, the child of God therefore does *apply* the call of every pericope of every book of Scripture—not for gaining

---

24. Mounce, *Pastoral Epistles*, 423.

25. Mounce, *Pastoral Epistles*, 425.

26. Also see LXX Ps 135:4 [English 134:4] employing περιουσιασμός, *periousiasmos*, "own possession."

27. Regardless of genre, authors *do* things with what they say, and that authorial *doing* in each pericope directs readers everywhere and in every age to respond. Thus, every pericope of every book of every Testament of the canonical Scriptures is *applicable*, profitable as they are for "for teaching, for reproving, for correcting, for training in righteousness, so that that the person of God may be capable, fully equipped for every good work" (2 Tim 3:16–17). This I consider an emergent property of the canon.

TITUS

merit, but because one has already been blessed—a living into, if you will, of Christ that the believer has already been clothed with: a "faith-full" obedience.[28]

And with that, we return to a recapitulating imperative for Titus to "speak" (2:15), in relation to the ethical exhortations earlier in the chapter (2:1–10). Even if someone disrespects his authority, Titus is to carry on boldly, for these matters of which he was to "speak" were critical for the soundness of the faith and excellence of praxis of the church.

SERMON MAPS

> **THEOLOGICAL FOCUS OF PERICOPE 17 FOR PREACHING**
>
> 17   God's people, irrespective of age, gender, and social standing, demonstrate exemplary godliness within community in word and in deed—grounded in the work of God in Christ redeeming people for his own—for the enhancement of the reputation of God and the furtherance of his economy (2:1–15).

Much of this pericope is a series of lists pertaining to the godly behavior of a variety of people: older men, older women, younger women, younger men, and slaves. The unifying theme is, needless to say, godliness within community, manifest in good works.

Possible Preaching Maps for Pericope 17

I.   Exhibition of Godliness in Community
    All believers, everywhere (2:1a, 3a, 6a, 9a)
    Exemplars of good works (2:1b–2, 3b–5a, 6b–8a, 9b–10a)
    Move-to-Relevance: If even slaves can . . .
II. Explanation of Godliness
    The work of God: Becoming the people of God (2:11–14)
    Enhancers of divine reputation (2:1, 5b, 8b, 10b)
    Move-to-Relevance: How our lives do not enhance God's name
III. *Execution of Godliness: Be God's People!*
    How specifically we can start doing this in community

---

28. See Kuruvilla, *Privilege the Text!*, 151–209. It is also interesting to note that the progressive movement from ἀνομία, *anomia*, "lawlessness," is to καλόι ἔργα, "good works" (Titus 2:14). One might have expected "lawfulness" instead of "good works." Quite likely, they are equivalent: to do good works is what it means to be obedient to divine demand = lawfulness in the current age/dispensation—again "faith-full" obedience.

Another option, that is more symmetric in its pre-application moves:

I. The Work and Goal of God
    God's work: Becoming the people of God (2:11, 13–14a)
    God's goal: effectuating believers' good works (2:12, 14b–15)
    Move-to-Relevance: How God's work accomplishes his goal
II. The Work and Goal of Believers
    Believers' work (2:1–5a, 8a, 9–10a)
    Believers' goal: Enhancing God's reputation (2:5b, 8b, 10b)
    Move-to-Relevance: If even slaves can . . .
III. *Execution of Godliness: Be God's People!*
    How specifically we can start doing this in community

PERICOPE 18

Showing God's Grace: Societal Godliness

Titus 3:1–15

[Behavior of God's People in Society; Extending Divine Grace to Others]

REVIEW, SUMMARY

Review of Pericope 17: The second pericope of Titus (Pericope 17: Titus 2:1–15) dealt for the most part with behavior within community. All believers engage in godliness, grounded in the divine work that effectuates those human works, and thus enhance God's reputation and further his economy.

> **Summary of Pericope 18:** The third and final pericope of Titus (Pericope 18: Titus 3:1–15) parallels the structure and logic of the previous pericope, except that it deals with behavior in society. Because a gracious and merciful God saved sinful people for good works, believers engage fruitfully in good works towards all, extending the grace and mercy of God to those without the community, within society, promoting God's mission.

18 *Titus 3:1–15*

THEOLOGICAL FOCUS OF PERICOPE 18

18 Believers' behavior in society involves submission to authority and utmost consideration for all people, avoiding all manner of ungodliness and fractious behavior (and rejecting those who unrepentantly engage in such sinful and unfruitful lifestyles), for God saved his people in Christ and through the Spirit so that they may be ready for, and constantly engage in, good works, demonstrating the same kindness and love for mankind that he had for his people (3:1–15).

OVERVIEW

As was noted in Pericope 17: Titus 2:1–15, that pericope and the major portion of this (3:1–11) are structurally similar: both have exhortations to behavior (2:1–10; 3:1–2), then a section on the theological bases for these exhortations (2:11–14; 3:3–7), and both conclude with an exhortation regarding false teachers (2:15; 3:8–11). In the previous pericope, the exhortation to "good works" (2:7, 14 [using καλός, *kalos*]) dealt, for the most part, with behavior within the community.

> Underlying the instruction is the realisation by believers that they now form a separate group in society . . . . They must take a positive attitude to society as good citizens, both by doing good and by avoiding strife. Their outgoing attitude of patient gentleness to everybody is backed up by the example of God's own patience to them; the unspoken implication would seem to be that this attitude may lead to the conversion of unbelievers.[1]

In this pericope, "good works" (3:1 [using ἀγαθός, *agathos*], 8, 14 [using καλός]) deals with behavior in society, with those outsiders scrutinizing the church.[2]

18   Titus 3:1–15

THEOLOGICAL FOCUS 18

18   Believers' behavior in society involves submission to authority and utmost consideration for all people, avoiding all manner of ungodliness and fractious behavior (and rejecting those who unrepentantly engage in such sinful and unfruitful lifestyles), for God saved his people in Christ and through the Spirit so that they may be ready for, and constantly engage in, good works, demonstrating the same kindness and love for mankind that he had for his people (3:1–15).

TRANSLATION 18

3:1   *Remind them to be subject to rulers, authorities, to obey, to be ready for every good work,*

3:2   *to blaspheme no one, to be non-quarrelsome, gentle, demonstrating all consideration for all people.*

3:3   *For we also were once foolish ourselves, disobedient, deceived, enslaved to various lusts and pleasures, spending lives in evil and envy, hateful, detesting one another.*

3:4   *But when the kindness and mankind-love of God our Savior appeared,*

3:5   *He saved us, not by works which we ourselves did in righteousness, but according to His mercy, through washing of regeneration and [through] renewal of the Holy Spirit,*

3:6   *whom He poured out upon us richly through Jesus Christ our Savior,*

3:7   *so that, being made righteous by His grace, we might be made heirs according to the hope of eternal life.*

---

1. Marshall, *Pastoral Epistles*, 298–99.
2. The only other instances of "good works" in Titus are in 1:16; 3:1 (both with the adjective ἀγαθός); there is also οἰκουργοί ἀγαθαί, "good home-workers," in 2:5.

TITUS

3:8 This statement is trustworthy; and concerning these things I want you to confidently assert, so that those who have believed God will be careful to engage in good works. These things are good and profitable for people.

3:9 But avoid foolish controversies and genealogies and strife and quarrels about the law, for they are unprofitable and futile.

3:10 Reject a factious person after the first and second warning,

3:11 knowing that such a person has been perverted and is sinning, being self-condemned.

3:12 When I send Artemas or Tychicus to you, make every effort to come to me in Nicopolis, for I have decided to spend the winter there.

3:13 Make every effort to send Zenas the lawyer and Apollos on their way so that there may be no lack for them.

3:14 Now our people must also learn to engage in good works to meet pressing needs, so that they may not be unfruitful.

3:15 All who are with me greet you. Greet those who love us in the faith. Grace be with you all.

NOTES 18

18 Believers' behavior in society involves submission to authority and utmost consideration for all people, avoiding all manner of ungodliness and fractious behavior (and rejecting those who unrepentantly engage in such sinful and unfruitful lifestyles), for God saved his people in Christ and through the Spirit so that they may be ready for, and constantly engage in, good works, demonstrating the same kindness and love for mankind that he had for his people (3:1–15).

Titus 3:1–2 is a single sentence in the Greek, with seven items that Titus is to remind the Cretan Christians of, an asyndetic list. Obedience and subjection is to be directed towards rulers and authorities[3]; the rest towards fellow citizens in society. Here, too, as in 2:1–10, a contrast is being made with the opponents of 1:10–16:

Christians (3:1–2)	Opponents (1:10–16)
ὑποτάσσω, *hypotasso* (3:1) "be subject"	ἀνυπότακτοι, *anypotaktoi* (1:10) "rebellious"
πειθαρχέω, *peitharcheō* (3:1) "obey"	ἀπειθήω, *apeitheō* (1:16) "disobedient"
"ready for every good work" (3:1)	"rejected for every good work" (1:16)

Unlike their opponents, Christians are to live a godly life both in community (2:1–10) and in society (3:1–2). These latter appeals, like the former, have a clear missiological goal that furthers the economy of God. "The church's subjection to the state, worked out in public Christian service, has the redemption of creation as its goal, not simply peaceful coexistence

---

3. Loyalty to foreign states and governments was a theme even in the OT days when the Israelites were in exile or ruled by a gentile government: Ezra 6:9–10; 7:23; Jer 29:7; 1 Macc 7:33. Of course, in the PE, this notion was already encountered in 1 Tim 2:1–2; elsewhere in the NT, see Rom 13:1, 5; 1 Pet 2:13.

with the secular power structure."[4] This is a poignant exhortation, particularly in light of the circumstances of the Christians in Crete: "It would be impossible to find except in some rare instances personal conduct more treacherous or a public policy more unjust than in Crete" (Polybius, *The Histories*, 6.47.5).[5] Subjection and obedience to rulers and authorities are to be part of the Christian life, no matter what the character of those in power or the character of the society's civics. That being said, God's people, everywhere and always, are ultimately to "obey God rather than people" (Acts 5:29). So any act of obedience to government cannot counter what Scripture has commanded. "Thus we must see this as a general exhortation that excludes any capitulation to clearly non-Christian conduct. . . . The purpose of the remark is so that a Christian will be as good a citizen as possible, causing no unnecessary offense, other than the offense of the gospel itself."[6] The scope of the exhortation in Titus 3:2 is broad: it begins with "no one" and ends with "all people." Altogether we have πᾶς occurring thrice in 3:1–2: "*every* good work," "*all* consideration for *all* people." "Where believers . . . come into contact with other people, they are to embody the highest ideals of human virtue as they imitate the pattern of behavior embodied by Christ himself."[7] Only such a lifestyle can promote the divine mission and further the divine economy.

All the instructions in 3:1–2 are based on theological grounds (3:3–7; following the same pattern in the previous pericope: instruction, 2:1–10; followed by theological bases, 2:11–14): 3:3 has γάρ introducing the turn to the doctrinal bases of the exhortations (as also did 2:11).

Perhaps intentionally, there are seven "vices" to avoid in 3:3, corresponding to the seven "virtues" to adopt in 3:1–2. No doubt, the foul attitudes and behaviors in 3:3 were destructive to the believing community, but in context, these vices are being painted as injurious to society as a whole. Then we have a contrast with δέ, *de*, "but," that commences the single sentence comprising 3:4–7. The "appearance" of divine "kindness" and "mankind-love" (3:4) is equivalent to the "appearance" of divine "grace" in 2:11. Both these appearances commenced the work of God in Christ (and both God and Christ are called "our Savior": 3:4, 6; as also in 2:11, 13). In fact, 3:4–6 is Trinitarian: "God the Father as the planner and initiator . . . , Jesus Christ as the agent of redemption . . . , and the Holy Spirit as the instrument of regeneration and renewal."[8] The pair of nouns χρηστότης and φιλανθρωπία (*chrēstotēs* and *philanthrōpia;* "kindness" and "mankind-love") were almost idiomatic in contemporary Greek literature to indicate the proper attitudes of a wealthy patron.[9] In contrast, here God is depicted as the ideal ruler, the patron *par excellence*—the Savior!

Notice the number of plurals in the single sentence of 3:4–7—pronouns: ἡμῶν (*hēmōn*, "our," 3:4, 6), ἡμᾶς (*hēmas*, "us," 3:5, 6), and ἡμεῖς (*hēmeis*, "we," 3:5); and verbs: ἐποιήσαμεν (*epoiēsamen*, "we . . . did," 3:5), δικαιωθέντες (*dikaiōthentes*, "[we] being made righteous") and γενηθῶμεν (*genēthōmen*, "we might be made," 3:7). Though the focus is on the divine work, its being directed towards the people of God ("us") takes

---

4. Towner, *Letters to Timothy and Titus*, 772.
5. Polybius, *Histories*, 3:417.
6. Witherington, *Letters and Homilies*, 155–56.
7. Towner, *Letters to Timothy and Titus*, 773.
8. Mounce, *Pastoral Epistles*, 447.
9. For instance, see Isocrates, *Evagoras* 43; Plutarch, *Comparison of Demosthenes and Cicero* 3.3–4.

prominence here—i.e., God's "labors and intentions" for the sake of his children.[10] And the time frame here, as in the theological section of 2:11-14, encompasses not just the past and present, but also the future: "that . . . we might be made heirs according to [in accordance with] the hope of eternal life" (3:7). Seeing that Paul has been exhorting godliness in the here and now, this emphasis on an inheritance in the there and then, i.e., rewards in eternity, is quite appropriate.[11] Thus what "we" did—acts of unrighteousness (3:3) and fleshly acts of righteousness (3:5)—is contrasted with what *God* did for "us"(3:4-7), hinting at what we must now do, how we must now live henceforth—in godliness towards "all people" (3:2)—particularly in light of those future rewards. The salvific (justification, sanctification, and glorification) work of God in Christ was not based on works, but according to his mercy (3:5). Notice the emphatic first-person plural pronoun at the commencement of the sentence, as well as the position of the verb of divine action at the very end of the clause: "Not by works which we *ourselves* did in righteousness [ἃ ἐποιήσαμεν ἡμεῖς, *ha epoiēsamen hēmeis*]—but according to His mercy *he saved us*" (3:5). Later, in 3:7, δικαιωθέντες ("being made righteous" by *God's* grace) stands in striking contrast with δικαιοσύνη, *dikaiosynē*, in 3:5 ("righteousness" by *mankind's* works).

The mercy of God that motivated his work is further explicated in 3:5b-6: "through *washing* of *regeneration* and [through] *renewal* of the Holy *Spirit*" (3:5). This is a tricky phrase to decipher, but it might be best to see the four main genitives (italicized above and shown below[12]) as being organized thus:

A	"washing"
B	"regeneration"
B'	"renewal"
A'	"Spirit"

The four genitives are organized "chiastically with the most distinguishable terms first and last ['washing' and 'Spirit': *A* and *A'*] and with the terms for the result, the transformation, in the center ['regeneration' and 'renewal': *B* and *B'*]."[13] The first pair ("washing" and "regeneration": *A* and *B*) point backwards to the past life of sin; the second pair (["renewal" and "Spirit": *B'* and *A'*]) forwards to the future life of righteousness. In other words, "washing" (*A*) accomplished by the Spirit, i.e., spiritual cleansing (*A'*),[14] brings about regeneration (*B*) and renewal (*B'*) of believers, thus preparing them for a life of godliness and good works.

And then, after the Spirit's regeneration and renewal—i.e., after being made righteous by Christ[15]—God expects them, aside from their own pre-conversion "works" (ἔργα, *erga*,

10. Mounce, *Pastoral Epistles*, 438.

11. Rewards in the PE are referred to in 1 Tim 6:19; 2 Tim 1:18; 2:5-6, 10, 11-12; 4:8. Also see Rom 8:17; Eph 1:18; Jas 2:5 for rewards, heirs, and inheritances. See Dillow, *Reign of the Servant Kings*, 43-110, 135-45, for an excellent accounting of the OT and NT concepts of "inheritance" and "rewards."

12. There are actually five genitives, counting ἁγίου, *hagiou*, "holy," but that only qualifies πνεύματος, *pneumatos*, "Spirit."

13. Knight, *Pastoral Epistles*, 343-44.

14. Washing and the Spirit are associated elsewhere in Scripture, in Ezek 36:25-27; John 3:5; 1 Cor 6:11; all involve inner transformation. Also see Fee, *1 and 2 Timothy, Titus*, 205.

15. Multiple salvific events and terms are referred to in 3:4-7. "The temptation to analyze the whole statement as if it yields a chronological formula or sequence of the experience of salvation must be

3:5), to be ready for every "good work" (ἔργον ἀγαθός, *ergon agathon*, 3:1) and to be careful to engage in "good works" (καλοί ἔργα, *kaloi erga*, 3:8, 14), these being performed post-conversion. In sum, the "works which we ourselves did in righteousness" (3:5) are those done in the flesh; the "good works" we are expected to do after regeneration and renewal (3:5) are works done in the Spirit. Thus the adjective "good" qualifies those deeds done by God's people in the Spirit, not those done in the flesh.

All that to say, just as God demonstrated "kindness" and "philanthropy" ("mankind-love") to us (3:4) when we did not deserve it (3:3), and when our own works of righteousness were of no avail (3:5)—a salvation accomplished at great cost to the Godhead—so also, the saved must extend these beneficences to members of the society at large, those without the community of God, those without Jesus Christ, perhaps at great cost to themselves. No doubt, that temporal cost is immeasurably offset by the heirs' eternal rewards (3:7). In sum, this is to engage in "good works" (3:1, 8, 14), emphasized in 3:8 with a duplication of καλός: "good deeds" are "*good* and profitable."

The trustworthy statement (3:8) likely refers back to the single sentence of 3:4–7. And "these things" that Paul would have Titus speak confidently about (3:8) probably points to all of 3:1–7. The delegate is exhorted to assert the importance of "good works" that all God's people must be careful to "engage in" (προΐστημι, *proistēmi*, "go after," 3:8)—things that are "good and profitable [ὠφέλιμος, *ōphelimos*]." Then Paul proceeds to make a contrast with what he wants Titus (and his audience) to "avoid" (περιΐστημι, *periistēmi*, "go around")—things that are "unprofitable [ἀνωφελής, *anōphelēs*] and worthless" (3:9):

	Action	Object	Value	
3:8	προΐστημι	Good works	good	profitable
3:9	περιΐστημι	Inutile dissensions	worthless	unprofitable

Later we are told that "good works" are "not . . . unfruitful" (3:14). It is worth noting that in 3:8 the doers of these "good works" are "those who have believed God"—i.e., Christians—but the ones who profit from these "good deeds" are "people"—i.e., non-Christians, those without the community. As Archbishop William Temple (1881–1944) declared: "The church exists primarily for the sake of those who are outside it."[16] As had been noted in Pericope 17: Titus 2:1–15, there is a deliberate structuring of the whole Epistle based on "good works" in community (2:1–14) and on "good works" in society (3:1–8)[17]:

---

resisted" (Towner, *Letters to Timothy and Titus*, 786). No *ordo salutis* is being delineated in this text. However, the fact that Jesus Christ is the one who sends the Spirit, "whom He [God] poured out upon us richly through Jesus Christ" (Titus 3:6; also see Acts 2:33; John 14:16; 15:26; 16:7), makes the equivalence between the work of Christ and that of the Spirit understandable. Ultimately, the overwhelming force of the text views all of this almost synchronically, as a snapshot of the wondrous work of God in Christ by the Spirit—the amazing grace of God! The only sense of a sequence in all this is that after conversion *not by works* (Eph 2:8–9), comes a life of godliness *marked by works* (Eph 2:10): Titus 3:5 followed chronologically by 3:8, 14.

16. Cited as Temple's personal dictum by Guiana, "Letter from the Archbishop," 242.

17. Modified from Fee, *1 and 2 Timothy, Titus*, 210; and Quinn, *Letter to Titus*, 260.

Introduction	"faith," 1:4; "grace," 1:4; ἀπέλιπόν, *apelipon*, "left"; τὰ λείποντα, *ta leiponta*, "what is left," 1:5	1:1–9
A Warnings against false teachers		1:10–16
B "Good works" in community		2:1–14
C Warnings against false teachers		2:15
B' "Good works" in society		3:1–7
A' Warnings against false teachers		3:8–11
Conclusion	λείπω, *leipō*, "lack," 3:13; "faith," 3:15; "grace," 3:15	3:12–15

Most of the terms in 3:9 are also used of the false teachers of Ephesus: "foolish" (2 Tim 2:23); "controversies" (1 Tim 6:4; 2 Tim 2:23); "genealogies" (1 Tim 1:4); "strife" (1 Tim 6:4); "quarrels" (2 Tim 2:23; "word-quarrels," in 1 Tim 6:4; "word-quarrel," in 2 Tim 2:14; in Titus 3:9). The note about "quarrels about the law" suggests a Jewish link (also see Titus 1:14–15); this in turn might point to "genealogies" being arcane, invalid, and futile speculations about Genesis. Thus these false teachers may well have been Jewish Christians. At any rate, their "unprofitable and futile" activities (3:9) are characteristic of "factious" people (3:10; αἱρετικός, *hairetikos*, from which we get "heretic") who sow strife. They must be rejected, but after appropriate warnings. Clearly there is an intent at correction even of these apostates, but if that fails, damage control by rejection is the only option.

And with that negative conclusion, the major portion of the Epistle ends. However, Paul does not let go without a final reference to "good works" and exhorting their engagement upon Cretan Christians ("our people," 3:14; and "those who love us in the faith," 3:15).[18] No doubt, good works are to be a critical aspect of believers' lives. The present imperative μανθανέτωσαν, *manthanetōsan*, indicates that their "learning" to "engage in good works" was to be an ongoing, lifelong affair, for all of God's people, everywhere. This is what it means to be fruitful unto God.

SERMON MAPS

THEOLOGICAL FOCUS OF PERICOPE 18 FOR PREACHING

18 Behavior in society involves submission to authority, and utmost consideration for all people, avoiding all ungodly and fractious behavior (and persons), as believers engage in good works, demonstrating the same kindness and love for mankind that God had for them (3:1–15).

This pericope is quite parallel in structure and logic to the previous one (Pericope 17: Titus 2:1–15), therefore I have kept the sermon maps for Pericope 18 parallel to those for Pericope 17.

---

18. The identical phrase καλῶν ἔργων προΐστασθαι, *kalōn ergōn proistasthai*, "to engage in good works" (3:14), was also employed in 3:8.

Possible Preaching Maps for Pericope 18

I. Exhibition of Godliness in Society
   To authorities and to all (3:1a, 2)
   Exemplars of good works (3:1b, 8, 14–15)
   Eschewing bad works and bad workers (3:9–13)
   Move-to-Relevance: Our less-than-good works in society
II. Explanation of Godliness
   The work of God's people as sinners (3:3)
   The work of God to save sinners (3:4–7)
   Move-to-Relevance: Our work reflecting God's work
III. *Execution of Godliness in Society!*
   How specifically we can start doing this in society

The more symmetric option:

I. The Work of God
   What we once were (3:3)
   How God saved us (3:4–7)
   Move-to-Relevance: How God's work implies how we should now work
II. The Work of Believers
   Godliness towards authorities and to all (3:1a, 2)
   Exemplars of good works (3:1b, 8, 14–15)
   Eschewing bad works and bad workers (3:9–13)
   Move-to-Relevance: Our less-than-good works in society
III. *Execution of Godliness in Society!*
   How specifically we can start doing this in society

CONCLUSION

*"Make every effort to present yourself approved to God,
a worker who does not need to be ashamed,
clearly expounding the word of truth."*

2 Timothy 2:15

In 1525, Desiderius Erasmus (1466–1536) launched his first attack on Martin Luther (1483–1546), publishing *On the Freedom of the Will*. In it, the Dutch philosopher, Christian scholar, classicist, and humanist declared: "I confess that it is right that the sole authority of Holy Scripture should outweigh all the votes of all mortal men. But the authority of the Scripture is not here in dispute. The same Scriptures are acknowledged and venerated by either side. Our battle is about the meaning of Scripture."[1] It always has been so. And in this endeavor to secure "the meaning of Scripture," the lot of the homiletician is not easy, neither is the responsibility of such a one minimal: each week, the preacher has to negotiate this formidable journey from ancient text to modern audience to expound, with authority and relevance, a specific biblical pericope for the faithful. "What is 'the meaning of Scripture?'" is the first question that must be asked if this august responsibility is to be discharged. And so, quite soon in the encounter with the sacred writ, commentaries are broken open.

But unfortunately, commentaries, generally written by biblical scholars not particularly acquainted with preaching, have tended towards what I call "a hermeneutic of excavation"—the exegetical turning over of tons of earth, debris, rock, boulder, and gravel: a style of interpretation that yields an overload of biblical and Bible-related information, most of it unfortunately not of any particular use for one seeking to preach a relevant message from a specific text.[2] Karl Barth's indictment is appropriate:

> My complaint is that recent commentators confine themselves to an interpretation of the text which seems to me to be no commentary at all, but merely the first step toward a commentary. Recent commentaries contain no more than a reconstruction of the text, a rendering of the Greek words and phrases by their precise equivalents, a number of additional notes in which archaeological and philological material is gathered together, and a more or less plausible

---

1. Erasmus, "On the Freedom of the Will," 43.
2. Much of the following paragraphs are taken from the conclusion in Kuruvilla, *Judges*, 303–5.

arrangement of the subject matter in such a manner that it may be made historically and psychologically intelligible from the standpoint of pure pragmatism.³

I have given heed to Barth, and attempted to go beyond the "first step toward a commentary," to deliver not so much what the author was *saying* in comprehensible fashion, but also the nuggets—clues from the text as to what the author was *doing* with what he was saying: the theology of the pericope. With an abiding interest in preaching, I come to this task of commentary writing with the hope of providing preachers what they can profitably use to create sermons. In other words, *1 and 2 Timothy, Titus: A Theological Commentary for Preachers* is one attempt in a larger endeavor to help the preacher move safely, accurately, and effectively across the gulf between ancient text and modern audience. Thereby, this intrepid soul, aided by the Holy Spirit, becomes the pastoral agent of the life-transforming truths of Scripture.⁴

The PE, like other books of the Bible, are designed to induce (seduce?) its readers to change their lives in thought, in feeling, and in action, to comply with the precepts, priorities, and practices of God's world (i.e., the theology of the pericope) that is displayed in, with, and through the inspired writing. All this so that pericope by pericope, God's people would be moved towards Christlikeness—a *christiconic* mode of interpreting Scripture.⁵

That is to say—again!—that the author of the PE is *doing* something with what he is saying. This theological agenda of the writer mandates that interpreters, particularly those who interpret for preaching purposes, attend not only to what is being said, but also to what is being *done* with what is said. In aiding the preacher, this commentary has approached the PE in a unique fashion, undertaking a form of exegesis geared towards discerning the theology of the pericope—*theological* exegesis.⁶ It is a foundational conviction of this work that valid application of a pericope of Scripture may be arrived at only via this critical intermediary between text and praxis, pericopal theology.⁷ The hermeneutical philosophy behind this commentary also holds that such valid application to change lives for the glory of God is the appropriate goal of every sermon. And so the task of the preacher with a pastoral heart ought to include the delineation of specific ways in which the theological focus of the pericope may be translated into the real lives of real people.

Here, again, are the broad theological foci of 1 and 2 Timothy and Titus that, individually and together, reflect how leaders of the divine household promote God's economy:

---

3. Barth, "Preface to the Second Edition," 6.

4. See Kuruvilla, *Vision for Preaching*. It bears repeating that the commentaries in this current series are only "theological" commentaries, not "preaching" commentaries. They take the preacher only part of the way to a sermon, from text to theology (the hermeneutical step). It remains the preacher's burden to complete the crossing by moving from theology to application, i.e., making concrete application that is specific for the particular audience, and presenting all of this in a sermon that is powerful and persuasive (the rhetorical step).

5. See Kuruvilla, *Privilege the Text!*, 238–69; *Vision for Preaching*, 131–48; and "Christiconic Interpretation."

6. See introduction; Kuruvilla, *Privilege the Text!*, 33–65; and "Pericopal Theology," 265–83.

7. In the commentary, a crystallization of pericopal theology shows up as the "Theological Focus."

CONCLUSION

1 Timothy: Shepherding the Saints

The leaders of the divine household promote God's economy by rightly handling Scripture for the goal of love, the manifestation of godliness, discharging one's ministry faithfully, engaging in corporate prayer for all, accepting the respective critical roles of men and women in the corporate gathering, leading by modeling godliness, undertaking intense spiritual disciplining and persevering in godliness for future reward, caring for the deserving needy, celebrating godliness in others and thereby guarding the holiness of the church, serving one another selflessly with good works, thus enhancing God's reputation, and relentlessly pursuing godliness marked by humble contentment and rich generosity.

2 Timothy: Completing the Course

The leaders of the divine household promote God's economy by undertaking the divine commission faithfully and unashamedly, empowered by the Spirit, seeking single-mindedly to please God, pursuing righteousness and being beneficial to God for good works (especially right speech), continuing in Scripture that makes them fully equipped for good works, preaching God's word at every opportunity, and demonstrating lifelong faithfulness to God, thus being confident of ultimate deliverance and eternal reward.

Titus: Exemplifying the Excellent

The leaders of the divine household promote God's economy by correcting false teachers, manifesting exemplary godliness in community, and likewise in society, engaging in good works, expressing to others the love God had for them.

And to repeat myself, the PE are all about leading the household of God for the promotion of the divine economy. Indeed, to lead the household of God to further God's mission is the task of *every* child of God, for each of them is a leader empowered by the Spirit of God, appointed by God to various stations and arenas of life. And by doing so, the child of God becomes more like the Son of God.

Inasmuch as the application propounded by homileticians in each sermon is faithfully assimilated into listeners' lives, creating Christian dispositions and forming Christlike character, the people of God will have aligned themselves to the will of God for the glory of God—the goal of preaching. Text will have become praxis, the people of God will have experienced and enjoyed divine blessings, and Christlikeness will have been inculcated in God's children: the economy of God furthered. Here, in the PE, one important aspect of such Christlikeness is the godliness of God's leaders, functioning in any and every ecclesial situation. Preaching the individual books of the PE week by week and pericope by pericope, preachers are called to fulfill the solemn responsibility, aided by the Holy Spirit, to align the people of God to the divine goal of establishing and maintaining godly leadership of the household of God, and being such leaders themselves. And as God's people develop into godly leaders, God's mission is being promoted, and the microcosmic scope of God's household is expanding into the macrocosm of God's world—"thy Kingdom come!"

BIBLIOGRAPHY

Aristotle. *Nicomachean Ethics*. Translated by H. Rackham. LCL 73. Cambridge: Harvard University Press, 1926.

———. *Politics*. Translated by H. Rackham. LCL 264. Cambridge: Harvard University Press, 1932.

Augustine. *On Christian Doctrine*. In *The Nicene and Post-Nicene Fathers, Volume 2*, series 1, edited by Philip Schaff, 513–97. 14 vols. 1886–89. Reprint. Peabody, MA: Hendrickson, 1994.

Barnett, Paul W. "Wives and Women's Ministry (1 Timothy 2:11–15)." *Evangelical Quarterly* 61 (1989) 225–38.

Barrett, C. K. *The Pastoral Epistles in the New English Bible*. Oxford: Clarendon, 1963.

Barth, Karl. "Preface to the Second Edition." In *The Epistle to the Romans*, by Karl Barth, translated by Edwyn C. Hoskyns, 2–15. London: Oxford University Press, 1933.

Baugh, Steven M. "'Savior of All People': 1 Tim 4:10 in Context." *Westminster Theological Journal* 54 (1992) 331–40.

Best, Ernest. *A Critical and Exegetical Commentary on Ephesians*. International Critical Commentary. Edinburgh: T. &. T. Clark, 1998.

———. "The Reading and Writing of Commentaries." *Expository Times* 107 (1996) 358–62.

Beyer, Hermann W. "ἐπισκέπτομαι, κτλ." In *Theological Dictionary of the New Testament, Volume 2*, edited by Gerhard Kittel and Gerhard Friedrich, translated by G. W. Bromiley, 599–622. 10 vols. 1964–76. Grand Rapids: Eerdmans, 1965.

Blomberg, Craig L. "Not Beyond What Is Written: A Review of Aída Spencer's *Beyond the Curse: Women Called to Ministry*." *Criswell Theological Review* 2 (1988) 403–21.

———. "Women in Ministry: A Complementarian Perspective." In *Two Views of Women in Ministry*, edited by James R. Beck, 128–72. Grand Rapids: Zondervan, 2005.

Bowman, Robert M. "Jesus Christ, God Manifest: Titus 2:13 Revisited." *Journal of the Evangelical Theological Society* 51 (2008) 733–52.

Bruce, F. F. *Paul, Apostle of the Heart Set Free*. Grand Rapids: Eerdmans, 1977.

Callimachus, Lycophron, and Aratus. *Hymns and Epigrams, Lycophron: Alexandra, Aratus: Phaenomena*. Translated by A. W. Mair and G. R. Mair. LCL 129. Cambridge: Harvard University Press, 1921.

Campbell, R. A. "ΚΑΙ ΜΑΛΙΣΤΑ ΟΙΚΕΙΩΝ—A New Look at 1 Timothy 5.8." *New Testament Studies* 41 (1995) 157–60.

Carson, D. A. "Do the Work of an Evangelist." *Themelios* 39 (2014) 1–4.

Christian, Ed. "Women, Teaching, Authority, Silence: 1 Timothy 2:8–15 Explained by 1 Peter 3:1–6." *Journal of the Adventist Society* 10 (1999) 285–90.

Chrysippus. *Fragmenta Moralia cum Generali Stoicorum Doctrina Composita*. Edited by Johannes von Arnim. Stoicorum Veterum Fragmenta 3. Leipzig: Teubner, 1903.

Chrysostom. *Homilies on Titus 4*. In *The Nicene and Post-Nicene Fathers, Volume 13*, series 1, edited by Philip Schaff, 531–35. Repr. Peabody, MA: Hendrickson, 1994.

Cicero. *On Duties*. Translated by Walter Miller. LCL 30. Cambridge: Harvard University Press, 1913.

———. *On the Republic, On the Laws*. Translated by Clinton W. Keyes. LCL 213. Cambridge: Harvard University Press, 1928.

Clement. *The Apostolic Fathers, Volume I: I Clement, II Clement, Ignatius, Polycarp, Didache*. Edited and translated by Bart D. Ehrman. LCL 24. Cambridge: Harvard University Press, 2003.

BIBLIOGRAPHY

Cooper, Marjorie J., and Jay G. Caballero. "Reasoning through Creation Order as a Basis for the Prohibition in 1 Timothy 2:12." *Presbyterion* 43 (2017) 30–38.

Couser, Greg A. "'The Testimony about the Lord,' 'Borne by the Lord,' or Both? An Insight into Paul and Jesus in the Pastoral Epistles (2 Tim 1:8)." *Tyndale Bulletin* 55 (2004) 295–316.

Cranfield, C. E. B. *The Epistle to the Romans.* International Critical Commentary. 2 vols. Edinburgh: T. & T. Clark, 1979.

Delgado, José Miguel Jiménez. "Mycenaean Words Related to Στρέφω and Τρέπω: A Story of Conflation." *Indo-European Linguistics* 4 (2017) 31–48.

Demosthenes. *Orations, Volume VI: Orations 50–59: Private Cases, In Neaeram.* Translated by A. T. Murr. LCL 351. Cambridge: Harvard University Press, 1939.

Dillow, Joseph C. *The Reign of the Servant Kings: A Study of Eternal Security and the Final Significance of Man.* Hayesville, NC: Schoettle, 1992.

Epictetus. *Discourses, Books 3–4, Fragments, The Encheiridion.* Translated by W. A. Oldfather. LCL 218. Cambridge: Harvard University Press, 1928.

Erasmus. "On the Freedom of the Will." In *Luther and Erasmus: Free Will and Salvation,* edited by E. Gordon Rupp and Philip S. Watson, 35–98. Philadelphia: Westminster, 1969.

Fee, Gordon D. *1 and 2 Timothy, Titus.* New International Bible Commentary. Rev. ed. Peabody, MA: Hendrickson, 1988.

Feldman, Emanuel. *Biblical and Post-Biblical Defilement and Mourning: Law as Theology.* New York: Yeshiva University Press, 1997.

Friesen, Garry, with J. Robin Maxson. *Decision Making and the Will of God.* Rev. ed. Portland, OR: Multnomah, 2004.

Fuller, J. William. "Of Elders and Triads in 1 Timothy 5.19–25." *New Testament Studies* 29 (1983) 258–63.

Gibson, Scott M., and Matthew D. Kim, eds. *Homiletics and Hermeneutics: Four Views on Preaching Today.* Grand Rapids: Baker, 2018.

Gourgues, Michel. "Jesus's Testimony Before Pilate in 1 Timothy 6:13." *Journal of Biblical Literature* 135 (2016) 639–48.

Guggenheimer, Heinrich W. *The Jerusalem Talmud: Tractate Berakhot.* Studia Judaica 18. Berlin: De Gruyter, 2000.

———. *The Jerusalem Talmud: Tractates Sotah and Nedarim.* Studia Judaica 31. Berlin: De Gruyter, 2005.

Guiana, Alan (Knight). "Letter from the Archbishop of the West Indies." *Theology* 59 (1956) 240–43.

Guthrie, Donald. *The Pastoral Epistles: An Introduction and Commentary.* Tyndale New Testament Commentaries. Rev. ed. Grand Rapids: Eerdmans, 1990.

Hall, Stuart George, and Rachel Moriarty. "Gregory, Bishop of Nyssa: Homilies on Ecclesiastes." In *Gregory of Nyssa: Homilies on Ecclesiastes,* Proceedings of the Seventh International Colloquium on Gregory of Nyssa (St. Andrews, 5–10 September 1990), edited by Stuart George Hall, 31–144. Berlin: de Gruyter, 1993.

Hartley, John E. *Leviticus.* Word Biblical Commentary 4. Dallas: Word, 1992.

Himes, Paul A. "Rethinking the Translation of Διδακτικός in 1 Timothy 3:2 and 2 Timothy 2:24." *The Bible Translator* 68 (2017) 189–208.

Hoehner, Harold. "Can a Woman Be a Pastor-Teacher?" *Journal of the Evangelical Theological Society* 50 (2007) 761–71.

———. *Ephesians: An Exegetical Commentary.* Grand Rapids: Baker, 2002.

Holmén, Tom. *Jesus and Jewish Covenant Thinking.* Leiden: Brill, 2001.

Hugenberger, Gordon P. "Women in Church Office: Hermeneutics or Exegesis? A Survey of Approaches to 1 Tim 2:8–15." *Journal of the Evangelical Theological Society* 35 (1992) 341–60.

Hutson, Christopher R. "'A Little Wine': 1 Timothy 5:23 and Greco-Roman Youth." *Lexington Theological Quarterly* 45 (2013) 79–98.

Isocrates. *To Demonicus, To Nicocles, Nicocles or the Cyprians, Panegyricus, To Philip, Archidamus.* Translated by George Norlin. LCL 209. Cambridge: Harvard University Press, 1928.

Johnson, Luke Timothy. *The First and Second Letters to Timothy.* Anchor Bible Commentary 35A. New York: Doubleday, 2001.

Knight, George W. *The Pastoral Epistles: A Commentary on the Greek Text.* New International Greek Testament Commentary. Grand Rapids: Eerdmans, 1992.

Köstenberger, Andreas J. "Ascertaining Women's God-Ordained Roles: An Interpretation of 1 Timothy 2:15." *Bulletin for Biblical Research* 7 (1977) 107–44.

———. *Commentary on 1–2 Timothy and Titus*. Biblical Theology for Christian Proclamation. Nashville: Broadman and Holman, 2017.

———. "A Complex Sentence: The Syntax of 1 Timothy 2:12." In *Women in the Church: An Interpretation and Application of 1 Timothy 2:9–15*, edited by Andreas J. Köstenberger and Thomas R. Schreiner, 117–62. Wheaton, IL: Crossway, 2016.

Kuruvilla, Abraham. "Christiconic Interpretation." *Bibliotheca Sacra* 173 (2016) 131–46.

———. "Christiconic View." In *Homiletics and Hermeneutics: Four Views on Preaching Today*, edited by Scott M. Gibson and Matthew D. Kim, 43–70. Grand Rapids: Baker, 2018.

———. *Ephesians: A Theological Commentary for Preachers*. Eugene, OR: Cascade, 2015.

———. *Genesis: A Theological Commentary for Preachers*. Eugene, OR: Resource, 2014.

———. *Judges: A Theological Commentary for Preachers*. Eugene, OR: Cascade, 2017.

———. *A Manual for Preaching: The Journey from Text to Sermon*. Grand Rapids: Baker, 2019.

———. *Mark: A Theological Commentary for Preachers*. Eugene, OR: Cascade, 2012.

———. "Pericopal Theology." *Bibliotheca Sacra* 173 (2016) 3–17.

———. *Privilege the Text! A Theological Hermeneutic for Preaching*. Chicago: Moody, 2013.

———. *Text to Praxis: Hermeneutics and Homiletics in Dialogue*. Library of New Testament Studies 374. London: T. & T. Clark, 2009.

———. "Time to Kill the Big Idea? A Fresh Look at Preaching." *Journal of the Evangelical Theological Society* 61 (2018) 825–46.

———. *A Vision for Preaching: Understanding the Heart of Pastoral Ministry*. Grand Rapids: Baker, 2015.

———. "'What Is the Author *Doing* with What He Is *Saying*?' Pragmatics and Preaching—An Appeal!" *Journal of the Evangelical Theological Society* 60 (2017) 557–80.

Laertius, Diogenes. *Lives of Eminent Philosophers, Volume I: Books 1*. Translated by R. D. Hicks. LCL 184. Cambridge: Harvard University Press, 1925.

———. *Lives of Eminent Philosophers, Volume II: Books 6–10*. Translated by R. D. Hicks. LCL 185. Cambridge: Harvard University Press, 1925.

Lea, Thomas D. "The Early Christian View of Pseudepigraphic Writings." *Journal of the Evangelical Theological Society* 27 (1984) 65–75.

Lewis, Charlton. T., et al. "*Beneficium*." In *A New Latin Dictionary: Founded on the Translation of Freund's Latin-German Lexicon*, 231–32. New York: American, 1907.

Liddell, Henry George, and Robert Scott. "διάκονος." In *Greek-English Lexicon*, revised by Henry Stuart Jones and Roderick McKenzie, 398. Oxford: Clarendon, 1996.

Liefeld, Walter L. *1 and 2 Timothy, Titus*. New International Version Application Commentary. Grand Rapids: Zondervan, 1999.

Lincoln, Andrew T. *Ephesians*. Word Biblical Commentary 42. Nashville: Thomas Nelson, 1990.

Luther, Martin. "Sermon for the First Sunday After Easter, John 20:21–29." In *Sermons on the Gospel of St. John Chapters 17–20, Volume 69 of Luther's Works*, edited by Christopher Boyd Brown, translated by Kenneth E. F. Howes, 330–31. St. Louis: Concordia, 2009.

Maccoby, Hyam. *Ritual and Morality: The Ritual Purity System and Its Place in Judaism*. Cambridge: Cambridge University Press, 1999.

Malherbe, Abraham J. "How to Treat Old Women and Old Men: The Use of Philosophical Traditions and Scripture in 1 Timothy 5." In *Scripture and Traditions: Essays in Early Judaism and Christianity in Honor of Carl R. Holladay*, edited by Patrick Gray and Gail R. O'Day, 263–90. Leiden: Brill, 2008.

———. "Overseers as Household Managers in the Pastoral Epistles." In *Light from the Gentiles: Hellenistic Philosophy and Early Christianity: Collected Essays, 1959–2010*, edited by Carl R. Holladay et al., 559–74. Leiden: Brill, 2014.

Marcus, Joel. *Mark: A New Translation with Introduction and Commentary*. Anchor Bible Commentary 2. New Haven: Yale University Press, 2002.

Marshall, I. Howard (with Philip H. Towner). *The Pastoral Epistles*. International Critical Commentary. Edinburgh: T. & T. Clark, 1999.

Meier, John P. "*Presbyteros* in the Pastoral Epistles." *Catholic Bible Quarterly* 35 (1973) 323–45.

BIBLIOGRAPHY

Merkle, Benjamin J. "Are the Qualification for Elders or Overseers Negotiable?" *Bibliotheca Sacra* 171 (2014) 172–88.

Metzger, Bruce. *The Canon of the New Testament: Its Origin, Development, and Significance.* Oxford: Clarendon, 1987.

Milgrom, Jacob. "Rationale for Cultic Law: The Case of Impurity." *Semeia* 45 (1989) 103–9.

Moffat, James. *The New Testament: A New Translation.* New York: Doran, 1922.

Moo, Douglas J. "The Interpretation of 1 Timothy 2:11–15: A Rejoinder." *Trinity Journal* 3 NS (1981) 198–222.

———. "What Does It Mean Not to Teach or Have Authority Over Men? 1 Timothy 2:11–15." In *Recovering Biblical Manhood and Womanhood: A Response to Evangelical Feminism,* edited by John Piper and Wayne Grudem, 178–93. Wheaton, IL: Crossway, 1991.

Mounce, William D. *Pastoral Epistles.* Word Biblical Commentary 46. Nashville: Thomas Nelson, 2000.

Onasander, et al. *Aeneas Tacticus, Asclepiodotus, and Onasander.* Translated by the Illinois Greek Club. LCL 156. Cambridge: Harvard University Press, 1928.

Paschke, Boris A. "The *Cura Morum* of the Roman Censors as Historical Background for the Bishop and Deacon Lists of the Pastoral Epistles." *Zeitschrift für die neutestamentliche Wissenschaft* 98 (2007) 105–19.

Pausanias. *Description of Greece, Volume II: Books 3–5.* Translated by W. H. S. Jones and H. A. Ormerod. LCL 188. Cambridge: Harvard University Press, 1926.

Perry, Gregory R. "Phoebe of Cenchreae and 'Women' of Ephesus: 'Deacons' in the Earliest Churches." *Presbyterion* 36 (2010) 9–36.

Philo. *On the Decalogue, On the Special Laws, Books 1–3.* Translated by F. H. Colson. LCL 320. Cambridge: Harvard University Press, 1937.

———. *On the Special Laws, Book 4, On the Virtues, On Rewards and Punishments.* Translated by F. H. Colson. LCL 341. Cambridge: Harvard University Press, 1939.

———. *Questions on Genesis.* Translated by Ralph Marcus. LCL 380. Cambridge: Harvard University Press, 1953.

Pietersen, Lloyd K. "Women as Gossips and Busybodies? Another Look at 1 Timothy 5:13." *Lexington Theological Quarterly* 42 (2007) 19–35.

Plato. *Laws, Volume II: Books 7–12.* Translated by R. G. Bury. LCL 192. Cambridge: Harvard University Press, 1926.

———. *Republic, Volume I: Books 1–5.* Edited and translated by Christopher Emlyn-Jones and William Preddy. LCL 237. Cambridge: Harvard University Press, 2013.

Pliny the Younger. *Letters, Volume II: Books 8–10, Panegyricus.* Translated by Betty Radice. LCL 59. Cambridge: Harvard University Press, 1969.

Plutarch. *Moralia, Volume II: How to Profit by One's Enemies, On Having Many Friends, Chance, Virtue and Vice, Letter of Condolence to Apollonius, Advice About Keeping Well, Advice to Bride and Groom, The Dinner of the Seven Wise Men, Superstition.* Translated by Frank Cole Babbitt. LCL 222. Cambridge: Harvard University Press, 1928.

———. *Moralia, Volume VI: Can Virtue Be Taught? On Moral Virtue, On the Control of Anger, On Tranquility of Mind, On Brotherly Love, On Affection for Offspring, Whether Vice Be Sufficient to Cause Unhappiness, Whether the Affections of the Soul are Worse Than Those of the Body, Concerning Talkativeness, On Being a Busybody.* Translated by W. C. Helmbold. LCL 337. Cambridge: Harvard University Press, 1939.

Polybius. *The Histories, Volume III: Books 5–8.* Translated by W. R. Paton. Revised by F. W. Walbank and Christian Habicht. LCL 138. Cambridge: Harvard University Press, 2011.

———. *The Histories, Volume IV: Books 9–15.* Translated by W. R. Paton. Revised by F. W. Walbank and Christian Habicht. LCL 159. Cambridge: Harvard University Press, 2011.

———. *The Histories, Volume V: Books 16–27.* Translated by W. R. Paton. Revised by F. W. Walbank, and Christian Habicht. LCL 160. Cambridge: Harvard University Press, 2012.

Porter, Stanley E. "Pauline Chronology and the Question of Pseudonymity of the Pastoral Epistles." In *Paul and Pseudepigraph,* edited by Stanley E. Porter and Gregory P. Fewster, 65–88. Leiden Brill, 2013.

Quinn, Jerome D. *The Letter to Titus.* Anchor Bible Commentary 35. New York: Doubleday, 1990.

Quinn, Jerome D., and William C. Wacker. *The First and Second Letters to Timothy*. Eerdmans Critical Commentary. Grand Rapids: Eerdmans, 2000.

Ramelli, Ilaria. *Hierocles the Stoic: Elements of Ethics, Fragments, and Excerpt*. Translated by David Konstan. Atlanta: SBL, 2009.

Reumann, John Henry Paul. "The Use of *Oikonomia* and Related Terms in Greek Sources to About A.D. 100, as a Background for Patristic Applications." PhD diss., University of Pennsylvania, 1957.

Rudolph, David J. "Jesus and the Food Laws: A Reassessment of Mark 7:19b." *Evangelical Quarterly* 74 (2002) 291–311.

Saucy, Robert L. "Women's Prohibition to Teach Men: An Investigation into Its Meaning and Contemporary Application." *Journal of the Evangelical Theological Society* 37 (1994) 79–97.

Scheidel, Walter. "Human Mobility in Roman Italy, I: The Free Population." *The Journal of Roman Studies* 94 (2004) 1–26.

———. "Human Mobility in Roman Italy, II: The Slave Population." *The Journal of Roman Studies* 95 (2005) 64–79.

Schnabel, Eckhard J. "Paul, Timothy, and Titus: The Assumption of a Pseudonymous Author and of Pseudonymous Recipients in the Light of Literary, Theological, and Historical Evidence." In *Do Historical Matters Matter to Faith?: A Critical Appraisal of Modern and Postmodern Approaches to Scripture*, edited by James K. Hoffmeier and Dennis R. Magary, 383–404. Wheaton, IL: Crossway, 2012.

Schreiner, Thomas R. "An Interpretation of 1 Timothy 2:9–15: A Dialogue with Scholarship." In *Women in the Church: An Analysis and Application of 1 Timothy 2:9–15*, edited by Andreas J. Köstenberger and Thomas R. Schreiner, 85–120. Grand Rapids: Baker, 2005.

Seneca. *Epistles, Volume I: Epistles 1–65*. Translated by Richard M. Gummere. LCL 75. Cambridge: Harvard University Press, 1917.

———. *Epistles, Volume III: Epistles 93–124*. Translated by Richard M. Gummere; LCL 77. Cambridge: Harvard University Press, 1925.

———. *Moral Essays, Volume III: De Beneficiis*. Translated by John W. Basore. LCL 310. Cambridge: Harvard University Press, 1935.

Sirilla, Michael G. *The Ideal Bishop*. Thomistic Ressourcement Series. Washington, DC: Catholic University of America Press, 2017.

Skeat, T. C. "'Especially the Parchments': A Note on 2 Timothy IV.13." *Journal of Theological Studies* NS 30 (1979) 173–77.

Snodgrass, Klyne R. "Galatians 3:28—Conundrum or Solution?" In *Women, Authority and The Bible*, edited by Alvera Mickelson, 161–80. Downers Grove, IL: InterVarsity, 1986.

Thiering, B. E. "*Mebaqqer* and *Episkopos* in the Light of the Temple Scroll." *Journal of Biblical Literature* 100 (1981) 59–74.

Thornton, Dillon T. "Sin Seizing an Opportunity through the Commandments: The Law in 1 Tim 1:8–11 and Rom 6–8." *Horizons in Biblical Theology* 36 (2014) 142–58.

Towner, Philip H. *1–2 Timothy and Titus*. IVP New Testament Commentary. Downers Grove, IL: InterVarsity, 1994.

———. *The Letters to Timothy and Titus*. New International Commentary on the New Testament. Grand Rapids: Eerdmans, 2006.

van Nes, Jermo. *Pauline Language and the Pastoral Epistles: A Study of Linguistic Variation in the Corpus Paulinum*. Linguistic Biblical Studies 16. Leiden: Brill, 2017.

Van Neste, Ray. *Cohesion and Structure in the Pastoral Epistles*. Journal for the Study of the New Testament Supplement Series 280. London: T. & T. Clark, 2004.

Wall, Robert W. "Empire, Church, and *Missio Dei*: On Praying for Our Kings (1 Timothy 2:1–2)." *Wesleyan Theological Journal* 47 (2012) 7–24.

Wallace, Daniel B. *Greek Grammar Beyond the Basics: An Exegetical Syntax of the New Testament*. Grand Rapids: Zondervan, 1997.

Westermann, William Linn. "Between Slavery and Freedom." *The American Historical Review* 50 (1945) 213–27.

White, Benjamin L. "How to Read a Book: Irenaeus and the Pastoral Epistles Reconsidered." *Vigilae Christianae* 65 (2011) 125–49.

BIBLIOGRAPHY

Wieland, George M. "Roman Crete and the Letter to Titus." *New Testament Studies* 55 (2009) 338–54.

Wilder, Terry L. "Does the Bible Contain Forgeries?" In *In Defense of the Bible: A Comprehensive Apologetic for the Authority of Scripture,* edited by Steven B. Cowan and Terry L. Wilder, 165–82. Nashville: Broadman and Holman, 2013.

Wilson, Walter T. *The Sentences of Sextus*. Wisdom Literature from the Ancient World. Atlanta: SBL, 2012.

Winter, Bruce W. *Roman Wives, Roman Widows: The Appearance of New Women and the Pauline Communities*. Grand Rapids: Eerdmans, 2003.

Witherington, Ben. *Letters and Homilies for Hellenized Christians, Vol. 1: A Socio-Rhetorical Commentary on Titus, 1–2 Timothy and 1–3 John*. Downers Grove, IL: InterVarsity, 2006.

Wolters, Al. "ΑΥΞΕΝΤΗΣ and its Cognates in Biblical Greek." *Journal of the Evangelical Theological Society* 52 (2009) 719–29.

———. "A Semantic Study of αὐθέντης and its Derivatives." *Journal of Biblical Manhood and Womanhood* 11 (2006) 44–65.

Xenophon. *Hellenica, Volume II: Books 5–7*. Translated by Carleton L. Brownson. LCL 89. Cambridge: Harvard University Press, 1921.

Zamfir, Korinna. "Is the *Ekklēsia* a *Household* (of God)? Reassessing the Notion of Οἶκος Θεοῦ in 1 Tim 3.15." *New Testament Studies* 60 (2014) 511–28.

———. *Men and Women in the Household of God: A Contextual Approach to Roles and Ministries in the Pastoral Epistles*. Novum Testamentum et Orbis Anitquus / Studien zur Umwelt des Neuen Testaments 103. Göttingen: Vandenhoeck and Ruprecht, 2013.

Zamfir, Korinna, and Joseph Verheyden. "Text-Critical and Intertextual Remarks on 1 Tim 2:8–10." *Novum Testamentum* 50 (2008) 376–406.

MODERN AUTHORS INDEX

Barnett, Paul W., 33
Barrett, C. K., 158
Barth, Karl, 230, 231
Baugh, Steven M., 92
Best, Ernest, 5, 119
Beyer, Hermann W., 69
Blomberg, Craig L., 55, 60, 61
Bowman, Robert M., 218
Bruce, F. F., 194
Bunyan, John, 33

Calvin, John, xi
Campbell, R. A., 103
Carson, D. A., 189
Christian, Ed, 55
Cooper, Marjorie J., 60
Caballero, Jay G., 60
Couser, Greg A., 45, 146
Cranfield, C. E. B., 24

Delgado, José Miguel Jiménez, 188
Dillow, Joseph C., 95, 226

Erasmus, 230

Fee, Gordon D., 178, 212, 226, 227
Feldman, Emanuel, 89
Friesen, Garry, 44
Fuller, J. William, 113, 114

Gourgues, Michel, 128
Guggenheimer, Heinrich W., 54
Guiana, Alan (Knight), 227
Guthrie, Donald, 6

Hall, Stuart George, 120
Hartley, John E., 89
Himes, Paul A., 68
Hoehner, Harold, 69, 120
Holmén, Tom, 208
Hugenberger, Gordon P., 55
Hutson, Christopher R., 115

Johnson, Luke Timothy, 8, 11, 12, 18, 21, 30, 73, 84, 104, 105, 106, 114, 122, 123, 130, 132, 135, 136, 144, 166, 171, 172, 178

Knight, George W., 26, 33, 34, 35, 52, 69, 78, 121, 123, 177, 182, 209, 216, 226
Köstenberger, Andreas J., 34, 55, 61, 62, 63, 76, 86, 87, 124, 177, 190
Kuruvilla, Abraham, 1, 2, 3, 4, 22, 23, 24, 25, 27, 28, 38, 46, 57, 58, 60, 81, 90, 95, 116, 118, 148, 157, 188, 215, 220, 230, 231

Lea, Thomas D., 6
Lewis, Charlton, T., 124
Liddell, Henry George, 69
Liefeld, Walter L., 88
Lincoln, Andrew T., 118
Luther, Martin, 57, 160, 230

Maccoby, Hyam, 90
Malherbe, Abraham J., 67, 74, 93
Marcus, Joel, 90
Marshall, I. Howard, 8, 26, 40, 54, 80, 86, 87, 93, 144, 148, 160, 165, 169, 177, 182, 186, 223
Meier, John P., 110, 112, 113
Merkle, Benjamin J., 73
Metzger, Bruce, 6
Milgrom, Jacob, 89
Moffat, James, 189-90
Moriarty, Rachel, 120
Moo, Douglas J., 56, 58
Mounce, William D., 5, 22, 33, 40, 44, 49, 51, 56, 59, 69, 70, 77, 88, 102, 103, 105, 110, 111, 123, 125, 129, 132, 146, 157, 160, 169, 170, 180, 181, 190, 201, 219, 225, 226

Paschke, Boris A., 67
Perry, Gregory R., 76
Pietersen, Lloyd K., 10, 179
Porter, Stanley E., 6

Modern Authors Index

Quinn, Jerome D., 11, 22, 33, 42, 43, 45, 51, 61, 73, 74, 79, 93, 102, 130, 151, 183, 189, 203, 204, 205, 206, 207, 212, 216, 227

Ramelli, Ilaria, 99
Reumann, John Henry Paul, 21
Rudolph, David J., 90

Saucy, Robert L., 56
Scheidel, Walter, 119
Schnabel, Eckhard J., 6
Scott, Robert, 69
Sirilla, Michael G., 6
Skeat, T. C., 92
Snodgrass, Klyne R., 61

Thiering, B. E., 67
Thornton, Dillon T., 23
Towner, Philip H., 6, 8, 9, 24, 26, 35, 42, 45, 79, 87, 91, 99, 102, 104, 105, 114, 123, 124, 129, 134, 136, 146, 149, 151, 156, 161, 162, 169, 171, 176, 177, 182, 188, 190, 192, 193, 204, 207, 215, 217, 218, 225

van Nes, Jermo, 7
Van Neste, Ray, 9, 18, 20, 30, 32, 34, 71, 84, 109, 118, 137, 167, 201, 206

Wacker, William C., 11, 22, 33, 42, 43, 45, 51, 61, 79, 93, 102, 130, 151, 183, 189
Wall, Robert W., 43
Wallace, Daniel B., 57, 218
Westermann, William Linn, 118
White, Benjamin L., 6
Wieland, George M., 207
Wilder, Terry L., 6
Wilson, Walter T., 53
Winter, Bruce W., 105, 202, 215
Witherington, Ben, 7, 33, 49, 61, 130, 177, 200, 206, 225

Verheyden, Joseph, 49

Zamfir, Korinna, 9, 49, 54

SCRIPTURE INDEX

OLD TESTAMENT

Genesis

1–3	60
1:4	88n12
1:10	88n12
1:12	88n12
1:18	88n12
1:21	88n12
1:25	88n12
1:26	120
1:28	62
1:31	89
2	60
2:7	60
2:8	60
2:15	60
2:18	61
2:19	60
3:1	60
3:2	60
3:4	60
3:6	60
3:9–12	60n43
3:12	60
3:13	60, 60n43
3:15	60
3:16	60, 60n44
3:17	60
6:5	22n19
9:3	89
20:11	44, 79n41
49	11

Exodus

4:21	22n19
5:14	26
19:5	219
20:4–6	26
20:7	26
20:8	26
20:12	26
20:13	26
20:15	26
20:16	26
20:24	50n5
21:5	123
22:22–23	102
23:22	219
30:19–21	51

Leviticus

1:3	45
1:4	45
4:1–35	33n9
10	209n36
11	209n36
11:6	89
11:7	89
11:8	89
11:10	89
11:11	89
11:12	89
11:20	89
11:23	89
11:26	89
11:27	89
11:28	89
11:29	89
11:31	89
11:45	89
12	209n36
13	209n36
17:4	45
18:2–5	89
18:24–25	89
19:5	45
19:12	26
19:32	99

Scripture Index

Leviticus (continued)

20:23–26	89
22:14	33n9
22:19	45
22:20	45
22:21	45
23	209n36
23:11	45
41	209n36
42	209n36

Numbers

3:7–8	60
8:26	60
15:22–51	33n9
16:5	170
18:7	60
28	189n14

Deuteronomy

5:16	26
5:17	26
5:18	26
5:19	26
5:20	26
6:4	9n36
7:6	219
7:8	219
8:2	22n19
10:18	102
11:16	60
12:13	50n5
12:30	60
13:4–5	60
14:2	219
14:29	102
15:16	123
17:6	113
19:15	113
19:17	113
19:21	113
20:6	158
24:17	102
25:4	110n2
26:11	89
26:18	219
27:19	102
28:50	99
28:58	192n30
31:11–12	94n37
33	11

Joshua

1:8	192n30
22:5	60
23—24	11

2 Samuel

13:17	75
23:1–7	11

1 Kings

7:17	78
8:42	50
9:6	60

2 Kings

25:13	78

1 Chronicles

27:24	192n3
27:31	76n36
29:6	76n36

2 Chronicles

3:15	78
4:12	78
6:32	50
8:10	76n36
24:11	76n36

Ezra

6:9–10	9n36, 43n6, 224n3
7:23	9n36, 43n6, 224n3

Nehemiah

8:8	94n37

Job

1:6	113n13
1:21	131n15
2:1	113n13
28:28	44, 79n41

Psalms

4:6	104
5:12	104
7:2	104
9:11	104
10:14	61

10:16	9n36	20:29	99
15:1	104	21:27	209n36
17:3	104	23:4–5	131n10
22	193	23:5	75
22:1	193	23:17	95n41
22:4	193	27:18	158
22:5	193	29:27	209n36
22:8a	193		
22:8b	193	**Ecclesiastes**	
22:20	193	2:7	120
22:21	193	3:12–13	89
22:27	193	5:12–13	131n10
22:28	193	5:15	131n15
24:4	51	5:18	89
26:6	51		
29:10	9n36	**Isaiah**	
30:10	61	1:15	51
39:6	131n10	1:17	102
49:6–10	131n10	2:2	176
49:17	131n15	11:2	44, 79n41
52:7	131n10	26:10–11	170
54:4	61	26:13	170
68:5	102	26:14	170
68:5	103	29:13	207n26
72:12	61	33:6	44, 79n41
73:13	51	55:4	45n19
77:11	123	59:3	51
81:1	113n13	66:1	50
82:3	102		
103:22	50n5	**Jeremiah**	
118:43	168	10:10	9n36
119:54	60	16:11	60
134:4	219n26	29:7	9n36, 43n6, 224n3
146:9	102		
		Ezekiel	
Proverbs		16:49	105
1:7	44	36:25–27	226n14
3:6	168		
11:1	209n36	**Daniel**	
11:4	131n10	1:12	114
11:5	168	7:9–11	113n13
11:16	131n10	9:2	192n3
11:20	209n36		
11:28	131n10	**Amos**	
12:22	209n36	6:10	75
15:8	209n36		
15:9	209n36	**Micah**	
15:25	102	4:1	176
15:26	209n36		
16:12	209n36		
17:15	209n36		
20:4	158		
20:23	209n36		

Scripture Index

Zephaniah
2:11	50

Zechariah
7:6	102

Malachi
1:11	50
3:14	60

NEW TESTAMENT

Matthew
6:25–34	131n10
6:9	26
7:22	150n32
7:23	162n18
10:10	110n2
10:33	162
13:22	131n10
13:49–50	113
15:4	110n2
16:27	113, 113n13
18:15–16	113
18:16	113
18:17	113
19:12	72
19:16–30	131n10
19:18	25n33
19:28	162n18
20:28	68
22:37–40	22
23:11	68
24:31	113n13
25:31	113n13
26:41	80n47
28:19–20	56

Mark
1:44	208n34
3:31–35	99
7:9–13	102n7
7:10	110n2
7:18–19	90
7:18	90
7:19	89n23, 90
7:20–21	90
8:38	113n13, 162n18
9:35	68
10:19	25n33
10:43	68
12:10	182
12:28–34	208n34
12:30–31	22
13:1–27	87
13:9	45n19
13:26	218n18
13:27	113n13
14:38	80n47
16:19	80n49

Luke
1:53	131n10
3:22	92
4:14	147n18
4:17	192n3
4:21	182
8:21	99
9:5	45n19
9:26	113, 113n13
10:7	110n2
10:12	150n32
10:27	33
10:34	74
10:35	74
11:2	26
12:9	113n13, 162n18
12:13–21	131n10
12:48	35
14:4	54n16
14:14	169
15:10	113n13
16:14–15	131n10
16:14	177n3
19:20	25n33
21:34	150n32
22:25–27	123
22:25	123
22:26	68, 69n18
22:30	162n18
23:34	33n9
23:56	54n16

John
1:14	80n46
1:31	80n46
3:5	226n14
3:6	80n47
3:10	78
6:51	80n46
6:63	80n47
7:38	182

8:17	113	15:21	94n37
10:10	33, 136	15:22–23	68
12:16	80n49	15:29	89n17
12:23	80n49	15:37–39	192
12:26	69n18	16:1–3	144n6, 180n14
13–17	11	16:1	204n18
14:16	81	16:2–3	147n21
15:26	81	16:4	68
16:7	81	16:14	26
19:26–27	99	16:24	20
19:38	182	17:4	26
		17:14–15	147n21
		17:17	26

Acts

1:2	80n49	17:23	7n28, 44n10
1:8	147n18	17:31	169
1:10	80n48	17:32	146
1:17–18	56	18:2–3	194n34
1:20	110n2	18:7	26
2:11	5	18:18–19	194n34
2:17	176	18:26	58, 194n34
3:17	33n9	19:6	114n15, 147
4:9	123	19:11	10
5:28	20	19:19	10
5:29	225	19:22	147n21, 194n34
6	69	19:28	78
6:1–6	69	19:34	78
6:1	102	19:35	5
6:5	147n18	20:4	194n34
6:6	114n15	20:17	68, 69
6:8–10	69	20:28–31	10
6:8	69, 147n18	20:28–29	67
8:17–19	114n15	20:28	68, 69, 69n17
8:17–18	147	20:29–30	87n9
9:12	147	20:37	144n10
9:17	147	21:9	58
10:38	123	21:14	54
10:45	206	21:18	68
11:2	206	21:29	194n34
11:18	54	27	5
11:30	68	28:16	192
13:1–3	69n17, 147		
13:2	35	## Romans	
13:3	114n15	1:3–4	80n47
13:14–52	180n14	1:4	80n47
13:15	94n38	1:5	25
13:43	26	1:7	123
13:50	26	1:8	31
14:1–5	180n14	1:24	22n19
14:6–20	180n14	1:29–31	176
14:23	68, 69	2:27	26
15:1–20	90	3:3	162
15:2–6	68	3:8	20n7
15:20	89n17	3:20	23, 23n24

Romans (continued)

4:3	182
4:15	24n28
4:25	80n47
5:2	147n18, 160n13
5:12–20	60n43
5:12–14	20n6
5:12	59n41
5:13	23
5:17	59n41
5:20	24n28
6:14	24n28
6:17	22n19
7:1–4	24n27
7:1–3	73
7:5	24n28
7:6	24n27
7:7–12	23
8:1	24, 24n27
8:3–5	25
8:3	23n24, 80n46
8:4	80n47, 81
8:5	80n47
8:6	80n47
8:7	56n26
8:9	80n47
8:12–16	81
8:13	80n47
8:15	147n18
8:18	160n13
8:21	218n18
8:29	2, 188n11
8:34	81
9:17	182
9:18	44n12
9:23	218n
10:11	182
11:2	182
11:14	95n43
11:28	123
11:33–36	148
12:8	69n17, 75, 110
12:13	68
12:17	43n7
12:18	43n7
13:1–7	123
13:1	55, 55n22, 216, 224n3
13:4	69n18
13:5	55, 224n3
13:9	25n33
14:6	88n13, 89n16
14:17	87n10
15:8	68
15:13	147n18
15:19	147n18
15:30	147n18
16:1–2	69n18, 76n36
16:1	76n36
16:2	76n36
16:3–4	194n34
16:13	99
16:21	19n4, 147n21
16:22	7
16:23	194n34
16:25	77n37
16:26	19n2, 25

1 Corinthians

1:4	31
1:18—2:16	120
1:23	146
2:1–3	147n21
2:2	77n37
2:4	147n18
2:7	77n37
2:7–8	77n37
2:8	218n18
2:12	147n18
3:2	56n26
3:5	69n18
3:9–10	8n33
3:13	150n32
3:15	61n54
3:16	55
4:1	8n33, 77n37, 171n14, 204n20
4:3	56n26
4:16–17	147n21
4:17	19n4, 93
4:18	20n7
4:19	44n12
5:1	20n7, 56n26
5:5	80n47
6:11	226n14
6:13	89
7:1–40	89
7:1	89
7:6	19n2
7:8–9	73
7:16	95n43
7:20–24	120
7:21	121
7:25	19n2
7:26	87
7:32–40	72
7:39–40	73
8:1–13	89n15

8:8	89n16
9:7	158
9:14	110n2
9:22	95n43
9:27	95
10–11	49n4
10:16	88n13
10:30	88n13
10:32	72
11:1–16	56
11:1–3	49n4
11:2	136n33
11:3	49n4
11:4–6	51
11:4	49n4
11:5–6	49n4
11:5	49n4, 58
11:7–9	49n4
11:12	49n4
11:13–16	49n4
11:13	49n4
11:14	56n26
12:5	147n18
12:7	147n18
12:7–11	58
12:11	44n12, 69n17
12:12–26	58
12:13	61, 123
12:18	44n12, 69n17
12:21–33a	58
12:27–30	57
12:28	69, 69n17
14:21	56n26
14:26	56
14:28	54
14:30	54
14:31–35	49
14:34	54, 55, 56, 216
14:37	150n33
15:1–2	95
15:2	62
15:12	20n7, 169
15:13	56n26
15:16	56n26
15:21–22	60n43
15:24	187n6
15:28	215n8
15:38	44n12
15:44	80n47
15:51–52	77n37
15:56	23
16:10	19n4, 147n21, 216
16:16	55, 55n22
16:19	194n34
16:21	7

2 Corinthians

1:1	19n4
1:19	19n4, 147n21
1:22	147n18
2:13	202n12
3:1	20n7
3:2	43n7
3:6	69n18
3:12	75
3:18	160n13
4:4	218n18
4:6	218n18
4:17	160n13
5:5	147n18
6:4	69n18
6:16	55, 78
7:1	80n47
7:4	75
8:8	19n2
8:23	202n12
11:2	73
11:3–4	59n39
11:3	60n43
11:5	69n18
11:23–27	146
11:23	69n18
12:9	131n16
13:1	113

Galatians

1:7	20n7
1:9	209
2:3	56n26, 202n12
2:5	56n26
2:12	20n7, 206
2:15	26
2:19	24n27
3:3	80n47
3:6	20n6
3:8	182
3:10	192n3
3:19	23
3:19—4:7	23
3:28	61, 123
4:29	80n47
4:30	182
5:16	80n47
5:17	80n47
5:19	80n47

Galatians (continued)

5:22	147n18
5:23	147n18
6:6	55
6:10	8n33, 74, 103n13, 171n14, 204n20
6:11	7
6:13	56n26

Ephesians

1:8–10	22n15, 148n28
1:9–10	45, 77n37, 187n6
1:9	77n37, 180
1:10	80n49, 187n6
1:13	168
1:15	33n8
1:16	31
1:17	218n18
1:18	218n18
2:10	8n33, 171n14, 204n20
2:14–18	24
2:19–22	8n33, 74
2:21–22	55
3:3–4	77n37
3:3	77n37
3:7	69n18
3:8–9	77n37
3:9	77n37
3:16	147n18, 218n18
4:1	187n6
4:8	187n6
4:11	68, 69, 69n17, 189n12
4:18	33n9
5:18	68
5:21	55, 55n22, 216
5:22–23	215n8
5:22	55, 216
5:24	216
6:1–4	121
6:4	58
6:5–9	120
6:6–7	216n15
6:9	120
6:19	75
6:21	7, 69n18, 192

Philippians

1:1	19n4, 68, 69, 77, 143n4
1:3	31
1:7	20n6
1:15	20n7
2:9	80n49
2:12	95
2:19–24	147n21
2:19–22	19n4
2:20	19n4
2:22	93
3:17	216n12
3:21	80n49, 218n18
4:5	43n7
4:8	44

Colossians

1:1	19n4
1:3	31
1:4	33n8
1:5	168
1:7	69n18
1:8	147n18
1:11	218n18
1:13	187n6
1:22–23	95
1:22	80n46
1:23	69n18
1:25–27	77n37
1:25	69n18
1:27	44n12, 218n18
2:2	77n37
2:5	80n47
3:11	61, 123
3:16	56, 58
3:18	55, 216
3:19	55
3:22—4:1	120
3:22	216n15
4:1	120
4:3	77n37
4:5	72
4:7	7, 69n18, 192
4:10–11	192
4:11	206
4:14	192
4:17	69n18

1 Thessalonians

1:1	19n4, 143n4
1:3	33n8
1:5	147n18
1:6	216n12
1:7	216n12
2:12	160n13
2:13	150n33
2:15	43n7
2:19	190

3:2–3	147n21	1:5–6	136
3:2	19n4, 69n18	1:5	36, 63, 86, 201
3:6	147n21	1:6–7	9
4:2	20	1:6	201
4:8	147n18	1:6	32, 36
4:11	54n16	1:7–8	206n25
4:12	72	1:7	9, 10, 10n38, 32, 37n17, 57, 205, 216n11
4:16	113n13	1:8–11	30
5:7–8	68	1:9–10	9n36
5:12–13	69, 69n17, 110	1:9	129n3
5:12	55n22, 75	1:9	32, 33
		1:10	7n27, 10n38, 56n30, 73, 121n15, 166n2, 201, 205, 208n33, 216n11

2 Thessalonians

1:1	19n4, 143n4	1:11	30n1, 31, 32, 202n9
1:3	31, 33n8	1:12–20	12, 17, 21, 39, 40, 43, 45
1:6–7	113n13	1:12–17	7, 20n5
1:7	113n13	1:12–14	40, 190n21
1:10	80n49, 150n32	1:12	200
2:1–13	87	1:12	8n33, 68, 204n18
2:1–2	169	1:13	143, 161, 180
2:2–10	7	1:14	22n20, 63
2:13	31	1:15–17	40
2:14	160n13	1:15–16	43
2:15	136n33, 150n33	1:15	7, 8n33, 62n56, 71, 92, 95, 160
3:12	54n16	1:16–17	142
3:6–7	150n33	1:16	62n56, 68, 143, 216n12
3:6	136n33	1:17	9n36, 10, 135, 135n25, 148
3:9	216n12	1:18–20	40, 91, 133
		1:18–19	40, 77

1 Timothy

(Also see within the appropriate pericope for particular verses of that chapter.)

1–3	78, 86, 86n3	1:18	11, 19n4, 20, 93, 95n40, 133, 134, 136, 147n20, 157n4, 158
1	201	1:19–20	43
1:1–11	9n36, 12, 29, 33, 33n9, 35, 36, 39, 40, 205, 209	1:19	9, 20n7, 63, 77n37, 86, 87, 103, 134n20, 150n33, 179, 181n19
1:1–2	143	1:20	9, 21, 72, 85, 169n10, 193
1:1	45n16, 45n20, 143	2:1—3:13	10
1:2	11, 63, 93, 136, 137, 142, 143	2	49n4, 57, 60
1:3–20	10	2:1–7	12, 29, 48, 49, 49n1, 51
1:3–17	24, 91	2:1–6	123
1:3–11	30	2:1–2	224n3
1:3–7	133	2:1	49n3, 50, 51, 57n33
1:3–5	36	2:2	7n28, 49n3, 53, 54, 54n16, 68, 73, 74, 79, 129n3
1:3–4	87, 95	2:3–6	62n56
1:3	9, 10, 30, 36, 37n17, 50, 56n30, 57, 129, 144n10, 201, 216n11	2:3–4	92n29, 95
		2:3	20n5
1:4–5	31	2:4	87, 218n20
1:4	8, 9, 32, 44n13, 63, 75, 122, 167n4, 201, 204, 206n25	2:5–6	45n19
		2:5	7, 9n36, 73

1 Timothy (continued)

2:6	105, 147n23
2:7	8, 10, 10n38, 35, 49n4, 86, 205, 216n11
2:8–15	13, 39, 40, 65, 66
2:8	41, 42, 73, 76
2:9–15	121, 178
2:9	66, 68, 76., 112n9, 130, 214
2:10	7, 7n28, 44, 79n41, 121n16, 136n30, 181n17, 208n32, 215n5
2:12	10, 41, 73, 216n11
2:13–15	7, 24
2:15	22n20, 41, 66, 68, 73, 89n16
3	57, 66, 204
3:1–16	13, 40, 48, 51, 54, 58, 83, 86, 95, 104, 115, 115n20
3:1–15	126
3:1–13	101
3:1–7	63
3:1–2	57n33, 58
3:1	7, 33n5, 92, 121n16, 136n30, 208n32, 215n5
3:2	50n6, 53n14, 57, 89n16, 104, 110, 130, 157, 172n18, 203, 204n17, 214, 215
3:3	115, 130, 99n4
3:4–6	98
3:4–5	8n33, 22n18, 55, 89n16, 103, 110, 171n14, 204n20
3:4	44, 55n21, 68, 110, 150n33
3:5	110
3:6–7	85
3:6	93, 114, 130, 203
3:7	123, 131, 150n33, 203, 215
3:8–13	91
3:8	32, 44, 115, 130, 130n7, 214, 215
3:9	86, 150n33
3:10	32, 114, 123, 203, 215
3:11–12	50n6
3:11	86, 204n18, 214, 215
3:12	22n18, 32, 55, 89n16, 103, 104, 110, 171n5, 204n20
3:13	32, 59n38, 63, 203
3:14—4:16	10
3:14–15	57n33
3:14	125n33, 128
3:15	103n13, 135, 169n12, 171n5, 204
3:15	8, 22, 22n18, 45, 49, 55, 87, 99
3:16	7, 7n28, 85, 129n3
4	91, 93
4:1–16	13, 65, 97, 98, 109, 115, 208n34
4:1–5	133
4:1–3	21, 114, 206n25
4:1–2	1, 208
4:1	9, 10, 10n38, 20n7, 21, 32, 37, 56n30, 57, 63, 103, 205, 216n11
4:2	22n19
4:3–5	208n34
4:3	87n10, 132
4:4	135n28
4:6–16	133
4:6	10, 10n38, 32, 56n30, 69n18, 125n33, 128, 205, 216n11
4:7–10	158
4:7–8	59
4:7	7n28, 9, 21, 79, 129n3, 158, 206n25
4:8	7n28, 33, 79, 129n3, 142
4:9	33n5
4:9	55n21
4:9	7
4:9	71
4:10	20n5, 43, 45n16, 78, 123, 134, 135, 158
4:11–16	57, 62,
4:11–12	63
4:11	10, 20, 56, 56n30, 125n33, 128
4:12	22n20, 63, 68, 73, 79n44, 98, 100, 114, 216, 216n12
4:13	10, 10n38, 56, 205, 216n11
4:14	35, 68, 69n17, 77, 114n15, 133, 147n20
4:15	125n33, 128
4:16	10, 10n38, 56, 59, 98, 205
5:1—6:2	9, 10, 118, 125
5:1–16	13, 83, 108, 109, 118, 126
5:1–2	8n33, 22n18, 84, 93, 171n5, 204n20, 214
5:1	69, 109, 112n9, 216
5:1b	112n9
5:2	55n21, 73, 114
5:3	109, 110, 112, 112n9, 118, 123
5:3–16	109, 118
5:3–25	109
5:3—6:2	98, 109
5:4	7n28, 44n10, 45, 59, 109, 112n9, 129n3, 130
5:5–6	112
5:6	112

5:7	20, 67, 84, 109, 125n33, 128	6:6	7n28, 79
5:8	109, 123, 130, 161	6:7	55
5:9–10	53n12	6:9–10	61
5:9	50n6, 72, 73n25, 73n28, 214n2	6:9	71n22
		6:10	20n7, 32, 36, 63, 71n22, 208
5:10	7, 53, 55, 68, 109, 121n16, 136n30, 181n17, 208n32, 215n5	6:11–16	7, 84, 91
		6:11	7n28, 22n20, 63, 79, 86n3, 125n33, 161
5:11–15	109, 178	6:11	215
5:11	59, 109	6:12–15	33n6
5:12–15	55	6:12	63, 86n3, 142, 158
5:12	109	6:13	20, 45n19, 142, 147n23, 166
5:13–15	9	6:14	57, 218n21
5:13	10	6:15–16	148
5:14–16	207	6:15	10, 34n12
5:14–15	61, 62, 121	6:16	55, 142
5:14	62, 73n25, 89n16, 123	6:17–19	9, 68
5:15	20n7, 36, 86, 136	6:17	20
5:16	130	6:18	7, 53, 181n17, 208n32, 215n5
5:17–25	9, 13, 68, 68n12, 97, 98, 99, 117, 118	6:18a	121n16
		6:18b	121n16
5:17–18	59, 68	6:19	33, 142, 226n11
5:17	10, 10n38, 24, 57, 58, 69, 69n17, 74, 110, 118, 123, 157, 158, 205, 215, 216n11	6:20–21	84, 136
		6:20	157n4
		6:21	11, 20n7, 32, 37, 63, 142
5:18	84n2, 182		
5:19–25	203		

2 Timothy

(Also see within the appropriate pericope for particular verses of that chapter.)

5:20	56, 56n30
5:21–23	84
5:22	73, 77, 125n33, 128, 166
5:22	203
5:23	89n16
5:24–25	53
5:24	20n7
5:25	7, 121n16, 136n30, 181n17, 208n32, 215n5
6:1–2	13, 108, 109, 127, 128
6:1–2	216n13
6:1	10, 32, 109, 10n38, 110, 205, 216n11
6:2	7n29, 10, 56, 84, 98, 128, 204n18, 216n11
6:2b	128
6:3–21	10, 13, 117
6:3–10	71n22, 91
6:3–5	208
6:3–4	56n30
6:3	7n27, 7n28, 9, 10, 10n38, 20, 57, 79, 79n43, 166n2, 205, 208n33, 216n11
6:4	21n12, 32, 167n4, 228
6:5	7n28, 79
6:6–10	68

1:1—2:13	165
1:1–18	13, 154, 156
1:1	19n3, 172, 192
1:2	11, 19n4, 93
1:3–14	7
1:3	20, 22n19, 159n12, 200
1:4	159n12
1:5	58, 63, 159n12, 178n10, 181n19
1:6–14	155
1:6	11, 69n17, 94n40, 95n40, 114n15, 155, 159n12
1:7	22n20, 63, 155
1:8–10	62
1:8	7n29, 11, 45, 77, 155, 157n4, 161, 169
1:9–10	155
1:9	155, 180
1:10	135n24, 155, 218n21
1:11–12	155
1:11	8, 10, 10n38, 35, 205, 216n11
1:12	7n29, 56, 155, 156, 157n4, 169

Scripture Index

2 Timothy (continued)

1:13–14	11
1:13	7n27, 22n20, 63, 155, 166, 166n2, 167, 180, 181n19, 208n33, 216n11, 216n12
1:14	56, 79n44, 155, 157n4
1:15–18	155n1
1:15	156
1:16–18	7, 156
1:16	155, 169
1:18	7n29, 155, 155n1, 226n11
2:1	19n4, 93, 152, 190n21, 193
2:1–13	13, 141, 145, 164, 165, 190n18
2:1–9	11
2:2	10, 35, 68, 144n8, 149n30, 167, 204n18, 215, 216n11
2:3–13	142
2:3–4	165
2:3	7n29, 142n3
2:5–6	226n11
2:5	7n29
2:6	7n29
2:7	59, 182
2:8–10	123
2:8	7, 165, 167, 169
2:9	7n29, 142n3, 168
2:10	7n29, 142, 226n11
2:11–12	226n11
2:11	7, 33n5, 59n38, 71, 92, 142, 169
2:12–13	178
2:12b–13	165, 167, 169
2:12	7n29, 129n3, 150n32
2:13	167, 204n18
2:14—4:8	165
2:14–26	13, 154, 174, 175, 183, 194
2:14–16	11
2:14	9, 68, 144n12, 159n12, 228
2:15	77, 179, 230
2:16–18	56n30
2:16	7n28, 59, 129n3, 175, 179n13
2:17–18	9, 37, 208
2:17	20
2:18	63, 87n10, 144n8, 175, 179, 181n19
2:19	182
2:20–21	103n13
2:20	8n33, 22n18, 78n39, 204n20
2:21	7, 121n16, 136n30, 181n17, 192, 208n32, 215n5
2:22–24	11
2:22	22n20, 63, 93, 144n8, 175, 180, 181n19, 216
2:23–26	178
2:23	9, 21n12, 56n30, 228
2:24	7n29, 68
2:25–26	9, 37n17, 123, 208
2:25	44, 175, 178, 179
2:26	61, 72, 86, 131, 177, 181
3:1–17	13, 164, 185, 186, 194
3:1–9	87
3:1	188
3:5–6	59
3:5	7n28, 79, 129n3, 150n33, 208
3:6–7	9
3:6	73, 186, 207
3:8–9	206n25
3:8	9, 10, 21n10, 63, 144n8, 159n12, 193
3:10—4:8	186
3:10–17	145
3:10–14	11
3:10–12	142
3:10–11	186
3:10	10, 10n38, 22n20, 63, 161, 186, 205, 215, 216n11
3:11–12	7n29
3:11	142n9
3:12	7n20, 161
3:13	9, 10
3:14—4:4	186
3:14	159n12
3:15	63
3:16–17	2, 219n27
3:16	10, 10n38, 24, 186, 187, 205, 216n11
3:17	7, 121n16, 136n30, 186, 208n32, 215n5
3:21	183
4:1–22	13, 172, 174
4:1–5	11
4:1–2	56, 57
4:1	135n24, 166, 218n21
4:2–5	56n30
4:2–3	59
4:2	10, 10n38, 56, 182, 205, 216n11
4:3–4	87
4:3	7n27, 9, 10, 57, 166n2, 182, 205, 208n33, 216n11
4:4	9, 21, 179, 182
4:5–8	142
4:5–6	59
4:5	7n29, 142n9, 157n4, 206n25

4:6–8	33n6, 134n20, 145	1:15	22n19, 161, 214
4:6	165	1:16	7, 121n16, 136n30, 181n17, 214, 215n5, 218n23, 223n2, 224
4:7	63, 134		
4:8	7n29, 135n24, 142, 151n35, 218n21, 226n11	2:1–15	14, 118, 199, 222, 223, 227
4:9–22	142	2:1–14	227
4:9–10	59	2:1–10	9, 223, 224, 225
4:9	144, 152	2:1	7n27, 10, 10n38, 56, 166n2, 205
4:10	152		
4:11	59	2:2–6	22n18
4:13	92n29	2:2	7n27, 44, 53n14, 63, 68, 69, 74, 161, 166n2, 201n4, 208n33
4:14–16	152		
4:14–15	7n29		
4:14	9, 20, 182	2:3–5	121
4:15	59	2:3–4	58
4:17–18	7n29, 182	2:3	10n38, 68, 76
4:17	43	2:4–5	7, 53n12
4:18	7n29, 142, 145	2:4	68, 89n16
4:19	151n35, 187n19	2:5	53n14, 55, 68, 223n2
4:22	11, 144, 152, 178n19	2:6	56, 68, 76
4:22	142	2:7	7, 10, 10n38, 44, 53, 68, 74, 121n16, 136n30, 181n17, 205, 223

Titus

(Also see within the appropriate pericope for particular verses of that chapter.)

		2:8–10	123
1	66, 73	2:8	7n27, 166n2
1:1–16	5, 13, 172n21, 211	2:9–10	120
1:1–9	213	2:9	55, 55n22
1:1	7n28, 44, 63, 79, 79n43	2:10	10n38, 20n5, 45n16, 63, 201n4, 205
1:2	142		
1:3	20n5, 45n16	2:11–14	7, 33n6, 223, 225, 226
1:4	11, 19, 63, 142, 213	2:11–12	79n44
1:5–9	58, 68, 69, 89n16, 213	2:11	43, 135n24, 225
1:6–9	63, 66	2:12	7n28, 79n41
1:6	50n6, 66n5, 67, 68, 103, 123, 215	2:13	20n5, 135n24, 225
		2:14	7, 53, 121n16, 136n30, 181n17, 223
1:7	8, 22, 22n18, 66n5, 68, 69, 75, 99n4, 103n13, 115, 130, 215		
		2:15	56, 56n30, 118, 207, 223
1:8	53n14, 67, 68, 214, 215n3	3:1–15	14, 126, 211
1:9	7n27, 10, 10n38, 56, 56n30, 57, 67, 68, 110, 157, 166n2, 172n18, 216n11	3:1–11	212
		3:1–7	213
		3:1–2	123, 212
		3:1	7, 55, 55n22, 121n16, 123, 136n30, 181n17, 208n32, 212, 215n5, 216
1:10–16	213, 214, 224		
1:10	9, 10, 21n10, 92n29, 214, 224	3:2	68
1:11	9, 10, 56n30, 57, 68, 214, 216n11	3:3–7	62n56, 212
		3:4–7	7
1:12	7	3:4	20n5, 45n16, 135n24, 212, 218n21
1:13	7n27, 9, 37n17, 56n30, 63, 68, 166n2, 214, 216n11		
		3:5	212, 218n21
1:14–16	9, 21n10	3:6	212
1:14–15	228	3:7	142
1:14	21	3:7	212

253

Titus (continued)

3:8–11	212, 213
3:8–10	212
3:8	7, 33n5, 53, 71, 74, 92, 121n16, 123, 136n30, 160, 181n17, 201n4, 212, 215n5
3:9–11	56n30
3:9	9, 21n10, 21n12, 59, 68, 206, 206n25
3:10–11	9
3:10	37n17, 207
3:12–15	213
3:12	59, 192n25, 213
3:14	7, 53, 74, 121n16, 136n30, 181n17, 215n5
3:15	11, 63, 201n4, 201n5, 213

Philemon

1	19n4, 143n4
4	31
7	121
8	75
10–21	120, 121
16	121
20	121
24	192

Hebrews

1:2	176
1:8–10	110n2
3:6	95
3:14	95
5:7	80n46
5:12	56, 58, 68
7:25	81
9:15	92n28
9:19	192n3
9:24	81
9:26	80n46
10:7	192n3
10:20	80n46
10:22	23n21
10:28	113
12:5	94n38, 183n24
12:7	183n24
12:9	80n47, 183n24
12:22–24	113n13
12:22	78
13:2	68
13:5	68
13:7	69, 69n17
13:17	55n22, 69, 69n17
13:20	73
13:22	94n38
13:23	157n6
13:24	69, 69n17

James

1:10–11	131n10
1:12	190
1:27	102
2:6–7	131n10
2:23	182
4:7	55n22
4:8	51
5:3	176
5:3–5	131n10
5:14	68
5:20	95n43

1 Peter

1:20	80n46, 176
1:21	80n49
2:1	55
2:5	55
2:6	110n2
2:6	182
2:12	72
2:13–17	43n6, 123
2:13	55n22, 216, 224n3
2:18–25	120
2:18	55
2:25	73
3:1–6	55
3:1	216
3:1	55, 55n23
3:3	55n23
3:4	44, 54n16, 55n23
3:5	55, 55n23, 216
3:6	55n23
3:7	55n23
3:18	80n46, 80n47
3:20	61n54
4:1	80n46
4:9	68
4:10	69n17
4:13	218n18
4:17	8n33, 55
5:1–5	67, 68, 69
5:2	68
5:3	68
5:4	73, 190
5:5	55n22

2 Peter

2:16	167
2:20	157n7
2:22	110n2
3:3–7	87
3:4	92n28
3:16–17	182

1 John

1:2	80n46
2:1	81
2:18	87
2:22–23	103
3:5	80n46
3:8	80n46
4:2	80n46

2 John

1	68
7	80n46

3 John

1	69

Jude

17–18	87
23	95n43

Revelation

1:3	94n37
1:6	162n18
2:10	190
3:5	113n13
3:17–18	131n10
3:21	162n18
4:4	162n18
5:10	162n18
5:12–13	81
7:2	78
8:1	54
11:16	162n18
13:16	123
14:10	113n13
17:4	52
18:7	105
18:9	105
20:4	162n18
20:5–6	169
20:6	162n18
21:14	170n13
22:5	162n18

APOCRYPHA

1 Esdras

8:52	183n24
9:48	94n37

Wisdom

7:6	131n15
8:1	21n13
8:14	21n13
12:18	21n13
15:1	22n13

1 Maccabees

2:66	93
7:33	9n36, 43n6, 224n3
14:34	183n24
16:2	93

2 Maccabees

1:27	209n36
6:11	44n11
6:13	123
6:28	44n11
8:15	44n11
9:26	123
15:9	94n38

Sirach

7:21	120n11
25:24	59n41
33:31	120n11
38:1	102n7
39:33	88n12

ANCIENT SOURCES INDEX

CLEMENT OF ROME

1 Clement

29:1	51
42:4	69
44:1–5	69
44:4	67
47:6	69

AELIUS ARISTIDES

Orations

23.31	9

AESCHINES

Timarchus

30	75

APOLLODORUS

Library

2.4.8	202

Apostolic Constitutions

8.19.1–2	76

ARISTOTLE

Nicomachean Ethics

8.11.7	119

Politics

1.2.14	119
1.1254b13–14	215
1.1259b1–2	217
1.1260a9–14	217

ARIUS DIDYMUS (IN STOBAEUS, *ANTHOLOGY*)

2.7.26	215
2.149.5	215

ATHENAEUS

The Learned Banqueters

13.571	78

AUGUSTINE

On Christian Doctrine

4.27.59	5

CALLIMACHUS

Hymns 1, To Zeus

6.1.8–9	207

CELSUS

On Medicine

1.8.1–2	115

CHRYSIPPUS

Fragmenta Moralia

9.7.611	62

CHRYSOSTOM

Homilies on Ephesians

13.11–17	59

CHRYSOSTOM (CONTINUED)

Homilies on First Timothy

10	67
16	123
17	131

Homilies on Second Timothy

9	190

Homilies on Titus

4	216

CICERO

On Duties

1.13.41	119

On the Republic

3.9.15	207

COUNCIL OF NICAEA

Canon

19	76

DEMOSTHENES

In Neaeram 59.122   73

DIO CHRYSOSTOM

Discourses 45

3	33

DIOGENES LAERTIUS

Lives

6.50	131

DIONYSIUS OF HALICARNASSUS

Antiquitates romanae

3.23.17	33

DIOSCORIDES

De Materia Medica

5.7.1	115

EPICTETUS

Discourses

3.13.21	114

GREGORY OF NYSSA

Homilies on Ecclesiastes

4	120

HERMAS

Similitudes

1.7	102
6.2	157

HIEROCLES (IN STOBAEUS, *ANTHOLOGY*)

79.53	99

HIPPOCRATES

On Ancient Medicine

13	115

HOMER

Iliad

2.649	188

IGNATIUS

Polycarp

4.1	102
6.1	67

IRENAEUS

Against Heresies

2.22.5	93
3.2.2	69
3.3.1–3	69

ISOCRATES

Nicocles

19	75
41	9

Evagoras

43	226

JOSEPHUS

Jewish Antiquities

10.210	181
13.168	181
14.10.12–13	5
16:6.1–7	5
17.117	208
17.120	208
19.16.132	33

Jewish War

1.10.4	9
1.624.62	208
2.17.2	9

Against Apion

1.54	181
2.6.77	9

JUSTIN MARTYR

1 Apology

1.67	94

LUCIAN

Pro imaginibus

24	168

ONASANDER

The General

1.1	66–67

OTHER

Codex Theodosianus

6.8.14	68

Damascus Document

5:17–18	178
13:8–10	67

Exodus Rabbah

On Exod 9:7	178

Letter of Aristeas

45	9
234	21
254	21

Pirque Abot

6.4	114

Rule of the Community

6:4–6	88
6:10–20	67
9:19–22	67
10:14–15	88

Targum Pseudo-Jonathan

1:3	178
7:2	178
40:6	178

Testament of Judah

19.1	131

Tractate Baba Batra

58b	115
119b	54

Tractate Berakhot

7.2	54
51a	115

Tractate Menahot

85a	178

Tractate Sanhedrin

94b	54

Tractate Sotah

3.4	54

PAUSANIAS

Description of Greece II

5.24.9	158

POLYBIUS

Histories

3.412–13	207
6.4.5	99
6.46.3	207
6.47.5	225
9.2.1	21
10.22.5	67
18.12.5	93

PHILO

Flaccus
7.49	9

On the Life of Moses
2.47	21
2.6	183

On the Life of Abraham
98	94

On the Contemplative Life
68	94
75	181
78	181

On the Creation
2	21
36.105	93, 214

On the Confusion of Tongues
21	21

Special Laws
1.19.102	52
2.8.33	214
2.66–68	119

Special Laws (continued)
2.89–91	119
3.9.51	52
3.137–43	119

Questions on Genesis
1.33	59

On the Virtues
57	74

On the Decalogue
119–20	102
167	119

The Worse Attacks the Better
110	168

On Husbandry
19.99	177

PLATO

Timaeus
22A–B	21
33D	131

Laws
7.810E	168
879C	100

Epistle VIII
352C	158

PLINY THE ELDER

Natural History
23:22	115
30.2	178

PLINY THE YOUNGER

Epistle 10
97.8	121

PLUTARCH

Advice to Bride and Groom
9	53
26	53
31–32	54–55

On Brotherly Love
479F	102

Advice About Keeping Well
19	115

Aemilius Paulus
23.6	202

Lysander
20.2	202

Whether an Old Man Should Engage in Public Affairs
792E	215

Comparison of Demosthenes and Cicero
3.3–4	225

POLYCARP

Philippians
6:1	67

PSEUDO-PHYCYLIDES

Sentences

223–27	119

SENECA THE YOUNGER

Epistle 94

40	68

Epistle 47

1	119
10	119
11	119
13	119

De Beneficiis

3.18	121
18.2	124
18.4	124
19.1	124
21.1–2	124
22:1–2	124

SEXTUS

Sentences of Sextus

235	53

SEXTUS EMPIRICUS

Against the Professors

253	21

Sibylline Oracles

7.69	56
8.309	56

SOPHOCLES

Antigone

661–62	75

STRABO

Geographica

8.2	21

SUETONIUS

Lives of the Caesars 2: The Deified Augustus

58	9

TERTULLIAN

Apology

39	2

Against Marcion

5.21	6

THEODORE OF MOPSUESTIA

Commentary on 1 Timothy

5:9	104

THUCYDIDES

The Peloponnesian War

2.100	168

XENOPHON OF EPHEUS

Anthia and Habrocomes

1.11.5	78

www.ingramcontent.com/pod-product-compliance
Lightning Source LLC
Chambersburg PA
CBHW081329230426

43667CB00018B/2874